WAKE UP!

An Analysis of African-American History from a Glorious Past to the Present Crisis

ROBERT L. BRADLEY

ISBN 1-886225-62-1

Cover illustration by Sharon Morton

Cover production by Angie Johnson

Library of Congress Cataloging-in-Publication Data

Bradley, Robert L.
  Wake up! : an analysis of African-American history from a glorious past to the present crisis / Robert L. Bradley.
    p. cm.
  Includes bibliographical references and index.
  ISBN 1-886225-62-1
  1. African Americans--History. 2. African Americans--Ethnic identity. 3. African Americans--Social conditions. 4. Blacks--America--History. 5. Africa--History. 6. Slavery--United States--History. 7. Slavery--America--History. I. Title.
  E185 .B813 2001
  305.896'073--dc21

                                                    2001006497

Dageforde Publishing, Inc.
128 East 13th Street
Crete, Nebraska 68333

Dedication

*This book is dedicated to my mother,
Rosie Bradley.*

Contents

Acknowledgments

It took eleven years of hard work to write *Wake Up!* However, without the support and inspiration of others, this book would have never become a reality.

A special thanks is given to my wife, Rosilyn, and to my children, Michael, Alicia, and Janae, for their support and understanding in the completion of this book. I know it was frustrating at times for you all because the completion of this book took a lot of my time, but thanks a million for hanging in there with me. Again thanks Rosilyn for your support and patience.

Thank you Mama for your kindness, inspiration, and support over the years. You have stuck by me through thick and thin. I wouldn't have made it without you.

Special thanks Daddy (Robert L. Bradley, Sr.) for introducing me to black history. You were the first person I ever heard talk about the history of black people. When I was about seven or eight years old, you told me fascinating stories about slavery times that had been told to you by your grandfather. Your stories were so good that they inspired me to study the history of black people.

A special thanks is given to the following members of my family for their support and interest in this book: sister Betty Bradley, sister Sennie Bradley, sister Bobbie Bonner, sister Roxie Turner, and her husband

Gregory Turner, niece Melba Bradley, and niece Trina Bradley.

A special thanks is given to Uncle Larry Scott, Uncle Willie Scott, Aunt Ruthie Coulter, and Cousin Willie Nunley for helping me in my youth, a time when I was struggling and trying to get myself together. Thanks, Uncle Larry for your kindness and generosity to me. You would give me financial support and would never ask for anything in return. Thanks, Uncle Bill, for your kindness to me. You took me to the driving station to take the test to get my first driver's license. Thanks, Aunt Ruthie, for your kindness and generosity to me. You would give me financial support and would never ask for anything in return. Thanks, Cousin Willie, for your kindness to me. You would take me to work when I didn't have a car and would never ask for anything in return. Thank you all for your help, and it hasn't been forgotten.

A special appreciation is given to the Whiteside brothers, Tim and Dave, for their interest in this book. They live out of town, but whenever I saw them they would ask me, "How is your book coming along?" Thank you all for your interest in this book.

A special thanks to a man of wisdom and insight, who is none other than Mikal El-Amin. Thank you for reading some of my chapters and offering constructive suggestions.

A special appreciation is given to artist, Sharon Morton, for taking the time to do the cover illustration of this book.

Special thanks to the publisher and staff at Dageforde Publishing, Inc. for their patience and professionalism in the publishing of this book.

Lastly, special thanks to the many scholars whose works I have used in the writing of this book. The list is too long to name here.

Preface

The dictionary defines a crisis as "a time of great danger or trouble, whose outcome decides whether possible bad consequences will follow." Many African-Americans don't want to hear the word crisis. They say, "Please don't talk about the bad that is happening in the black community. Instead, let's talk about the good that is happening in the black community." We all agree that some good is happening in the black community. For example, there are many successful blacks in Black America today. Also, black homicides are down as compared to seven or eight years ago. However, we must talk about the bad because if we continue to ignore it, it will only get worse in the future.

Today, the beginning of the twenty-first century, is a time of crisis for Black America. The increasing number of HIV/AIDS cases in the black community threatens the very survival of African-Americans. AIDS is now the leading cause of death among blacks between the ages of twenty-five and forty-four. Crime and violence in the black community destabilizes neighborhoods and fills us with fear and distrust. Low scores on achievement tests by black children cause them to suffer from low self-esteem and impair their ability to reach their full potential. A decline in morals and values in the black community over the last thirty-five years has led to an increasing lack of self-respect among blacks. The increasing number of households headed by black females in the black community denies black kids the presence of a father to love and guide them. The increasing imprisonment and mass deaths of young black males shrinks the pool from which black females select mates, thereby denying them husbands. The destructive, negative behavior of blacks toward one another causes divisiveness and distrust in the black community.

This serious, survival-threatening crisis in Black America is not seen by everyone because it is deceptive. It is deceptive because it appears less dangerous than what it really is. For example, the growing number of black millionaires and the large number of successful blacks in this country lead some people to believe that there is no serious crisis in Black America. However, what they fail to realize is while some blacks are moving forward economically, many others are moving backwards socially and spiritually.

Some African-Americans see this serious crisis. Some blacks see this serious crisis and try to warn others about it. Some blacks see this serious crisis, but it is so painful and frightening that they close their eyes to it. On the other hand, many blacks are asleep. They don't see this serious crisis facing Black America.

When you are asleep you are unconscious. Things can be going on around you, but you won't realize it. Because many need to be awakened, this book is entitled *Wake Up!*

Many African-Americans need to become more conscious historically. Our history is our road map. It will give us direction and will also be our guiding light in times of trouble. Those who are not aware of history or choose to ignore history shall repeat it.

Many African-Americans need to become more conscious politically. Our right to vote didn't come easy. It came as a result of hard struggles in which some people lost their lives. We need to exercise our right to vote. Our votes do count and can make a difference.

Many African-Americans also need to become wiser voters. We must learn to judge political candidates more by their track records than by their promises, smiles, and handshakes.

Many African-Americans need to become more conscious economically. African-Americans are mainly consumers. We spend over $400 billion annually, but very little of it with black businesses. African-Americans need to become sellers and producers of goods instead of being mainly consumers. If we become sellers and producers of goods, we will create jobs for ourselves. We won't have to rely on the federal government and private industry for most of our jobs. Other ethnic groups such as Asian-Americans and Jews have many small businesses that provide jobs for their communities. They use their capital to create jobs for themselves. We need to learn to spend our money wisely and to use it to empower ourselves economically.

Many African-Americans need to become more conscious socially in terms of how we treat one another. Negative behaviors toward one another—disrespect, slickness, envy, and selfishness—cause divisiveness and mistrust in the black community. These psychological chains prevent us from moving forward.

Lastly, many African-Americans need to become more conscious educationally. We need to be more committed to helping our children get a quality education. As the United Negro College Fund says, "A mind is a terrible thing to waste." A scholar or master teacher needs to be as respected in the black community as an athlete or entertainer.

Solutions to these problems will not be given to us on a silver platter. Instead, we will have to solve them ourselves through hard work, critical analysis, solid planning, organization, and a change of attitudes.

African-Americans trying to solve cultural problems can be compared to an individual trying to solve a personal problem. If a woman visits a psychologist for treatment of a rape that occurred when she was a child, the first thing the psychologist will do is to have her fill out a history form. Her history is necessary for the psychologist to correctly diagnose her problem and to prescribe the appropriate treatment. What is true for this woman is also true for African-Americans. Our history is necessary to find both the reasons for and solutions to our problems. In essence, our history will tell us who we are, where we have been, what we have accomplished, where we are now, and how to get where we want to go.

We turn now to the subtitle of this book, An Analysis of African-American History from a Glorious Past to the Present Crisis. This subtitle will no doubt confuse some readers. They might say, "African-Americans don't have a glorious past. Their history began in 1619 when a Dutch slave ship brought twenty of their ancestors to America. Before their ancestors were brought to America and civilized, blacks had no history or culture. The continent of Africa waited in darkness for Europeans to bring them the light of civilization. There is no way African-Americans have a glorious past."

African-Americans do have a glorious past. Our ancestors built cities and civilizations in Africa long before contact with Europeans in the fifteenth century, as we shall see.

I have written this book to give African-Americans an analysis of our history. It differs from most black history books, which generally offer historical data, achievements, and/or heroes, but very little analysis. African-Americans, mired in a serious crisis, need a book that will give inspiration, direction, and analysis. This book attempts to give them that.

I will attempt to answer the following questions and many more. How did blacks fall from pyramid builders to ghetto dwellers? How did we lose our "self-confidence and historical memory?"[1] Since blacks built great cities and civilizations in the past, why aren't we today rebuilding the boarded-up houses and buildings in our communities, a much simpler task? Did slavery impact blacks mentally as well as physically? Why are blacks generally shown laughing and clowning on television and at the movies? Why are images of blacks mostly negative? What were our strengths and weaknesses in history? How did blacks survive the most dehumanizing and brutal slavery known to man? How were blacks vulnerable in history? How can the study of history help blacks to survive in the future? In short, a critical analysis of black peoples' history can not only answer these questions but also tell us what to do now to overcome our problems.

Introduction

The term African-American denotes a person of African descent living in America. So then, the history of Africa is also the history of African-Americans.

The aim of this book is to investigate and analyze the history of African-Americans. It begins with our ancestors' origin in Africa in prehistoric times. It continues with our ancestors' development of cities and civilizations in antiquity to the Middle Ages and the transatlantic slave trade, and down to the present.

This book also deals with Africa as a whole, because blacks once occupied the entire continent, instead of just the sub-Saharan region they occupy today. A predominately black sub-Saharan Africa and a predominately white North Africa is what it became, not what it was. In ancient times blacks occupied all of North Africa, from Egypt across to Morocco. The ancient people who inhabited North Africa— Egyptians, Libyans, Numidians, and Moors—were black. Both human fossil remains and ancient historical records support the view that blacks once occupied the whole of North Africa. A number of factors changed North Africa from black to white, including invasions and conquests by foreigners from Europe and western Asia, migrations of foreigners into North Africa, blacks being forced from North Africa, blacks being killed in wars of resistance against invaders, and race mixing between

Africans and foreigners. Race mixing may have had the biggest impact in transforming the region from black to white because modern anthropologists classify mulattoes in North Africa as white.

This book takes the view that African-Americans have a glorious past. It discusses a period in African history before the slave trade when our African ancestors built great cities and civilizations in Africa. It discusses the rise and fall of great ancient African civilizations such as Egypt and Carthage. It discusses the rise and fall of vast medieval empires in West Africa such as Ghana, Mali, and Songhay. It tells of famous African figures: Thutmose III, a great pharaoh of ancient Egypt; Imhotep, the world's first known genius; Hannibal, the great Carthaginian general; and Queen Nzinga, the great queen of Angola who resisted the slave trade.

Many people today do not believe African-Americans have a glorious past. However, it is understandable why they think this way. One reason is our recent enslavement. Many people in the modern world have become so accustomed to seeing blacks being dependent and serving others that they can't visualize us at any time in history doing things without other peoples' assistance. A second reason is the mountain of negative literature written about blacks during the past 500 years. This negative literature implies that blacks are inferior. Since blacks have been labeled inferior, many people believe that there is no way we could have built architectural wonders—pyramids and sphinxes—in our distant past. A third reason is the negative portrayal of blacks as clowns and buffoons at the movies and on television. These negative images imply that blacks are a people that you don't take seriously when it comes to serious matters. How can you take a people serious when they are always laughing? Therefore, when the people of the world see blacks laughing, clowning, and disrespecting themselves at the movies and on television, these negative images reinforce in their minds the belief that blacks are an inferior people. They say to themselves, "Just look at those blacks laughing and clowning. There is no way they belong to the same race of people that built the great pyramids and the sphinx. African-Americans don't have a glorious past."

Yet historical records prove that blacks indeed have a glorious past. The question is, what caused us to fall from pyramid and sphinx builders in ancient history to mostly consumers and non-producers in modern times? This question will be answered in the coming chapters.

We turn now to a preview of the thirteen chapters in this book.

Chapter 1 explains the significance of black history. Some people don't believe that black history is important. They say, "Slavery and that old stuff happened a long time ago. We can't do anything about the past. So let's forget about it and concentrate on the present. The present is what's important, not the past." However, they fail to understand that what happened yesterday effects what is happening today. The present is inevitably linked to the past.

Chapter 2 addresses human origins. After many years of searching, most scientists now believe Africa is the birthplace of mankind.

Chapter 3 takes the view that ancient Ethiopia is the mother of civilization. The ancient Ethiopians developed the arts and sciences, hieroglyphic writing, and other knowledge, and took it northward to Egypt. Ancient Egypt was the daughter of ancient Ethiopia. Ancient Ethiopia also had other daughters, including ancient Sumer of Mesopotamia.

Chapter 4 discusses the rise and fall of the great civilization of ancient Egypt. It also discusses the great personalities of ancient Egypt such as Menes, Imhotep, Queen Hatshepsut, Thutmose III, Amenhotep IV, Ramses II, and Ramses III.

Chapter 5 discusses the rise and fall of the celebrated North African city-state of Carthage. Included in this discussion are the three Punic Wars between Carthage and Rome. This chapter also tells of the great Carthaginian general, Hannibal Barca, who led the Second Punic War against Rome. In addition, this chapter describes the Battle of Cannae in Italy between Hannibal and the Romans, considered by some historians the most famous battle of all antiquity.

Chapter 6 discusses North Africa under Roman and Vandal rule. The Romans, after their defeat of Carthage in the Third Punic War, began the conquest of North Africa. By 30 B.C. they had conquered all of North Africa. In A.D. 429 Roman North Africa was invaded by a wandering Germanic tribe called the Vandals. By 439 the Vandals were in control of Roman North Africa.

Chapter 7 deals with the Moors of North Africa and their occupation of Spain. In 711, Muslim forces, mostly African Moors led by Tarik, invaded and conquered Spain. The Moors occupied Spain for hundreds of years but were finally driven out in 1492.

Chapter 8 discusses the empires and states of West Africa. The great empires of Ghana, Mali, and Songhay flourished in West Africa during the Middle Ages. They and the lesser states of West Africa—notably the Mossi States, the Hausa States, and the states of Kanem-Bornu—reached high cultural achievements.

Chapter 9 discusses the Arab slave trade and the European slave trade in Africa. It also looks at the origins of slavery. In addition, it tells of Queen Nzinga of Angola, the great slave abolitionist.

Chapter 10 discusses blacks in slavery in the Caribbean, in mainland Latin America, and in the United States to the present. This chapter portrays many heroes, from Toussaint L'Ouverture to Harriet Tubman.

Chapter 11 deals with the psychological effects of slavery on black people. Although slavery has been over for more than a century, its evil spirit still haunts blacks today.

Chapter 12 is a historical analysis of three subjects that have had a big impact on black history: invasions of Africa, the mulatto, and the weaknesses and strengths of black people. These subjects are seldom mentioned in discussions of black history.

Chapter 13 deals with today's crisis in the black community. Can black people overcome it? Yes, we can. This chapter offers eight propositions that can help black people overcome this crisis.

This book's approach to African-American history is a little different from most books' approach to the subject. One way its approach is different from most books is it doesn't begin African-American history with the slave trade; instead, it begins in ancient times, thus, including Africa's glorious past as a part of African-American history. Another way its approach is different from that of other books is with its investigative-analysis of African-American history in addition to historical facts, heroes, and achievements.

This book's approach to African-American history was created out of necessity. African-Americans need a book that will do more than make us feel good about ourselves. We need a book that will also investigate our history for weaknesses, vulnerabilities, mistakes, and blunders. By knowing our weaknesses and vulnerabilities, we will understand how to become strong. By understanding our mistakes and blunders, we can learn to avoid repeating them. Thus, our history can become a guiding light that will help us overcome our problems.

Chapter 1

The Significance of Black History

In the 1500s Europeans began transporting enslaved Africans directly from Africa to the New World for sale. This infamous trade, which uprooted millions of Africans from their homeland and brought them to America to labor on plantations, became known as the transatlantic slave trade. To justify the cruelty of the transatlantic slave trade, Europeans began depicting Africans as a people who lacked a history and culture, and were, therefore, done a favor by being brought to America and civilized.

This denial of history and culture to blacks has continued from the slave period down to the present. For example, there are still some history books that ignore the cultural achievements of blacks. These history books concentrate mostly on our slave history while ignoring our achievements and heroes.

To counter this neglect, black historians have been writing books for over a century to show the world that we indeed have a history and culture. In 1883 George Washington Williams published *History of the Negro Race in America*. In 1887 Edward W. Blyden published *Christianity, Islam, and the Negro Race*. W.E.B. Du Bois, a Harvard Ph.D. graduate, wrote a number of books about black history, including *The Suppression of the African Slave Trade to the United States, 1638-1870*, published in 1896, and *The Negro*, published in 1915. However, the person most responsible for laying the foundation for the study of black history was Carter G. Woodson, a Harvard Ph.D. recipient and great organizer. He founded the Association for the Study of Negro Life and History in 1915. He established Negro History Week in 1926. He also wrote sixteen books. His best-known work is probably *The Mis-education of the Negro* (1933). Many other black scholars have also published works on black history.

Despite the large number of books written on black history, some people still believe that black history is insignificant. The following story illustrates this point.

▲▲▲

Once upon a time, a black student named John decided to enroll in a white university and major in math. He progressed very well at the white university, maintaining a B average. During the spring semester of his senior year, he decided to take a black history course as an elective. The teacher of the course was Dr. Dorsey, a black man and chairman of the Black Studies Department.

When John got in the black history class he expected it to be a breeze, but soon found it much tougher than he had expected. He was required to do a ton of reading and lots of written assignments. One day John decided that he had enough of Dr. Dorsey and his black history class, and he stopped by his office to tell him so.

John said to Dr. Dorsey, "Dr. Dorsey, I think your black history class is too demanding. It requires too much reading and too many written assignments. I am a math major. I have other demanding courses, you know."

Dr. Dorsey said, "Young man, I don't think my class is too demanding. History requires lots of reading and written assignments. Remember, you get out of something what you put into it."

John said, "Dr. Dorsey, I am going to be frank with you. What good is all of this black history anyhow? It can't help me. As far as I am concerned, it is insignificant. When I go look for a job after I graduate, the white people at the employment office are not going to ask me about this old black stuff. No, sir. They are going to want to know if I am qualified to do the job that I'm applying for. This old black stuff is insignificant. Do you know what I mean?"

Dr. Dorsey replied, "Calm down, young man. I know how you feel, but history is a valuable subject. Let me explain what I am talking about. You are a math major, but math by itself can't help you. However, if you use it as a tool, it can help you. For example, engineers used math to help construct the building we are sitting in. Also, John, you use math in ways that you may not be aware of. For example, when you play basketball with your friends, you use math. Your 360-degree dunk shot is an application of math. Your bank shot off of the backboard is an application of math. In addition, when you dance with your girlfriend, you are using math. Your dance steps and body movements require the use of math. For example, you use math when you do a dance that requires two steps up and two steps back. You use math when you do a dance that requires a turn of 180 degrees or 360 degrees. Furthermore, you know that a good dancer has to have rhythm and balance, and rhythm and balance involve mathematics. John, my point is, math is valuable if you use it as a tool, but by itself it can't help you. The same thing is true of history. History by itself can't help you, but if you use it as a tool, it can help you."

John said, "Dr. Dorsey, I understand what you mean. If you apply history as a tool it can help you, but by itself it can't help you."

Dr. Dorsey said, "Yes, young man, history is a valuable subject if you use it as a tool. For example, you can learn from history. If you made a mistake in the past, you can benefit from it by not repeating it. Also, if you know history, it will help you to avoid falling into traps and pitfalls, and it will enable you to understand the present and predict the future. In addition, history is your road map. It tells you your point of origin. As long as you know your point of origin, you will never get lost. But if you don't know your point of origin, you won't know where you came from, and if you don't know where you came from, you won't know where you are going."

John said, "Thanks, Dr. Dorsey, for the knowledge that you have shared with me today. You are a very wise man. I will never again question the significance of black history. You have showed me that both math and history can be used as tools to help myself."

▲▲▲

There are at least six reasons why the study of black history is significant to black people: (1) it will clear-up the confusion surrounding our identity; (2) it will give us role models to emulate; (3) it will give us dignity, self-respect, and pride; (4) it will help us respond to crises; (5) we will learn from history; and (6) it will give us direction.

Identity

Black people in the United States might be the most confused of all people of African descent throughout the Diaspora concerning their identity. When a historian recently went into the black community and asked individuals what they called themselves, he got a number of different responses. The responses included *colored, Negro, black, Creole, mixed, black Hebrew, black Indian, German,* and *African-American*. The most appropriate answer is African-American or *African living in America* because it identifies a place of origin or historical location. The person who said he was German was probably the most confused of all. If a black kid was born and raised in Germany while his father was stationed in the military there, this would not make him a German. To be a German, his historical roots must be there.

When one hears the word *Chinese-American*, it is easy to associate this person with a place of origin. The same is true of the word *Italian-American*. But when one hears the words colored, Negro, Creole, and mixed, it is difficult to associate these words with a historical location.

The transatlantic slave trade gave birth to the word Negro. Prior to this time, names such as Ethiopian, Moor, and *blackamoor* were used to describe Africans or black people. The ancient Greeks and Romans originally used the word Ethiopian to describe black people. Writer Frank Snowden gives the following description of the ancient Ethiopians:

> The classical evidence relating to physical characteristics, geographical location, and tribal identification demonstrates that the Greeks and Romans classified as Ethiopians several physical types of dark and black peoples inhabiting different parts of Africa. However classified by modern scholars, to Greeks and Romans these peoples were all Ethiopians.[1]

The word Moor came into use after the word Ethiopian to describe black people. The historian J.A. Rogers says, "To the... Greeks, the Moors were 'a black or dark people' (*Mauros*) and to the Romans... [Maurus] a black wooly-haired people, known synonymously as *Ethiops*, *Niger* (*Negro*), and *Afer* (*African*)."[2] Later the Moors amalgamated with the invading Arabs. As amalgamation continued over the centuries, there came to be two types of Moors. The first type consisted of Arabs and mulattoes (African-Arab offsprings). The mulattoes were sometimes called Tawny-Moors. The second type consisted of dark and black-skinned Africans, the original Moors. They now were called blackamoors.

The word Negro came into use in the fifteenth century with the beginning of the European slave trade in Africa. This word means black in both Portuguese and Spanish. It refers to a color, not a race. When the

Portuguese and Spanish arrived in West Africa to obtain slaves, they used the term to describe the Africans inhabiting this region. Also blackamoor was another term used by the Spanish and Portuguese to describe West Africans.

Historian the Rev. Sterling M. Means says, "The term 'Negro'... [originally] meant Black Moor; but the term has been converted to mean a separate group of Africans—the most inferior to all races of mankind and who from time immemorial have been slaves and have never been able to rise above the environments of servitude."[3]

The word Negro also makes it possible for writers of black history to misclassify the black race. They make the Africans associated with the slave trade a different group than the ones associated with the great cultures of ancient Egypt and Ethiopia. The Africans associated with the slave trade are classified as Negroes, while those associated with ancient Egypt and Ethiopia are instead classified as *Hamites* or dark-skinned whites. However, classifying the ancient Egyptians as dark-skinned whites is incorrect. The ancient Egyptians and the Africans who were associated with the slave trade both belonged to the same race.

Because the word Negro can so easily be used to confuse, one can understand why it is probably the most misleading and misused of all words in describing black people.

What black people in America choose to call themselves has varied from time to time. At first they called themselves Africans. The names African Methodist Episcopal Church, Free African Society, and Richmond African Baptist Missionary Society are indications of this. Next black people called themselves colored or Negroes. There is an overlap in the time period when black people used these words to identify themselves. Examples from when they called themselves colored are First Colored Grand Lodge, Institute for Colored People, and National Association for the Advancement of Colored People. Examples of when they called themselves Negroes are Universal Negro Improvement Association, National Negro Business League, and United Negro College Fund. Specific time periods for usage of these three terms are difficult to give because there is overlap, but approximate time periods are: the word African, from the arrival of blacks in the United States in 1619 to the 1820s; the words colored and Negro overlap each other; the word colored, from the 1820s to about 1900; the words Negro and colored are both used from about 1890 to about 1966, but the word Negro is dominant between 1900 and 1966. About 1966 the slogans "Black Power" and "Black is Beautiful" appeared. They made the words colored and Negro obsolete. Negroes and coloreds, who had been ashamed to be called black a few years earlier, now took pride in being called black. Many wore the African dashiki and displayed the Afro hairstyle as expressions of pride in their heritage. In the late 1980s some blacks became dissatisfied with being called black and Afro-American. As a result, they made it known to the media that they wanted to be called African-Americans. The words black and African-American are in at the present time, but in the future blacks may want to be called another name.

From knowledge of self, gained by studying his history, the black man will no longer need anyone to tell him who he is because he will know who he is. There will be no need to claim someone else's identity because he will already have an identity. Also he will find that it does not matter so much what he is called, but what he is, what he has done, and what he is doing. The black man will not cease to be what he is by calling himself something else. He will have to work hard and make a contribution to the world like he once did in ancient Egypt and Ethiopia. Then the world will learn to respect him and look upon him as a contributor rather than an imitator.

Models to Emulate

Black people can find models to emulate by studying their history. Besides being entertainers, African-Americans have also been famous scientists, inventors, physicians, educators, scholars, and leaders.

Reading about famous African-Americans may inspire black youth to want to be like them. After reading Dr. Martin Luther King's biography, a black boy may aspire to become a civil rights leader so he can help fight against injustice and inequality in society. After reading Malcolm X's biography, a teenage black male with a juvenile delinquency past may aspire to turn his life around like Malcolm X did. After reading George Washington Carver's biography, a black girl with an interest in science may aspire to become a scientist and discover a new way to feed the world's hungry people. After reading about Mary McLeod Bethune, a black girl may aspire to become an educator so she can help black kids strive for excellence in academics. After reading about Dr. Charles Drew, a black boy with an interest in medicine may aspire to become a physician so he can discover a cure for cancer. After reading about Magic Johnson, a little black boy may aspire to become a millionaire pro basketball player who uses some of his money to empower the black community economically. After reading about Jackie Joyner-Keerse, a little black girl may aspire to become a famous track star who uses her fame to help raise money to build a youth center in her old neighborhood. If black kids read about famous African-Americans, they may become inspired to want to be like them.

Even if black youths never become a Magic Johnson or a Jackie Joyner-Keerse, they can still benefit from reading about them. Their reading can help them learn some of the outstanding qualities of Magic Johnson and Jackie Joyner-Keerse that made them champions. For example, they can learn about these two athletes' great determination and perseverance, and can use these two qualities to help themselves in life. There is no substitute for determination and perseverance. These are what helped Magic Johnson and Jackie Joyner-Keerse to be champions in sports, and they can help black youth become champions in the game of life.

If our ancestors achieved greatness, so can we. If our ancestors used religion as a source of inspiration, so can we.

Religion is probably the one thing that inspires black people the most. History indicates that we have always been a very religious people. Religion inspired the early blacks of the Nile Valley to build the great civilization of Ethiopia-Egypt. African-American historian Chancellor Williams points this out.

> Because religion to the Africans was far more than ritual reflecting beliefs, but a reality reflected in their actual way of life, religion from the earliest times became the dynamic force in the development of all the major aspects of Black civilization.[4]

> This belief in life after death was the great inspiration for building on so grand a scale, trying to erect structures that would stand forever. Necessity, therefore, gave birth to the mathematical sciences required for building the amazing pyramids and the architectural designs for the most elaborate system of temple building the world had ever known.[5]

Religion also played a major role in enabling black people to endure the pain and suffering of slavery. By maintaining a strong belief that somehow God would deliver us from bondage, we were able to cope with this inhumane situation.

If religion was once the dynamic force that inspired black people to build a great civilization and to survive slavery, then it can become the dynamic force that inspires us to continue to struggle for freedom and equality, survival, and advancement.

Dignity, Self-Respect, and Pride

Slavery was a devastating experience for black people. It cut us off from our history and culture. It conditioned us to feel inferior. It stripped us of our dignity, self-respect, and pride.

Although slavery has been over for 136 years, it still haunts African-Americans psychologically. Many of us still have a slave mentality. We often do things that show a lack of dignity, self-respect, and pride. However, it is not hard to understand why we are lacking in these qualities.

Dignity is a thing of great value to a people. Take away their dignity and they have nothing left. It gives them the right to hold their heads up high, to feel good about themselves, to do things for themselves, to think and plan, to strive for excellence. But once their dignity is removed, they are a shattered people.

African-Americans without dignity will do embarrassing things. We will accept degrading roles in movies, saying and doing foolish things that demean black people in the eyes of the world, or just clowning in general because we don't know better.

African-Americans do not respect one another like we should. This behavior is a scar from slavery. To the average black, another black is not as important as someone—anyone—of another race.[6] This lack of respect for one another is manifested in many different ways. For example, the painful black-on-black homicides in the black community are caused by a lack of respect for black life. Black life is considered cheap. Therefore, the penalty for taking a black life is not as severe as for taking a white life.

Blacks often display a lack of pride in being themselves. Some are not comfortable being identified as Americans of African descent and would rather be called something else. Some have no love for self or sense of pride. Anything black is perceived as being inferior. This lack of pride is another scar from slavery.

It is difficult for a people to maintain dignity, self-respect, and pride when they are constantly confronted with racism, suffering, and oppression. Nevertheless, some African-Americans are able to maintain these qualities, despite the obstacles we face. Even during slavery, there were men and women who maintained dignity, self-respect, and pride in the midst of the most difficult conditions. Their spirit could not be broken.

The mentality of black people will change with a true knowledge of our glorious history. Blacks' inferiority complexes will change to an awareness of equality with all peoples of the world. With this new mentality, black people will begin to feel good about themselves. Eventually this good feeling will grow into love for self. Once we possess love for self, we will start to regain lost dignity, self-respect, and pride.

Help in Responding to Crises

African-Americans have a rich source of knowledge from which to draw when dealing with crises. Black history in America is a history of survival and dealing with crises. Our forefathers survived the cruelties of slavery, the rough times of the Great Depression, and the injustices of segregation. We can learn how to deal with the present crisis through knowledge learned from dealing with past crises.

How did African-Americans survive past crises? We survived through our faith in God, our concept of the extended family, our concept of sharing and caring, and our creative genius.

During times of crisis our forefathers turned to God as a source of strength and inspiration. Their strong belief in God enabled them to have hope when it looked as if there were no hope. No matter how hard times got, they kept on believing that things were going to get better, and they did.

The African-American concept of the extended family was a thing of beauty a generation ago. Children took care of their parents when they got old and sick. Instead of putting grandma in the old folks' home, her daughter would take her in and provide for her. When children's parents died, someone in the family would take the kids in and raise them, instead of sending them to an orphanage.

There was a time when the concept of sharing and caring was alive in the black community. Relatives shared with one another and cared for one another. For example, an uncle would give a nephew money to buy a pair of shoes and wouldn't expect anything in return. Friends shared with one another and cared for one another. For example, Dave would give his friend Walter a sack of flour and a ham to feed his family and wouldn't expect anything in return. Neighbors shared with one another and cared for one another. For example, a neighbor would share his car with another neighbor and wouldn't expect anything in return.

Throughout their sojourn in America, black people have used their creative genius to survive. During slavery times, slaves took the leftovers from a hog that Old Massa didn't want and used them for food. They turned the hog's feet, tail, ears, neck, head, and guts (chitterlings) into delicacies. Our grandmothers and mothers also turned leftover food into delicacies. They used leftover rice to make a mouth-watering rice pudding. They used leftover biscuits to make a delicious biscuit pudding.

There is strength in the old traditional values and ways of our forefathers. The black community must draw strength and knowledge from that history to confront the present crisis before it is too late. The descendants of a people who survived the most destructive and cruel slavery known to man have the strength and ability to deal with the present crisis if we put our minds to it.

Learn from History

We African-Americans must study our history so that we can learn from it. Historian Chancellor Williams emphasizes this point.

> We study our past for the express purpose of learning what things made the race great in the past, what explains subsequent failures and weakness, and what, in the light of that history, we can do now—if we have the will. This is what the study of history should mean for African people in particular.[7]

All peoples have strengths and weaknesses. A probing analysis of our history will reveal our strengths and weaknesses.

One thing that made black people vulnerable in history was putting blind trust in foreigners and strangers before thoroughly checking them out. As a result of this lack of caution, black people became easy prey for those who had hidden motives of exploitation and manipulation.

A second thing that made black people vulnerable in history was the disunity that made it easier for invaders to divide and conquer.

A third thing that made black people vulnerable was lack of foresight. For example, they failed to see the long-term disaster of the slave trade.

For black people to better learn from history, egos will first have to be put aside. Many times when weaknesses, vulnerabilities, and mistakes in history are mentioned, black people go into a state of denial or say that other peoples have those weaknesses, too.

For centuries, black people have been so preoccupied with the day-to-day struggle for survival that concern about their future has been lacking. We need to start seriously planning our future; we can't continue to leave it up to chance.

Direction

Lacking direction, a ship far out to sea will drift and drift. Unless it finds its direction, the ship will eventually become lost at sea.

The same is true of people without their history. They will go around in circles, confused, frustrated. Unless they find their history for direction, they will never learn how to get where they want to go. African-American historian John Henrik Clarke emphasizes the importance of history in giving direction.

> Without history people are without direction. History in the final analysis is the compass that people use to find themselves on the map of human geography and it is the clock they use to tell their special time of day. History tells a people where they have been and what they have been; where they are and what they are. Most important, history tells a people where they still must go and what they still must be.[8]

A traveler on a long journey needs a road map because he will eventually come to a crossroads. His decision at the crossroads is critical because it will determine whether he continues his journey or becomes lost.

The African-American community in the United States is at a crossroad. Our history can be our road map. We need to carefully study our history and use it as a guide to determine which road to travel. The current road is dangerous. It is a road of disunity, self-hate, declining morals and values, drug abuse, and lack of respect for one another. It can no longer be followed. We must awaken to reality and choose another road to travel because the very survival of black people is at stake. We must choose the right direction before it is too late.

Chapter 2

Africa: Birthplace of Mankind

Most scientists use the word hominid to refer to man's early ancestors. Scientists' hominids comprise near-human and humans. However, in this chapter all of man's early ancestors will be humans, and will be called prehistoric humans or prehistoric men.

The first prehistoric humans are called australopithecines. They lived roughly between four million and two million years ago. Their diet consisted of foods such as vegetables, seeds, fruits, and nuts. Fossils of australopithecines have been found only in Africa.

The australopithecine type of prehistoric human eventually evolved into a type of prehistoric human called Homo habilis, who first appeared about two million years ago. Homo habilis prehistoric humans were slightly more advanced than the australopithecines, having larger brains. The Homo habilis prehistoric humans ate meat as well as vegetables, fruits, and nuts. They are believed to be the first toolmakers. Their fossils have also been found only in Africa.

The Homo habilis type of prehistoric human eventually evolved into a type of prehistoric human called Homo erectus, who lived roughly between 1.5 million years ago and 500 thousand years ago. The Homo erectus prehistoric humans were more advanced than the Homo habilis prehistoric humans. For example, they made better tools. Also Homo erectus prehistoric humans are believed to have known how to use fire. Fossils of Homo erectus have been found in Africa, China, and Java (Indonesia).

Between about 300 thousand and 500 thousand years ago, Homo erectus prehistoric humans evolved into a type of prehistoric human called Homo sapiens. Homo sapiens are the ancestors of modern man.

During the nineteenth century most scientists believed that Europe or Asia, not Africa, was the birthplace of mankind. However, scientist Charles Darwin was an exception. He thought that Africa was probably the birthplace of mankind. The reason so few scientists considered Africa was because of the misconceptions about her during this period. Africa was widely thought of as a primitive land without a history or culture, not the kind of place where the human race would originate.

It was in Europe where the first fossil remains of prehistoric humans were found. In 1856 workmen in Germany found parts of a skeleton of a prehistoric man while "digging for limestone"[1] in a cave. This prehistoric man was named Neanderthal man after the Neanderthal River that flowed nearby. Neanderthal man lived between 130 thousand and thirty-five thousand years ago. In 1868 Cro-Magnon man was discovered in Les Eyzies, France. Cro-Magnon man lived 40 thousand to 10 thousand years ago.

In 1887 a Dutchman named Eugène Dubois left Europe and went to Asia (Indonesia) to search for the missing link between modern man and his original ancestors. By the academic world he was considered mad for wanting to look outside Europe for man's prehistoric ancestors. However, in 1891 he proved to the academic world that he had made the right decision. That year he struck pay dirt. He found the remains of an earlier prehistoric human which was named Java man. Java man was the first *Homo erectus* type of prehistoric human ever found. He probably lived between one million and 700 thousand years ago.

In the 1920s Peking man was discovered in China. Peking man belonged to the Homo erectus type of prehistoric human. He resided in China roughly between 600 thousand and 250 thousand years ago.

We turn now to the African continent, which was generally ignored in the nineteenth century and the early twentieth century as a source of prehistoric human fossil remains. In 1913 Homo capenses, or Boskop man, was discovered in South Africa. Also in 1913 Dr. Hans Reck, a German geologist, unearthed a skeleton of a prehistoric man in Olduvai Gorge, located in Tanzania, East Africa. This skeleton was first "believed to be one million years old; but later investigations showed this to be an error, and the fossil is now rated as being only twenty thousand years of age,"[2] which makes it a Homo sapiens type of prehistoric human.

In 1921, Dr. Albert Churchward's book *The Origin and Evolution of the Human Race* was published. In his book Churchward differed with the position that man had originated in Asia or some other part of the world. Instead, he argued that man had originated in Africa. Churchward, an Englishman, was a noted anthropologist, archaeologist, and physician. His position is further explained by African-American historian John G. Jackson.

> The earliest members of the human species appeared in Central Africa two million years ago, Churchward argued. From the Great Lakes region they spread over the entire continent. Certain groups of these early men wandered down the Nile Valley, settled in Egypt, and then spread out and colonized the entire world. The first migration was of primitive little men, known as Pygmies. Afterward came waves of Nilotic Negroes who also spread out over the world. As these early Africans wandered over the world, they differentiated into the various human subspecies that now inhabit the globe. Men who remained in the tropics and the equa-

torial regions retained their dark complexions; those who settled in temperate zones lost some of their pigmentation and developed a fairer skin.[3]

Dr. Churchward's position was not "favorably received by his contemporaries."[4] His viewpoint that the human race had originated in Africa two million years ago was considered ridiculous. Time has proven his position to be valid.

In 1924 Raymond Dart discovered the skull of a prehistoric human in Taung, South Africa. This was the first australopithecine type of prehistoric human ever found. It became known as the Taung child. The Taung child is "estimated to be two million years old."[5]

The Taung child and other promising discoveries on the continent sparked interest in searching for further fossil remains of prehistoric man in Africa. South Africa soon yielded other prehistoric human fossils. In 1936 fossil remains of a prehistoric human were found in a cave at Sterkfontein, South Africa. In 1938 Robert Broom discovered fossil remains of a prehistoric man in Kromdraai, South Africa. In 1948 fossil remains of a prehistoric man were discovered at Swartkrans, South Africa. In 1949 Dart discovered fossil remains of a prehistoric man at Makapansgat, South Africa. These four prehistoric humans were australopithecines. The Makapansgat remains are thought to be about three million years old. The Sterkfontein prehistoric human is thought to be about 2.5 million years old. The Kromdraai prehistoric man comes next and is followed by the Swartkrans prehistoric man.

The most famous person to search for human origins in Africa was Louis Leakey. He was born of English missionary parents in Kenya in 1903. He grew up among the Kikuyu, played with the children of the tribe, and spoke their language.[6] When he was sixteen he went to England to attend school. There he studied archaeology and anthropology. In 1926 he graduated from Cambridge University. After graduation Leakey returned to Africa to begin his search for the origins of man. The academic world at that time thought Leakey was going in the wrong direction. But after his nearly fifty years of fossil hunting, he had convinced the academic world that Africa was the place to do serious searching for human origins.

Leakey searched for human origins in East Africa. His favorite place was Olduvai Gorge in Tanzania. In 1931 Leakey was a member of an expedition that searched "for Stone Age artifacts at the Olduvai site."[7] The expedition found splendid examples of ancient stone tools but was unable to locate fossil remains of the prehistoric men who had lived there.

In 1932 Leakey searched "at Kanam and Kanjera" (sites in Kenya) for fossils of prehistoric men. There "he found fossil skulls of Homo sapiens, of uncertain age."[8]

Throughout the 1930s, 1940s, and most of the 1950s, Leakey searched for fossil remains of prehistoric men at Olduvai Gorge but always came up empty. Finally, on July 17, 1959 the skull of a prehistoric man was found at Olduvai Gorge. The person who made the discovery was his wife Mary Leakey, a respected paleontologist in her own right. The prehistoric man was estimated to have lived about 1.75 million years ago. This was the first australopithecine discovered in East Africa. In 1960 Jonathan Leaky, son of Louis and Mary Leakey, discovered another prehistoric man at the Olduvai Gorge site. This prehistoric man, named Homo habilis, lived between two million and one million years ago.

In 1972 a skull of a prehistoric man was found at Lake Turkana in Kenya. The skull was found by Bernard Ngeneo and identified by Richard Leakey, another son of Louis and Mary Leakey. The skull also belonged to the Homo habilis type of prehistoric man. It is the oldest of this type yet found. He is estimated to have lived about two million years ago.

In November 1974 in the Ethiopian desert, Don Johanson, a fossil hunter, made an extraordinary discovery. He located the partial skeleton of a three-million-year-old prehistoric woman. She was given the nickname Lucy. In her lifetime, Lucy was about three-and-a-half feet tall and weighed about sixty pounds. Lucy's skeleton was the most complete of all the australopithecine type of prehistoric humans that had been found until 1998. Lucy is also the most famous prehistoric human found in Africa.

In 1975 Richard Leakey discovered fossil remains of a prehistoric human at Lake Turkana. It was of the Homo erectus type who lived about 1.8 million years ago.

In 1984 a Kenyan named Kamoya Kimeu discovered the partial skeleton of a prehistoric boy at Lake Turkana. The skeleton was also of the Homo erectus type and was estimated to be over 1.6 million years old.

In 1994 at Lake Turkana, Peter Nzube Mutiwa discovered the remains of the oldest australopithecine type prehistoric human ever found.

In 1998 another australopithecine type prehistoric human skeleton was found at Sterkfontein, South Africa. This skeleton was the first australopithecine ever to be found complete.

The discovery in Africa of a number of prehistoric human remains over a million years old provides convincing evidence that mankind originated there. Many of the prehistoric fossils found in Africa are older than the ones found anywhere else in the world. For example, Lucy is at least one million years older than Java man of Asia and over 2.8 million years older than Neanderthal man of Europe. As a result of this evidence, scientists now believe that man first appeared in Africa, then spread to Asia and Europe and elsewhere.

Geneticists have now joined the search for the ancestors of modern man. They are "trained in molecular biology"[9] rather than anthropology. They work with genes in "laboratories instead of"[10] examining bones and stone tools at fossil sites.

Recent genetic studies have also traced the origin of modern human beings back to Africa. This is known as the Noah's Ark Theory. According to this [theory], modern human beings evolved in Africa and branched off in different directions several hundred thousand years ago.[11] By comparing the genes of modern people, one research team has linked every person now on Earth to a fully human common ancestor—a woman who lived in Africa 100 thousand to 300 thousand years ago.[12]

A 1988 article in *Newsweek* magazine, "The Search for Adam and Eve," comments on the woman scientists say is our common ancestor.

> Scientists are calling her Eve, but reluctantly. The name evokes too many wrong images—the weak-willed figure in Genesis, the milk-skinned beauty in Renaissance art, the voluptuary gardener in *Paradise Lost* who was all "softness" and "meek surrender" and waist-length "gold tresses." The scientists' Eve—subject of one of the most provocative anthropological theories in a decade—was more likely a dark-haired, black-skinned woman, roaming a hot savanna in search of food...She was not the only woman on earth, nor necessarily the most attractive or maternal. She was simply the most fruitful, if that is measured by success in propagating a certain set of genes. Hers seem to be in all humans living today: 5 billion blood relatives. She was, by one rough estimate, your 10,000[th] great-grandmother.[13]

A 1988 *World Press Review* article "The Mother of Us All" explains the method by which geneticists compared the genes of modern people and came up with the view that all modern people evolved from the same family tree.

Geneticists can measure the degree of relationship between different people, or between different species. To tell how long ago two individuals diverged from a common ancestor, geneticists consult a "molecular clock." A genetic study based on such clocks, conducted by Allan Wilson and his colleagues at the University of California at Berkeley, has given a boost to the Noah's Ark theory. Wilson's team studied a peculiar sort of DNA [deoxyribonucleic acid, the chief constituent of the chromosomes, which transmit hereditary characteristics]. It sits in each cell's power generator—known as mitochondria—rather than in the nucleus, where the bulk of the DNA is stored. Although all human beings get half of the nuclear DNA from their mothers and half from their fathers, they get all of their mitochondrial DNA from their mothers. So all of the changes in the mitochondrial DNA down a line of females will be random code changes, or mutations, that represent ticks of the clock.

The Berkeley team compared mitochondrial DNA from 147 people of all races. The samples, from around the world, looked pretty similar. The Berkeley team then fed all the measurements into a computer programmed to link them according to their genetic similarity. The result was a sort of family tree of individuals connecting those people with the closest genes to the same branch and linking the closest branches by common ancestors.[14]

This family tree was rooted in Africa, because the DNA from all 147 people in the study could be traced back to a common African ancestor.

It seems that this ancestor—the most recent woman to extend a line of female descendants to everyone alive today—lived in Africa, because of the way she was related to the Africans in the sample. Assuming that the mitochondrial DNA is a reliable molecular clock, "Eve" lived

100,000-300,000 years ago. She therefore fits in with the theory that all of us are descended from one group of modern H. sapiens in Africa. Africa should then sport the greatest diversity of genes, since its population has had the longest time to develop them. Sure enough, the mitochondrial DNA from Africans proved the most varied.[15]

Evidence by both anthropologists and geneticists supports the theory that Africa is the birthplace of mankind. It is now generally accepted by scientists, with only a few exceptions, that Africa is the birthplace of mankind. They believe that humans first appeared in Africa, then later spread to Asia and Europe and other places.

The Stone Age

Early man spent a long time in the Stone Age—over a million years. The Stone Age was characterized by man's use of stone tools, implements, and weapons before he acquired the knowledge necessary to produce metals and build civilizations. Archaeologists subdivide the Stone Age into three periods: Paleolithic, or Old Stone Age; Mesolithic, or Middle Stone Age; and Neolithic, or New Stone Age.

The Paleolithic or Old Stone Age was a period of enormous length. It began about two million years ago and ended about 10,000 B.C. During this period man learned to make tools from stone and bones. He obtained his food by hunting wild animals, by fishing in streams and lakes, and by gathering wild plants. He also created cave art. Paintings of animals such as deer, bison, and horses have been found in many caves.

The Mesolithic or Middle Stone Age was a transition period between the Old Stone Age and the New Stone Age. It began about 10,000 B.C. and ended about 5,000 B.C. The people of the Mesolithic period gave us items such as flint axes, crude pottery, and fishhooks made of bones. They also domesticated the dog.

The Neolithic or New Stone Age was a period in which man made crucial steps toward civilization. It began about 5,000 B.C. and ended about 3,500 B.C. During this period man developed polished stone tools, the art of weaving textiles from fibers or hair, better pottery, and began raising stock, and developed agriculture techniques. Now that he had become a farmer and a herdsman, he no longer had to depend entirely upon food gathering, fishing, and hunting for his meals. He was now a producer of food rather than a gatherer of it. With food in abundance, he was able "to settle permanently in villages...."[16]

Now man, settled permanently in villages, had time to concentrate on other things. He became specialized in his activities. He advanced socially in terms of religion, thought, family structure, etc. Then he discovered the art of metalworking, which marked the end of the Stone Age. With food in abundance and hard metal tools of copper and bronze, the villages eventually grew into cities and civilizations.

Note: The dates given here for the periods of the Stone Age (Old, Middle, and New) are approximate. It is possible that these three periods ended earlier than the dates given here. Some scholars cite evidence that an advanced civilization existed on the earth before 5,000 B.C.

Chapter 3

Ethiopia: Mother of Civilization

The word Ethiopian was used by the ancient Greeks to identify the dark and black-skinned people of both Africa and Asia and means sunburnt faces. The ancient Greeks thought the blackness of the Ethiopians was caused by the heat from the sun.

There were times in ancient history when all Africans were considered Ethiopians and the whole continent of Africa was considered Ethiopia. Historian Chancellor Williams mentions an ancient "Ethiopian Empire" in Africa. This ancient empire encompassed a large area. Before circa 3500 B.C., it extended from the source of the Nile in present-day Ethiopia to the Mediterranean Sea in the north. It roughly comprised the modern countries of Egypt, Ethiopia, Sudan, and a part of Somalia.

The Greek historian Herodotus said that there were two types of Ethiopians: Western or African Ethiopians and Eastern or Asiatic Ethiopians. Eastern Ethiopians...differed physically from African Ethiopians, according to Herodotus, only in that those of Asia were straight-haired and those of Africa the most wooly-haired of all men.[1]

The large area stretching from Africa to India was once called Ethiopia by the Greeks, and all the dark-skinned and black-skinned inhabitants of this area were called Ethiopians. According to Homer and

Herodotus, the inhabitants of the following territories were Ethiopians: the Sudan, Egypt, Arabia, Palestine, Western Asia, and India.[2]

In far ancient times black people were very numerous and widespread. They occupied areas of the world that are now occupied by Caucasoid (white) people. They formed a belt of black humanity that stretched from Africa to Malaya. Dr. Bertram Thomas, in his book *The Arabs,* comments on this black belt of humanity:

> The original inhabitants of Arabia...were not the familiar Arabs of our own time, but a very much darker people. A protonegroid belt of mankind stretched across the ancient world from Africa to Malaya. This belt, by environmental and other evolutionary processes, became in parts transformed, giving rise to the Hamitic peoples of Africa, to the Dravidian peoples of India, and to an intermediate dark people inhabiting the Arabian peninsula. In the course of time two big migrations of fair skinned peoples came from the north, one of them, the Mongoloids, to break through and transform the dark belt of man beyond India; the other, the Caucasoids, to drive a wedge between India and Africa.[3]

The big Caucasoid migration into the black world of India and western Asia began roughly about 2000 B.C. These Indo-European migrants, well armed, desired to leave their homeland in the Eurasian steppes. "Since the late...[nineteenth] century, the Indo-European homeland has been placed somewhere in the vast Eurasian steppes between the frontiers of China on the east and the plains of central Europe on the west."[4] Historian Runoko Rashidi describes the Indo-Europeans and their big migration into the black world of India and western Asia.

> Now armed with military technologies second to none, by the end of the third millennium B.C., the Indo-European tribes, including the Aryans, were in full motion, carrying their families and

all worldly possessions on their backs and in their wagons. Whether motivated by drought, excess populations, or forces and factors that have not been fully explained, these northern nomads were heading like a great human juggernaut toward new and unknown lands, uprooting whole peoples in their path. The southern world, ill prepared to defend itself against the onslaught, was rocked to its foundations.[5]

The Indo-Europeans settled down in India and western Asia. They had a big impact on this black world. Race mixing became widespread. Today, modern anthropologists classify the people of this region as mostly Caucasoid racially. However, black people do live today in India, Saudi Arabia, and Yemen. The nation of India has millions of blacks, called *untouchables* and *Dalit*. "Some of the tribals in Central India closely resemble the African blacks in their physical features. The black untouchables of Tamil Nadu, on the southern end of India, perhaps more than any other group, retain their original physical features, including dark skins and broad noses."[6] Arabia was originally inhabited by blacks. Descendants of these original blacks still reside in the southern part of Arabia.

In ancient times the name Ethiopian was more respected than it is now. In her book, *A Tropical Dependency*, writer Lady Lugard describes how favorably the ancient world saw the Ethiopians.

> The fame of the Ethiopians was widespread in ancient history. Herodotus describes them as "the tallest, most beautiful and long-lived of the human races," and before Herodotus, Homer, in even more flattering language, described them as "the most just of men; the favorites of the gods." The annals of all the great early nations of Asia Minor are full of them. The Mosaic records allude to them frequently; but while they are described as the most powerful, the most just, and the most beautiful of the human race,

they are constantly spoken of as black, and there seems to be no other conclusion to be drawn, than...at that remote period of history the leading race of the Western world was a black race.[7]

"A number of scholars, both ancient and modern, have come to the conclusion that the world's first civilization was created by... the Ethiopians,"[8] says historian John G. Jackson.

Civilization is a word often used by archaeologists, anthropologists, historians, and other social scientists in their writings, but they rarely define it. One definition says that civilization is the condition of being civilized. This makes sense. For a society to be truly civilized, its citizens must be courteous and mannerly toward others. In other words, the society must have humanity. Another meaning of civilization deals with the general stage of man's development. According to this definition, civilization is reached when a society achieves a high stage of social and cultural development. A final definition states that civilization comes into existence when a society has acquired the knowledge of writing, metalworking, large-scale building, and humane conduct toward others.

The world's first civilization was created by the Ethiopians on the African continent. This civilization in its infancy arose in the interior of the African continent, around the Great Lakes area, far back in prehistoric times. Then it slowly traveled northward up the Nile Valley. The cities of Meroe and Napata were at the center of this ancient black civilization, where hieroglyphic writing, sculpture, large-scale building, and other knowledge originated. This ancient black civilization continued to "spread northward, reaching its most spectacular achievements in what became known as 'Egyptian Civilization.'"[9] Continuing on, this ancient black civilization spread to western Asia from the Nile Valley.

There has been much controversy concerning the origin of Egypt, the greatest civilization of the ancient world. Some scholars believe that Egyptian civilization was a white civilization of European or Asian origin. However, abundant evidence shows that Egyptian civilization was of African origin. The ancient writer Diodorus of Sicily was of the opinion that the Egyptians evolved from the Ethiopians. He states:

> The Ethiopians say that the Egyptians are one of their colonies which was brought into Egypt by Osiris. They even allege that this country was originally under water, but that the Nile, dragging much mud as it flowed from Ethiopia, had finally filled it in and made it a part of the continent....They add that from them, as from their authors and ancestors, the Egyptians get most of their laws. It is from them that the Egyptians have learned to honor kings as gods and bury them with such pomp; sculpture and writing were invented by the Ethiopians. The Ethiopians cite evidence that they are more ancient than the Egyptians, but it is useless to report that here.[10]

Modern writer Colonel Alexandre Braghine, an archaeologist, supports the view that ancient Egypt's roots are in Ethiopia. In his book, *The Shadow of Atlantis,* he comments on Egypt's origin:

> The most interesting hypothesis concerning the origin of the Egyptians and their culture is the Ethiopian one.... Diodorus affirms that the ancient Egyptians took their hieratic writing, sculpture and some of their other knowledge from the Ethiopians. The Ethiopians themselves have a tradition supporting this statement. ...[Theophrastus], in his biography of the famous magician Apollonius of Tyana, relates that the latter, after his education in India and Egypt, came to Ethiopia in order to enlarge his knowledge by learning from the Ethiopian mystagogues. The same Apollonius, according to

...[Theophrastus], claimed that Pythagoras learned from Egyptian priests only what the latter themselves had learned from the Ethiopians. Very possibly the prehistoric Ethiopian culture was superior to that of their neighbors.[11]

Ethiopia was the mother of Egypt. The highly advanced civilization of ancient Egypt was nurtured to maturity by the Ethiopians. Egypt dazzled the ancient world with her pyramids, sphinxes, temples, and obelisks. Egyptian civilization was an African creation. Ancient Egyptians were Ethiopians.

Ethiopia was also the mother of ancient Sumer in western Asia. The ancient Sumerians were a black people. They were Asiatic Ethiopians. It is believed the Sumerians came from the Nile Valley. "The myths, legends, and traditions of the Sumerians [all] point to... Ethiopia as...[their] original home...."[12]

Ancient Sumer corresponds roughly with the southeastern part of modern-day Iraq, the southern part of the ancient region of Mesopotamia. Mesopotamia means between rivers. Mesopotamia was located roughly between the Tigris and the Euphrates rivers. The ancient Sumerians began to develop their civilization about 3500 B.C. They tilled the soil, practiced irrigation, erected cities, ...[raised] cattle, and invented a system of writing which they bequeathed to their Semitic successors.[13] This system of writing was called cuneiform. Important Sumerian cities were Ur, Umma, Uruk, Lagash, and Kish.

In the 2300s B.C., Sumer was invaded by a Semitic people known as the Akkadians. The Akkadians, led by Sargon, eventually conquered the whole of Sumer.

Another ancient people of western Asia were the Elamites. Scholar Harry Johnston says "the Elamites of Mesopotamia appeared to have been a Negroid people with kinky hair...."[14] Their ancient kingdom, Elam, was located in the southwestern part of modern-day Iran. The capital of Elam was Susa, a famous ancient city. The biblical name for Susa is Shushan. Elam was another daughter of Ethiopia. Her roots were in the Nile Valley. There are "numerous similarities between the material cultures of early Elam and the Nile Valley, including: arrowheads, polished stone implements, pressure-flaking, mace heads, scripts, pottery forms, stone vases, female figurines, art motifs, and metal mirrors."[15]

The original inhabitants of India and Pakistan were black. They were Asiatic Ethiopians. Their ancient Indus Valley civilization began about 2500 B.C. These early blacks have been called Dravidians. Scholar Will Durant describes these early Dravidians as "a dark-skinned, broad-nosed people...."[16] The Indus Valley civilization was highly advanced. Historian John G. Jackson describes it in the following manner:

> The first great civilization of India was established by...Asiatic Ethiopians in the Indus Valley. They built large cities; the principal ones being Mohenjo Daro, Chanhu Daro, and Harappa. Their cities were well built: Mohenjo Daro was two square miles in area, with regularly laid out main and side streets lined with attractive two-story brick houses. Bathrooms were common, and they were fitted out with runaway drains leading to brick sewers which were laid under the streets...These people had domesticated cattle, sheep, and elephants; they cultivated wheat and cotton, possessed boats and wheeled carts, and were skillful workers in bronze and iron.[17]

The early blacks of the Indus Valley also created a writing system and a system for weighing and measuring things.

About 1500 B.C., maybe earlier, northern India was invaded by a migrating white people called Aryans. This invasion caused many blacks to move southward to southern India.

Some scholars are of the opinion that the Sumerian civilization of Mesopotamia is older than the Egyptian civilization of the Nile Valley. This view is inaccurate.

Egyptian civilization is much older than the Sumerian civilization. For one thing, Egypt began its dynastic history before Sumer. Egypt's dynastic history began about 3100 B.C., whereas Sumer's dynastic history began about 2700 B.C. Egypt had also created a calendar before Sumer was born. Sumerian civilization began about 3500 B.C. However, 736 years earlier, "4236 B.C. Egypt had already invented a calendar...."[18] It takes thousands of years to acquire the knowledge to create a calendar. African scholar Cheikh Anta Diop believes that it took the Egyptians "not less than 5,000 years"[19] to acquire the knowledge to create a calendar. This would put Egyptian history "back almost as far as 8,000 or 10,000 years...."[20]

Egyptian civilization is much older than the Sumerian civilization. According to Sir Gaston Maspero, the Egyptians made their first appearance on the stage of history about eight thousand to ten thousand years B.C.[21] In comparison, the Sumerian civilization began about 3500 B.C.

African scholar Cheikh Anta Diop agrees that the Egyptian civilization is much older then the Mesopotamian civilizations (Sumer and Elam). He states as follows:

> Egyptian civilization goes far back in "prehistoric" antiquity. If man as we know him was born in the region around Kenya (to the exclusion of all other regions) some 120,000 years ago, and if he began to colonize the Nile Valley from the area of the Great Lakes and on into Egypt, then there is nothing strange about the fact that there should already be an established civilization in this valley dating to 10,000 years ago. All of which will explain the precocity of this civilization at a time when the rest of the world was in barbarism. Egypt was the first to emerge, all ideology put aside. It is not possible—it clashes with chronology—to establish a parallel between Mesopotamia and Egypt, even though the first Mesopotamian civilizations

were black...But the movement was out of Egypt, the Egyptian influence spread through all of western Asia. It was much later, compared to Egyptian history, that these regions, that this black world was also to emerge to civilization.[22]

The black people who were known to the ancient world as Ethiopians created the world's first civilization. This black civilization began in the interior of the continent and traveled northward up the Nile Valley, reaching its greatest height in what became known as Egyptian civilization. This black civilization then spread to western Asia.

While Ethiopia was the mother of civilization, she also had daughters. Egypt was her greatest daughter; Sumer, Elam, and India were also her daughters.

Godfrey Higgins, an English scholar, bears witness to blacks' influence on early Asia in his work, *Anacalypis,* first published in 1836. He says, "There were two Ethiopias, one to the east of the Red Sea, and the other to the west of it; and a very great nation of Blacks from India did rule over almost all Asia in a very remote era, in fact beyond the reach of history or any of our records."[23]

Black people are the original people of the earth. We originated in Africa and spread out over the world in prehistoric times. For thousands of years, we were the only people inhabiting the earth.

Higgins says, "We have found the black complexion or something relating to it whenever we have approached the origin of nations."[24] Concerning blacks' influence on the world in remote antiquity, Higgins states as follows:

I shall, in the course of this work, produce a number of extraordinary facts, which will be quite sufficient to prove, that a black race, in very early times, had more influence...[over] the affairs of the world than has been lately suspected; and I think I shall show, by some very striking circumstances yet existing, that the effects of this influence have not entirely passed away.[25]

It is most unfortunate that the modern world has suppressed the black man's ancient history. It is one of the world's best-kept secrets. However, the truth is slowly emerging. Books such as *African Presence in Early Asia*, 1995; *African Presence in Early America*, 1995; *Egypt: Child of Africa*, 1995; and *Egypt Revisited*, 1993, bear witness to this truth. One day the truth about the black man's ancient history will emerge in full view to the world, and it will set our minds free.

Chapter 4

Egypt: Great Civilization of the Nile Valley

"For there is nothing covered, that shall not be revealed; neither hid, that shall not be known."
—Luke 12:2

Who Were the Ancient Egyptians?

The ancient Greek and Roman writers, eyewitnesses of that remote period in history, observed the physical characteristics of the ancient Egyptians. All were in general agreement that the ancient Egyptians were black-skinned people with wooly hair.

The Greek historian Herodotus visited Egypt about 450 B.C. He, therefore, was an eyewitness to the physical characteristics of the ancient Egyptians. He describes them as having "black skin and wooly hair."

Evidence that Herodotus considered the ancient Egyptians black is found in *The History of Herodotus, Book II*. In this book he mentions a black, wooly-haired people called Colchians who, he said, were physically and culturally similar to the Egyptians. He also believed the Colchians were descended from the Egyptians. Comparing the Colchians to the Egyptians, Herodotus states:

> There can be no doubt that the Colchians are an Egyptian race. Before I heard any mention of the fact from others, I had remarked it my-

self....My own conjectures were founded, first, on the fact that they are black-skinned and have wooly hair, which certainly amounts to but little, since several other nations are so too; but further and more especially, on the circumstances that the Colchians, the Egyptians and the Ethiopians, are the only nations who have practiced circumcision from the earliest times.... I will add a further proof to the identity of the Egyptians and the Colchians. These two nations weave their linen in exactly the same way, and this is a way entirely unknown to the rest of the world; they also in their whole mode of life and in their language resemble one another.[1]

The Colchians are important because they can be used to establish the racial identity of the ancient Egyptians. Herodotus described them as black with wooly hair, and said they belonged to the Egyptian race. If the ancient Egyptians hadn't been black, Herodotus would not have said that the Colchians were an Egyptian race.

Herodotus was told by Egyptians that the Colchians were descended from the soldiers of Sesostris, a pharaoh of the Twelfth Dynasty. Sesostris is said to have made military conquests in Asia.

The ancient Colchians lived on the eastern shore of the Black Sea, and area the Greeks called Colchis. Ancient Colchis was located in what is now the modern republic of Georgia, a former republic of the Soviet Union. Today there are blacks who still reside in this area near the Black Sea. Some scholars believe these black Russians are survivors of the ancient Colchians.

Another Greek writer who said the ancient Egyptians were black was Lucian. In a writing of his, two Greeks are having a conversation, one of them describes an Egyptian boy to the other. He says, "This boy is not merely black; he has thick lips and his legs are too thin...."[2]

Still another Greek writer who attested to the blackness of the ancient Egyptians was Aristotle, the philosopher. Correlating cowardice and courage to the amount of melanin in the skin, he states, "Those who are too black are cowards, like for instance, the Egyptians and Ethiopians. But those who are excessively white are also cowards as we can see from the example of women, the complexion of courage is between the two."[3]

When Herodotus observed the similarities between the Egyptians and the Colchians, he was certain that the Colchians were of Egyptian origin. So, according to these descriptions by the ancients, who were eyewitnesses, the ancient Egyptians would be members of the black or so-called Negro race. However, most modern writers have disagreed with the ancients about the race of the ancient Egyptians.

The racial identity of the ancient Egyptians has been a topic of much controversy. Bitter arguments and debates have raged over what was the race of the ancient Egyptians. This controversy has divided scholars into two schools of thought. One side is of the opinion that the ancient Egyptians were not *true Negroes*. Instead they were dark-skinned whites (Hamites), but definitely not a black people. However, these scholars have failed to point out that there are variations among indigenous Africans. Not all indigenous Africans fit the so-called true Negro model. Some scholars, recently, in the face of so much evidence of a black ancient Egypt, have backed away from saying that the ancient Egyptians were whites; they now say that the ancient Egyptians were a racially mixed people. The other side, supported by overwhelming evidence, advocates that the ancient Egyptians were of African origin. Therefore, they belonged to the black or so-called Negro race.

"There are at least six variants of the indigenous African...."[4] One type is the Elongated variant. This variant is distinguished by an elongated body build;

narrow head, face, and nose; dark skin; spiraled hair; and thick but not everted lips.[5] The Elongated Africans are a "contrast to the classical Negro type but are indigenous, unmixed Africans."[6] The Elongated type includes the Fulani, the Tutsi, and the Hima (Rwanda), the Masai (Kenya), the Galla (Ethiopia), the Somalis (Somalia), and the Beja (northern Sudan).[7] A second type of indigenous African is the Nilotic variant. "The Nilotic variant...is taller than the elongated type with a narrower head, a lower and wider nose, a very slender body, with extremely long legs and little fat. These Nilotic...include the Nuer, the Dinka, the Shilluk, and the Anuak, all of whom occupy the Nile River basins in the Southern Sudan."[8] A third type of indigenous African is the Bushman variant. The Bushman variant has tight, wooly hair, short stature, and a yellowish-brown skin color. They reside in the desert regions of southern Africa. A fourth type of indigenous African is the Pygmy variant. The Pygmy variant is very short (less than five feet tall) with kinky hair, and a black-brown skin color. This variant resides in the forests of Central Africa. A fifth type of indigenous African is the Madagascar variant who lives on the island of Madagascar, off the southeastern coast of Africa. The indigenous people of Madagascar are called Malagasies. Scientists hypothesize that the Malagasies are a mixture of original black Africans and Indonesians, who migrated to the island hundreds of years ago. The sixth type of indigenous African is the best known of all, the so-called True Negro variant. He is characterized by a wide nose, thick lips, wooly hair, dark skin, and tall stature.

There are wide variations among indigenous Africans. Not all fit the stereotyped "true Negro" model. Some indigenous Africans don't have thick lips. Some indigenous Africans have brown or yellowish-brown skins. Some indigenous Africans have narrow noses, a trait associated with Caucasoid people. Climate and the environment have no doubt played a role in causing the variations among indigenous African people. Some scientists believe that adaptation to a particular environment over a long period of time can change people physically. A cooler climate is said to lighten the skin. A dry, hot climate is said to narrow the nose.

These variations among indigenous Africans were generally not taken into consideration by early anthropologists doing skull studies on the ancient Egyptians. They selected only skulls of the true Negro type to be representative of Africans. These anthropologists assumed that the skulls of the Elongated and Nilotic Africans, which varied from the true Negro type, were skulls of Caucasoid people or people mixed with Caucasoids. They therefore concluded that the ancient Egyptians were not true Negroes but Hamites, a dark-skinned Caucasoid people.

This classification of the ancient Egyptians as mainly Caucasoid or non-African people has been reflected in skull analyses that give the racial identity of the ancient Egyptians by percentages. "An Oxford team—David Thomson and Randall McIver—declared in 1905 that only 25 percent of the ancient Egyptians were Negroid. Sir Arthur Keith challenged this, showing that if these parameters were used, then 30 percent of England's population would be classified as Negroid."[9] Later, Falkenburger did a study on pre-dynastic Egyptian skulls. His results were as follows: 36 percent Negroid, 33 percent Mediterranean (dark-skinned white), 11 percent Cro-Magnoid (European), and 20 percent mixed.

As we can see, anthropologists have used the variations among Africans to make some of them into Caucasians, dark-skinned Caucasians (Hamites), and mixed bloods. Africans such as the Galla of Ethiopia and the Somalis of Somalia, who have narrow noses (a Caucasian trait), have been made into Caucasians by anthropologists. Some anthropologists have even made Negroes such as the Masai of Kenya and the Dinka and the Shilluk of the Sudan into Caucasians. This is ridiculous. Yet anthropologists, when classifying Europeans, don't divide them into different races because of their physical variations. Europeans vary physically just like Africans. Northern Europeans tend to have blonde hair and a light skin. Southern Europeans tend to be shorter in stature and have darker skins and darker hair than northern Europeans. There is quite a contrast between a blonde Scandinavian and a dark-skinned Spaniard or Italian. The Scandinavian could be called a *true white* person, while the Spaniard and Italian could be denied membership in the Caucasoid race. Just as there is a physical variation between a blonde Scandinavian and a dark Italian, there is also a physical variation between a brown Galla from Ethiopia (East Africa) and a dark Wolof from Senegal (West Africa). However, when Africans vary from the so called true Negro model, they are generally classified as Caucasians by anthropologists. On the other hand, when Europeans vary from the so-called true Caucasoid model, anthropologists still classify them as white.

We find that skull analysis can be somewhat misleading and arbitrary. However, more reliable methods can be used to determine the racial identity of the ancient Egyptians. Recent studies by scientists provide further evidence that the ancient Egyptians were indigenous Africans. Analysis of hair and melanin content of the skin, studies of dental traits, and analysis of DNA and blood types show that the ancient Egyptians were related to the other blacks of Africa.

The Caucasoid trait of a narrow nose in the Elongated African such as the Galla of Ethiopia and the Somalis of Somalia is now thought by geneticists to be caused by an adaptation to dry heat. Genetic analysis and ancestral relationships show ...[that the Elongated African] clusters with other African populations and emerges distinct from European or Asiatic races....[10]

The view that the ancient Egyptians were dark-skinned Caucasians or Hamites is a misconception. Much evidence shows that the ancient Egyptians were indigenous Africans. They were as African as blacks from tropical Africa.

Controversy over the race of the ancient Egyptians could have been avoided if modern scholars had accepted Herodotus' description of them. The father of history, a reliable eyewitness, could hardly have been wrong. Why have modern scholars disagreed with the ancients about the race of the ancient Egyptians? To answer this question, we have to go back into history.

In 1798, French troops commanded by Napoleon Bonaparte invaded Egypt. They defeated the Mamelukes in a battle fought near the Pyramids at Giza. By establishing a base in Egypt, Napoleon hoped to disrupt the trade between Great Britain and the Middle East. But in 1801, after three years of occupying Egypt, French troops were forced to withdraw after suffering heavy losses against the Ottoman Turks and British forces.

Napoleon's expedition into Egypt also included a number of French scientists and scholars. They observed the pyramids, sphinxes, statues, and other wonders of ancient Egypt. They were amazed at the perfection and splendor of this past civilization. They were even more amazed to discover that a black race had created this great civilization. "This rediscovery by Europeans of ancient Egypt, and the disclosures of a powerful Negro-African element in the ancestry of a civilization to which Europe owed so much, came as an embarrassment. It came also at a most inopportune time."[11] Africans were being enslaved in masses by Europeans. To justify this cruel and inhuman activity, the myth of black innate inferiority had been invented. With the disclosure of a black ancient Egypt, this myth was in jeopardy of being exposed as a falsehood. How could an inferior race have created such an advanced civilization? To solve this problem, the African origin of ancient Egyptian civilization simply was denied and a clever new twist was invented. Instead of being classified as Africans or Negroes, the creators of this great civilization were now classified as members of the Hamitic branch of the Caucasian race, or dark-skinned whites. As a result, most modern scholars would talk of a white Egypt, disagreeing with the testimony of the ancients.

The viewpoint that the ancient Egyptians were of African origin has been supported by a number of modern white scholars, including Count C.F. Volney, Arnold Heeren, Gerald Massey, and Albert Churchward. However, some of their works have been largely ignored. Few are well known to the general reading public.

C.F. Volney (1755-1805) was a famous French scholar and traveler. He authored *Travels in Syria and Egypt*, (1787) and *The Ruins* or, *Meditation of the Revolutions of Empires: and the Law of Nature*, (1793).

Volney, visited Egypt between 1783 and 1785, a time when Africans were being victimized by slavery. When Volney observed the appearance of the Great Sphinx of Gizeh (Giza), he said that it solved for him the riddle of why the native Egyptians were so Negroid in appearance. Speaking of the Sphinx, Volney said, "On seeing that head, typically Negro in all its features, I remembered the remarkable passage where Herodotus says: 'As for me, I judge the Colchians to be a colony of the Egyptians because, like them, they are black with wooly hair....'"[12] Volney goes on to say, "In other words, the ancient Egyptians were true Negroes of the same type as all native-born Africans. That being so, we can see how their blood, mixed for several centuries with that of the Romans and Greeks, must have lost the intensity of its original color, while retaining nonetheless the imprint of its original mold."[13]

Looking at the Negroid appearing Sphinx, a symbol of power and supreme achievement, it was hard to believe that an enslaved race, a symbol of inferiority and servitude, had in its distant past, erected such an awesome monument. How could history have been so violently reversed?[14] "Reflecting on the ...state of the

Egyptians compared with what they had been,"[15] Volney said, "Just think that this race of black men, today our slave and the object of our scorn, is the very race to which we owe our arts, sciences, and even the use of speech!"[16] Unfortunately, Volney lived at a time when the enslavement of Africans was flourishing. Those who supported the lucrative slave trade were strongly opposed to the statement that Negroes had created a great civilization like Egypt. They needed to maintain the image of the African as a slave. Henceforth, they would try hard to erase the memory of a Black Egypt.

Arnold Heeren (1760-1842) was a noted scholar and professor of history and politics at The University of Gottingen, Germany. In his work, *Historical Researches: African Nations*, he comments on the African origin of Egyptian civilization:

> The ancient civilization of Egypt spread, as we know from south to north, and...there is seemingly no doubt that the earliest center of civilization in Africa was the country watered by the Upper Nile....The principal state of this Ethiopian country bore the well-known name of Meroe....This is not the place, nor am I competent to discuss the arguments which form the ground of belief that the civilization of Meroe precedes that of Egypt. It is enough to say very briefly that on the site of the City of Meroe, there exist remains of temples and pyramids from which archaeologists have drawn the conclusion that the pyramids were a form of architecture native to Meroe, and only afterwards brought to perfection in Egypt....The carvings of the monuments of Meroe show a people in possession of the arts and luxuries of civilization and having some knowledge of science. On the base of one of the monuments a zodiac has been found....This remarkable spot is regarded by the ancients as the cradle of the arts of science, where hieroglyphic writing was discovered and where temples and pyramids had already

sprung up while Egypt still remained ignorant of their existence.[17]

Gerald Massey (1828-1907) was a famous English poet, literary critic, and Egyptologist. He did extensive research on African and Egyptian history. His writings support the view that Egypt was of African origin. He was the author of *A Book of the Beginnings* (1881), *The Natural Genesis* (1883), and *Ancient Egypt, the Light of the World* (1907). In *A Book of the Beginnings*, vol. 1, Massey says, "Egypt is often called Kam, the black land, and Kam does signify black; the name probably applied to the earliest inhabitants whose type is the Kam or Ham of the Hebrew writers."[18] In another passage Massey comments on the African origin of Egyptian Civilization:

> It will be maintained in this book that the oldest mythology, religion, symbols, language had their birthplace in Africa, that the primitive race of Kam came thence, and the civilization attained in Egypt, emanated from that country and spread over the world. The most reasonable view on the evolutionary theory...is that the black race is the most ancient, and that Africa is the primordial home.[19]

Albert Churchward was an English physician, anthropologist, and archaeologist. In his book *The Origin and Evolution of the Human Race* he supports the view that ancient Egypt was of African origin.

We deeply appreciate white scholars C.F. Volney, Arnold Heeren, Gerald Massey, and Albert Churchward, whose works transcend modern racism and tell history as it was. Their scholarly works have been used by a number of black scholars.

Baron Viviant Denon, who was part of Napoleon's expedition into Egypt, made a sketch of the Great Sphinx in 1798. He had this to say about it: "The character is African...the lips are thick. Art must have been at a high pitch when this monument was executed."[20]

The view that the ancient Egyptians were Africans is also supported by a number of black scholars, including J.A. Rogers, Chancellor Williams, John G. Jackson, John Henrik Clarke, Cheikh Anta Diop, Yosef ben-Jochannan, Wayne B. Chandler, Runoko Rashidi, Asa G. Hilliard III, Charles S. Finch III, and others.

J.A. Rogers (1883-1966) was an internationally known scholar, researcher, and historian. He traveled throughout the world researching the history of black people. He was an early advocate of the view that the ancient Egyptians were black. This view is supported in his books *World's Great Men of Color*, vol. I, 1947; *Sex and Race*, vol. I, 1940; and *Africa's Gift to America*, 1961.

Chancellor Williams (1893-1992) was a renowned scholar, historian, and professor at Howard University. He was a very alert historian, skillful at reading the abstract and the implied, and a great history analyst. He did regional field studies in Africa, seeking the true history of black people. He was a strong defender of Africa and black people. His great work, *The Destruction of Black Civilization* (1976), strongly supports the view that the ancient Egyptians were a black people.

John G. Jackson (1907-1993) was a famous historian and scholar. He began early in his life writing about the history of back people. He wrote articles for Marcus Garvey's newspaper, *Negro World*, while he was still in high school. He strongly defended the view that the ancient Egyptians were a black people in *Introduction to African Civilizations* (1970).

John Henrik Clarke (1915-1998) was a brilliant historian, scholar, and professor at Hunter College in New York. He was mostly self-educated. He worked long and hard, restoring the missing pages of African history to world history. He was very good at analyzing history and connecting the past to the present. He strongly defended the view that the ancient Egyptians were a black people in articles and in his work, *Notes for an African World Revolution: Africans at the Cross-roads* (1991).

Cheikh Anta Diop (1923-1986) was born in the African nation of Senegal. He gained international fame as a multi-discipline scholar and Egyptologist. He was a leader in the struggle to reclaim ancient Egypt as an African civilization. In 1974 in Cairo, Egypt, he participated in a big debate over the racial identity of the ancient Egyptians. In this debate he was aligned with fellow African scholar, Theophile Obenga, against an array of international scholars. Witnesses say the big debate was marked by "passion and prejudice," but Diop and Obenga came prepared, and were victorious, shattering the theses of their opponents. Diop's work, *The African Origin of Civilization* (1974), strongly defends the view that the ancient Egyptians were a black people.

Josef ben-Jochannan was born in 1917 in Ethiopia. He is a noted scholar, author, and Egyptologist. He is affectionately called Dr. Ben by his colleagues, students, and friends. He has spent many years researching the ancient history of the Nile Valley. He is a strong defender of Africa and an even stronger defender of the view that the ancient Egyptians were a black people. His books include *Africa: Mother of Western Civilization* (1971) and *Black Man of the Nile and His Family* (1972).

Maulana Karenga has achieved widespread fame as a scholar, community activist, and leader. He was active in the Civil Rights Movement of the 1960s. He also created the popular African-American holiday called Kwanza, which is celebrated from December 26 to January 1. He has strongly defended the view that the ancient Egyptians were a black people in his lectures, articles, and books. He is currently professor and chairman of the Department of Black Studies at California State University, Long Beach.

Ivan Van Sertima was born in the South American country of Guyana. He is an internationally known anthropologist, linguist, and scholar. He is a professor at Rutgers University in New Jersey. He is a strong leader in the defense of the view that the ancient Egyptians were indigenous Africans. He edited books, *Egypt Revisited* (1993) and *Egypt: Child of Africa* (1995), which strongly defend this view.

Wayne B. Chandler is a well known scholar, author, lecturer, and anthrophotojournalist. He is very active researching and lecturing in the United States and abroad, and has produced numerous works on black history. In his articles in *Journal of African Civilizations*, he has strongly defended the view that the ancient Egyptians were a black people.

Runoko Rashidi is a famous historian, lecturer, and scholar. He is a specialist on the history of blacks in early Asia. He has traveled throughout the world lecturing about the African contribution to world history. He has written articles in *Journal of African Civilizations*, strongly defending the view that the ancient Egyptians were black.

Asa G. Hilliard III is a well known scholar, educator, administrator, and lecturer. He is a professor at Georgia State University in Atlanta, Georgia. He has strongly defended the view that the ancient Egyptians were a black people in *Journal of African Civilizations*.

Charles S. Finch III is a well known physician and scholar. He teaches at the Morehouse School of Medicine in Atlanta, Georgia. He has written articles in *Journal of African Civilizations*, strongly defending the view that the ancient Egyptians were black.

We applaud these black scholars for their well documented and strong defense of the view that the ancient Egyptians were a black people. Their scholarly works are an inspiration to blacks everywhere.

Egypt's crossroads location put her under constant pressure from foreigners for thousands of years. "Egypt is located at the cross roads of three continents—a meeting place for cultures and conflicts," writes Clarke. "The tragic uniqueness of Egypt is that it is an African nation that has been ruled by invaders for more than two thousand years."[21] She eventually succumbed to the Persians in 525 B.C. Wave after wave of invaders followed. The Greeks arrived after the Persians in 332 B.C., the Romans in 30 B.C., the Arabs in A.D. 639, the Turks in 1517, the French in 1798, and the British in 1882. As a result, these uninterrupted invasions practically erased the memory of an original Black Egypt.

The racial identity of the inhabitants of a nation or a geographic area can change over a period of time due to migrations, invasions and conquests, slavery, amalgamation, and other factors. For example, the racial makeup of the United States today consists of African-Americans, Asian-Americans, European-Americans, Hispanic-Americans, and Native Americans. But six hundred years ago the Indians were the only Americans here. They are the only Americans who are native. Their ancestors built the Mayan and Incan civilizations in Central and South America. The same is true of Egypt. The indigenous Africans of the Nile Valley built the ancient Egyptian civilization. The current rulers of Egypt, the Arabs, are not native to Egypt, although they have been there for over thirteen hundred years. They are the descendants of the Arabs who invaded and conquered Egypt in the seventh century.

The Egypt of today is much different from the Egypt of yesterday. Present-day Egypt is part of the Asian Middle East, a region characterized and united by the Islamic or Muslim faith. Therefore, the Egypt of today is an African nation that has been taken geographically and culturally out of Africa. It is now a part of the Arab world. Thus the name change from Egypt to the United Arab Republic. The Egypt of yesterday was created by the indigenous Africans of the Nile Valley and ruled by them until the wave of invasions came. But if one did not know about the early role of Africans in ancient Egyptian history, coupled with the Africans' subservient position in the world over the last five hundred years, one would naturally conclude that black Africans had no part in Egyptian history and culture, except maybe as slaves. This is why Egyptian history is so confusing and so misleading.

To understand Egyptian history completely, one has to know what happened before and after the invasions. The invasions impacted the physical appearance of the original black Egyptians. The crossbreeding between conquerors and conquered resulted in more and more Egyptians becoming mixed or mulattoes, transforming them from black to different shades of brown and even near-white in complexion. In short, the invasions obscured the early creating role of Africans in Egyptian civilization, leaving the impression that although Egypt is located in Africa, Africans had nothing to do with the origin of its civilization. Nothing could be further from the truth.

History recorded on stone reveals that ancient Egypt was of African origin. The Reverend Sterling M. Means reflects on the undeniable truth that monuments reveal.

> A monument is history recorded on stone and a photograph chiseled or sculptured on polish marble features the likeness of the people who erected it. This being true it gives license to say that without a shadow of doubt, a monument is more reliable than history and tells a truth more real than tradition and demonstrates a fact that is "stranger than fiction."[22]

German historian Arnold Heeren, says, "A monument bears witness of a fact more clearly and certain than could be done by the statement of a writer. The fact that the people who erected this monument had attained a degree of civilization without which they could not have erected it."[23]

The indigenous blacks of the Nile Valley built awesome monuments in their likeness, as if they knew modern history would falsely attribute their achievements to some other race. Wise and spiritual people, they knew their civilization was finite. It would not last forever. But they tried to build their monuments to last for eternity. Therefore, these monuments would bear witness to generations unborn who the creators of the Nile Valley civilization were. The Great Sphinx, located in the Nile Delta in Egypt, has unmistakably African features: thick lips and a broad nose. It would be hard for anyone, "even a fool,"[24] to "seriously doubt that this"[25] monument was a portrayal of an African.

The struggle to reclaim Egyptian history has been long and hard and emotional. But it must continue. African history will remain incomplete until it includes Egyptian history. The two are inseparable. Ancient Egypt will play the same role in African history as Greece and Rome do in European history. Black scholars who research and write about African history must deal with Egypt. African scholar Cheikh Anta Diop says, "The African historian who evades the problem of Egypt is neither modest nor objective, nor unruffled; he is ignorant, cowardly, and neurotic."[26]

Diop invented a chemical process for determining the amount of melanin in the skins of Egyptian mummies called the Melanin Dosage Test. Melanin is the substance that determines the skin's darkness or lightness. Dark skin has more melanin than light skin. "Melanin...is...insoluble and is preserved for millions of years in the skins of fossil animals."[27] By analyzing the amount of melanin in the skins of Egyptian mummies, one can determine what color the ancient Egyptians were.

Diop studied Egyptian mummies at the Museum of Man in Paris, France. These were mummies that Auguste Mariette, a French archaeologist, had excavated in the Nile Delta and brought to the museum. In these mummies, Diop found a melanin level that could only belong to a black skin. From his analysis, Diop said, "the evaluation of melanin level by microscopic examination...enables us to classify the ancient Egyptians unquestionably among the black races."[28]

Who were the ancient Egyptians? They were a black people. The evidence is so overwhelming that no scholar can seriously challenge it. The opposite view that the ancient Egyptians were dark-skinned whites has no convincing evidence to support it. In fact, it is based more on emotion than evidence.

The Rise and Fall of Egypt

The ancient Egyptians never used the word *Egypt* to refer to their country. They called their country *Khem, Kemet,* or *Kam,* meaning Black Land, referring to the black people who lived there. The word Egypt is of Greek origin, derived from the Greek word *Aigyptos.* The word Aigyptos was the Greek way of saying *Hikuptah,* an ancient name for the city of Memphis. So the Greeks unintentionally gave the name of a city to a country.

The word *Ethiopia* is also of Greek origin, meaning sunburnt faces. The ancient Greeks believed that the heat from the sun made the Ethiopians' skin black. The Greeks referred to all dark and black-skinned people of Asia and Africa as Ethiopians.

But what did the Ethiopians call themselves? The Ethiopians called themselves the *Anu* people.

In far ancient times, a group of Ethiopians led by Osiris migrated down the Nile River from Ethiopia into Egypt and established a colony. This colony over time grew into the greatest civilization of the ancient world.

The ancient blacks of Ethiopia and Egypt were both Anu people. In their early history they "were one and the same."[29] This is why the ancients said the Egyptians were Ethiopians.

The magnificent Nile Valley civilization of Ethiopia-Egypt was one of the greatest civilizations the world has ever known. As early as 10,000 years ago, there already was an established civilization in this valley. This civilization in its infancy began in the Great Lakes region of Central Africa far back in prehistoric times. Then it spread northward, entering the Nile Valley and developing into the world's first civilization. The ancients called this early civilization Ethiopia. The famous ancient city of Meroe was at the center of this civilization, where temple and pyramid building, religion, the arts and sciences, and hieroglyphic writing originated. This civilization continued to spread northward and reached its greatest glory in what became known as Egyptian civilization. Egypt, then, was the daughter of Ethiopia.

Ancient Ethiopia was a large empire, stretching from the Mediterranean Sea in the North to the source of the Nile in the South, comprising *Nubia* (Sudan), *Khem* (Egypt), *Punt* (Somalia), and *Kush* (Ethiopia). Egypt was located in the northeastern part of this empire.

Archaeological evidence, old and new, reveals that the culture of this ancient empire was of African origin. This culture went up the Nile Valley, in a south-to-north direction. To illustrate this point, an article in *Archaeology* magazine entitled "The Lost Pharaohs of Nubia" comments on a new archaeological discovery that reveals evidence of black pharaohs of Nubia ruling in the Nile Valley before the beginning of the historic First Dynasty in Egypt.

> Direct evidence for kings in the Nile Valley before the reign of Narmer has finally emerged in context, but in a place and culture that no one had expected—Qustal in Lower Nubia, very near the present-day border of Egypt and the Sudan. The inhabitants of Lower Nubia in this period... were long thought to have had too simple a culture and too small a population to establish and support the complex political institutions and centralization implied by the presence of pharaohs. How could they possibly have achieved some "first Dynasty" of their own?[30]

This finding is rendered even more startling by the fact that advanced political organization was not believed to have come to Nubia, or anywhere south of Egypt, for another 2,500 years.[31]

This shocking evidence reverses the thinking about the relationship between ancient Egypt and the land to the south of her. It had been assumed "for a long time that Egypt's"[32] great civilization had moved slowly downward to the primitive people "in the South."[33] But this evidence indicates that the reverse is true—"the South brought things up."[34] For example, the various "religious and political symbols"[35] that were found to have been used by Nubian royalty were the same ones that appeared later in dynastic Egyptian royalty. In addition, this ancient Nubian kingdom has been dated 3300 B.C., preceding by 200 years the appearance of the first Egyptian Dynasty, dated 3100 B.C. This discovery of black pharaohs in the Nile Valley before the rise of the First Dynasty in Egypt is, without a doubt, "the most important single find in Africa the last two...centuries."[36] It proves that ancient Egyptian civilization was of African origin.

About 3100 B.C. Menes (Narmer) united the kingdoms of Lower Egypt and Upper Egypt, creating the world's first nation-state. The kingdom of Lower Egypt was the Delta, or northern region. The kingdom of Upper Egypt was the southern region. The king of Upper Egypt wore the white crown and the king of Lower Egypt wore the red crown. Menes was the first king to wear the double crown, symbolizing the unification of Lower and Upper Egypt. Egypt's dynastic period, then, began with Menes as pharaoh. However, Egypt's civilization was already intact. "Writing, virtually the same calendar that we use today, sophisticated astronomy... [and other knowledge were] all in place."[37]

"In the third century B.C.,...Manetho, a learned Egyptian priest,...[wrote] a history of Egypt from the earliest times up to his own day. Unfortunately the greater part of this history was lost in the destruction of the Alexandrian Library, but among the surviving fragments are Manetho's list of the kings of Egypt."[38] His list divided the kings of Egypt into thirty dynasties, from the first king Menes to Nectanebo II.

Egyptologists today have combined and grouped the dynasties into the following periods: the Old Kingdom, the First Intermediate Period, the Middle Kingdom, the Second Intermediate Period, the New Kingdom, the Late Period, and the Saite Period. In 525 B.C. Egypt was conquered by the Persians, ending indigenous rule.

During one of the longest reigns in history, Menes brought about the kind of stability and innovations in administration that not only provided a solid foundation for a first dynasty, but also the economic and social conditions necessary for the more uniform expansion of religion, the arts, crafts, and the mathematical sciences.[39]

The capital of Memphis was built at the boundary of the two kingdoms (Lower and Upper Egypt). Memphis was named in Menes' honor. Memphis rose to become "one of the greatest cities of Egypt and the world from the First to the Twentieth Dynasty when it yielded to Thebes again, but it was still a great city when Alexander the Great arrived in 332 B.C."[40]

Menes' death brought his long and glorious reign to a close. He "was succeeded by his son Teta, who was a brilliant physician and built the royal palace in Memphis."[41]

Sources adequate enough to give a detailed account of the kings of the First and Second Dynasties of the Old Kingdom have not survived. Little is known about the various kings of these two dynasties except their names. The First Dynasty ended in 2884 B.C. and the Second Dynasty ruled from 2883 to 2665 B.C.

The last part of the Old Kingdom, the Third through Sixth Dynasties, was a period of remarkable achievements. It was Egypt's first golden age. During this period a highly organized central government was established, providing the kind of internal peace and stability necessary for the blossoming of Egyptian creative genius.

The Third Dynasty, 2664 to 2615 B.C., introduced the Great Pyramid Age. Imhotep designed and built the famous stepped pyramid tomb for Pharaoh Zoser at Sakhara near Memphis. This pyramid was the world's first large stone structure. The building methods used in the construction of this pyramid revolutionized the architecture of the ancient world.[42]

Imhotep was an extraordinary figure in the court of Pharaoh Zoser. He was not only a brilliant architect but an outstanding physician as well. He also was a poet and philosopher. In addition, he was an astronomer and magician, and held the post of chief physician to the monarch.[43] He was probably the world's first multi-genius.[44] In later days he was deified and became the god of medicine.[45]

The Fourth Dynasty continued the brilliant achievements of the Third Dynasty. Trade and contacts with other countries flourished. There was progress in all fields: agriculture, the arts and sciences, crafts, mining, engineering, architecture, and industry. The great pyramids and temples built during this Dynasty reflect the skill and genius of the ancient Egyptians. The great pyramid of Khufu (Cheops) at Giza is an example of amazing skill in engineering, architecture, and mathematics; it stands 481 feet and covers 13 acres at its base. It remained the tallest building in the world until modern times, a period of over four thousand years. The second pyramid at Giza was built by Pharaoh Khafre (Chephren). It is not quite as large as the one built for Khufu, but it is still impressive. The third pyramid at Giza was built by Mycerinus, the last great leader of the Fourth Dynasty. His pyramid is the smallest of the three.

The Fourth Dynasty was characterized by great leaders—Snefru, Khufu, Khafre, and Mycerinus. The Giza pyramids symbolize the power and prestige of the pharaoh during this period. His power was supreme. During this dynasty the power of the monarchy reached its peak. The Fourth Dynasty ended in 2502 B.C.

The Fifth Dynasty began with Userkaf as pharaoh in 2501 B.C. This dynasty was characterized by the significance of the sun god Ra. During this period, the pharaohs began calling themselves *Sons of Ra.* Their pyramid-temples were constructed at Abusir, north of Sakhara. During the Fifth Dynasty there were achievements in architecture, the arts and sciences, philosophy, and building. Also foreign trade continued to flourish. Toward the end of the Fifth Dynasty the lords of the provinces began to grow in power and wealth. Pharaoh Unis was the last ruler of the Fifth Dynasty. His pyramid tomb was constructed at Sakhara. Engraved on the walls were the famous Pyramid Texts, a composition of prayers. The Fifth Dynasty ended in 2342 B.C.

The Sixth Dynasty was the last of the Old Kingdom. During this period, the power of the monarchy began to decline due to the increasing power of the priests and the lords of the provinces. As a result, the central government began to slowly weaken. Near the close of The Sixth Dynasty, the weakening of the central government accelerated, especially during the last half of Pepi II's "ninety-year reign."[46] Pepi was "a strong leader and a mighty king during the first fifty years of his reign,...[but a] general upheaval began when he had become too old to govern or even know what was going on in the country."[47] With a weak central government, the provinces began to break away and establish independence. Eventually the central government collapsed, ending the Sixth Dynasty. Egypt's first golden age had come to an end. The year was 2180 B.C.

The period that followed the Old Kingdom was called the First Intermediate Period. It included the Seventh through Tenth Dynasties and part of the Eleventh Dynasty, 2180 to 2052 B.C. This was a time of chaos in Egypt. Lacking centralized authority, various provinces fought for power and control. The civil strife became more intense and bitter as the largest and strongest provinces, such as Thebes, tried to force the others back into a state of national unity.[48] There was often confusion about who actually was pharaoh of all Egypt. For example, there were times when kings in Lower Egypt, ruling from Avaris or Sais, and kings in Upper Egypt, ruling from Thebes or Memphis, claimed the throne at the same time when actually none had control over the whole nation. The problem was, too many kings wanted the same thing—to be pharaoh of all Egypt.

During this period of decentralization and civil disorder, more foreigners—mainly Asians—entered Egypt. They first settled in the Nile Delta area and Lower Egypt, but as the centuries passed they spread throughout the country. Egypt, located at the crossroads of three continents, with her advanced culture, wealth, and great agricultural system that produced an abundance of food, was a magnet for foreigners. As the centuries passed, the foreigners' descendants and later arrivals, contributed to Egypt's downfall, as we shall see.

Meanwhile, a family of lords centered at Heracleopolis in Middle Egypt had grown in power and influence. They formed the Ninth and Tenth Dynasties. In Upper Egypt, a powerful family from Thebes had founded the Eleventh Dynasty. Friction developed between the two families and a civil war erupted. The family from Thebes triumphed over the family from Heracleopolis. Afterward, the Thebans succeeded in reuniting Lower and Upper Egypt into a single nation, thereby ending the period of chaos in Egypt. This was the second time that southerners had united Egypt.

The Middle Kingdom, 2052 to 1786 B.C., included part of the Eleventh Dynasty and the whole Twelfth Dynasty. The Eleventh Dynasty began with a powerful family from Thebes, the Mentuhoteps. It was the great Mentuhotep II who first defeated the lords of the Tenth Dynasty from Heracleopolis, thereby uniting Upper

Egypt, and then led the struggle that reunited both Lower and Upper Egypt. The Eleventh Dynasty revived centralized government in Egypt and "ushered in another golden age"[49] of prosperity and progress. "African ships of commerce sailed the seas again, nation-wide reconstruction was pushed and the revival of learning, science, [and] the arts and crafts marked the Eleventh and Twelfth Dynasties."[50] The first pharaoh of the Twelfth Dynasty, Amenemhet I, was an outstanding leader. He was the greatest of the Twelfth Dynasty rulers. He erected many temples and built forts. He was followed by his son, Sesotris I. The Dynasty closed with a woman pharaoh, Queen Sebeknefrure. With the closing of the Twelfth Dynasty in 1786 B.C., almost 350 years of prosperity, political stability, and progress came to an end.

The Thirteenth Dynasty brought in another period of breakdown in centralized government in Egypt. This period of decentralization was called the Second Intermediate Period, 1785 to 1544 B.C. It included the Thirteenth through Seventeenth Dynasties. Again there was confusion as to who was pharaoh of all Egypt. A family forming the Thirteenth Dynasty ruled from Memphis, while a rival family forming the Fourteenth Dynasty ruled from Xoïs in the Delta. Both families claimed to be legitimate successors to the Twelfth Dynasty. As before, more Asians came into Egypt during this time of internal strife. They could now move in unchallenged.[51]

This "period of turmoil was also the opportune time for great armed invasions."[52] Suddenly a large group of nomadic people from Asia, called Hyksos or shepherd kings, invaded Egypt. They defeated the Egyptians and settled in the Delta, making Avaris their capital. Growing in power, they moved up the river and settled in parts of Middle Egypt also. Scholars differ on how much of Egypt they actually controlled, but they never were in control of the whole country. The Hyksos conquest was made easier by support from Asians who had already settled in Egypt. This was the first time that foreigners, attacking from within and without, had been able to conquer the indigenous Africans of Egypt. The Hyksos were ruthless and barbaric. They formed the Fifteenth and Sixteenth Dynasties. The Fifteenth Dynasty ruled from Avaris in the Delta; the Sixteenth ruled from Middle Egypt. The Seventeenth Dynasty was founded by Africans at Thebes. Weary of foreign domination, the Egyptians organized a liberation movement during the Seventeenth Dynasty. Pharaoh Sekenenre, a member of a strong family from Thebes which had founded the Seventeenth Dynasty, began an all-out war of liberation to rid the country of the Hyksos. He was killed on the battlefield and was succeeded by his son Kamose, who continued the war of liberation. Kamose was succeeded by his brother Ahmose I. The great Ahmose I finally liberated Egypt from foreign domination. He defeated the Hyksos, drove them out of Egypt into the Sinai desert, and reunited Egypt again, thus ending the Second Intermediate Period. This was the third time a southern king had united Egypt.

The Eighteenth Dynasty ushered in a new period in Egyptian history, the New Kingdom, 1554 to 1075 B.C. It included the Eighteenth, Nineteenth, and Twentieth Dynasties. This was Egypt's third golden age and also its period of expansion. The Egyptians were now conscious of foreign invasion. Their nation had to be protected against foreign aggression. One way to contain aggression from western Asia was to check it at its source. Therefore, Egypt's military expansion into foreign territories during the New Kingdom grew out of her wish to protect her borders.

Egypt returned to greatness again with the arrival of the Eighteenth Dynasty. A strong, centralized government was established. There was the usual revival of domestic industry, agriculture and foreign trade, along with the expansion of imperial rule in Palestine and Syria to the Euphrates in Mesopotamia.[53] Egypt also expanded her rule over Nubia, a fellow black nation to the south. Wealth from trade and wealth in the form of tribute from conquered nations poured into Egypt. Caravans, heavily loaded, brought ivory, gold, silver, and spices into Egypt. Magnificent temples and palaces were built. Egypt's glory and imperial power reached its peak during this dynasty.

The great Eighteenth Dynasty had a line of famous kings and queens. This was the most outstanding dynasty since the fabulous Fourth. Ahmose I, the founder of the Eighteenth Dynasty, had liberated Egypt from the Hyksos. His famous wife, Nefertari, was deeply loved and honored by her people. Thutmose I introduced the new expansionist foreign policy of the Eighteenth Dynasty. He was a mighty conqueror and leader. He led military campaigns into Nubia, Palestine, and Syria. He was succeeded by his son, Thutmose II, who married his half-sister Hatshepsut. Thutmose II's reign did not last long because of an early death. He was succeeded by his son, Thutmose III, who was too young to rule. So his stepmother and aunt, Hatshepsut, served as coregent with him. But "during the second year of her stepson's reign she took over all authority from the young ruler and was crowned...[queen] of Upper and Lower Egypt."[54]

Hatshepsut was an extraordinary queen, considered by some scholars to be one of the greatest female rulers of all times, if not the greatest. Using her feminine charm, brilliant mind, and aggressiveness, she maneuvered herself into the position of pharaoh of all Egypt and ruled for twenty years. Naturally, there was opposition to a female in a traditional male role. To counter this threat, "she often dressed in royal male attire, including the false beard and wig."[55]

Hatshepsut's major contributions were in terms of art, trade, and architecture. Dazzling temples, pyramids, and obelisks were built during her reign. The famous trading expedition she sent to Punt (present-day Somalia) is recorded on the walls of her terraced mortuary temple at Deir el-Bahari. A variety of products were brought back, including myrrh, incense, gold, ebony, and ivory. Her death brought her dramatic reign to an end.

Thutmose III had waited impatiently for his time to rule. "On ascending the throne, he continued the conquests begun by his mighty ancestor,...[Ahmose I], who had"[56] driven the Hyksos out of Egypt. "Leading the way at the head of his army, 'mighty like a flame of fire,'...[Thutmose] III brought back to Egypt the kings of other nations to grace his triumphs, and such wealth of golden thrones, royal chariots, gold, jewels, gold and silver vessels, and cattle as had never fallen to Egypt before."[57]

Thutmose III commanded a huge army. He made at least sixteen military campaigns. His mighty conquests increased Egypt's power and influence abroad. He conquered the then-known world, including Nubia, Libya, Syria, and northern Mesopotamia. He was the "mightiest conqueror and administrator of Far Antiquity."[58] He built the first real empire and is thus the first character possessed of universal aspects, the first world hero.[59] Of all the black men who ruled ancient Egypt, Thutmose III is considered by many to be the mightiest and the most enlightened. He also was a merciful ruler; he did not kill the conquered like "most conquerors of antiquity"[60] did. Death claimed Thutmose III when he was eighty-two years old. However, his name was long remembered after he was gone.

Another outstanding pharaoh of the Eighteenth Dynasty was Amenhotep III. His chief wife was the famous Queen Tiye. During his reign, Egyptian glory reached its peak. The empire was well organized and stable. Foreign trade flourished with Punt, western Asia, Nubia, and Libya. Wealth and greatness were reflected everywhere. Historian John G. Jackson describes the splendor of the city of Thebes during the great Eighteenth Dynasty.

Thebes itself expanded into a great metropolis with walls nine miles in circumference. On the outskirts of the city were the elegant mansions of the nobility, some containing fifty or sixty rooms, and halls with the walls covered with colorful paintings, and embellished with costly inlaid furniture, beautiful vases, and attractively carved ornaments and utensils of ebony, bronze, and ivory. Along the great river, temples were built by the order of the king, and were linked together by avenues of sphinxes. Around the mansions and temples were tree-shaded boulevards and flower gardens; and the environing landscape was enhanced by a series of lakes. Since the vanquished Hyksos had introduced horses into Egypt, an improved system of transport was adopted: Bigger and better roads were constructed and Egyptian gentlemen traveled over the highways in horse-drawn chariots.[61]

Amenhotep III's long and outstanding reign came to an end with his death. He was succeeded by Amenhotep IV, better known as Akhenaton, the Heretic King. Akhenaton, the son of Queen Tiye and Amenhotep III, was a remarkable king. His wife was Queen Nefertiti, who bore him seven daughters. He was a spiritual man, preaching a doctrine of love and peace instead of war and conquest. African-American historian J.A. Rogers describes Akhenaton:

> Living centuries before King David, he wrote psalms as beautiful as those of the Judean monarch. Thirteen hundred years before Christ he preached and lived a gospel of perfect love, brotherhood, and truth. Two thousand years before Mohammed he taught the doctrine of the One God. Three thousand years before Darwin, he sensed the unity that runs through all living things.[62]

Unfortunately, Egypt was not ready for Akhenaton's religious revolution. His belief in one universal God, Aton, symbolized by the flaming disc of the sun, was in direct conflict with the belief system associated with the Egyptian God Amon and the other lesser gods of the hierarchy. The powerful priests opposed Akhenaton, regarding him as a dangerous heretic. Dedicating himself to spiritual matters, the king neglected his earthly duties. The empire fell apart as subject nations rebelled. As these subject nations seceded, the rich tribute they used to bring in fell off.[63] Egypt's power was declining and her empire was shrinking. But Akhenaton held firmly to his principles, amid all trials, till his death at the age of thirty-one.[64]

King Tutankhamen, known as King Tut, came to power near the end of the Eighteenth Dynasty at a very young age. During his reign, the priests of Amon were returned to power. He died at the young age of eighteen. The abundance of treasure found in his tomb reflects the fabulous wealth of the Eighteenth Dynasty.

The last ruler of the Eighteenth Dynasty was Haremheb, a general who became pharaoh of Egypt. He ruled from 1335 to 1304 B.C. He re-established law and order in the whole country, and extricated Egypt from the chaos into which Akhenaten and his co-religionists had plunged her.[65]

The Nineteenth Dynasty, 1304 to 1192 B.C., was outstanding but not as great as the Eighteenth. This dynasty began with Ramses I as pharaoh. He was appointed to the position by Pharaoh Haremheb instead of inheriting it. His reign was short. His son, Seti I, succeeded him.

Seti I was a mighty conqueror. He conquered Palestine and fought against the Syrians, Libyans, and Hittites, with whom he made a peace treaty. He also was a famous builder. His most noted monument is his mortuary temple at Abydos. His son, Ramses II, succeeded him. Ramses II is the most famous of all the pharaohs. He is said to be the pharaoh of the biblical Exodus. He was a mighty conqueror like his father, winning a great victory over the Hittites. He also built

many monuments, including the famous temples at
Abu Simbel. His reign lasted sixty-seven years. He had
many wives and fathered about one hundred children
by them.

Next Merneptah, son of Ramses II, came to the
throne. During his reign, Egypt was threatened by a
large group of migrating Indo-Europeans called the
Sea Peoples. This group aligned themselves with the
Libyans against Egypt, but they were defeated by the
Egyptians. As a result, they were prevented from settling in Egypt.

The Twentieth Dynasty, 1192 to 1075 B.C., the last
Dynasty of the New Kingdom, began with Setnakht as
pharaoh. His son, Ramses III, succeeded him. Ramses
III was a great ruler and a mighty warrior; he was the
last of the great pharaohs of Egypt. During his reign,
Egypt had to deal with a new threat from the Sea
Peoples. Again the Sea Peoples allied themselves with
the Libyans, but Ramses III successfully stopped three
invasions by this coalition. Ramses III also defeated
the Libyans in a battle in the Nile Delta. "Ramses
III...was succeeded by eight kings all bearing the name
Ramses, but none of them attained the status of greatness."[66] Toward the end of the Twentieth Dynasty
problems arose. The royal temples were looted, the
government grew corrupt, and the high priests of
Amon became increasingly powerful and wealthy, so
much so that they eventually considered themselves
the ruling power in the country. The Dynasty ended in
corruption and anarchy in 1075 B.C., bringing the New
Kingdom, Egypt's third great period to an end.

For the third time there was a breakdown in centralized government in Egypt. This period of decentralization covered the Twenty-first, Twenty-second,
Twenty-third, and Twenty-fourth Dynasties, 1075 to
710 B.C. It was a period marked by anarchy and foreign domination. As usual a breakdown in central government meant that both Lower Egypt (the north) and
Upper Egypt (the south) became independent again.

The north had a large concentration of foreigners (Libyans, Asians, etc.). They had come into Egypt over the centuries as conquering invaders, friendly settlers looking for a home, or as slaves. The south was mostly African. During the Twenty-first Dynasty kings in Lower Egypt, ruling from Tanis, and high priests in Upper Egypt, ruling from Thebes, both claimed to be the legitimate rulers of Egypt. The Twenty-second Dynasty began with Sheshonk I, a Libyan, who ruled from Tanis in the Delta. He invaded Palestine, captured Jerusalem, and plundered the temple of King Solomon. The Twenty-second and Twenty-third Dynasties overlapped each other. The Twenty-fourth Dynasty's rulers were Tefnakhte and his son, Bocchoris.

The Twenty-fifth Dynasty has been called the Kushite or Ethiopian Dynasty.[67] During this period the Ethiopians moved northward and conquered Egypt. The circumstances that led to this event began when Tefnakhte, the Asian king from Sais in the Delta, became aggressive and started taking over the Delta, forcing the other Asian kings into a new northern coalition. His objective was to move southward and gain control over all Egypt. After capturing Memphis, Thebes, and other territory, he marched to take the city of Heracleopolis.

Meanwhile, the Ethiopians in the south had been watching these developments very closely. They declared an all-out war to stop the advance of the foreign invader. Their military was commanded by Piankhi, the black king of Nubia. His capital was located at Napata.

Piankhi carefully devised his battle plans, then started his campaign northward to suppress the alien invaders and conquer Egypt. His fleet and transports were so numerous that they stretched for miles down the river.[68] As he marched down the Nile, he captured town after town. Hermopolis, ruled by Prince Nimrod, was taken; Tefnakhte was defeated at Heracleopolis; and the city of Memphis was also captured. Next he continued toward the city of Heliopolis, the site of the temple of the sun god Amon-Ra. He captured the city, entered the temple, and "was solemnly and ritually crowned Pharaoh of Upper and Lower Egypt."[69] With his mission accomplished, Piankhi returned to his home in the south, the city of Napata.

Piankhi, the great warrior-king, was very religious, believing that he was predestined by the god Amon (Amen) to rule. He baptized his vast army in the river before proceeding into battle.[70] He urged his soldiers to put their trust in Amon. His army's fanatical devotion to Amon gave the soldiers a feeling of destiny and purpose, making them formidable in battle.

Next Shabaka, the brother of Piankhi, came to power in 710 B.C. At that time, there was rebellion in the Delta, caused by Bocchoris, the son of Tefnakhte. To put this rebellion down, Shabaka invaded the Delta and put Bocchoris to death. This invasion reestablished Ethiopian control over Lower Egypt and, therefore, "firmly established the Twenty-fifth Dynasty."[71] This dynasty inspired a cultural rebirth in Egypt. Once again pyramids were built, temples were renovated, and monuments were restored. Shabaka was succeeded by his nephew, Shabataka.

Meanwhile, a new threat had emerged in western Asia. The Assyrians, armed with iron weapons, had invaded and conquered Palestine and Syria. Now they threatened Egypt. When Assyria began to harass Palestine again, the ruler of Judah, Hezekiah, asked Egypt for support. Egypt responded by sending a large army to help Palestine. This large Egyptian army was led by Taharqa, the son of Piankhi. The Assyrians were under the command of King Sennacherib. The two armies met at the Battle of Elteka. The Reverend Sterling M. Means describes the great battle between the Africans and the Assyrians.

> In this battle the Ethiopians and Egyptians were under the command of...Taharqua but they were repulsed and Taharqua made a

strategical retreat which shortened his line of battle and he fell back to save Egypt from Assyrian invasion. But in the meantime an epidemic broke out among the Assyrian army and the next morning one hundred and eighty-five thousand Assyrian soldiers lay dead upon the ground. Taharqua attributed this disaster to the destruction wrought by the God Amon and the Jews claim that it was Jehovah their God, who sent an angel to slay the enemies of Jerusalem. Sennacherib never attempted another expedition and died soon after.[72]

In 690 B.C. Taharqa became ruler of Ethiopia (also Egypt) by seizing power. He established his capital at Tanis in the Delta, where he could keep a watchful eye on the Assyrians. They presented a constant threat of invasion to Egypt. In 673 B.C. Assyrians, under the command of King Esarhaddon, fought Taharqa and his troops in the Delta but were driven back by the Egyptians. In 671 B.C. Esarhaddon successfully invaded Egypt, captured the city of Memphis, and drove Taharqa southward. Still full of fight, Taharqa regrouped, and in 669 B.C. led his forces northward and retook the city of Memphis. Three years later, in 666 B.C., Ashurbanipal, the son of Esarhaddon, renewed the fight against Egypt. In this engagement, Taharqa was defeated. He returned to Napata and died there in 664 B.C.

Taharqa was a great warrior-king, determined and very energetic. He fought the Assyrians until he became too old to fight them. His enemies and contemporaries, the Assyrians, had a deep respect for him.

"Kings like Taharka would appear in the van of their forces, riding on a swift chariot. He made a spectacular sight. His horses were brilliantly caparisoned...To see the black king Taharka galloping across the battlefields of Jerusalem, at Tanis in the Delta, and in the sacred city of Thebes, was never to forget him...The Assyrians have immortalized him."[73]

"Esarhaddon had a portrait of him carved upon a stele at Sinjirli...."[74]

Taharqa was succeeded by his nephew, Tanutamon.[75] Tanutamon organized an army and then took the offensive against a coalition of feudal lords of the Delta who were loyal to the Assyrians. This offensive thrust by Tanutamon resulted in the recapture of Memphis and put "the Africans in a dominant position in Northern Egypt once again."[76] However, the Assyrians responded in a ruthless manner to Tanutamon's offensive thrust. In 661 B.C., led by Ashurbanipal, they attacked Egypt, looted and burned the ancient city of Thebes, and drove Tanutamon back to Napata.

The sacking of Thebes by the Assyrians was a big blow to the Africans. Thebes, the Eternal City of the Blacks, was an important religious center. Its origin was so ancient that it went "far back...[into] prehistory."[77] "The fall of the most venerable city of all Antiquity aroused deep emotion in the world of that time," says African scholar Cheikh Anta Diop. "That date also marked the decline of Black political supremacy in Antiquity and in history."[78]

Having lost Egypt to the Assyrians, Tanutamon continued to rule from Napata in Nubia. His reign came to a close in 656 B.C. This marked the end of the Twenty-fifth Dynasty. All the "kings from Piankhi to Tanutamon were all buried in the great pyramids they and their ancestors had built at Napata."[79]

The relationship between Egypt and her fellow African nations to "the south was both good and bad, depending on the period and the dynasty in power."[80] For example, the relationship between Egypt and the Nubians of Kush (Ethiopia) varied. At times Egypt invaded Nubia and forced her to pay tribute, and at other times they were at peace. The Nile River was the great cultural highway that linked Egypt and the nations to the south of her.

The black pharaohs of Nubia gained center stage "in the dawn and in the sunset of ancient Egypt...."[81] In the beginning, they helped to develop the political and religious ideas that later appeared in dynastic Egypt. In the end, "these kings formed the last bastion of Egyptian civilization against the advance of the alien."[82] In a supreme effort, they defeated the alien kings in the north; established Ethiopian control over both Lower and Upper Egypt; and fought "the Assyrians, holding that great power at bay for nearly a century until they were eventually outclassed by the heavier concentration of iron weaponry in the Assyrian forces."[83] For one brief century they restored Egypt to her former glory, renovated her temples, [and] gave new life and moral authority to the sun god, Amon-Ra, who had become in that time the chief god among both Nubians and Egyptians.[84]

Africans' lack of iron weapons was the main reason they were defeated by the iron-armed Assyrians. Why didn't the Africans adopt iron weapons? It maybe because they were acquiring so much wealth from foreign trade that it blinded them to the danger of falling behind their enemies technologically. Sometimes too much prosperity can lull a nation to sleep and cause it to drop its guard. Historian Chancellor Williams comments on the African's failure to adopt iron weapons:

> Iron was the basis of the technological revolution in warfare. That the Assyrians, Hittites, Persians and other Asiatic nations were equipping their armies with new type iron weapons, and that these were devastatingly more effective than stone and copper weapons had to be well-known to the Africans. And it was not news. As mentioned before, they not only knew about the uses of iron but they had long since developed the iron smelting processes. The trouble was the highly secretive royal monopoly. No secret was more zealously guarded than the smelting of iron. This meant rigidly limited production. Here was fear outmatching both reason and the

most elementary common sense. This over-secretiveness which inhibited the expansion of iron production was to contribute mightily to the success of Assyrian arms over them.

Prosperity, too, may have blurred the African's vision. Too much success can be dangerous. In this case so much wealth was being piled up from foreign trade, especially in gold, ivory, and copper that the question of iron, if raised, may have been dismissed as "economically unsound." Whatever the reasons were, the fact is that the great iron industries which developed in this center and spread over Africa could have started centuries before they did.[85]

The Twenty-sixth Dynasty, 664 to 525 B.C., began with Psamtik I as pharaoh. This period witnessed the liberation of Egypt from Assyrian control (about 655 B.C.) and saw an increased influx of foreigners into Egypt— mainly Greeks, Syrians, Jews, and Carions. Also during this period, the Egyptian army became increasingly dependent upon foreign mercenaries to defend Egypt against foreign invasion. This was a sign of weakness and proved to be a costly mistake for Egypt.

The Persians, led by Cambyses, the son of Cyrus the Great, were the next power to invade Egypt. The Persians overpowered the Egyptians and conquered them in 525 B.C. This is an important date in African history because it marks the end of indigenous Egyptian rule and the beginning of foreign domination of Egypt. It also marks the end of the greatness of ancient Egypt.

After Persian rule in Egypt, more invasions followed. Alexander the Great arrived in Egypt in 332 B.C. and established Macedonian-Greek rule, which lasted until 30 B.C. The Romans followed the Greeks and ruled until A.D. 642. The Arabs, led by their general Amr ibn-al-As, invaded and conquered Egypt in the seventh century. The Turks arrived under Selim I in 1517. The French, led by Napoleon, invaded Egypt in 1798. The British arrived in Egypt in 1882.

All of these invaders left their mark on Egypt. They impacted her culturally, socially, and politically. Also, foreign domination has blurred the memory of an ancient Egyptian civilization that was created and ruled by indigenous Africans. In short, Egypt is an African nation that has been under foreign domination for over 2,500 years.

The Greatness of Egypt

Ancient Egypt was the peak of a great Nile Valley civilization that had its roots in inner Africa. This Nile Valley civilization in its infancy began in the Great Lakes area far back in prehistoric times, then moved northward into the Nile Valley. What modern scholars call Egyptian civilization is in reality African.

The indigenous Africans of this Nile Valley civilization made some remarkable achievements. They were the first people to write. They were the world's first brick and stone masons. They were the first people to construct large buildings in stone. In addition, they were pioneers in agriculture, law, government, religion, and the arts and sciences.

Ancient Egypt was the light of the ancient world. She was for many centuries the storehouse of knowledge. Peoples throughout the ancient world traveled to Egypt "to drink at the fount of scientific, religious, moral, and social knowledge, the most ancient such knowledge that mankind had acquired."[86] The Greeks considered Egypt to be the land of wisdom and knowledge. Pythagoras the mathematician, Solon the statesman, and Plato and Thales the philosophers, all traveled to Egypt to study and learn. This knowledge from Egypt was handed down to succeeding generations. Author Margaret Murray in her book *The Splendor That Was Egypt* highlights Egypt's influence on the Greeks.

> In every aspect of life Egypt has influenced Europe, and though the centuries may have modified the custom or idea, the origin is clearly visi-

ble. Centuries before Ptolemy Philadelphus founded his great temple of the Muses at Alexandria, Egypt was to the Greek the embodiment of all wisdom and knowledge. In their generous enthusiasm the Greeks continually recorded that opinion; and by their writings they passed on to later generations that wisdom of the Egyptians which they learnt orally from the learned men of the Nile Valley.[87]

Ancient Egypt provides an example of one of the longest lasting civilizations in history. Her greatness covered a period of thousands of years. For example, "where Greece and Rome can count their supremacy by the century Egypt counts hers by the millennium, and the remains of that splendor can even now eclipse the remains of any other country in the world."[88] In addition, "of the Seven Wonders [of the ancient world] the Pyramids of Egypt alone remain almost intact, they still tower above the desert sands, dominating the scene, defying the destroying hand of Time and the still more destructive hand of Man."[89] In short, ancient Egypt's civilization was so dynamic that even in ruin and desolation, it mystifies the modern world.

The ancient Egyptians were a very religious people. Their religion was African and so were their gods. The Egyptians believed in one supreme god and other gods. The most important god was the sun god Ra. The chief goddess was Isis, who was the goddess of fertility. Osiris was the brother and husband of Isis; he was the god of the lower world and judge of the dead. Horus was the son of Isis and Osiris; he was the sky-god, represented by the head of a falcon.

Although the Egyptians worshiped their main deities, they also worshiped lesser gods and goddesses. The various towns and cities had their own particular gods. Some of these local gods in time became important national gods. For example, Amon, the local god of Thebes, a sun god, became over time a god of national importance and was identified with the great sun god Ra, which changed the name of Egypt's greatest god from Ra to Amon Ra.

The ancient Egyptians enjoyed life and believed it would continue after death. The bodies of their dead had to be mummified to prevent them from decaying in the next life. Great tombs were built for the burial of kings and queens. Food, clothing, jewelry, and other items were put in the tombs for use in the afterlife.

Religion was an inspirational force among the ancient Egyptians. Their belief in an afterlife inspired them to build amazing pyramids, colossal temples, and great tombs. Built to last for eternity, these structures had to be of excellent quality, the best that man could build. To produce such magnificent and amazing structures, great skill and knowledge was required. Thus, the need to build on such a great scale led to the development of great architectural and engineering skills among the Egyptians.

We now turn to the Egyptian pyramids, the origin and purpose of which have been cloaked in mystery for thousands of years. The three large pyramids at Giza are the most famous of the Egyptian pyramids. They were built during the Fourth Dynasty.

Who built them? There have been all kinds of wild answers to this question, including beings from another planet. Some people don't believe the ancient Egyptians had the expertise to build such architectural wonders. However, putting follies aside, a number of scholars believe the ancient Egyptians built the pyramids using their expert knowledge of science. It probably took thousands of workers over a number of years to build each one of the big pyramids at Giza. Also, the ancient Egyptian priests may have used secret knowledge in building the pyramids that has been lost to the modern world.

What were the pyramids used for? It was first thought that the pyramids were tombs. However, this has been questioned by some scholars in recent years.

Scholar Margaret Murray comments on the use of the pyramids:

> The question as to the use of the early pyramids has never been satisfactorily answered. It is usually stated that they were burial-places; this may be true of the later ones, but there is no proof that this was their original purpose. But there is evidence that they were used for some special religious ceremonies in connection with the Divine King, though whether he was alive or dead is uncertain. It must also be remembered that many Pharaohs had both a burial-place and a cenotaph, and it is possible that the pyramid was the cenotaph.[90]

Scholar Wayne B. Chandler believes "in regards to their esoteric meaning, the pyramids appear to have symbolized the fusion of heaven and earth or, more correctly stated, spirit and matter."[91]

Thebes was a great religious center and educational center in ancient Egypt. It also had many splendid temples, some of which were of huge size. The origin of Thebes goes far back into prehistoric times. "One...[Nineteenth] Dynasty poet said that it had existed since the beginning of time."[92] An early name of Thebes was Nowe. Thebes also was called Waset, No, and Na-Amun. Today Thebes is called Luxor. In ancient times Thebes was called such colorful names as: *The City*, *The University City*, and *The Mother of Cities*. The Greek poet Homer called Thebes *The City of a Hundred Gates* in his work, the *Iliad*. Historian Chancellor Williams seems to get very sentimental when discussing the great African city of Thebes in *The Destruction of Black Civilization*. He says, "Thebes was the most important single city in the entire history of the Black people."[93] He also makes the following statements about Thebes:

> But let us never forget the central fact about Thebes—not even for a moment. For if the Blacks had never left a single written record of their past greatness, that record would still

stand, defying time, in the deathless stones of Thebes, of her fallen columns from temples, monuments, and her pyramids—a city more eternal than Rome because its foundation was laid before the dawn of history, and its plan was that copied by other cities of the world. If the Blacks of today want to measure the distance to the heights from which they have fallen, they need go no farther than Nowe (Thebes).[94]

The ancient Egyptians are credited with having invented the calendar. It must have taken thousands of years for them to accomplish this remarkable feat. As early as 4236 B.C. the calendar was already in use in Egypt. Therefore, "it is to Egypt that we owe our divisions of time; the twelve months and the three hundred and sixty-five days of the year; the twelve hours of the day and the twelve hours of the night are due to the work of the Egyptian astronomers."[95]

The Egyptians were also the inventors of the clock. The earliest clocks, the *clepsydrae*, were the invention of Egyptian physicists.[96]

The ancient Egyptians had other achievements. They are credited with inventing the pen, paper, and ink. They were highly skilled in embalming the dead and mummification. They were skilled in metalworking, producing beautiful gold jewelry and other objects in bronze and copper. Their craftsmanship in producing gold jewelry was outstanding. No country ancient or modern (with the possible exception of the Renaissance jewellers of Italy) ever reached the Egyptian standard of beauty of design or delicacy of craftsmanship.[97]

The Nile River was very important to ancient Egypt. Its annual flood left a deposit of rich soil on the land. This rich soil enabled Egypt to produce an abundance of food, so much that she became the Bread Basket of the Ancient World. Water from the Nile was used for irrigation. The Nile served as a great highway for Egypt—her principal transportation route. The Nile was indispensable to Egypt; it was both a source of transportation and a source of nourishment.

Egypt was the greatest nation of the ancient world. She was famous for her power, long history, splendor, mystery, wealth, knowledge, and wisdom. The modern world is still in awe of some of the amazing achievements that this ancient African nation made. Egypt was first in introducing to the world many aspects of civilization. Modern science and technology, flaunted before our very eyes, have their roots in this Nile Valley culture, which was created by indigenous Africans. The modern world is indebted to these ancient black men of the Nile who introduced to the world the basic fundamentals of human knowledge.

Chapter 5

Carthage: Celebrated City-State of North Africa

Ancient North Africa

Present-day North Africa can be divided physically into three areas. The first area is "a strip of narrow plains and river valleys [that] borders the Mediterranean Sea."[1] The second area is the Atlas Mountains. The third area is the great Sahara Desert. The Sahara is the largest desert in the world. However, it "has not always been a desert."[2] Seven or eight thousand years ago, the climate of the Sahara was much wetter. It was covered with green forests and grasslands that contained rivers, lakes, and streams. Wild animals and birds were plentiful. Rhinoceroses, antelopes, elephants, lions, giraffes, and hyenas roamed the forests and grasslands. Fish of all kinds swam in the streams and lakes. Drawings found in caves by scientists, who have explored the Sahara for clues about its early history, show that the early inhabitants of this region were hunters and herdsmen.

The word *Sahara* means desert. It derives from the Arabic word, *sahra*. The Sahara Desert covers an area about the size of the continental United States. It stretches across North Africa from the Red Sea in the east to the Atlantic Ocean in the west.

The Sahara began to dry up about seven or eight thousand years ago because of a change in climate. Through the centuries, the Sahara has slowly increased in size, aided at times by animals overeating the grasses and scrubs, and people indiscriminately chopping down trees.

The great Sahara Desert divides Africa into two divisions: (1) North Africa, a region inhabited by a predominately Caucasoid Arab-Berber people and (2) Black Africa, or Africa south of the Sahara, inhabited by a predominately Negroid people. If one did not know this continent's ancient history, he would probably assume that Africa, from the earliest times, had always been divided into a Caucasoid North Africa and a Negroid sub-Saharan Africa. However, this assumption is far from the truth, as we shall see. Africa was once the land of the blacks, meaning that blacks once occupied the whole continent.

North Africa was originally inhabited by a Negroid people; anthropology and historical documents support this viewpoint.

Caucasoid people are not indigenous to North Africa. They migrated to North Africa, probably in prehistoric times. These whites amalgamated with the indigenous blacks of North Africa. One group of Africans with which they amalgamated was the original black Libyans. During the Nineteenth Dynasty of Egypt, a group of Euro-Asian whites called the Sea Peoples formed a coalition with the Libyans and invaded Egypt. And also during the Twentieth Dynasty these same Sea Peoples again aligned themselves with the Libyans and invaded Egypt.

The coming of groups such as Indo-Europeans, Greeks, Romans, Vandals (a Germanic tribe), and Arabs into North Africa has impacted the indigenous Africans both culturally and physically. These movements of foreigners into North Africa, whether by migrations or invasions, caused some of the indigenous Africans to be pushed out of the North, whereas others crossbred with the foreigners, resulting in a modification of the "Negroid character of the"[3] original population. However, a Negroid strain is evident in many inhabitants of present-day North Africa. In his book, *A History of the Colonization of Africa*, Harry H. Johnston comments on the presence of blacks in ancient North Africa.

> But from the little we possess in the way of fossil human remains and other evidence it seems probable that every region of Africa, even Algeria and Egypt, once possessed a Negro population. In Mauritania (Morocco to Tripolitania) these ancient Negroes were partly driven out by... Caucasian invaders and partly absorbed by intermarriage, the mixture resulting in the darkened complexions of so many of the North African peoples.[4]

Scientists have also found prehistoric rock paintings in the Sahara Desert that portray ancient people of Negroid stock.

The existence of an ancient black people in present-day Libya provides additional evidence that North Africa was originally inhabited by a Negroid people. These ancient black people are called the Dawada, or "Worm Eaters." They are thought to be survivors of the original people of North Africa. The Dawada live in an inaccessible area of the desert in Libya called Ramla El Dawada (country of the worm eaters).

In his book, *Lost Worlds of Africa*, James Wellard describes his visit to the Dawada homeland. He and his caravan, which consisted of a guide, a camel boy, and the camels they rode, had to travel across fifty miles of sand dunes just to reach their villages. This fifty-mile stretch of wasteland was void of both plant and animal life. Wellard says that "unless one knew otherwise, one would be forced to conclude that there was no possibility of human life beyond the towering hills of sand."[5] When the author finally arrived in the village of the Dawada people, his guide introduced him to their leader, an old black man. The leader gave Wellard a warm and friendly welcome. The people in the village were also hospitable to him. The Dawada lived in "huts called zeriba made of the fronds of palms set down in the sand."[6] According to Wellard, between four and five hundred people lived in the villages. The Dawada spoke Arabic and were Muslims. They lived a very simple life. Worms found in the lakes near their villages, along with dates, were their main source of food. However, they supplemented their diet with a few vegetables grown in their gardens and a few goats and chickens they raised.

The Dawada people fascinated Wellard. "Who are the Dawada?" he asks, "and how did they get to such a remote corner of the desert?"[7]

> Without a careful anthropological study, the first of these two questions cannot be answered. All one can conclude from observing them is that they are Negroid stock, though without the markedly wide nostrils and everted lips of the central African. On the other hand, the possibility of their having Arab blood is unlikely, for the Arab invaders of the seventh and eighth centuries could not have penetrated this region. It is much more probable, therefore, that they are the last survivors of some ancient Negro race who were driven into this wilderness by invaders and have lived there ever since. A French doctor who saw them describes them as "living fossils."[8]

The invasions of foreigners and the expanding Sahara Desert put tremendous pressure on the indigenous Negroid people of North Africa. The expanding desert caused some of them to migrate from it, whereas others remained in it and tried to adapt to its life-threatening conditions. The indigenous Negroid people of North Africa responded to the invasions in several ways. Some resisted the invaders and went down fighting. Others accepted conquest and enslavement. Still others fled to inaccessible areas rather than accept conquest and enslavement.

The ancestors of the Dawada might have fled to this remote area of the desert during the Roman conquest of North Africa. In an area that provided only the barest of necessities—food, water, and a place to live and sleep—just about all the Dawada could do was try to survive. Circumstances prevented them from creating a kingdom or an empire. Instead of being looked down upon as primitive savages, the Dawada should be commended for defying the odds and surviving for so many centuries in such a hostile environment. They are an outstanding example of African people who have survived despite the overwhelming odds against them.

Who Were the Phoenicians?

The Phoenicians were a great seafaring people. They were the founders of the North African city-state of Carthage. In addition to Carthage, they established other colonies on the North African coast, including Lixus (Morocco), Leptis Magna (Libya), Utica (Tunisia), and Hadrumetum (Tunisia).

The Phoenicians lived in western Asia. They "occupied the coastal strip of the eastern Mediterranean in an area that now consists of northern Israel, Lebanon and southern Syria."[9] The Phoenicians "called themselves Canaanites; the name Phoenicians was bestowed upon them by the Greeks. These ancient mariners were manufacturers of a famous dye known as 'royal purple', which the Greeks called 'Phoenix,' and as a result they were nicknamed Phoenikes or Phoenicians."[10] The Canaanites were a black people who were descended from Canaan. In the Bible, Canaan is the youngest son of Ham, who had three other sons: Mizraim (Egypt), Cush (Ethiopia), and Phut (Libya). African scholar Cheik Anta Diop says that "the man found in Canaan in prehistoric times, the Natufian, was a Negroid."[11] Also, "there is a tradition that the ancestors of the Phoenicians originally came from the land of Punt, in East Africa."[12] Later, as invaders came to the Phoenician homeland, crossbreeding occurred. The Negroid Phoenicians became increasingly racially mixed and lost their black identity.

Phoenicia was never a centralized nation. Like Greece, she was made up of "many independent city-states, each ruled by its own king...."[13] Phoenicia's two most important cities were Tyre and Sidon.

The Phoenicians, according to tradition, were the founders of Carthage. The ruthless brother of Phoenician Princess Elissa, King Pygmalion, "on succeeding to the throne, murdered her husband for the sake of his wealth."[14] "Distraught with grief at the death of her beloved husband and fearful for her own safety,"[15] Princess Elissa—called Dido in Virgil's *Aeneid*—fled from her native city of Tyre. A group of aristocrats who disliked King Pygmalion accompanied her. The party, led by Princess Elissa, departed secretly from Tyre "in a little fleet of...trading vessels known...as 'round ships'...."[16] After a long journey at sea, these Phoenician refugees landed safely on the North African coast in 814 B.C. The indigenous people they encountered allowed them to stay and build a town. They named their town Kart Hadasht, meaning New Town in Phoenician. The Latin word for Kart Hadasht is *Carthago,* or *Carthage.* So, according to tradition, this is how the great city-state of Carthage was born.

Who Were the Carthaginians?

The Carthaginians were a Negroid people. Both anthropology and historical data provide evidence of this.

"Bertholon and Chantre, leading authorities on the anthropology of North Africa,"[17] have examined ancient graves there. "Some characters possess marked Negroid traits. And such are not always persons of no importance. Indeed, the celebrated priestess of Tanit showed numerous Negroid traits, marked prognathism, flat, wide nose, long forearm, and had the physical traits of the Neolithic Negroes..."[18] The priestess was found buried in a cemetery of ancient Carthage. Author Eugene Pittard describes the splendor of her tomb.

> Those who have recently visited the Lavigerie Museum in Carthage will recall that magnificent sarcophagus of the Priestess of Tanit, discovered by Father Delattre. That sarcophagus, the most ornate, the most artistic yet found, whose external image probably represents the goddess herself, must have been the sepulcher of a very high religious personage. Well, the woman buried there had Negro features. She belonged to the African race![19]

To which African scholar Cheikh Anta Diop replies:

> The conclusion that the author draws from this passage is that several races coexisted in Carthage. Obviously, we agree. Nevertheless, there is one conclusion that the author did not draw, but which is even more compelling: Among the various races in Carthage, the one most highly placed socially, the most respected, the one that held the levers of political command, the one to whom they owed that civilization, if we are to judge by the material proofs presented instead of interpreting them in line with prejudices we have been taught, was the Negro race.

> If an atom bomb destroyed Paris but left the cemeteries intact, anthropologists opening the graves to determine what the French were like would similarly discover that Paris was inhabited not only by Frenchmen. On the other hand, it would be inconceivable that the corpse buried in the most beautiful tomb, as exceptional as that of Napoleon at the Invalides,...[was] that of a slave or some anonymous individual.[20]

Pittard's prejudices about black people kept him from understanding that the Negro woman buried in the tomb was the very high religious personage he was looking for. She was not a slave. But because she wore a black skin, Pittard thought she was out of place buried in the most beautiful tomb of all the tombs examined. Why? Because it is so natural to think of African as slaves or servants. The image of Africans as slaves or servants has been so deeply ingrained in the minds of the peoples of the modern world that they naturally look to find Africans in that same position in the ancient world. However, if ancient history is interpreted correctly, it tells a different story. It points out that blacks were the most advanced people of the ancient world. Writers of that remote period, such as Herodotus and Diodorus of Sicily, confirm this viewpoint. It is very difficult for most modern scholars to interpret the history of blacks in the ancient world objectively. Their vision has been blurred by the recent enslavement of African people.

Negroid Carthage and North Africa in general changed physically with the coming of foreigners. When North Africa became part of the Roman Empire, large numbers of Romans migrated there. In the fifth century, the Vandals migrated to North Africa. Later, in the seventh century, the Arabs moved into North Africa.

The Rise and Fall of Carthage

Carthage was a great city-state of the ancient world. It was located near the modern-day Tunisian city of Tunis.

Carthage was founded by the Phoenicians about 814 B.C. as a trading post. As time passed, Carthage grew in wealth and power. In 654 B.C. she began to expand, establishing a colony on the island of Ibiza, near the Iberian Peninsula. About 550 B.C. a man named Mago came to power in Carthage, founding the Magonid dynasty. Mago brought energy and changes to Carthage. Carthage, from now on, ceased to be a city of the Western Phoenicians among many others;

she claimed leadership and imposed her military authority throughout the Western Mediterranean.[21] By the end of the sixth century B.C. Carthage already had become famed for her riches, envied for her profitable overseas trade, and feared for her navy.[22]

Like the Canaanites and Phoenicians before them, the Carthaginians felt a special kinship with the open sea and a thirst for high adventure, especially when it meant opening up new markets abroad and reaping huge financial rewards.[23] The stories of the voyages of Hanno, who sailed from Carthage to the coast of West Africa, and Himilco, who traveled from Carthage to Brittany, show the daring and skill of these Carthaginian navigators. These voyages also show the great distances they were willing to travel to find new markets.

The voyages of Hanno and Himilco were remarkable feats, especially at this point in history. Hanno's voyage to West Africa, according to some scholars, occurred about 465 B.C. Other scholars give an earlier date, 520 B.C. "Hanno set sail [from Carthage] with [a fleet of] sixty ships, each manned by fifty oarsmen, and carrying altogether 30,000 men and women."[24] The expedition sailed through the Pillars of Hercules and on around the west coast of Africa, stopping at various points along the way, perhaps traveling as far south as present-day Sierra Leone, Ghana, and Cameroon before returning to Carthage. Himilco's voyage is said to have occurred about the same time as Hanno's. Himilco's voyage took him around present-day Spain, France, and on to Brittany, perhaps as far north as the British Isles.

In 600 B.C., long before the voyages of Hanno and Himilco, the Phoenicians were sent by the Egyptian Pharaoh Necho on a voyage of exploration that sailed around the continent of Africa. The Phoenicians, stopping along the way to plant and harvest grain, started the voyage by sailing down the Red Sea and then continuing around Africa, passing through the Pillars of Hercules and finally back to Egypt by the way of the Mediterranean Sea. Herodotus said "this voyage around Africa took about three years to complete."

As Carthage continued to expand, establishing new colonies and trading posts, she came into conflict with the Greeks, who also were founding colonies. About 535 B.C. the Carthaginians united with the Etruscans (founders of Rome) to defeat the Phocaeans (Greeks who had settled Corsica) in a great sea battle off the coast of that island. This battle caused the Phocaeans to leave Corsica.

The rivalry between the Carthaginians and the Greeks intensified as both struggled for control of the island of Sicily. The island's strategic location and fertile soil made it attractive for colonization. The Carthaginians had cities and towns on the island's western end, the Greeks on its east.[25] In 480 B.C. the Greeks and Carthaginians clashed on Sicily at Himera; in this battle the Carthaginians were defeated. In 410 B.C. fighting started again between the Carthaginians and the Greeks. In 409 B.C. the Carthaginians captured the cities of Selinus and Himera. In 406 B.C. they sacked the city of Agrigentum. They later captured the cities of Gela and Camarina. The Greeks responded to the Carthaginian invasion by waging a war of revenge. In 398 B.C. the Greeks, led by Dionysius of Syracuse, besieged the Carthaginian colony at Motya and destroyed it.

The Carthaginians and Greeks continued to battle, with one side gaining the advantage and then the other, but neither side was able to deliver a knockout blow. In 338 B.C. a peace treaty was signed between the two sides.

In 311 B.C. fighting broke out once again in Sicily between Carthage and the Greeks. In a battle at Ecnomus, the Carthaginians defeated the Greeks, who were led by Agathocles, the tyrant from Syracuse. This victory put Carthage in control of nearly all of Sicily except Syracuse, where Agathocles retreated for protection. Next, the Carthaginians besieged the city of Syracuse by land and sea. Facing what seemed like certain defeat, Agathocles made a surprising and bold move that saved Syracuse. He invaded the Carthaginian homeland in Africa, knowing "that the Carthaginians had virtually no army at home, and that their civilians were accustomed to luxury and inexperienced in war."[26] This surprise move by Agathocles caught Carthage off guard, enabling the Greeks to raid and plunder the countryside. Although Agathocles won some victories, he was never able to capture Carthage. The fighting spirit of the Carthaginians prevented him from doing this. He died in 289 B.C.

In 280 B.C. a Greek general named Pyrrhus invaded Italy and waged war against the Romans, defeating them twice. But his victories (Pyrrhic victories) were costly in terms of the number of soldiers he lost. Next, he moved into Sicily and clashed with the Carthaginians, pushing them back westward to the town of Lilybaeum, but was unable to conquer them. Subsequently, he gave up and left the island of Sicily. This was the last "direct warfare between Carthage and the Greeks."[27]

Though unsuccessful in his attempt to conquer the Carthaginians on the island of Sicily, Pyrrhus was successful in predicting the future. When he left Sicily in 276 B.C., he predicted that Rome and Carthage would eventually clash for control of the island. The course of history would eventually lead them to the inevitable, a life-and-death-struggle that would leave one of them destroyed.

In 332 B.C. the Greeks, led by Alexander the Great of Macedonia, captured Tyre, the mother city of Carthage. With the fall of Tyre, Carthage inherited the leadership of the Phoenician world. At this point in history Carthage was wealthy and powerful, and possessed a large Mediterranean empire. She was the "Queen of the Western Mediterranean" and "the Pearl of North Africa." General Donald Armstrong describes the Carthaginian Empire at its peak.

> When Alexander was besieging Tyre, in 332 B.C., Carthage was the capital of an empire that stretched along North Africa's coast from the Greek colony of Cyrene on the east to and beyond the Strait of Gibraltar on the west. She had possessions in Spain that extended from her trading posts on the Mediterranean to Cadiz on the Atlantic coast. She occupied the west of Sicily, the coasts of Sardinia, and at least portions of every other large Mediterranean island.[28]

African scholar J.C. de Graft-Johnson describes the splendor and wealth of the capital city.

> The city of Carthage round about 300 B.C. was the epitome of grandeur and pomp. It contained several imposing temples, a fortress, and many magnificent buildings. It was encircled by a triple line of fortifications which secured it against all comers. Immediately beneath the towering walls were rows of tall houses, six storeys high, on either side of three streets which led down to the harbours. To the north and again to the west of the city lay the great suburb called Megara. Megara was full of villas and lovely gardens, the property of the idle rich, the homes of prosperous Carthaginians.[29]

Also at this time, "Carthage possessed libraries, baths, restaurants or public messes, and theatres."[30]

Rome was founded about 753 B.C., according to legend. In 509 B.C. Rome ended Etruscan domination and declared herself a republic. From here on she began to grow and expand. She did not get involved in the centuries of warfare between the Greeks and the Carthaginians; instead she concentrated on matters inside Italy. Carthage and Rome were on friendly terms. They signed treaties of friendship in 509 B.C., 348 B.C., and 306 B.C. Another "treaty in 279 was a pact against the common enemy Pyrrhus."[31]

While Carthage was busy establishing and defending her empire, carrying on foreign commerce, and accumulating wealth, Rome was busy in internal affairs, developing her military and gradually bringing the other cities in southern Italy under her control. By 275 B.C. Rome had almost all of the Italian Peninsula under her control. She had become a force to be reckoned with, strong enough to challenge mighty Carthage, the supreme power in the western Mediterranean, for supremacy of the Mediterranean world. It was only a matter of time before something triggered the inevitable—a clash between Carthage and Rome.

The struggle between Carthage and Rome broke out in 264 B.C. From 264 to 146 B.C. these two powers fought three wars, the Punic Wars. The word *Punic* was the Latin word for Phoenicia, referring to both Phoenicia and Carthage.

The First Punic War began when Carthage and Rome became involved in Sicily in a conflict between the city of Messina (located across the strait from Italy) and Syracuse. The city of Messina was controlled by a ruthless group of mercenaries who "called themselves Mamertines or sons of Mars." They lived by looting and raiding "their neighbors in Sicily."[32] In 270 B.C. Hieron II, the king of Syracuse, became tired of their plundering and decided to do something about it. He led an offensive against the Mamertines, and was so successful that he managed to blockade the latter in Messina.[33] The Mamertines, fearing that they might have to pay for their past evil deeds, asked Carthage for help. The Carthaginians, under the command of Hanno, responded by occupying the city of Messina. "The Mamertines soon began to resent this occupation...."[34] Subsequently, the Mamertines appealed to Rome for help against Carthage. Rome accepted the invitation. The First Punic War was on.

General Armstrong describes the ensuing conflict in Sicily.

> As the struggle in Sicily continued, Carthage and Syracuse forgot their hundreds of years of warfare and joined forces against the Romans. But the alliance was short-lived. The Romans defeated them both and Syracuse sued for peace and offered to become an ally of Rome. The Romans gladly accepted.[35]

During the early years of the war, Carthage's superior navy gave her the advantage. Rome lacked a strong navy; her strength was in her large, well-disciplined, well-organized army. As the war progressed, the Romans began to recognize the importance of a strong navy. So, "using a captured enemy warship as a model, they built a fleet and trained its crews ashore, on rowers' benches."[36] In 260 B.C. the Romans defeated Carthage in the sea battle of Mylae, off the coast of Sicily. In 256 B.C. the Romans, led by Regales, won a navy battle at Ecnomus. The following year the Carthaginians, using elephants, defeated the Romans in a land battle near Carthage in Africa. In 249 B.C. a Carthaginian admiral named Adherbal defeated the Romans in a navy battle at Drepanum.

Meanwhile, the Romans were busy building another fleet to challenge Carthage. By 241 B.C. the Romans were ready to fight. In the sea battle of the Aegates Islands, off the coast of Sicily, the Romans soundly defeated the Carthaginians. This battle brought the long, exhausting First Punic War to an end. Although the Romans were the victors, both sides had suffered heavy losses in men and had absorbed much damage. The peace treaty required Carthage to give up Sicily and pay a huge, crippling indemnity of 3,200 talents to Rome. The indemnity was to be paid within a ten-year period.

The long, costly war and the Roman indemnity brought economic hardship to Carthage. And when her mercenary soldiers (thousands of fellow Africans— Libyans and Numidians—as well as men from Spain, Gaul, and Sardinia) demanded their pay, she failed to pay them. This led to the Revolt of the Mercenaries. The Carthaginian general, Hamilcar Barca, known for his daring raids during the war against Rome, was called on to suppress them. In 238 B.C., after three and a half years of war, the mercenaries were defeated. Meanwhile Rome, knowing that a weakened Carthage was in no condition to challenge her, seized two Carthaginian possessions, Corsica and Sardinia. Rome also demanded that Carthage pay her an additional 1,200 talents or go to war. A weakened Carthage sub-mitted to the treachery of Rome to avoid a war she was unprepared to fight.

"Carthage's one hope of salvation now was to de-velop her Spanish empire to redress the balance of her losses elsewhere, and Hamilcar Barca, her foremost general...had himself chosen for the task."[37] With a small army, and...his young son Hannibal, Hamilcar sailed to Spain in 237 B.C.[38] Before his death in battle in 229 B.C., Hamilcar had gained control of most of southern and eastern Spain. He was succeeded by his son-in-law Hasdrubal. Hasdrubal began to organize and consolidate the Carthaginian territory in Spain. He founded a town on the southeast coast of Spain in 228 B.C., calling it New Carthage. In 226 B.C. he made a treaty with Rome, who also had interests in Spain. The treaty made the Ebro River a boundary that sepa-rated Carthaginian and Roman interests in Spain. "The crossing of the Ebro was...[henceforth] regarded by the Romans as a declaration of war."[39]

In 221 B.C. Hasdrubal was killed. This brought Hannibal, the son of the legendary Carthaginian gen-eral Hamilcar Barca, to the forefront. Hannibal was immediately named the commanding general in Spain, although he was only twenty-six years old. The young leader had been schooled since infancy in every aspect of military life; he had learned the tricks of the trade from the greatest Carthaginian and mercenary leaders and had years of invaluable practical experience in warfare against various Iberian tribes.[40]

Hannibal Barca, born in 247 B.C., "was a full-blooded Negro with wooly hair, as his coins show."[41] According to tradition, Hannibal was always identified as a black man—that is, until the rise of modern racism. [An African slave of Peter the Great of Russia was given the name Hannibal.] This African, known as the Negro of Peter the Great, became a well-known Russian general. In ancient times, Hannibal was called Hannibal the Afer, meaning Hannibal the African.

Meanwhile, "in the first three years of his service as commander in Spain, Hannibal came into conflict with Roman interests there."[42] He clashed with a Roman ally in Spain, the town of Saguntum, which infuriated the Romans. In 218 B.C. the Romans demanded that the Carthaginians hand Hannibal over to them or else war would be declared. The Carthaginians refused, and the Second Punic War was on.

Militarily, Rome was in great shape. She had a large army and a powerful navy. Her navy, stronger than that of Carthage, would prevent a landing anywhere on the Italian coast.[43] And if Carthage invaded from the north, she had to deal with the dangerous Alps, considered impossible for an army to cross.

Rome planned to attack the Carthaginians in Spain and in North Africa. But to Rome's astonishment, Hannibal moved first, with daring and total surprise.[44]

Hannibal decided to invade Italy by land, since Rome controlled the Mediterranean Sea. In April 218 B.C., he left the town of New Carthage in Spain and started his historic march toward Italy with an army of ninety thousand infantry, twelve thousand cavalry, and thirty-seven elephants. (Note: scholars differ on how many men and elephants Hannibal had.) He marched northward "up through southern Spain,"[45] crossed the Ebro River and the Pyrenees Mountains, and continued on into Gaul (France), crossing the Rhone River and finally the mighty Alps into Italy. His march was filled with danger and adversity. "The mountains, the rivers, the weather, and hostile native forces all resisted his advance...."[46] However, nothing could prevent Hannibal from reaching his goal—Italy.

Hannibal's crossing of the Alps is probably the most daring and the most dangerous march ever accomplished by an army. Hannibal and his army had to deal with snow and ice, snowstorms and avalanches, bitter cold, and the hostile mountain tribes that resisted their advance. Soldiers and animals were killed when these mountain people dropped big stones on them from above.

Hannibal paid a price for his daring march. When he reached Italy in October of 218 B.C., his army had been greatly reduced. Scholars differ on how many men he lost. "Polybius says Hannibal reached Italy with scarcely 20,000 infantry and 6,000 cavalry, and gives no figures for the elephants, either at the start or the finish. Appian puts the figures at 48,000 infantry, 8,000 cavalry, and 15 of the 37 elephants with which Appian believes he set out."[47]

With an army weakened by its long march from Spain and greatly reduced in size, Hannibal faced the greatest military power of the then-known world. If she needed to, Rome could raise a force of about eight hundred thousand men. The odds were overwhelmingly against the Carthaginians but they had one thing going for them. They had Hannibal.

The Romans were unprepared for Hannibal. They had underestimated his daring and skill. Hannibal was able to recruit much-needed men from the Gauls, enemies of the Romans. His first two battles against the Romans occurred near rivers, the Ticinus (Ticino) and the Trebia. In his first battle, at Ticinus, Hannibal was victorious. His superb Numidian cavalry put the Romans to flight. The Roman commander Publius Scipio was badly wounded in this battle. In December of 218 B.C. Hannibal engaged the Roman consul Sempronius in the battle at Trebia. In this battle Hannibal lured the Romans into a trap and crushed them. The Romans lost 30,000 (killed or taken prisoner) of their 44,000 men in this battle.

Hannibal and his troops spent the winter in Bologna, Italy. In the spring of 217 B.C., Hannibal and his troops crossed the dangerous Apennines Mountains of central Italy to engage the Romans in battle. After crossing the Apennines, Hannibal and his troops ran into soft, wet marshland. There Hannibal had a stroke of bad luck. He contracted a harmful eye infection which caused him to lose vision in one of his eyes.

Meanwhile, Rome elected two new consuls to deal with Hannibal. They were Gaius Flaminius and Servilius Geminus. Consul Flaminius was full of confidence and was anxious to engage Hannibal in battle so he could rid Italy of him.

After Hannibal learned of the Roman consul's overeagerness for battle, he decided to exploit the situation by setting a deadly trap for Flaminius. Hannibal was aware that Flaminius and his men had to take a road by way of Lake Trasimene. He, therefore, hid his troops "in the hills above and parallel to the road along the shore of Lake Trasimene,"[48] and waited on Flaminius and his men to appear so he could ambush them. In history's greatest ambush, Hannibal charged the long marching column and Flaminius was unable to form a line of battle.[49] He was completely unprepared for Hannibal's surprise attack. "Surrounded... Flaminius and his men were massacred...."[50] The defeat at Lake Trasimene in June of 217 B.C. was a big blow to the Romans. Of the forty thousand Roman soldiers in the battle, fifteen thousand were killed and another fifteen thousand were taken prisoner. By contrast, Hannibal lost only about fifteen hundred men at the battle of Lake Trasimene.

Hannibal's success on the battlefield was a tribute to his military genius. He showed the Romans that there was an art to warfare and that by using clever strategy and tactics, a smaller force could overcome a much larger one. "Hannibal was...a master at using the physical features of a landscape, often selecting sites for ambush that put the enemy at a disadvantage—trapped in a valley, jammed up in a confined pass or backed up against a river."[51]

Meanwhile, the Romans had selected a new leader, Dictator Fabius Maximus. Fabius decided that the best way to deal with Hannibal was not to fight him in a head-to-head battle, but rather to harass him and try to wear him down or catch him in a trap. Fabius began to stalk and watch Hannibal as he plundered the countryside. Finally, Fabius trapped Hannibal "in a narrow pass."[52] Certain that he had him, Fabius decided to wait until the next day to attack Hannibal. This gave Hannibal time to devise a plan of escape. That night he tied burning sticks to the horns of a herd of cattle, causing them to stampede. The Romans, thinking that it was Hannibal who was trying to escape over the hills, abandoned their posts, after which Hannibal easily broke through and went off to take up his winter quarters in peace.[53]

The Romans after a while became tired of the "delaying tactics"[54] of Fabius Maximus. He was allowing Hannibal to ravage and plunder the countryside. He also had allowed Hannibal and his men to escape when he had them in a trap. As a result, the Romans replaced Fabius with two consuls, Aemilius Paulus and Terentius Varro.

Roman patience with Hannibal was wearing thin. In 216 B.C. the Romans decided to move on him and bring the war to an end. They raised an army of ninety thousand men to confront Hannibal.

In June of 216 B.C., Hannibal captured the Roman town of Cannae, where supplies were stored. The Romans sent their forces there to fight him. The Roman consuls Varro and Paulus arrived at Cannae with a force of about ninety thousand men, compared to Hannibal's fifty thousand men. The battle that took place at Cannae on August 2, 216 B.C. is the most famous battle of all antiquity. African-American historian J.A. Rogers describes the great battle at Cannae.

> The battle began on a bright...[August] morning in 216 B.C. The Romans, driving down on the Carthaginians, struck them full in the center as Hannibal had anticipated. Finding little resistance there, they pushed on inwards, sure of victory. But their ranks were broken. The effect was precisely that of one who hurls himself against a door he believes is locked to find that it isn't.
>
> When the Romans had thus penetrated far enough, Hannibal sent his African infantry in solid formation to attack them on both flanks while his cavalry galloped to the rear to attack them there.
>
> The Romans, thus surrounded, were slaughtered like sheep...[Consul Paulus] was slain and with him eighty Roman senators and seventy thousand men.[55]

The tactical skill Hannibal displayed in defeating this greatly superior force is unparalleled in military history.[56] This battle at Cannae, also called the Battle of Annihilation, is still studied in military schools.

Following the victory at Cannae, Maharbal, Hannibal's chief of cavalry, advised him to attack the city of Rome at once. Hannibal refused. Some scholars blame Hannibal for not attacking Rome and delivering a knockout blow when he had the chance to do so. However, his chance of capturing Rome was not very good. Rome was over two hundred miles distant, well walled, and...a large force...could be quickly gathered to protect it.[57] Furthermore, "Hannibal lacked a siege train and his army was too small to storm the city's walls—good reasons for not pressing on at the time."[58]

"Hannibal's younger brother Mago...carried to Carthage the news of the victory at Cannae."[59] Mago told "the Carthaginian Senate"that Hannibal urgently needed money and men to finish the task in Italy. Unfortunately, the Carthaginian Senate was divided: there was a pro-Hannibal side and an anti-war side. The pro-Hannibal side wanted to send aid to him, whereas the anti-war side was more interested in making money than in defeating the Romans. Due to the disunity at home, Hannibal never received the amount of reinforcements that he needed. He would have to try to acquire them in Italy.

Hannibal's overwhelming victory at Cannae attracted allies to his cause, but not enough of them to have an impact on Rome. Many towns in Lower Italy came over to his side. Also the wealthy and luxurious city of Capua came over to his side. In 215 B.C. Hannibal and Philip V of Macedon became allies. The following year, 214, "Syracuse rebelled against Rome to give Carthage still another ally and deprive Rome of a valuable naval base in Sicily."[60] On the other hand, central Italy would not desert Rome. She stayed loyal and "became the core of Roman nationalism and resistance."[61] If Hannibal had been able to persuade more of the Italians to defect to his cause, he could have conquered Rome without aid from Carthage. Unfortunately for him, most of the Italians chose to fight rather than to defect.

Roman resistance kept Hannibal's new allies from helping his cause. The Roman navy prevented Philip V of Macedon from aiding him. Rome recaptured the cities of Syracuse and Capua in 211 B.C. Rome also attacked the other towns that had defected to Hannibal and forced most of them to come back over to her side. The tide was slowly turning in Rome's favor.

In 211 B.C. the Roman commanders in Spain, Publius Scipio and his brother, were killed in battle. The next year the Romans appointed Publius' son, P. Cornelius Scipio, as commander in Spain. The young Scipio "had observed firsthand Hannibal's flexible forces and carefully orchestrated battle plans, as well as the extreme discipline of his troops."[62] He, therefore, began to copy Hannibal. "By using Hannibal's own tactics,"[63] he became successful on the battlefield against the Carthaginians in Spain. In 209 B.C. he captured the Carthaginian headquarters at New Carthage and in 208 B.C. he won a victory over Hannibal's brother, Hasdrubal.

Meanwhile, back in Italy, the Romans were avoiding an all-out fight with Hannibal. They were using delaying tactics instead, hoping that time would slowly wear him down and eventually do him in.

After their defeat at Cannae, the Romans realized that it was unwise to fight Hannibal in an all-out battle because in this type of fighting Hannibal could use his strengths: his tactical skills and his excellent cavalry. So they returned to the strategy of Fabius Maximus—follow Hannibal, harass him, prevent him from getting reinforcements, wear him down, but avoid an all-out battle with him.

The delaying tactics of the Romans were slowly sapping the strength from Hannibal's troops. Their numbers were decreasing. It was difficult to replace his veteran African troops, the core of his army. Hannibal desperately needed reinforcements from Carthage, men and supplies.

In 208 B.C. Hasdrubal decided to leave Spain to help his brother, Hannibal, in Italy. He crossed the Pyrenees over into Gaul (France), where he spent the winter. He arrived in Italy by way of the Alps in 207 B.C. He had sent a letter by his scouts to give to

Hannibal, describing the route he was going to take and where they were going to join forces. Unfortunately, the Romans seized the letter before it reached Hannibal. After reading the letter, the Romans set a trap for Hasdrubal in a valley near the Metaurus River. The Roman consuls, Claudius Nero and Marcus Linius, who were enemies, joined forces and annihilated Hasdrubal and his army. Then, "Nero...announced the defeat to Hannibal by flinging Hasdrubal's severed head into his camp."[64] This "grim incident marked the turning point in the Second Punic War"[65] because it prevented Hannibal from getting the reinforcements that he so desperately needed. If the combined forces of the Barca brothers had been able to march on Rome, they probably would have been too much for the war-weary Romans and Rome probably would have asked for peace.

Hannibal's last chance to reverse the course of the war was gone. All he could do now was to hope that good fortune would come his way.

By 206 B.C. Scipio had gained control of Spain. Next, he decided to invade Africa. This move, if successful, would force Hannibal to leave Italy and return home to defend Carthage. Scipio invaded Africa in 204 B.C. He devastated the Carthaginian countryside, capturing towns and cities. He forced Carthage to appeal for peace and ask Hannibal to return home. Peace had almost been concluded when people from Hadrumetum arrived in Carthage with the announcement that Hannibal had just disembarked beneath their city walls.[66]

Hannibal's arrival in Africa lifted the spirits of the Carthaginian people; they were ready to fight again. He had been in Italy from 218 to 203 B.C. There he had never lost a battle.

The final battle of the Second Punic War occurred at Zama in 202 B.C. Hannibal "took the field with 55,000 men, mostly raw recruits, and 80 elephants."[67]

Scipio arrived with about forty-thousand battle-tested men. Scipio's ally Masinissa, the Numidian king, had four thousand cavalry and six thousand infantry. In all, Scipio's cavalry outnumbered Hannibal's cavalry sixty-seven hundred to two thousand. In a comparison of the two armies, Scipio's troops were far superior to Hannibal's ragtag army.

Scipio had made an alliance with the Numidian king, Masinissa, who had switched his loyalty from Carthage to Rome. As a result the superb Numidian cavalry, which had always been in Hannibal's camp, was now in Scipio's camp. During the battle, Hannibal's unseasoned elephants were a big disappointment. They were supposed to disrupt the Roman line and create confusion. However, as they approached the Roman line, they became frightened by the loud noise the enemy made, men shouting and blowing trumpets. The elephants turned around and ran back into the Carthaginian troops, creating confusion among them. Despite the misfortune with the elephants, "there were a few moments during the day-long struggle when Hannibal's veterans came close to victory."[68] However, in the end, the superb Numidian cavalry was the difference, for it turned the tide of battle in Rome's favor. The battle ended in a victory for the Romans. Hannibal had suffered his first defeat. He had won every battle except the last one. Unfortunately, the last battle determined the winner of the Second Punic War. The Romans had now defeated the Carthaginians in two straight wars.

Masinissa's excellent cavalry gave Scipio the edge at the battle of Zama, enabling him to defeat Hannibal. Masinissa had fought with the Carthaginians against the Romans in Spain. However, he changed sides because he blamed Carthage for an unhappy love affair.

Masinissa was a native of Numidia, an ancient country of North Africa that comprised present-day eastern Algeria and western Tunisia. The Numidians were a Negroid people.

In his youth Masinissa was sent to Carthage to get his education. While in Carthage, the young Masinissa met and fell in love with the beautiful and charming Sophonisba. Her father, Hasdrubal, promised him that he could marry his daughter. Masinissa was delighted. Afterwards, Masinissa and Hasdrubal went to Spain to fight against the Romans. In Spain Masinissa and his superb Numidian cavalry were very impressive against the Romans.

While things were going well for Masinissa in Spain, things back home in Carthage were beginning to go against him. Sophonisba's beauty and charm had attracted another man's attention. His name was Syphax, king of Numidia. And when Syphax heard of the future marriage between Masinissa and Sophonisba, he became angry and threatened to attack Carthage. To make peace, the Carthaginians forced Sophonisba to marry Syphax.[69] When Masinissa learned about the marriage in Spain, he was devastated.

"Massinissa thereupon resigned his command to return to his own country. Before leaving Spain, however, he went secretly to Scipio's camp and pledged himself to Rome. Henceforth Carthage would find him an implacable foe."[70]

Back in Africa, Masinissa and the Romans were very successful in their battles against Syphax and the Carthaginians. Eventually, Masinissa captured Syphax in a battle and made him a prisoner. Then he married his beloved Sophonisba. However, Scipio refused to accept the marriage. He forced Masinissa "to choose between Sophonisba and Rome."[71] If Masinissa chose Sophonisba it "would be the ruin of his people and himself."[72] On the other hand, if "he chose Rome,"[73] he would be without his love, Sophonisba. Masinissa, filled with sadness and heartbroken, chose Rome. He then gave his wife poison to drink. She "drank the poison"[74] and died.

In his book *The Reluctant Warriors*, General Donald Armstrong makes the following comments about Masinissa and his impact on the Battle of Zama.

> If Masinissa had been allowed to keep Sophonisba as his wife, his hatred of Carthage—which had been born of his frustrated love for the girl—might have mellowed: with the help of those Carthaginians who favored reconciliation with him and hoped for Carthage's union with Numidia, the rift might have been healed and the old association perhaps re-established. Such an outcome could have changed the course of history, for it was Masinissa's aid to Scipio at the battle of Zama that weighed the balance against Hannibal and won for Scipio the surname Africanus.[75]

A peace treaty between Carthage and Rome was signed in 201 B.C. Carthage was forced to pay a large indemnity to Rome. She was allowed to have only ten ships in her navy, and she could not go to war against any nation without Rome's approval.

Two strategic moves by the Romans sealed their victory over Carthage in the Second Punic War. The first was the decision to use delaying tactics against Hannibal. This policy, although unpopular at first with the Romans, eventually wore Hannibal down and reversed the course of the war in Rome's favor. The second was Scipio's decision to invade Africa. Once in Africa, the cunning Scipio took advantage of the rift between the Carthaginians and the Numidians. He used the strategy of divide and conquer to overcome the Africans. In short, strategic moves conceived off the battlefield led to a Roman victory on the battlefield.

Author Theodore Dodge believes the Carthaginian Senate's lack of support for the war was the major reason Hannibal was defeated. In his book, *Great Cap-*

tains, he makes the following comments about what caused Hannibal to be defeated in the end:

> Finally, long after Hasdrubal had made his way to Italy, and had been defeated by the consul Nero, Rome carried the war into Africa, and Hannibal was recalled from Italy and defeated at Zama by Scipio. It was, however, neither Scipio nor Zama that defeated Hannibal. The Carthaginian cause had been doomed years before. It was...[inaction], pure and simple, which brought Hannibal's career to a close—the lack of support of the Carthaginian Senate.[76]

Lack of support from a divided Carthaginian Senate prevented Hannibal from overcoming the Romans in Italy. The Romans were reeling after their devastating defeat at Cannae. If Hannibal could have secured additional men and supplies from Carthage, he probably could have delivered the knockout blow that would have defeated Rome. An early Roman defeat would have prevented two things, the successful delaying tactics of Fabius Maximus and the rise of Scipio Africanus.

After his defeat at Zama, Hannibal became politically involved in Carthage. With his intelligence, fairness, courage, and great understanding of people he became a good statesman. He reformed Carthage both politically and financially. However, in accomplishing this, he had to make decisions that were liked by some and disliked by others. Hannibal became a favorite of the masses because he fought to bring about justice for them. He had problems with the rich and powerful aristocracy, however, the same group of aristocrats who had not fully supported him during the war. His fight to end corruption in government made him unpopular with them—so unpopular, in fact, that "they sent word to Rome in 195 that Hannibal was plotting with King Antiochus of Syria to make war on Rome."[77] The Romans were suspicious of Hannibal and decided to investigate the matter. When a Roman commission arrived to investigate, Hannibal fled by sea to Tyre and then to King Antiochus in Ephesus.[78] Again fleeing the Romans, Hannibal went to the court of King Prusias of Bithynia (an old kingdom located in what is now Turkey). In 183 B.C. the Romans demanded that King Prusias surrender Hannibal to them. Hannibal, the great general and statesman, poisoned himself rather than become a prisoner of the Romans. One wonders what the Romans would have done to Hannibal if they could have taken him alive.

Hannibal Barca was a great general, one of the greatest of all time. He possessed daring, bravery, and skill. Despite these great attributes, some writers, ancient and modern, believe that his greatest attribute was his influence over men. His men were loyal to him despite all the hardships they had to deal with. Serving under his command were men from different races—Africans, Gauls, and Spaniards among them—and each group fought differently. Yet Hannibal was able to use them "in ways that brought out the best talents of each."[79]

Meanwhile, back in Africa, Carthage's old nemesis from the Second Punic War, the hated Masinissa, was causing problems for Carthage again. He was forcing the Carthaginian towns to pay him tribute, and he also was beginning to take more and more Carthaginian territory. When Carthage asked Rome for help, she failed to settle the disputes fairly. Rome sent arbitrators to Carthage who pretended to be neutral, but their decisions always favored Masinissa in one way or the other.

The reality of Rome's double-dealing with Carthage was this. Rome was using Masinissa as a tool to wage a subtle, hidden war against Carthage. Therefore, Rome was glad to have Masinissa on her side because his tactics kept Carthage "weak and on the defensive."[80]

In 154 B.C. Masinissa seized additional Carthaginian territory. The next year, 153 B.C., Rome sent a delegation to Carthage to settle the dispute. The delegation was led by Senator Cato, eighty-one years of age yet still energetic. Cato was "a conservative, self-righteous ascetic whose miserliness was the jest of Rome: he sold his slaves when they became too old to work in the fields, so that he would not have to feed them...."[81] Unfortunately for Carthage, this was the type of man she would have to deal with.

Cato did not expect to find Carthage in such good economic condition. Prosperity was reflected everywhere. The sight of a prosperous Carthage put fear into Cato's mind. He figured that it was only a matter of time before Carthage would challenge Rome again.

Upon arriving back in Rome, Cato immediately told the Roman Senate about the Carthaginian threat. He also warned them that as long as Carthage existed, Rome would not be safe. Afterwards, he ended every speech he made in the Roman Senate with the words "Delenda est Carthago" or "Carthage must be destroyed."

Cato's war talk put the Romans in a fighting mood. All they needed now was as excuse to invade Carthage. The excuse came in 150 B.C. when a war broke out between Carthage and Numidia. Carthage's participation in a war meant that she had violated the treaty of 201 B.C. In 149 B.C. Rome declared war on Carthage. Shortly afterward, she sent a large army and fleet to Africa.

Carthage surrendered immediately, giving up all its arms, and three hundred sons of leading officials were sent as hostages to the Romans.[82] Still the Romans were not satisfied. They demanded that the Carthaginians abandon their city and relocate at least ten miles inland so they could destroy it. The Carthaginians decided to fight to the death rather than give up their beloved city of Carthage.

The Third Punic War, the final war between Rome and Carthage, was a bitter struggle. It lasted from 149 to 146 B.C. To the Carthaginians it was a fight for survival; to the Romans it was a fight for world domination. During the first two years of fighting the Carthaginians won a number of victories over the Romans. But in the third year Rome was able to prevent Carthage from getting supplies. As a result, Carthage's heroic resistance crumbled, and she was defeated by combined Roman-Numidian forces in 146 B.C. The city of Carthage, the great metropolis of North Africa, was then looted and burned. The fifty thousand survivors of the last six days of furious street fighting were sold into slavery.

The bitter rivalry between Carthage and Rome was now over. Rome had finally conquered Carthage. It had taken three wars and 118 years for Rome to accomplish this difficult task. Senator Cato's dream had come true: Carthage was destroyed.

Both Cato and the Numidian king Masinissa, had worked hard to bring about Carthage's destruction, yet neither lived to see it happen. Cato died in 149 B.C. and Masinissa died in early 148 B.C., three and two years before Carthage was destroyed.

▲▲▲

Numidian support enabled Rome to destroy Carthage. For forty years the Numidians waged an indirect war against Carthage for Rome. Yet their support for Rome against their African brothers proved to be a big mistake. After conquering Carthage, Rome eventually fought a war with the Numidians and took their territory also. So, the reward for helping Rome was the loss of Numidian independence. By 30 B.C. Rome was in control of North Africa, a vast area stretching from Morocco to Egypt. This region was divided into five provinces (Africa Romana) and became a part of the growing Roman Empire.

Carthage did not commit herself totally to the struggle against Rome until it was too late. During the Second Punic War, a divided Carthaginian Senate prevented Hannibal from getting adequate reinforcements. Had he been able to get adequate support from Carthage, he could have defeated Rome. Before the beginning of the Third Punic War, Carthage was under the illusion that she could avoid war with Rome through appeasement. This led her to try to make peace with Rome at any cost. First Carthage surrendered unconditionally to Rome, but Rome was not satisfied. Next Rome asked Carthage for three hundred hostages and Carthage gave them, but Rome was not satisfied. Afterwards Rome asked Carthage to surrender all her arms and Carthage obeyed, but still Rome was not satisfied. Finally Rome asked the Carthaginians to leave their city and relocate inland so it could be destroyed. The Carthaginians' plea for mercy fell on deaf ears because Rome had already decided their fate beforehand. The Carthaginians, realizing at last that they had been led step by step into a deathtrap, refused Rome's last offer for peace and decided to fight to the end. Carthage made a superb last stand against Rome, giving it her all, committing herself totally to the war effort. Unfortunately, it came too late. Her inability to see the deathtrap in time caused her destruction.

The destruction of Carthage, the Pearl of North Africa, was one of the great tragedies of the ancient world. Carthage was a highly cultured city. She also had a great library. The library of Carthage is said to have contained about five hundred thousand volumes, and these no doubt dealt with the history and the sciences of Phoenicia as a whole.[83] The destruction of this library meant that a tremendous amount of irreplaceable knowledge was lost.

In their heyday both Egypt and Carthage were strong militarily. Egypt was feared because of her army, and Carthage was feared because of her navy. They both posed serious threats to foreign aggression in their particular domains of North Africa, although at different time periods. In 525 B.C. the Persians conquered Egypt and eliminated her as a threat to foreign aggression. In 146 B.C. the Roman conquest of Carthage removed her as a threat to foreign aggression. As a result, the fall of Egypt and Carthage left North Africa vulnerable to foreign invasion.

Carthage's destruction had a big impact on indigenous African rule. African-American scholar Yosef ben-Jochannan explains the far-reaching consequences.

> Carthage was in fact...destroyed....The beginning of the end to indigenous African rule in North Africa had begun and foreign colonialism was set in motion. It also proved to be the beginning of the end to indigenous African rule over the entire continent of Alkebu-lan—Mother Africa.[84]

The Roman conquest of Carthage in 146 B.C. opened the door to foreign penetration and domination of Africa. After conquering Carthage, the Romans expanded their control over all of North Africa. Roman control of North Africa ended in the seventh century when they were replaced by the Arabs. The Europeans arrived in West Africa in the fifteenth century. As the centuries passed, European penetration and control of Africa increased. By 1912 all of Africa except Liberia and Ethiopia was under European control.

Chapter 6

North Africa Under Roman and Vandal Rule

After their destruction of Carthage in 146 B.C., the Romans, through conquest, eventually brought all of North Africa under their control. From 112 to 105 B.C., the Romans fought a war against Jugurtha, a grandson of Masinissa. Jugurtha was ambitious and independent. His desire to expand the kingdom of Numidia had led him into conflict with the Romans. This seven-year war was called the Jugurthine War. Jugurtha was brave, cunning, and elusive. He and his men fought the Romans guerrilla style and gave them much trouble. However, the Romans were finally able to capture Jugurtha with the aid of his father-in-law, who betrayed him to the Romans for bribes. The Romans sent Jugurtha to prison in Rome. In 96 B.C. the Romans captured the city of Cyrene and absorbed it into their North African territory. Cyrene, located in Libya, was founded by the Greeks about 600 B.C. In 46 B.C. the Roman general Julius Caesar defeated the Numidian king Juba I, who was allied with the Pompeians, at the battle of Thapsus. Juba I, was a descendant of Masinissa. Following their victory at Thapsus, the Romans annexed the kingdom of Numidia to their North African territory. The Romans also absorbed the kingdom of Mauritania into their North African territory. In 30 B.C. the Romans conquered Egypt. All of North Africa, from Egypt to Morocco, was now under Roman control. Rome divided her North African land into five provinces: Mauritania Tingitana, Mauritania Caesariensis, Africa, Cyrenaica, and Egypt. Together these five provinces were known as Africa Romana.

The Romans developed North Africa into a land that produced wealth for them. They built towns and cities, they built roads, and they constructed aqueducts to carry water to areas that needed it. They built forts and observation posts so they could maintain control over their territory and protect it from raids by the indigenous Africans. The Romans took the most productive land and forced the indigenous Africans to live on the least productive land. The Romans also pushed the expansion of agriculture in North Africa and rebuilt the city of Carthage, which they had destroyed in 146 B.C.

Rome profited from her North African territory. North Africa supplied Rome with a variety of products, including fruits, olive oil, marble, ivory, wood, corn, and wheat. North Africa was called the granary of Rome because she supplied Rome with so much grain. North Africa also supplied Rome with wild animals, including lions, leopards, elephants, antelopes, hyenas, and bears. The Romans used these animals to entertain people at circuses and for games at the famous Colosseum in Rome. Many animals were killed during these games, which often pitted man against beast and beast against beast. For example, "the Emperor Augustus Caesar tells us that 3,500 African animals were slain in the twenty-six Games which he gave to amuse the people of Rome."[1] These violent and bloody games often attracted thousands of spectators. The famous Colosseum in ancient Rome could seat about 50,000 people.

Wild animals such as elephants and lions were found throughout North Africa during Roman times. Today they are extinct. Because the Romans slaughtered so many wild animals during their games of amusement, they are frequently accused of exterminating a number of wild animals that existed in North

Africa during their times. For example, it is believed that the Romans brought about the extinction of the elephant in North Africa. The Romans used the elephants in games at arenas, where they were killed for sport. Also, "elephants were killed by the Romans for their ivory."[2]

Most of the people of North Africa didn't fare very well under Roman rule. The African masses were used as laborers to produce wealth for the Roman Empire. They planted and harvested the crops; they obtained marble and stone from quarries; they erected buildings; they did other sorts of hard labor. On the other hand, some Africans fared well under Roman rule. Those who fared well were Romanized Africans. They were as Roman as the Romans who were born in Italy. These Romanized Africans took advantage of the benefits of Roman citizenship. They lived in the towns and cities, spoke Latin, attended schools, and visited public libraries. Also, some of "these Romanized Africans lived in splendid villas, became generals, professors, and governors, and when Christianity came they were made bishops."[3] One Romanized African even became emperor of the Roman Empire. His name was Septimus or Septimius Severus.

Septimus Severus was born in 146 A.D. in the ancient North African city of Leptis Magna (located in Libya). He was a well- educated man who spoke Latin as well as his native Punic language. He started his career as a civil magistrate and eventually became a skilled military leader. He seized the emperorship of Rome by military force. Following the murder of Emperor Commodus in 192, Septimus Severus, with the support of the military, proclaimed himself emperor of Rome in 193. But to remain emperor of Rome he had to defeat two other governors who had also claimed the throne. First, he defeated Pescennius Niger, governor of Syria. Afterwards, he defeated Clodius Albinus, governor of Britain in a showdown battle. Septimus reigned from 193 to 211. "During...[his] reign...African interests and affairs received special attention."[4] However, Septimus was probably more concerned about the interests of the upper class of North Africa than the masses. "Under Septimus Severus both the civil and military administration of the Empire took on a more military character, and retired army officers were often given jobs formerly done by civilians. Septimus Severus owed his rise to the army, and he never let the army down."[5] His death came in Britain in 211.

Septimus is said to have been responsible for camel-breeding in Africa.[6] He "realized the enormous value of camel-breeding and we know that the number of camels in Africa, hitherto small, increased very considerably during his reign."[7] The camel is not native to Africa, although most people believe it is. It was brought to Africa, probably from western Asia.

Africans were also involved in the development of the early Christian Church in North Africa. The Romans wanted these African Christians to give up their belief in Jesus Christ and worship the emperor. Those who refused to accept the emperor as their god were persecuted. The Romans interpreted this rejection of emperor worship by the Christians as an act of disloyalty to the state. Therefore, these early Christians were considered a threat to the stability of the empire. Among the many Africans who died for Jesus were St. Perpetua and St. Felicitas, two Carthaginian women. Their heads were cut off by a gladiator for refusing to deny their faith. This tragic event occurred in the sports arena in Carthage about 180. In addition to being martyrs, blacks also worked as leaders in the early North African church. The three most famous early African church leaders were Tertullian, Cyprian, and Augustine.

Tertullian (c. 155-230) was a distinguished early Christian writer. He was born in Carthage and was well educated. He spoke Latin and Greek, and was well trained in law. About 193 he converted to Christianity. Tertullian "campaigned vigourously against the licentious pagan life around him, warning converts against the fearful moral dangers of the circus, the races, the theatrical performances and the Roman tolerance of every kind of vice and self-indulgence."[8] Tertullian was a prolific writer, producing a number of works. He also had his own style of writing. Tertullian introduced Latin into the Christian Church. Some of his works are *De Praescriptione Haereticorum*, *De Carne Christi*, *Ad Matyras*, and *De Oretione*. He also "wrote the first exposition of the Lord's Prayer in any language."[9]

Writer and martyr Cyprian (c. 200-258) was a famous bishop of Carthage. He was from a wealthy family and was well educated. He became a professor at the University of Carthage, where "he taught rhetoric."[10] About 246 Cyprian accepted Christ as his savior and was baptized. Afterward he became a priest in the Christian Church and was later bishop of Carthage. As bishop, Cyprian's beliefs brought him into conflict with the emperor of Rome and Pope Steven I. Cyprian opposed "the emperor's edict which required all Christians to register and make public their religious preference."[11] He also opposed Pope Steven I's idea of allowing heretics to perform baptisms. Cyprian's opposition caused him to be looked upon by Rome as a dangerous troublemaker. In 257 the Roman emperor Valerian had Cyprian arrested and put on trial. After the trial he was exiled from Carthage. In 258 Cyprian was retried and "found guilty of crimes against Rome."[12] His penalty for being found guilty was death. He was then beheaded and made a martyr.

Augustine (354-430) was one of the greatest contributors to Christianity. His birthplace was Tagaste, Numidia. He attended college at the University of Carthage, where he studied rhetoric and philosophy. In his youth Augustine gambled, partied, and had a good time. He also lived with a woman for a number of years and had a son by her. Augustine's free-spirited life caused his mother much concern, and she constantly encouraged him to join the Christian Church.

He eventually joined the Christian Church and was baptized in April 387. In 391 Augustine became a priest. In 395 he became bishop of Hippo, a city in what is now Algeria. "From...[then] on...[Augustine was] engaged in all the religious, social, and political conflicts of his time."[13]

St. Augustine was a gifted writer. His writings have influenced religious people over the centuries. African-American historian Mark Hyman, in *Blacks Who Died for Jesus*, makes the following comments about St. Augustine's religious works:

> The religious writings of Augustine have become literary and spiritual monuments to the creative greatness of the bishop. *The Predestination of the Saints* and *The Gift of Perseverance* were among his first books. During his lifetime, he wrote 90 books. *The Confessions* and *The City of God* are the most renowned. He has been justly called the father of theology, or the inventor of the study of religion. These writings covered an enormous range of subjects such as morals, history, philosophy and heresy to name a few.[14]

St. Augustine died in 430, when North Africa was being invaded by the Vandals. He was seventy-five years old at the time of his death.

Blacks not only died and worked for Jesus, but they were also there when he was crucified at Calvary. A black man named Simon, who was from the North African city of Cyrene, helped Jesus carry the cross. Blacks were also a part of the Jesus Movement that was impacting people in Palestine and elsewhere. "Blacks were among the throngs who...heard Jesus speak," notes Hyman. "They followed Him to Jerusalem. They walked with Him as everyone else did. They touched Him."[15]

Three Africans served as pope or head of the church in Rome: Victor (189-198), Miltiades (311-314), and Gelasius (492-496). "Each made contributions which were as significant and lasting as...any of the others."[16]

Victor was the first African to head the church in Rome. He Latinized the church, which had previously been under "Graeco-Oriental influences."[17] He exerted his leadership in church matters and "was the most dynamic of the second-century...[popes]."[18] During his reign, he was involved in a controversy over the correct date to celebrate Easter. He wanted every church to celebrate Easter "on the Sunday following the four-teenth day of the Vernal Equinox. All of the churches obeyed except those in Asia Minor."[19] They continued to celebrate "Easter the fourteenth day after the Vernal Equinox, no matter on which day it fell."[20] For disobey-ing him, Pope Victor had the churches in Asia Minor excluded "from communion with Rome and the church."[21] About 192 Victor excommunicated Theodotus d'Tanner of Byzantium, leader of the Adoptionists, who taught that Jesus was not the true son of God but rather the adopted son of God. Victor also wrote some works that were in Latin. He "is the first pope known to have had dealings with the imperial household. He supplied Marcia, mistress of Emperor Commodus (180-92) and herself a Christian, with a list of Christians con-demned to the mines of Sardinia, and thus secured their release; they included a future pope, Callistus I, whose name he had deliberately withheld."[22]

Miltiades was the second black pope. During his reign, Christianity became tolerated, Emperor Constantine was converted to Christianity, and Chris-tians were granted freedom of worship.

In 313 controversy erupted in North Africa over whether Bishop Caecilian or Bishop Donatus was the lawful bishop of Carthage. Emperor Constantine was asked to arbitrate the differences between the two sides. He, however, commissioned Pope Miltiades to preside over the controversy in his place. "Miltiades shrewdly transformed the government commission of inquiry into a regular church synod [advisory council] by...adding fifteen Italian bishops."[23] Both Bishop Caecilian and Bishop Donatus were at the inquiry. When the synod announced the verdict, it ruled in Bishop Caecilian's favor, stating that he was the "lawful Bishop of Carthage;"[24] Bishop Donatus was excommunicated.

Pope Miltiades seemed to have had a good relationship with Emperor Constantine and his wife. She "gave him the luxurious Lateran Palace"[25] in which to live. This gave Pope Miltiades the distinction of being "the first [pope] to have an official residence."[26] Miltiades also "convinced the emperor to return the cemeteries and the churches which had been taken by the government."[27]

Gelasius was the third and last black pope. Historian Mark Hyman comments on him:

> Gelasius was born in Rome of African parents. They lived comfortably. He received a superior education. In his youth he was a member of the Roman clergy. As pope, he accomplished many significant things. Gelasius arranged several rules for the clergy. He ordered that the revenue of the church should be divided into four parts: One part for the bishops, one part for the clergy, one part for the poor and one part to support the churches and divine services. He tried to uproot a major competing religion called Manichaeism.[28]

During his reign, Gelasius exerted his leadership by resolving disputes and taking stands against issues he disagreed with. He resolved the issue "over using wine at the Holy Communion. Many Catholics felt wine should not be a part of it because they believed wine was sinful."[29] He "allowed the use of wine to those who chose to do so."[30] Gelasius also took a stand against those who wanted to revive the old pagan festival of Lupercadia. Hyman describes the pagan festival and the pope's stand against it:

The celebration of Lupercalia was a bothersome issue. Among the Catholics were those who revived the old pagan festival of Lupercalia. This was a ceremony in which men and boys beat women with thongs of goatskins. It was to insure the women's fertility. The petition to him favoring this rite drew the pope's anger. His recorded reply was "Really, you are neither Christian nor pagan, but rather men without faith or morals." After ordering Christians not to go near the festival of Lupercalia, he replaced this celebration with the Feast of Purification.[31]

"Next to Leo I, Gelasius was the outstanding pope of the...[fifth century], and he surpassed Leo in [the] theological grasp."[32] His writings and sermons have been quoted down through the ages.[33] It is believed by many present-day Catholics that *Gelasian The Sacrementary* was written by him.[34] Gelasius was well-respected and admired by his contemporaries. They saw him as humble, determined, vigorous, righteous, and compassionate. He was concerned about the poor and gave to them generously.

Gelasius was also for the separation of church and state. His view is expressed in the following manner:

> In a letter to the emperor Anastasius, he enunciated a theory of two powers ruling the world: the spiritual authority embodied in the pope, which dealt with spiritual goods, and the temporal power represented by the emperor, which cared for earthly matters. Both were from God and were subject to Christ, and each was independent in its own area; but the spiritual authority of the pope was superior since it offered eternal salvation to the earthly power. This approach influenced medieval theories on kingship and on the relationship between church and state.[35]

We have seen that early African Christians contributed to the growth and acceptance of Christianity in the Roman Empire. They served roles as martyrs, church leaders, and popes.

Emperor Constantine is given credit for making Christianity lawful within the Roman Empire. It is said that he had a vision, which influenced him to accept Christ. Before a battle with rival Maxentius in 312, Constantine had a vision in which he was told to write the first two letters of Christ's name on the shields of his soldiers. He did that, won the battle, and converted to Christianity. The next year he granted Christians religious freedom.

By 392, Christianity had triumphed over paganism in the Roman Empire and was the official religion of the empire, but victory hadn't come without a struggle. Emperor Nero had begun the persecution of Christians in 64 A.D., making them scapegoats for the fire he deliberately set that burned a big part of Rome. As scapegoats for the fire, many Christians were brutally murdered. For about 250 years Christians were persecuted. They were often blamed for the evils that happened in society by having angered the pagan Roman gods. They were also accused of being aloof from the social life of society, not attending the games at the Colosseum, not going to the theaters, and avoiding other popular entertainment. In 311 Emperor Galerius issued an edict that stopped the ruthless persecution of Christians within the Roman Empire. In 313 Christians were given religious freedom by Emperor Constantine of the West and Emperor Licinius of the East. In 392 Emperor Theodosius I prohibited paganism within the Roman Empire. This made Christianity the official religion of the empire.

Meanwhile, the Roman Empire had begun to weaken due to attacks by barbarians, power struggles, and other internal problems. It became increasingly difficult for one ruler to administer an area as large as the Roman Empire. So about 286, the empire was divided into two parts, with an emperor ruling in the east and an emperor ruling in the west. In 324 Emperor Constantine again united the Roman Empire when he beat co-emperor Licinius in battle. However, in 395, the Roman Empire was permanently divided into two parts: the Eastern Roman Empire with its emperor governing from Constantinople and the Western Roman Empire with its emperor governing from Rome.

In the early 400s, migrating Germanic peoples such as the Visigoths and Vandals put tremendous pressure on the Western Roman Empire. In 401 a Visigoth king named Alaric invaded Italy but was defeated by the Roman commander Stilicho. In 405 a German named Radagaisus invaded Italy but was defeated. In 406 Germanic hordes, mostly Vandals and Sueves, invaded Gaul and did much destruction. In 410 the Visigoth king Alaric and his men captured the city of Rome and looted it.

Roman North Africa was invaded by the Vandals in 429. The Vandals were a Germanic tribe that had been forced to leave "their original home near the shores of the Baltic by other, more powerful, tribes."[36] After leaving their original home, they had migrated in a southward direction, crossing the Danube River into Pannonia, then crossing the Rhine River into Gaul, next crossing the Pyrenees into northern Spain, and finally moving into southern Spain. While in southern Spain, the Vandals were invited to come over to North Africa by Count Boniface, a Roman legate in Africa. Count Boniface was involved in a dispute with Rome and thought he could use the Vandals as allies. This invitation was a stroke of luck for the Vandals, who had been pressured to move from one place to another for centuries. Subsequently the Vandals, about eighty thousand of them, loaded up their belongings and crossed the water (Strait of Gibraltar) over into North Africa. The Vandals were led by their lame and very cunning king, Genseric. Count Boniface soon regretted that he had invited the Vandals to Africa but "it was too late."[37] After arriving, the Vandals began to capture and loot the towns and cities in North Africa. It wasn't long before they had most of the significant towns and cities under their control. In 430 they captured the city of Hippo. In 435 at the Convention of Hippo, Rome acknowledged Genseric's conquests and in return he promised not to attack the city of Carthage. However, in 439 Genseric reneged on his promise, marched on Carthage, and seized it. He also took what jewels and gold he could find in Carthage and closed the doors of the Catholic Church. He now had Roman North Africa in his hands. Next he built a fleet that became involved in pirating ships in the western Mediterranean Sea.

In 455 the emperor of Rome, Valentinian III, was killed by a man named Petronius Maximus. His widow, Empress Eudoxia, asked Genseric for help against Maximus. This turned out to be a tragic error in judgment on her part, however. This invitation gave Genseric the chance to invade Italy. Genseric and his men invaded Rome, captured the city, and then looted it for two weeks. Their loot included bronze, gold, jewels, and other valuables. They also brought back to Africa Empress Eudoxia, the woman who had requested their help, and her two daughters, as captives. Empress Eudoxia's two daughters were Princess Placidia and Princess Eudoxia (same name as her mother). "Genseric married Princess Eudoxia to his eldest son. The former Empress Eudoxia and Princess Placidia, however, managed to escape from his Court, and eventually reached Europe."[38]

Genseric died in 477. He had reigned as king of the Vandals for almost fifty years, 428 to 477. During the years he had resided in North Africa, he had been a thorn in the side of the Romans and they had been unable to do anything about it.

The people of North Africa were probably better off under Roman rule than Vandal rule. The Vandals treated the Romans and Romanized Africans very badly. The non-Romanized Africans who had resisted Roman domination, such as the people in the mountains and countryside, fared a little better with the

Vandals. The Vandals took possession of the best land and forced the people of North Africa to take the worst land. They also forced the people of North Africa to pay high taxes. On the other hand, the Vandals enjoyed the fruits of the land. They ate and loved excessively, wore silk robes, took daily baths, and enjoyed the good life.

The Vandals also persecuted the Catholic Church in North Africa. The Vandals were Arians, and they wanted the Catholics in North Africa to change over to Arianism. Those who refused were cruelly treated.

Arianism evolved from an African named Arius. His interpretation of religious doctrine was that Jesus was not of the same substance as God, but was higher than all other created beings. On the other hand, an African named Athanasius believed that Jesus was of the same substance as God. This controversy over Jesus' relationship to the Father divided the Church, and in 325 a conference was held at Nicaea (located in present-day Turkey) to resolve the dispute. The Nicaea Conference of Bishops "condemned Arius' interpretation of the Father-Son relationship and declared it as follows: That Father and Son were of the same substance."[39]

Meanwhile, in 527 Justinian became emperor of the Eastern Roman Empire, or Byzantine Empire. The Western Roman Empire had fallen in 476 when the German forces replaced the Roman emperor with their leader, Odoacer. The year 476 is generally regarded as the date of the fall of the Roman Empire, although the eastern part continued to exist. As emperor of the Byzantine Empire, Justinian wanted to defeat the Vandals and recapture Roman Africa.

In 533 Justinian sent an army to North Africa commanded by General Belisarius. The Vandal forces that they faced were led by King Gelimer, the great- grandson of Genseric. The Vandals had first been looked upon as liberators from Roman oppression by some of the people of North Africa. But the Vandals' harsh treatment of the North African people had eroded their support with the passing years. The Vandals had worn out their welcome. They were now despised by most of the people of North Africa. In the war between the Vandals and the Byzantine army, the Vandals were soundly defeated. Vandal rule in North Africa had now come to an end.

The Vandals ruled North Africa for roughly a century. Nevertheless, this short span of time was a very dramatic chapter in North African history. The Vandals left a legacy of destroying and never rebuilding. In fact, they left such a bad reputation that even their name came to mean destruction.

The Byzantine Empire was now in control of North Africa. It tried to restore Roman Africa to her former splendor.

> Byzantine rule attempted to restore much of what the Vandals had destroyed. The Orthodox bishops and clergy, exiled by the Vandals because of their pro-Roman sentiments, were returned to power. In the cities, churches were built or rebuilt and were richly decorated in the Byzantine style. Lands and houses that had been seized by the Vandals were returned to Romanized loyalists. Latin underwent a renaissance among the learned classes, and the upper classes adopted a...life in the luxurious Byzantine style. North Africa was brought back into peaceful intercourse with the Mediterranean world. [40]

The conditions of the African masses, however, changed very little under Byzantine rule. They were exploited and treated cruelly as they had been under Vandal rule. This policy of oppression by the Byzantine authorities caused the indigenous Africans to frequently rebel against them. In 639 the Arabs invaded North Africa, marking the beginning of the end of Byzantine rule there. However, the Byzantine Empire continued to exist elsewhere. It continued to exist as the Eastern Roman Empire until 1453.

Chapter 7

The Moors of North Africa and their Occupation of Spain

The Rise of Islam

In the seventh century a new religion arose in Arabia that significantly influenced the course of history. This new religion was called Islam (submission). It was founded by a camel driver known as Muhammad (Praised One), who was born in Arabia about 570. Muhammad's father died before he was born, and his mother passed away when he was about six. Orphaned at an early age, he was raised by his grandfather and afterwards an uncle.

When he was seventeen, he became involved in his family's caravan trade business in Mecca. About the age of twenty-five, he married a rich widow named Khadija. She was fifteen years his senior. Muhammad had worked for this rich merchant before he married her. Their marriage produced six children. When Muhammad was nearly forty years old, he was called to be a messenger of God through a vision. "While he was in a cave on Mount Hara, engaged in religious meditation, the angel Gabriel appeared before him,"[1] commanding Muhammad to serve as a prophet of God. As time passed, the angel Gabriel appeared to him again, commanding him to serve as a prophet of God. For a while Muhammad had some doubts about these visions and commands. Later on, however, he accepted them as revelations from God.

Muhammad began to preach that there was no god but Allah, and that he was God's prophet. Muhammad also preached that when Judgment Day came in the hereafter, the righteous would be rewarded and the wicked would be punished. Muhammad's first convert was his wife, Khadija. Other early converts of Muhammad were Abu Bakr, a wealthy merchant, and Ali, a cousin. Most of Muhammad's early converts, however, came from the poor and slave ranks. They would listen to his message. Most of the wealthy and powerful people were opposed to Muhammad's message. Many ridiculed him. Muhammad followers were persecuted. About 615 some of them fled Arabia and took refuge in Ethiopia. Finally the people of Mecca became so angry with Muhammad that they plotted to kill him. In 622 he fled to the city of Medina. There he found the people more receptive to his message. He was able to win over many of them as converts. In 624 at Bedr (Badr), Muhammad and his followers were able to defeat a much larger force from Mecca. At Uhud in 625 Muhammad and his followers were overcome by Meccan forces led by Abu Sufyan. In 627 a strong force from Mecca, about ten thousand men, besieged the city of Medina, but Muhammad and his followers successfully defended the city against the attack. Muhammad's success on the battlefield helped to increase the ranks of his followers. These victories also increased the self-confidence and zeal of the Muslims. In 630 Muhammad and his followers returned to Mecca and captured it. The 360 idols there were destroyed. The forces of Islam were now in control of both Mecca and Medina. In 632 Muhammad became ill and died in Medina.

Among the early converts of Prophet Muhammad was a black man named Bilal. (Some sources say Bilal was Prophet Muhammad's first convert.) This Ethiopian slave became the first high priest and treasurer of the Islamic Empire. Bilal was also the man who created the "Call to Prayer." He became Islam's first *muezzin*, the crier who calls Muslims to prayer. Bilal had the ability to inspire others through prayer. "Whenever he prayed, the crowds sobbed aloud. After listening to him the soldiers of Muhammad, whipped to frenzy, were ready to hurl themselves against any foe."[2] Bilal was a firm believer that prayer could change things. "At the battle of Bedr, while the enemy was advancing and all seemed lost, he made the soldiers kneel and pray. Inspired by his impassioned zeal, they swept upon the foe, turning what seemed [like] certain defeat into victory."[3]

Bilal was important to the early development of Islam. He provided the new religion with inspiration, whereas Prophet Muhammad provided it with leadership. Without Bilal's inspiration at Bedr, where Muhammad and his followers were outnumbered about three to one, the battle more than likely would have been lost and the new religion of Islam probably never would have gotten off the ground.

Other blacks were also close to Prophet Muhammad. After the death of his mother, an African woman named Barakat helped to raise him. Muhammad had an adopted son who was an African. His name was Zayd (Zaid) ibn Harith.

> Zaid...[ibn] Harith, another convert of...[Muhammad], later became one of the Prophet's foremost generals... [Muhammad] adopted him as his son and made him governor of his tribe, the proud Koreish. He was later married into the Prophet's own family—the highest honor possible. Zaid... ibn Harith was killed in battle while leading his men against the armies of the Byzantines. The *Encyclopedia of Islam* hailed him as one of the first great heroes of that faith.[4]

Before Muhammad and Islam, the various tribes of Arabia fought among themselves. But when they were converted to Islam, things changed. This new faith became a unifying force, transforming them into a cohesive unit. Their leaders were able to redirect the energy they had used to fight among themselves to the conquest of other lands. Whether he conquered his foe or was killed in battle, the soldier of Islam felt that he had come out a winner. The reason being, if he died in battle he believed that he was going straight to paradise, and if he conquered his foe, he had the spoils of battle. This way of thinking made the soldiers of Islam formidable in battle.

After Muhammad's death in 632, his close friend and father-in-law Abu Bakr took the title *caliph* or successor. He forced the Arab tribes which had rebelled following the death of Muhammad to come back into the Muslim fold. Abu Bakr was a skillful organizer and administrator. Under his leadership, the Arabs began their program of military conquest of other lands.

The armies of Islam, united by their faith and spurred on by their religious zeal, pushed into Byzantine (Roman) and Persian territories. By 637, five years after the death of Muhammad, they had conquered Palestine, Syria, and Iraq. Afterwards they also conquered Persia (Iran), North Africa, and Spain. Within a century, the Muslims controlled an empire extending from Spain across North Africa and the Middle East to the borders of India and China. The rapid speed with which the Muslims conquered this large empire amazed the world. It was larger than the Roman Empire at its peak.

The unpopularity of Roman rule was one factor that worked in the Arabs' favor during their conquest of Roman territories. Some people in these territories welcomed the Arabs as liberators rather than as conquerors. As a result, support from these people made the establishment of Arab rule less difficult.

The Arab Invasion of North Africa

We turn our attention now to the Muslim invasion of North Africa. Arab forces led by Amr ibn-al-As, invaded Egypt in December of 639. Within three years Egypt was conquered and a part of the growing Islamic

Empire. The Arabs also conquered the Libyan region of Cyrenaica in 642. Because of the cruelty of Roman rule in Egypt and in Cyrenaica, the people in these regions offered little resistance to Arab conquest. They saw the Arabs as liberators instead of conquerors. Elsewhere in North Africa, however, Arab forces met fierce resistance from the Africans.

Between 647 and 648, the Arabs attacked and captured Tripoli. Afterwards they moved into Tunisia and Algeria but were bribed into leaving by the governor of Tunisia, who offered them a handsome sum of gold.

In 666 the Arabs renewed their attempt to conquer areas of North Africa not under their control (Tunisia, Algeria, and Morocco). They were led by their commander Oqbar ben Nafi. "By 672 the Moslem invaders...were firmly established in Tunisia and had founded the city of Kairouan to protect their lines of communication with Egypt and to serve as a permanent garrison of defense against native resistance."[5] Meanwhile, the Arab leader Oqbar ben Nafi was replaced by Abul-Muhajir Dinar. Dinar continued the Arab conquest of North Africa, pushing on into Algeria, where he met stiff resistance from African forces led by Prince Kuseila (Kusaila). The records of the wars between the Arabs and...[Prince Kuseila] have a legendary character.[6] Finally, however, about 678 "the Arabs defeated"[7] Prince Kuseila and his men and made him a prisoner. In 681 the Arab commander Abul-Muhajir Dinar was replaced by Oqbar ben Nafi. Once again Oqbar was leader of the Arab forces. Oqbar continued the Arab conquest of North Africa, pushing on across Morocco and eventually reaching the Atlantic Ocean.

The indigenous Africans of North Africa found Arab rule no better than the rule of their previous conquerors, the Romans and Vandals. The plundering and greed of the Arabs caused the indigenous Africans to rebel against them. The Africans were again led by Prince Kuseila, who had managed to escape from the Arabs. Under Kuseila's leadership the Africans fought bravely, defeating and killing Oqbar ben Nafi in a battle near Biskra in 682. Kuseila ruled as king of Mauritania for five years, but in 688 he was defeated and killed by fresh Arab forces.[8]

Kuseila's death, however, did not stop African resistance to Arab conquest. His position as leader of African resistance was quickly taken up by a relative—a woman named Dahia-al- Kahina.[9] She was the queen of her tribe and was of the Jewish faith. It was said that she had the ability to predict the future. Under her leadership the Africans fought back valiantly and drove the Arab army into Tripolitania.[10] However, in 698 the Arabs rallied under the leadership of General Hassan-bin-Numan and took Carthage. But his victory was short lived, for Kahina, rallying the African forces once more, drove Hassan from the city.[11]

This courageous woman continued her struggle against the Arabs, although her resistance was weakening. In a desperate attempt to stop the Arab advance, she had areas in southern Tunisia ravaged so that the Arabs couldn't live off the land. This move to discourage the Arab advance by denying them food and shelter failed, however. Kahina was finally defeated and slain by Hassa-bin-Numan in 705, and with her death came the end of one of the most resolute attempts to keep Africa for the Africans.[12]

Many thousands of Africans (Berbers) died resisting Arab conquest. Yet they fought well against the armies of Islam. Like the Arabs, they utilized speed and mobility. The Africans, in fact, gave the Arabs much greater resistance than the Byzantine and Persian armies of western Asia. It was in North Africa where the Muslim armies encountered some of their strongest resistance. However, the Arabs were able to convert large numbers of Africans to Islam, which brought them into the Muslim fold, thereby checking their resistance. The Africans' determined attempt to drive the Arabs out of Africa also fell short because they did not have the military muscle and organization to sustain a prolonged war against the well-organized armies of Islam. The Africans had been weakened by over seven hundred years of resisting Roman and Vandal rule.

In 708 the Arab general Hassin-bin-Numan, was replaced by Musa ibn Nusair. Continuing the conquest of the Arabs, Musa ibn Nusair pushed on across Morocco to the Atlantic Ocean. The Arabs now controlled all of North Africa, except Ceuta. Ceuta was an independent enclave in Morocco. Count Julian, the Byzantine governor of Ceuta, had successfully defended it against the Arabs.

The Muslim Conquest of Spain

The unfriendly relationship between Count Julian and the Arabs was now about to change. Count Julian had become angry with Roderick, king of the Visigoths in Spain, over matters concerning his daughter. While at Roderick's court at Toledo in Spain, his beautiful daughter had been raped by the pleasure-loving king. To pay King Roderick back for disrespecting his daughter, Count Julian decided to help the Muslims invade Spain. So Count Julian went to the Arab governor of North Africa, Musa, and suggested that they be friends instead of enemies. Afterwards he told Musa about how beautiful and rich the country of Spain was and that it was open for the taking. Count Julian also offered to loan the Arab governor of North Africa ships for the invasion of Spain.

Musa carefully thought over what Count Julian had told him about Spain and decided to move cautiously. In 710 he sent a small force of five hundred men, in four ships, to investigate and determine if Spain could be successfully invaded. The men raided the coast of Spain and returned home with their boats filled with spoils. After being informed about the success of the raid and how poorly Spain was defended, Musa decided to send a much larger military force into Spain.

In 711 an Islamic army commanded by the African Tarik invaded Spain. Tarik was a Moorish general who had been "converted to the Islamic faith during the Arab invasion of Morocco."[13] General Tarik had an army consisting of 12,000 men, mostly Africans, who were also called Moors. When King Roderick of Spain was told about the invading Moorish army, he raised a large force to meet them.

King Roderick's large army of about seventy thousand men looked awesome to the Moors as the two opposing armies came face to face. Tarik, however, was confident despite the odds. He yelled to his soldiers, "Men, before you is the enemy, and the sea is at your backs. By Allah, there is no escape for you save in valour and resolution." This electrified the Moorish army and they yelled in reply, "We will follow thee, O Tarik!" as they charged into the ranks of the enemy.[14]

The battle was fought near the Guadalete River. It was a long and bloody affair; it "lasted a whole week."[15] But in the end the Moors routed the Spaniards, and King Roderick was slain in the battle. The victorious Tarik and his soldiers had all but conquered Spain in one battle. What he had to do now was to capture the towns and cities that still offered resistance. When the Arab governor of North Africa, Musa, heard about Tarik's glory, he became jealous and sent word to him to stop his advance. Tarik, however, ignored his orders and pushed on, capturing town after town. Again becoming jealous after hearing of Tarik's glory in Spain, Musa decided to visit Spain himself. He and his army of eighteen thousand Arabs rushed across the Strait of Gibraltar in the summer of 712 so that they could take part in the conquest of Spain. They captured the towns of Carmona, Seville, and Merida. But the real conquest of Spain was done by African Muslims, not Arab Muslims.

Later Musa and Tarik met in the town of Toledo. Their meeting, however, was less than cordial. Musa was so jealous of and angry with Tarik that he rebuked him and had him thrown into prison for disobeying a superior officer. But when the *caliph* of the Islamic Empire at Damascus heard about the situation, he had Musa recalled to Syria, and Tarik the Moor was given back his command in Spain.

Who Were the Moors?

In modern times, much controversy has developed among scholars over the racial identity of the medieval Moors. This controversy has divided scholars into two groups. One group believes that the Moors of North Africa were not black Africans but rather dark- or brown-skinned whites, belonging to the Caucasoid race. The other group believes that the Moors were a black people, belonging to the Negroid race.

Both ancient and medieval records indicate that the Moors were a black people. The word Moor—*Mauros* in Greek and *Maurus* in Latin—means black. The Romans applied the word Maurus to the black people of northwestern Africa. Northwestern Africa was a Roman province called Mauritania. Procopius, the Roman (Byzantine) historian of the sixth century, described the Moors as black-skinned. The Roman writer Martial used the expression wooly hair like a Moor in a literary work. Another Roman writer, Juvenal of the second century, made the following statement about a Moor in a literary work: "Your cups will be handed you by the bony hand of a Moor so black you'd rather not meet him at midnight." Also, the Moors are described as blacks in the European literature of the Middle Ages. The *Cantigas of Santa Maria*, a collection of four hundred poems from medieval Spain, reveals that the Europeans of the Middle Ages saw the Moors as a black people. In the *Cantigas of Santa Maria*, "at least twenty-eight of the long poems deal primarily with Moors."[16] In the Cantiga 185 of King Alfonso the Wise of Spain (1254-86), three Moors attacking the Castle of Chincoya are described as "black as Satan."[17] The paintings from the Cantigas also show the Moors as blacks. In these paintings the black Moors are portrayed as aristocrats, noblemen, soldiers, musicians, menials, and servants.

The Moors were in the coats of arms of noble European families of the Middle Ages. They appear with wooly hair and black skin, which leaves no doubt that the Europeans of the Middle Ages saw the Moors as a black people. Europeans with Moors in their coats of arms include the English, French, Dutch, Spanish, Germans, Belgians, and Portuguese.

European names such as Morris, Moore, Morrow, Moorman, Moorhead, Maurice, Blackmore, Murray, and Morison suggest Moorish influence. For example, a Moor in England might have been called Peter the Moor. His descendants would have the surname Moore. The surname Morison also comes from the Moors. Morison means "Son of the Moor."[18]

In addition to being called Moors, the indigenous people of North Africa have been called Berbers. Some scholars believe the word Berber comes from the Latin word *barbari* (barbarian). Others believe the word Berber is African in origin, from the word *ber* or *bur*.

Most modern historians and geographers use the word Berber instead of the word Moor to identify the indigenous people of North Africa. They apply the word Berber to both the indigenous North Africans of today and the indigenous North Africans of ancient history. For example, they use the word Berber to refer to the Libyans, Moors, Numidians, and Carthaginians of ancient history.

There has been much controversy over whether the Berbers are of Negroid or Caucasoid origin. A number of scholars advocate that the Berbers have Negroid roots. On the other hand, many scholars are of the opinion that the Berbers resemble southern Europeans in appearance and, therefore, are of Caucasoid origin.

However, ancient Greek and Roman records describe the Berbers as black. The Greeks described the

Libyans of their day, who belonged to the Berber family, as black skinned. As modern geographer Preston James points out, "the people living in the northern part of Libya had black skins, and the Greeks assumed that they had been burned black by exposure to the sun."[19] Also, the Romans described the North African Berbers of their day as black skinned.

Over the centuries the indigenous black people of North Africa, called Moors and Berbers, have been impacted by three major factors: (1) the steadily expanding Sahara Desert, (2) the coming of foreigners into North Africa, and (3) the mixing of the races.

The expanding Sahara Desert dried up rivers, lakes, and streams, and turned green forests and grasslands into oceans of sand. To escape this threatening situation, some blacks migrated from North Africa to other regions of the continent where they found places with the resources to support them. Others, however, remained in North Africa but moved to oases in the desert where they were able to find enough food and water to survive.

Foreigners came into North Africa chiefly by migrations, slavery, and invasions. Foreigners migrated into North Africa from the earliest times. During the slave trade, whites were sold into Muslim North Africa. Foreign invasions put tremendous pressure on the indigenous blacks of North Africa. Some fiercely resisted the invaders and were exterminated. Sometimes whole tribes went down fighting. Others migrated to other regions of Africa to escape conquest and domination. Still others, however, remained among the foreigners and intermixed with them.

The mixing of the indigenous black people of North Africa with foreigners—Indo-Europeans, Greeks, Romans, Arabs, Europeans—modified their physical appearance. This explains why many present-day Berbers differ physically from the Africans who live south of the Sahara. Race mixing is a very sensitive subject, but it has had a big impact on the history of

North Africa. Today anthropologists classify the Berbers as a Caucasoid people, and they also classify the present-day Arab-Berber world of North Africa as Caucasoid.

The race mixing that has occurred in North Africa can be compared to the race mixing that has occurred in Brazil. Five hundred years ago, Brazil was inhabited by Indians; today it is a very mixed country. Over the centuries there has been a mixing of Europeans, Africans, and Indians in Brazil. The European-Indian mix is called a *mestizo*; the European-African mix is called a *mulatto*, and the African-Indian mix is called a *zambo*. Over the centuries there has been a mixing of Africans, Europeans, and Arabs in North Africa. The result of this mixing is the present-day Arab-Berber world of North Africa. However, there are still some black Africans who live in present-day North Africa, especially in the Sahara Desert.

The classification of present-day North Africans as white is misleading because it gives the appearance that North Africa has always been inhabited by a Caucasoid Arab-Berber people, which is far from the truth. Anthropologist Dana Reynolds has done extensive research on the roots of the original people of North Africa. Her deep probe into ancient North African history reveals that the people called Berbers and Moors have black African roots. In her extensive and well-documented essay, *The African Heritage and Ethnohistory of the Moors: Background to the emergence of early Berber and Arab peoples, from prehistory to the Islamic dynasties*, Reynolds comments about the blackness of the Berbers and Moors.

> Most of us are not aware that the peoples whom the classical Greek and Roman historians called Berber were "black" and affiliated with the then contemporary peoples of the East African area. The word Berber in fact was used to refer to peoples of the Red Sea area in Africa as well as North Africans. Similarly there was an ancient belief that the nomads dwelling in the same lati-

tudes in the deserts of Arabia were peoples whose ancestors had in times far distant roamed the deserts of East Africa. It was such populations that in large measure comprised the Moorish people, but because of the attribute of blackness which sharply distinguished them from the bulk of the European people, the word came to be generally used by Europeans to describe persons of black complexion in general.[20]

In medieval Europe the Moors were also called *Saracens*. Scholars disagree on the origin of the word Saracen, but it was often used to denote a Muslim. European literature of the Middle Ages describes battles between Saracens and Europeans. The *Song of Roland* (ca. 1100), the celebrated medieval epic poem, chronicles the eighth century Frankish invasion of northern Spain, and describes the Saracens in detail.[21] The following verses describe a black soldier in the Saracen army:

> At their head rides the Saracen Abisme...no worse criminal rides in that company, stained with the marks of his crimes and great treasons, lacking the faith in God, Saint Mary's son. And he is black, as black as melted pitch...[22]

Song of Roland also describes the large number of blacks in the Saracen army.

> Ethiope [Ethiopia], a cursed land indeed; The blackamoors from there are in his keep, Broad in the nose they are and flat in ear, Fifty thousand and more in company.[23]

The same epic poem continues to describe the blacks in the Saracen army:

> When Roland sees that unbelieving race, those hordes and hordes blacker than the blackest ink—no shred of white on them except their teeth...[24]

▲▲▲

The name whites have called black people has changed over the millennia. The ancient Greeks called the black people they saw Ethiopians, the word meaning sunburnt faces. The Greek historian Herodotus said that there were two types of Ethiopians, Western or African Ethiopians and Eastern or Asiatic Ethiopians. The ancient Romans also called black people Ethiopians. In ancient times the name Ethiopian became a general name for black and dark-skinned people. The Greeks and Romans also called black people by the name Moor, meaning black or dark-skinned. During the Middle Ages the name Moor became a general name for black people. As time passed the name Moor changed somewhat. Mulattoes began to be called Tawny-Moors, while black and dark-skinned Africans became known as Blackamoors. With the rise of the slave trade in the fifteenth century, black people began to be identified by the word Negro, meaning black in Portuguese and Spanish. Eventually, the names Moor and Blackamoor dropped from usage, and the word Negro became the general name to denote black people. The name Negro became identified with the slave trade and slavery, and caused black people to be looked upon as inferior in the eyes of the world. For centuries throughout the world black people were called Negroes, but in the 1960s the black consciousness movement awakened many blacks and caused them to want to define their own name. They subsequently told the media that they wanted to be called black instead of Negro. In the 1980s many black Americans chose to be called African-Americans. Today, in the United States, black people are called blacks and African-Americans. Today blacks in Africa are called Africans or black Africans. The name Negro, used to denote blacks for centuries, has just about dropped from use in today's world.

The point here is, what people are called is very important. Their name can bring them scorn and disrespect, or it can bring them prestige and respect.

Today the word Moor no longer refers to black people. The dictionary defines a Moor as a "Muslim person of Arab-Berber heritage," a Caucasoid type. However, the name Blackamoor still refers to black people. The dictionary defines a Blackamoor as a "black African or Negro."

The Moors in Spain

Today the countries of Spain and Portugal comprise the Iberian peninsula. But at the time of the Moorish invasion in 711, Portugal was a part of Spain. Portugal became independent from Spain in the twelfth century.

Spain became a province of the vast Islamic Empire when it was conquered by the Moors in the eighth century. The governor of Spain was appointed by a central ruler of the Islamic Empire called a caliph, who resided in Damascus, Syria. The caliph had the power to appoint and dismiss the governor of a province as he desired. The conquest of Spain had whetted the appetite of the Moors. They now desired to conquer all of Europe. So Muslim forces, Africans and Arabs, crossed the Pyrenees Mountains and invaded southern France. The invasion continued until it reached central France, where it was stopped by Charles Martel at the Battle of Tours in 732. In this battle the Moors were soundly defeated. A number of scholars consider this battle to be one of the most significant in world history because (1) it checked the Moors in their attempt to conquer Europe and (2) it determined whether Europe would remain Christian or become Muslim. If all western Europe had been brought into the Islamic Empire, instead of just Spain, history would have no doubt taken a different course.

After their defeat in France, the Moors turned their attention to ruling Spain. The Moors controlled most of Spain but not all of it because a few mountainous provinces in the north still remained in the hands of Spanish Christians. The conquered people of Spain were probably better off under Moorish rule than un-der their previous rulers, the Romans and Visigoths. For example, the new Moorish government allowed the people of Spain freedom of worship; the Christians and Jews could remain in their faith or become Muslims. On the other hand, under Visigoth rule, the Jews had suffered religious persecution. Also Spanish slaves were given their freedom if they became Muslims, and Christians and Jews could avoid the poll tax if they be-came Muslims.

The first governors of Moorish Spain had a difficult time trying to consolidate the country because of inter-nal problems among the Muslims. The Muslims were fighting one another over power and spoils, Arabs against Arabs and Arabs against Moors. These internal problems continued until a new and competent gover-nor was appointed by the caliph of Damascus. The new governor redivided the land and separated rival groups.

In 755 a fleeing Umayyad (Omayyad) prince from the Near East named Abd-al-Rahman arrived in Spain. His family in Syria, the Umayyads, had been forcibly removed from power by the rival Abbasids, and he had subsequently fled for his life. In Spain he found sup-port among the Syrian Arabs. After capturing Cordova in 756, Abd-al-Rahman officially announced that he was the emir of all Moorish Spain. This was the begin-ning of the Umayyad dynasty in Spain, which was es-tablished independently of the rival Abbasid dynasty in Syria.

Abd-al-Rahman continued his struggle against his rivals until he subdued all of them and brought them under his control. He also built up a strong army con-sisting of 40,000 mercenary Africans to protect himself and Spain. Most of all, however, he established order and stability in Spain, thus making it possible for the future great Moorish civilization to emerge.

Widespread Arab conquests enabled them to be-come acquainted with much knowledge. They learned

Greek philosophy and science; they learned Indian mathematics and philosophy; they also learned how to manufacture gunpowder and paper from the Chinese. This knowledge was spread throughout the Islamic Empire. It reached Spain through Africa and Europe through Spain.

The Moors developed Spain into a splendid and highly cultured country. They promoted agriculture, industry, trade, and learning. As a result of their efforts, prosperity and greatness were reflected throughout Moorish Spain.

The Moors were skillful farmers. They used irrigation and excellent farming techniques to expand agriculture in Spain. They tried to put every acre of land into use, turning barren land into green acres. The Moors also introduced a variety of fruits and plants into Spain, including rice, cotton, sugarcane, oranges, dates, lemons, and pomegranates.

The Moors developed a number of thriving industries in Spain, including the silk industry, the weaving industry, the carpet industry, and the pottery industry. The city of Almeria became well known for its excellent silk industry. The city of Cordova became famous for the production of excellent leather and for its fine weaving industry. It once had 130,000 weavers. It also produced wool, silk, and arms. The sword blades of Toledo were the most excellent and beautiful in all Europe, and a factory near Cordova had an output of twelve thousand shields per year.[25] The towns of Malaga and Valencia were known for their pottery, while the towns of Beza and Calcena were known for their carpet. Moorish Spain also produced glass, paper, mosaics, jewelry, and other fine products.

The Moors carried on a flourishing trade with lands near and far. Various goods made in Spain were sent to markets throughout the Islamic Empire, Europe, Africa, and other lands. People in places such as West Africa, Italy, India, Egypt, and Turkey could purchase goods made in Spain. On the other hand, goods such as ivory from Africa, glassware from Syria, spices from India, and ceramics from Persia could all be bought in markets in Spain.

The people of Moorish Spain held learning in high regard. There were numerous public schools and libraries throughout the country. Even the common people were given the opportunity to get an education. Many of them were literate in both Arabic and Latin. There were numerous colleges and universities in Moorish Spain where one could obtain a higher education. The noted University of Cordova attracted students from all over Europe and the Islamic Empire. In Moorish Spain, one could study various subjects, including geography, astronomy, chemistry, philosophy, physics, mathematics, medicine, literature, art, history, and botany. There were many scholars and learned men in Moorish Spain. They took scholarship and learning to a high level, perhaps the highest in the world at that time.

Muslim scholars of the Middle Ages made great contributions to science and mathematics. They are credited with the invention of algebra and trigonometry. They also introduced Arabic numbers (the decimal system and zero) to the world. Arabic numbers are thought to have first been used in India. Muslim scholars also knew that the world was a sphere and not flat, and that objects were held to the earth by gravity.

Cordova was the principal city of Moorish Spain. It reached the peak of its glory in the middle of the tenth century. It was famous for its dazzling beauty, prosperity, and high degree of civilization. It had miles of well-paved streets, which were lighted by lamps at night. It had sewers, sidewalks, beautiful gardens and parks, numerous public and private baths, and many beautiful buildings. It had markets, many homes, magnificent palaces, numerous colleges and universities, and a large number of public schools and libraries. The citizens of Cordova were well known for their knowledge, their fine tastes and manners, and their luxurious living. Doctors and surgeons, professors and teachers, scholars, and other learned people were common in Cordova. Students from all over the world came to Cordova to study and learn at her fine schools. Cordova was also famous for her fine architecture. The great mosque of Cordova, which has survived to modern times, is a testimony to the brilliant engineering skills of the Moors. The city of Cordova, during her glory years, was the brightest splendor of the world.

Moorish Spain was a shining light in the dark when compared to the rest of Europe during the Middle Ages. We know that after the fall of the Western Roman Empire in 476, Europe sank into the Dark Ages— a period of cultural decline and stagnation. In Moorish Spain there were many public schools and the overwhelming majority of the inhabitants could read and write, whereas in Christian Europe there were only a few schools and only a small part of the population— mostly the clergy—could read and write. During the tenth and eleventh centuries, there were only two universities in Europe, whereas Moorish Spain alone had seventeen famous universities. The city of Cordova, during her heyday, was the biggest, wealthiest, and most splendid city in Europe.

The founding of the Umayyad Dynasty in Spain has already been discussed. Its founder, Abd-al-Rahman I, died in 788. He was succeeded by his son Hisham I, a just and learned ruler. Hisham I ruled until 796, and he was followed by the rulers al-Hakam I, 796-822, and Abd-al-Rahman II, 822-852. After Abd-al-Rahman II's great reign, Moorish Spain endured a period in which the ineffective rulers Muhammad, Mundhir, and Abdullah reigned. In 912 Abd-al-Rahman III came to power in Spain. After a long struggle he reunited the country and ushered in a period of peace and prosperity. He also proclaimed himself caliph, or supreme religious head of the Muslims in Spain, thereby formally breaking ties with the Abbasid caliphs of Baghdad.

Abd-al-Rahman III's long and prosperous reign of almost fifty years ended in 961. He was succeeded by his son al-Hakam II, a lover of books and big supporter of education, who ruled until 976. Al-Hakam II's successor was his twelve-year-old son Hisham II, who reigned from (976 to 1009), (1010 to 1013). However, Hisham II never got the chance to develop into an effective ruler because a prime minister named Al Mansur, through charm and cunning, manipulated himself into power and ruled in his place from 976 to 1002. Al Mansur was an effective ruler who kept Moorish Spain united. He was also an able general, making numerous successful military campaigns against the Christians in northern Spain. His death came in 1002. Al Mansur was replaced by his son al-Muzaffar, who ruled until he "was poisoned by his brother and successor, Abd-al-Rahman"[26]in 1008. Abd-al-Rahman was so disliked by the people that he was soon put to death. Next Hisham II "was dragged out of his"[27] harem and put on the throne, but he was such a weak and ineffective ruler that he was forced to step down. After Hisham II's departure in 1009, a civil war broke out in Moorish Spain as rival factions fought for power and control. In 1010 the puppet Hisham II was put back on the throne again. Also the same year, the great city of Cordova was plundered and ravaged, and it was never the same. In 1013 the puppet Hisham II was forced to abdicate the throne again, "after which he disappeared in a mysterious way that has never been solved."[28] Also during this period of breakdown in cental authority, caliph after caliph was put on the throne in Moorish Spain; but in reality they had no authority because each was the puppet of some faction vying for power. In 1031 the Umayyad Dynasty, which had been declining since 1002, finally collapsed after being in power for 275 years.

With the collapse of the Umayyad Dynasty, Moorish Spain split up into various petty kingdoms ruled by Moorish, Slav, or Spaniard kings. A politically weak

Moorish Spain, torn by dissension, was now ripe for invasions from Christian Spain to the north. For centuries the Christians had been slowly recapturing territory from the Moors and pushing them southward. They now saw the opportunity to exploit a divided Moorish Spain. They, therefore, began to use the strategy of divide and conquer on the Moors, playing one ruler against the other, since each ruler was only concerned about his own little personal power. In 1085 the Christians, led by Alfonso VI, struck a big blow against the Moors, capturing the prized city of Toledo.

This victory left Moorish Spain vulnerable to conquest. It also opened the eyes of the Muslims to the danger of the situation. To deal with the increasing Christian threat, the Moors asked the Almoravids in Africa to help them. Some Moors, however, had reservations about doing this because they thought that once the fighting was over the Almoravids might want to remain in Spain. When asked, the king of the Almoravids, Yusuf I, accepted the invitation to come to Spain and gave his word that he would return to Africa when the Christians were defeated.

The Almoravids were a group of Islamized Africans, also called Berbers, from around the Senegal River and the Sahara Desert to the north. They had just recently become Muslims. As a result, they were fired up with religious zeal and were eager to spread the faith of Islam. This fanatical Muslim sect was known as the Marabouts or Saints, but in Spain they were called the Almoravids. They had rapidly conquered a large empire that stretched from Senegal in West Africa to Algeria in North Africa.

Yusuf I the leader of the Almoravids, was a black Berber. The *Roudh el Kartas*, a Moorish work of 1326, gives the following description of Yusuf: "Brown color; middle height; thin; little beard; soft voice; black eyes; straight nose; lock of Mohammed falling on the top of his ear; eye-brows joined; wooly hair."[29]

In 1086 Yusuf crossed over from Africa into Spain with an army of fifteen thousand men. "The pick of his army consisted of six thousand Senegalese, jet black and of unmixed descent, who were mounted on white Arab chargers as fleet as the wind. Utterly fearless, and knowing every trick of warfare, these picked horsemen were considered invincible."[30] The ten thousand Moorish forces of Spain were added to Yusuf's army of fifteen thousand men for a total force of twenty-five thousand men. United, the combined Muslim forces marched northward to fight the European Christians.

The Christians were led by Alfonso VI. Alfonso had raised an army of seventy thousand men, including thousands of knights from France. With such a large force, Alfonso was confident of victory. As he gazed at his fine army, he said, "With men like these I would fight devils, angels, and ghosts!"[31]

On the other side, however, Yusuf was not quite as sure. He hadn't expected the Christians to have such a large army. The two opposing armies met at Zallaka, Spain, on October 23, 1086. Before the battle, Yusuf tried a little psyche job on Alfonso. Sending a messenger to...[Alfonso], he audaciously offered him the choice of conversion to...[Islam, of paying tribute,] or the sword.[32] Alfonso replied sarcastically, "Islam has always paid tribute to me."[33] Not to be outdone, Yusuf said in return, "What will happen, you'll see."[34]

With the verbal jabbing over, both leaders were now ready to get on with the battle. Yusuf then asked Alfonso to choose the date for battle and Alfonso selected the Monday of the following week. Yusuf, believing that Alfonso's word was reliable, decided to leave camp and go pray with his men. However, the Moorish king Motamid, having fought the Christians before, was skeptical of Alfonso. He believed the Christians would try to surprise them.

Things happened just as Motamid had expected. Shortly after Yusuf and his soldiers left for prayer, the

Christians attacked. Rallying his men, Motamid hurried off a messenger to Yusuf, and resisted valiantly despite the desertion of a large number of his men, who, accustomed to defeat by the Christians, fled at the first onslaught.[35] When Yusuf learned "of the Christian treachery, he decided to beat them at their game."[36] Using the mountains as a cover, he and his men stealthily moved into a position behind the Christian's camp, then attacked them. Alfonso was now caught in a trap, being attacked from the front and rear, with not enough room to maneuver his troops. Despite the terrible position of the Christians, there was a furious battle between the two sides, with the momentum switching back and forth. However, toward the end of the day, Yusuf, with many years of experience on the battlefield, sensed that the time had come to deliver the knockout blow. He had been holding back "three thousand of his invincible black horsemen on their white chargers"[37] for use at this time. "Now he unleashed them. With blood-curdling yells, they swept down on the Christians, passing through their ranks with fearful carnage."[38] The charge of Yusuf's "invincible black horsemen" turned the battle into a rout. The battle ended in a great victory for the Muslims; thousands of Alfonso's best men were slain on the battlefield. The Muslims also reaped a tremendous amount of spoils from the battle. Now that he had defeated the Christians, Yusuf kept his word and went back to Morocco.

With Yusuf back home in Morocco, the Christians were again on the offensive in Moorish Spain. They were constantly attacking the Moors. So Yusuf was again asked to come to Spain and help the Moors fight the Christians. Yusuf returned this time not only to fight but to conquer the country as well. He began the conquest of Spain in 1090, capturing kingdom after kingdom. The Almoravids, however, ran into stiff opposition when they fought Rodrigo Díaz de Vivar, known to fame as the Cid, the hero of Christian Spain during this period. In June of 1094 the Cid captured the Muslim-controlled city of Valencia. When Yusuf and his Almoravid forces attacked Valencia, they were routed by the Cid and his troops. But in the end, Yusuf and his Almoravid forces were victorious over the Cid. In 1099 they routed the troops of the Cid. This defeat devastated the Cid and he "died of grief in"[39] July of 1099. By 1102 the Almoravids had conquered all of Moorish Spain except Toledo. The dynasty Yusuf founded in Spain was an African dynasty, in contrast to the Arab dynasty of the Umayyads.

With their conquest of Moorish Spain, the Almoravids now controlled an empire that extended from the Senegal River in West Africa to the Ebro River in Spain, called the Empire of the Two Shores. The Almoravids governed their empire from two courts, one in Spain and one in Morocco.

Yusuf continued to rule his empire until his death in 1106, at the age of 99. Following his death, the Almoravids were able to keep the Christians in check for a while, but eventually the luxurious and pleasurable life in Spain sapped their vigor and zeal. They became weak and thus unable to keep the Christians from raiding the country. By 1147 the Almoravid dynasty in Moorish Spain had collapsed.

The Almoravids were replaced in Spain by a new group of Africans called the Almohades, or Unitarians. The Almohades were religious zealots like the Almoravids. The founder of this Muslim group was a religious reformer named Muhammad ibn Tumart. The Almohades eventually became involved in a power struggle with the Almoravids. By 1147 they had defeated the Almoravids and were in control of Morocco. The Almohades then invaded and conquered Moorish Spain, establishing another African dynasty there in 1150 with Abd al Mumin as king. During their rule in Spain, the Almohades made significant contributions to the splendor of the country. They promoted learning, particularly philosophy and the sciences. They also built the Castle of Gibraltar and the splendid Giralda *minaret*, the tower from which the muezzin calls the people to prayer, in Seville.

In 1163 the reign of Abd al Mumin ended. He was succeeded by his son, Abu Yakub Yusuf, who ruled from 1163 to 1184. In 1184 the greatest of the Almohade kings came to power. His name was Yakub ibn Yusuf, known to fame as Yakub al-Mansur (The Invincible). He was never beaten in battle. He was a great warrior and organizer. In 1195 he met the Christian king Alfonso IX at the Battle of Alarcos. Alfonso IX had an army of three hundred thousand men. But Yakub al-Mansur inflicted a crushing defeat on Alfonso's army, killing 146,000 men. The Muslims also collected much booty from their victory. Yakub al-Mansur was called "the Black Sultan" by the common people. His reign ended with his death in 1199.

Tired of the Moors, European Christians decided to organize a united front to deal with the Moorish menace. Pope Innocent III, therefore, sent out a call to knights all over Europe, asking them to unite in a crusade against the Moors. Many knights "answered his call." The combined forces of the impassioned Christians and Crusaders met the Moors at Las Navas de Tolosa in July of 1212. The leader of the Christian forces was Alfonso VIII of Castile. The Moors were led by the Almohade king Muhammad al-Nasir. In this battle the Moors were handed a devastating defeat by the Christians, losing 180,000 men or more, whereas the Christians lost a very small number. This victory at Las Navas de Tolosa by the Christians finally broke the power of the Moors in Spain.

This disaster at Las Navas de Tolosa was "one of the worst defeats" ever inflicted upon a Muslim army. Much of the blame for this disaster has to go to the Muslim leader Muhammad al-Nasir. He was a weak leader and a procrastinator. His delay in fighting caused his army to have to spend the winter in Spain, where it suffered much. He also didn't have his soldiers prepared mentally, physically, and spiritually to fight the inflamed Christians. His army "was demoralized by inaction, hungry, almost in mutiny, and ready to let itself be beaten from hatred of its leadership."[40]

After 1212 the Almohade dynasty in Spain grew weaker and weaker. The Almohades were unable to prevent the Christians from recapturing various kingdoms and towns. By 1235 the Almohades had been pushed out of Spain, back into Africa.

Meanwhile the Christians were on the march. Their drive to recapture Spain had gained much momentum. They began to capture city after city from the Moors. Cordova was taken in 1236, Valencia in 1238, Murcia in 1243, and Seville in 1248. By the end of the thirteenth century, the Christians had recaptured all of Spain from the Moors except the kingdom of Granada. The Moors were able to hold Granada for almost two centuries, but in 1492 it also fell.

The marriage of Isabella of Castile and Ferdinand of Aragon in 1469 united Christian Spain. After their marriage the couple started the task of uniting all of Spain. But first they had to drive out the Moors. The Moors resisted the Christian forces for eleven years, until January 2, 1492, when the Moorish king Boabdil surrendered at the city of Granada. This ended 781 years of Moorish rule in Spain, 711 to 1492.

After their fall from power in Spain, some Moors returned to Africa. For a while, those who remained in Spain enjoyed freedom of worship. It had been stipulated in the terms of their surrender that they would be allowed religious freedom. But in 1499 the situation changed. Queen Isabella issued a decree that gave the Moors the choice of conversion to Catholicism or exile. Some Moors accepted forced conversion to Catholicism rather than leave their homes, whereas others refused to do so and were banished from Spain. Also mosques were closed and many Arabic manuscripts were burned. Isabella's aim was to achieve both political and religious unity in Spain. To do this, she had to force the infidel Moors and Jews out.

The people were now calling the Moors in Spain another name, *Moriscos*, meaning that they had been converted to Catholicism. In 1567 the Moors were ordered to change their way of dressing and wear Christian clothes, to quit bathing, to give up their Arabic language and speak Spanish; to change their names to Spanish names, and to give up their customs and ceremonies. A rebellion erupted in the Alpujarras district as a result of this order. This rebellion continued for two years (1568-70) before it was suppressed. The Moors who survived the rebellion were sold into slavery or exiled. In 1609 a decree was issued that forced the Moors to leave Spain. Many went to North and West Africa, while some found a new home in France.

The Spaniards celebrated the exile of the Moors from Spain. But they failed to realize the impact the departure of the Moors would have on their country. Gone were the skilled craftsmen and farmers, the scholars and professors, the wealthy merchants and professionals. For a while after the exile of the Moors, Spain enjoyed a period of greatness. She established a great empire in the New World and enjoyed great wealth and power. Then came decline and stagnation, and she has never been able to regain her lost glory.

The Muslims brought much knowledge to Spain. It spread to the rest of Europe from Spain. "Thus, whether it is in language or literature, art or architecture, craft or industry, science or philosophy, Spain as well as Europe at large are deeply indebted to the genius of the...[Moors]."[41]

Internal dissension played a major role in the Moors' fall from power in Spain. This dissension weakened the Muslims to the point that they were unable to resist the growing power of the Christians. By 1212 the Christians had broken the Moors' power in Spain. It was only a matter of time before the end of their rule, which came in 1492.

Chapter 8

Empires and States of West Africa

West Africa or the western Sudan is the ancestral home of most African-Americans. It was from this region that the most Africans were taken to be slaves in the Americas.

Over the years, many history books have reflected the view that West Africa lacked a history and culture before the arrival of Europeans. However, historical documents written by both African and Arab scholars prove this viewpoint is a misconception.

West Africa's history goes far back into ancient times. There was an early relationship between ancient Egypt and West Africa. In the early 1900s Lady Lugard, wife of British colonialist Lord Lugard, investigated the ancient history of West Africa. One of her sources was the *Tarikh-es-Sudan* (*History of the Sudan*), a book written by an African scholar named Abderrahman es Sadi. Drawing from this book, Lady Lugard comments about an interaction between the pharaoh of Egypt and magicians from the ancient West African town of Kaukau: "The 'Tarikh' tells us that, according to tradition, it was from this town that Pharaoh obtained the magicians who helped him in the controversy which is related in the Twentieth Sourate of the Koran as having taken place between him and Moses."[1] The pharaoh's request for help from the magicians who lived in the distant West African town of Kaukau to help him deal with Moses provides evidence of the ancientness of West African history. The controversy between Moses and the pharaoh of Egypt is believed to have occurred during the Eighteenth Dynasty. In ancient times the town of Kaukau was famous for its magicians. It "stood where Gao now stands."[2] Gao is located on the Niger River in the present West African nation of Mali.

Major Felix Dubois, author of the book, *Timbuctoo the Mysterious*, traveled in West Africa in the 1800s. When he looked at the architecture of the old West African city of Jenne, Dubois observed, "It is in the ruins of ancient Egypt, in the Valley of the Nile, that I have seen this art before."[3] The similarity of the architecture of Jenne to that of ancient Egypt provides more evidence of the relationship between ancient Egypt and West Africa. It also provides evidence of the ancientness of West African culture.

West Africa is a large area, about the size of the continental United States. From about 300 to 1600, three great empires arose and flourished in this area: Ghana, Mali, and Songhay. Several smaller states also arose in West Africa during this time. This chapter examines the three great trading empires of Ghana, Mali, and Songhay and a few of the smaller states.

Ghana

Ghana was the first of the three great trading empires that flourished in West Africa during the Middle Ages. At the apex of its political power it ruled over lands stretching westward to the Atlantic Ocean; eastward it extended to the great southward bend of the Niger; southward it expanded to a point near the headwaters of the Niger; and on the north the Empire of Ghana faded into the sandy wastes of the Sahara Desert.[4] According to tradition, the kingdom of Ghana was founded about A.D. 300. However, Ghana's history dates back much further, beyond the Christian era.

A people called the Soninkes were the original inhabitants of the kingdom of Ghana. They were a group of tribes related by a common ancestry; and each tribe was made up of a number of clans.[5] Some of the main clans of the Soninkes were the Kante, Sylla, Sisse, and Drame. These various clans worked together as a unit. Each contributed to the kingdom its own specialty.

The Soninkes did not call their kingdom Ghana. Instead they called it Ouagadou. Ghana was their word for king or leader. The people of North Africa mistakenly gave the king's title to the country.

The great Soninke leader Kaya Maghan came to power about 700. This strong leader united the Soninke people into a cohesive unit. And from hereon Ghana ceased to be just another kingdom; she began to expand by annexing other kingdoms through warfare or peaceful persuasion. By the tenth century or perhaps earlier, the kingdom of Ghana had grown and expanded into a wealthy and powerful empire.

Ghana's crossroads location helped her to become a great trading empire. The capital, Kumbi Saleh, became an important trading center. Goods were brought to the markets of Ghana from all directions. Merchants, using the great caravan trade routes, brought in merchandise such as copper and salt from mines in the Sahara Desert; wheat, sugar, and dried fruits from North Africa; and clothing and textiles from Europe, Arabia, and Egypt. From areas south of Ghana, merchants brought in gold, sheep, cattle, slaves, and ivory. There also were local items produced for trade, including leather, cloth, jewels, and metal artifacts. However, the two most important trade items were salt and gold. Gold was found in abundance in a region south of Ghana called Wangara. The mines at Taghaza, a town located north of Ghana in the Sahara Desert, contained plenty of salt. From her crossroads location, Ghana could control the flow of gold, salt, and other commodities entering and leaving the country. Her merchants, "acting as middlemen,"[6] made a handsome profit. Also the government of Ghana became increasingly wealthy by charging a tax on imports and exports. So, through trade, Ghana became a wealthy and powerful empire.

The empire of Ghana had an abundance of gold, so much that she was "called the land of gold." The government had to limit the flow of gold to keep it from losing its value on the market. The king kept all nuggets that came into the country but allowed the people to use the gold dust. Without this measure, the law of supply and demand would have rendered gold almost worthless. This seemingly unlimited supply of gold nuggets made the king of Ghana fabulously rich. One nugget was so large that it was used as a hitching post for the ruler's favorite horse.[7]

Ghana "controlled the greatest source of gold for both Europe and Asia."[8] Her fame became widespread in distant lands. She became the topic of conversation among merchants and travelers in places like Spain, Egypt, and Arabia.

Besides having plenty of gold, Ghana also had an iron industry. She produced both weapons and tools of iron. Iron weapons gave Ghana a military advantage over neighboring states, which did not have them. As a result, she was able to conquer neighboring states that resisted peaceful annexation.

The people of Ghana were also successful farmers and craftsmen. The farmers of Ghana produced a variety of crops such as cotton, millet, yams, and sorghum. They also raised cattle, goats, sheep, and horses. Skilled craftsmen produced various items in their shops. There were different types of craftsmen, including weavers, blacksmiths, goldsmiths, carpenters, coppersmiths, potters, and stonemasons.

Much of what is known about the empire of Ghana has come down to us from Arab writers. Some of these writers were eyewitnesses, whereas others obtained their information from merchants and travelers who had visited Ghana. The first known written reference to Ghana is found in the work of Arab astronomer Al Fazari, dated 773-774. He describes Ghana as being a land of gold. Geographer Al Yakubi wrote a book about 904 called *The History*. In it he describes "Ghana as having numerous gold mines and a great king who had a number of kingdoms under him." Ibn Kawoala of Baghdad traveled in Ghana in the early 900s. In his *Book of Ways and Provinces*, Ibn Kawoala said the king of Ghana was the richest in the world because of his gold.[9] He also describes the great trans-Saharan trade. One of the most important sources of information about the empire of Ghana comes from the Arab geographer El Bekri (Al Bakri), who was from Cordova, Spain. In 1067 he wrote a book called *Roads and Kingdoms* in which he gives a valuable description of Ghana. Information for his book came from the reports of travelers and merchants who had visited Ghana. El Bekri described Ghana at that time as being a rich and powerful empire. He also said that Ghana was ruled by a powerful king named Tenkamenin, who could field a formidable army of two hundred thousand men of whom forty thousand were archers. He described Tenkamenin as a man who loved justice. El Bekri said that the inhabitants of the country wore clothes made of "silk, cotton, and brocade." He reported that the empire was well organized and the king was well respected by the people.

Kumbi Saleh was the capital of the Ghana Empire and the main trading center in the western Sudan. It "was a twin city, composed of two towns about six miles apart connected by a long boulevard."[10] As time passed the space "between the two towns"[11] became covered with houses. One town was the Muslim town where Muslim merchants from North Africa stayed when they were in Ghana. The Muslim town also contained numerous houses built of stone and twelve mosques used for religious services. In the Muslim town resided scholars, theologians, and lawyers. Arabic was the language used for writing; it was a universal language like Latin was in Europe. The other town was the king's town. He lived there in a magnificent palace made of stone, with glass windows, and decorated with beautiful drawings and sculptures. Some of the inhabitants of the king's town lived in houses made of stone, whereas others lived in houses made of mud and thatch. The king's town was called Al-Ghaba, meaning the forest because it "contained a sacred grove of trees used for religious purposes by the Ghanaians."[12] This sacred grove of trees was carefully guarded to keep out intruders. It contained prisons, tombs of dead kings, and temples for religious ceremonies.

In the eleventh century, when El Bekri wrote about Ghana, the king and most of the people of the empire worshiped their traditional African gods. The people of Ghana believed that spirits existed in everything, both animate and inanimate, and that these spirits could be good or evil. They also believed that the spirits of their ancestors could influence their daily lives. There was a sizable Muslim population in Ghana, but mostly among the commercial classes. Some of the government officials were Muslims.

The people of Ghana, like all African people, "believed in life after death."[13] The following quote describes their preparation for the Ghana's afterlife:

> When a ruler died great care was taken to see that he lacked for nothing on his journey to the spirit world. A special hut was constructed for the dead Ghana's body and within it were placed comfortable rugs, his personal possessions, food and water and his domestic servants. Then the building was sealed off and completely covered with a thick layer of earth to form a huge mound. Later, sacrifices and libations would be made at shrines to the dead Ghana for he was now an ancestor who needed sustenance and whose aid was valuable to his people.[14]

Note that the afterlife preparations for the rulers of Ghana and the pharaohs of ancient Egypt were similar. However, the afterlife preparations for the pharaohs of Egypt were on a more elaborate scale.

The king of Ghana held court "in a domed pavilion."[15] Those occasions were characterized by extraordinary pomp and elegance. The king, sitting before a public audience, listened to the complaints and disputes of his subjects. He wore a beautiful robe and "a high cap decorated with gold and wrapped in turbans of fine cotton."[16] Tied near the domed pavilion were ten horses, each wearing a harness embroidered with gold. "The entrance to the pavilion was guarded by well-bred dogs wearing collars of gold and silver.... To the Ghana's right were assembled the sons of his tributary rulers expensively clad and with gold plaited into their hair."[17] The audience was called to order by the beating of a drum, or a daba.

The king was highly respected by the people of Ghana. They had special ways of showing him respect when they approached him. El Bekri says that "when the people who adhered to the same religion as the king approached him, they fell on their knees and sprinkled dust upon their heads; the Muslims greeted him by clapping their hands."

In 990 Ghana took the Sahara Desert town of Awdoghast from the desert Berbers, which put her in control of all trade in the western Sudan. The Berbers never forgave Ghana for doing this.

The Ghana Empire reached its peak in the eleventh century. At that time, it was wealthy and powerful. It had a well-organized and stable government, and a strong army. There also was an abundance of food in the empire and trade was thriving. Trade was Ghana's main source of wealth.

The dazzling wealth of Ghana had for centuries been very tempting to her neighbors. They envied her wealth and wanted it for themselves. For a long time Ghana's large and powerful army was able to protect the empire from invaders. "In 1020 North African forces with Arab assistance attacked the Empire, but were driven back. In 1042 the Almoravids made attacks on some of the outlying districts, but they avoided a direct clash with the main forces of the Ghana Empire."[18] The Almoravids were a fanatical Muslim sect. In 1062, led by Abu Bekr, the Almoravids launched an all-out invasion to conquer Ghana. The struggle between the two sides was bitter, with heavy losses on both sides. After fourteen years of determined resistance, the people of Ghana were defeated in 1076. Their capital, Kumbi Saleh, was captured and looted. The Almoravids demanded that the people of Ghana accept Islam or else they would be put to the sword. The people who resisted Islam were slain.

Who were these Almoravids, who wreaked such havoc on Ghana? The Almoravids were a desert African people who were also known as Berbers. They "occupied the southern desert from the coast to the north-eastern frontiers of Ghana."[19] About 1020 a group of these Berber tribes formed an alliance to deal with the growing threat of Ghanaian expansion. Tarsina, a tribal chief, was "appointed as their leader."[20] Tarsina became a Muslim and took the name Abdulla Abu Muhammad. When he died "his son-in-law Yahia"[21] replaced him. Yahia made the pilgrimage to Mecca and on the way back he stopped in the holy city of Kairouan in Tunisia. There Yahia met and talked to a learned Islamic theologian. Afterward, "Yahia decided to take back with him to his tribe someone capable of teaching the Koran to his people."[22] A man named Ibn Yasin was selected for the job. Ibn Yasin had a difficult time trying to teach Islam to the tribesmen; they did not want to give up their old ways of doing things. Refusing to give up, he decided to build a *ribat* (monastery) on "a small island in the Senegal River."[23] There he conducted his teachings. By the year 1042 he had a following of about one thousand people. Still he was unable to attract the large numbers he desired, so he decided to convert the tribesmen by force. He and his followers then went on a holy war to get rid of paganism. The tribesmen were offered the choice of accepting Islam or the sword. The Almoravids were very successful with their persuasive tactics. Within a short period, they had grown into a force of thirty thousand.

Soon the Almoravids developed into a formidable fighting force. They were driven by the religious motive of spreading their faith and by the desire to acquire booty. They retook the town of Awdoghast from Ghana in 1055. In 1059 their leader, Ibn Yasin, was killed fighting in Morocco. He was replaced by a man named Abu Bekr. Continuing their march, the Almoravids conquered Morocco, Algeria, Tunis, Ghana, and Spain. By 1102 the Almoravids were masters of an empire that stretched from the Senegal River in West Africa to the Ebro River in Spain.

Abu Bekr, the leader of the Almoravid forces which captured Ghana in 1076, was killed in 1087. Following his death, the Almoravids' control of Ghana disintegrated. This enabled the Soninkes to retake control of Ghana. However, because of the devastating blows Ghana had suffered at the hands of the Almoravids, she was unable to restore her political and economic dominance in West Africa. The Almoravids had disrupted Ghana's great trade, which was the source of her wealth; their large animal herds had brought about a depletion of water and agriculture resources in Ghana; their forced conversions of the people to Islam had caused many to flee the empire.

Weakened by her struggle with the Almoravids, Ghana was unable to prevent states such as Tekrur, Diara, and Susu (Sosso) from breaking away from the empire and establishing their independence. In 1203 the king of Susu, Sumanguru, attacked and captured Kumbi Saleh. So what remained of the Ghana Empire was now a part of the state of Susu. In 1235 the state of Susu was conquered by the Mandingo people from the kingdom of Mali. In 1240 the old capital of Ghana, Kumbi Saleh, was destroyed by forces from Mali. This event marked the end of a great state that had lasted for nearly a thousand years.

Mali

When Ghana passed into history, another state took her place and spread over her former territory. This state was called Mali or Melle. Mali started out as a kingdom and grew into an empire. The kingdom of Mali was founded by the Mandingo people in the seventh century. In 1050 the king of Mali, Barmandana (Baranmindanah), embraced Islam; afterwards he made a pilgrimage to Mecca. All kings who succeeded him made the pilgrimage to Mecca also.

After the Ghana Empire was conquered by the Almoravids, some of her tributary states broke away and established their independence. Mali (Kangaba) was one of those states. Her capital was at Jeriba.

Susu was another tributary state of Ghana that broke away and became independent. Her cruel king, Sumanguru, attacked and conquered Kumbi Saleh in 1203. Afterwards Sumanguru attacked the Mandingo people of Mali and established his rule in their kingdom. His rule was so harsh and ineffective that the people of Mali rebelled against him. In 1230 the inspirational and great warrior Sundiata became king of Mali. He immediately began to organize an army to liberate Mali from Sumanguru's harsh rule. However, he avoided an all-out battle with Sumanguru until he was ready. In 1235 Sundiata and his army met the feared Sumanguru and his army in a showdown at Kirina. In this historic battle Sundiata led his army to victory over Sumanguru and his men. Next Sundiata attacked and captured the city of Susu. Afterwards he conquered the Susu Empire and other new territories also. As a result, Sundiata turned a struggle for independence from Susu into the creation of the Mali Empire.

Sundiata became the first great king of Mali. He laid the foundation for Mali to become one of the most celebrated empires of her time. He consolidated his newly conquered territories and moved the capital of Mali from Jeriba to Niani. He promoted the expansion of agriculture. The production of cotton, millet, ground nuts, and other crops was increased. Sundiata's generals captured the lucrative gold fields of Wangara. Also, Mali took control of the great gold and salt trade that had once belonged to Ghana. When the legendary Sundiata died in 1255, after twenty-five years of outstanding rule, he left behind a prosperous empire that was well organized and well governed.

Sundiata's successor to the throne was his son Mansa Uli. The word *mansa* meant king or emperor. Mansa Uli was not the great leader his father was. During his reign his generals conquered new territories and added them to the Mali Empire. His reign ended with his death in 1270. Following Uli's rule several mediocre kings came to power but their reigns were short and unimpressive. In 1285 an ex-slave, Sakura, seized power and made himself king. Sakura was a remarkable warrior. He was successful in military campaigns against Songhay and Tekrur. Also during his reign trade increased in the empire. His rule ended in 1300 when he was killed while returning home from a pilgrimage to Mecca.

In 1307 Mansa Musa came to power in Mali and ruled for twenty-five years. He was an outstanding ruler with many talents. However, the one thing that made him famous was his spectacular pilgrimage to Mecca, 1324-25. The kings of Mali had made the pilgrimage to Mecca before, but not in the manner in which Mansa Musa did it. In 1324 Mansa Musa began his long journey to Mecca. He and his caravan made a spectacular sight as they rode across the landscape. Mansa Musa rode a magnificent horse decorated "with gold trappings."[24] In front of him rode five hundred servants, "each carrying a staff of gold weighing about six pounds.... Then came Mansa Musa's baggage-train of eighty camels, each carrying 300 pounds...weight of gold dust."[25] Altogether there were sixty thousand courtiers and servants in Mansa Musa's caravan. And they were all expensively clothed.

Mansa Musa and his caravan took a roundabout route to Mecca. After leaving the capital city of Niani, the caravan traveled to Walata, Tuat, and Cairo. From Cairo the caravan proceeded to the holy cities of Mecca and Medina. Everywhere Mansa Musa and his party stopped, they gave lavish gifts to the inhabitants and spent their gold freely. If a mosque was needed in a place, gold was given to build one. Also, there was a drop in the price of gold in Cairo due to the generous giving and extravagant spending of this precious metal by Mansa Musa and his party. Because of his generosity and extravagant spending, "he finally ran out of gold in Cairo."[26] He had to borrow money to pay the expenses of his trip back home to Mali.

The pilgrimage to Mecca by Mansa Musa was a magnificent display of the wealth and power of the Mali Empire to the outside world. The fame of Mansa Musa became widespread in Africa, Asia, and Europe. Long after he had come and gone, people in Cairo, Mecca, and other places he had visited talked about his spectacular pilgrimage.

> In the fourteenth century, cartographers of Europe published maps showing the location of Mali and calling attention to the wealth of its sovereign. In an atlas prepared for King Charles V of France, there is a drawing depicting Mansa Musa wearing regal robes and a kingly crown, and holding a scepter in one hand and a nugget of gold in the other.[27]

While Mansa Musa was in Mecca, he met the famous Moorish poet and architect Es-Saheli, who was from Granada, Spain. A friendship developed between the two men. Later Mansa Musa invited Es-Saheli to return to Mali with him. Es-Saheli accepted Mansa Musa's invitation and felt honored that he had been asked to serve the king. There were other distinguished men who were attracted to Mansa Musa's charm. They returned home with him also.

On his way back home to Mali, Mansa Musa received word that "one of his generals, Sagmandia,"[28] had been successful in a military campaign against the kingdom of Songhay. This victory brought Songhay into the Mali Empire as a tributary state, along with her cities, Gao, the capital, and Timbuktu. "Mansa Musa was so overjoyed at this new addition to his Empire that he decided to delay his return to Niani and to visit Gao instead. At Gao the King of Songhai came to make his personal submission, and his two sons, Ali Kolen and Sulayman Nar, were given up as hostages."[29]

Es-Saheli, the famous architect who accompanied Mansa Musa back to Mali from Mecca, directed the building of splendid mosques at Timbuktu, Gao, and other places. He also built for Mansa Musa an elaborate palace at Timbuktu.

There is a saying that "advertisement doesn't cost, it pays." This saying was certainly true for Mali. Mansa Musa's pilgrimage to Mecca advertised the wealth and power of Mali to the outside world. His advertisement paid off. It helped to bring about an interest in Mali from distant lands. As a result, many travelers, merchants, and learned men from throughout the Islamic world were attracted to Mali.

The Mali Empire was at its zenith during the reign of Mansa Musa. It was powerful, prosperous, wealthy, and well administered. It had a large standing army to prevent invasions and to maintain peace within the empire. In size, it encompassed "an area just about equal to that of western Europe."[30] The Mali Empire extended from the Atlantic Ocean in the west to the Hausa States of Nigeria in the east; in the north, it extended into the Sahara Desert; southward, it extended to Futa Jallon. Prosperity was reflected everywhere in Mali. Food was produced in abundance. A flourishing trade brought great wealth to the empire. Scholarship was encouraged by Mansa Musa. The city of Timbuktu became an important center for Islamic scholarship. There lawyers, scholars, doctors, and theologians were common. Other important centers for culture and scholarship in the empire were Gao, Niani, and Walata.

Mansa Musa was a devout Muslim. He encouraged others to embrace Islam also. For example, he sent a messenger southward to encourage the Wangara gold miners to embrace Islam. They refused to do so. They "even threatened to stop producing gold if they were forced to become Moslems."[31] Mansa Musa was disappointed with their response but he decided to leave them alone and let them continue to practice their traditional African religion.

The religion of Islam was practiced mostly by the people who lived in the towns. The people who lived in the small farming villages out in the rural areas overwhelmingly practiced the traditional African religion. The Mali king Barmandana was converted to Islam in 1050. All Mali kings who followed him embraced Islam. Since the Muslims controlled the caravan trade routes, the link to international trade, it was both economically and politically advantageous for a Mali king to be a Muslim.

The death of Mansa Musa in 1332 brought his glorious reign to an end. His successor to the throne was his son Mansa Maghan. After about a year of Mansa Maghan's weak rule, the Mali Empire was raided by the Mossi people of Yatenga. They captured the city of Timbuktu and burned it. Another sign of Mansa Maghan's weakness occurred when he relaxed the restrictions on the two hostages Ali Kolen and Sulayman Nar. The two princes took advantage of this situation and escaped back home to Gao, where they threw off Mali domination and made Gao independent again. Mansa Maghan's weak four-year reign ended with his death. His successor to the throne was "his uncle, Sulayman, [who was the] brother of Mansa Musa."[32]

Mansa Sulayman was able to stop the decline of the Mali Empire and preserve its greatness. He was a wise and able ruler. However, his thriftiness with money caused some resentment among the people. In 1351 he made a pilgrimage to Mecca, and in the following year the Mali Empire was visited by the great Seville and Tunisian historian, Ibn Battuta.[33]

For a description of how life was in the Mali Empire, we turn to Ibn Battuta, an eyewitness who visited the empire during the reign of Mansa Sulayman in 1352. Ibn Battuta was born in 1304 in Tangier, Morocco. He was an international traveler and scholar. He was also "an experienced observer,"[34] having traveled, lived, and taught in places like India, China, Spain, Arabia, and Turkey. Ibn Battuta was very impressed with the justice he observed in the Mali Empire. He said that of all people the blacks have a greater dislike for injustice. For example, the governor of Walata, "accused of robbing a merchant, had to come to Mali in person, where he was found guilty and disgraced by the king."[35] Ibn Battuta was equally impressed with the security he observed in the empire. If a white person carrying valuable goods died in the empire, his goods would not be confiscated; instead, they would be returned to a reliable person among the whites, who would keep the goods until a legitimate person claimed them. When the king held audiences in the palace yard, much pomp and glitter characterized those occasions. Ibn Battuta was impressed with the regularity with which the people attended their religious services. He was also impressed with the personal cleanliness of the people. For example, if a man had only one shirt, he made sure that it was washed before he wore it to the mosque on Friday.

Ibn Battuta disapproved of some of the things he observed in Mali. For example, he disliked seeing women servants and young girls walking around naked; he disapproved of the people eating the meat of asses; he disliked the submissive behavior the people displayed before the king. He said that of all people the blacks were the most submissive toward their king. For example, subjects would get down on all fours and throw "dust over their heads and shoulders" when they came before the king as a sign of deep respect and loyalty to him.

Ibn Battuta was observing the culture of Mali through the eyes of an outsider. No doubt the people of Mali also would have found certain customs in his country deplorable. Therefore, what people think about other cultures depends a lot upon how they have been taught to perceive the world.

Ibn Battuta's description of the Mali Empire in the fourteenth century is important because it provides documented evidence of the history and culture of West Africa before the devastating impact of the slave trade.

The Mali Empire lost a wise and able leader when Mansa Sulayman died in 1359. The kings who followed him were not as competent. His successor to the throne was his son Kamba, whose reign was short-lived. In a struggle for power Mari Jata II killed Kamba and took over as king. Mari Jata II's reign, 1360 to 1374, was marked by oppression and excessive spending. Mari Jata II was succeeded by the weak ruler Musa II, who reigned from 1374 to 1387. Between 1387 and 1390, three rulers—Maghan II, Sandiki, and an unnamed relative of Mari Jata—perished in the struggle for power before Maghan III, 1390 to 1400, eventually became mansa.[36]

In the 1400s internal problems and external pressure caused the Mali Empire to disintegrate. Some of the internal problems were weak leadership, disunity, power struggles, and religious conflicts between Muslim emperors and the masses who practiced the traditional African religion. Strong kings like Sundiata and Mansa Musa had the wisdom, charisma, and skill to hold the Mali Empire together, whereas the later, weaker kings did not have these qualities. A weak Mali could not withstand the attacks of the Mossi, Tuareg (people of the desert), and Songhay armies. The Tuareg seized the commercial towns of Arawan, Walata, and Timbuktu in about 1433 and ruined Mali's control of the trans-Saharan trade.[37] As Mali's power declined in the western Sudan, the kingdom of Songhay's power increased and she began to take Mali territory. About 1475 the Mali Empire was no longer the supreme power in the western Sudan because that position had been taken by the rising Songhay Empire. Mali continued to exist as a kingdom for almost two more centuries, but her days of glory were gone.

Songhay

Songhay began as a small state in the seventh century and eventually grew into an empire. The Songhay people were the founders of this state. According to tradition, the first significant dynasty of Songhay was the Dia dynasty, which came to power in 690. The fifteenth *dia* (king) of Songhay, Dia Kosoi (Kossoi), came to the throne in 1009. He was the first Songhay ruler to embrace Islam. During his reign the capital of Songhay was moved from Kukia to Gao. As time passed, Gao became an important trading center in the western Sudan.

In 1325 Mansa Musa's general, Sagmandia, was successful in a military campaign against Songhay. As a result of this conquest by the Mali army, Songhay, including the cities of Gao and Timbuktu, became a tributary state of the Mali Empire. We learned earlier that Mansa Musa was returning home from his pilgrimage to Mecca when he received word of this conquest. So, instead of going directly home, Mansa Musa went on to the capital city of Gao. There he received the personal submission of the Songhay king. As was the custom, Mansa Musa brought the Songhay king's two sons, Ali Kolen and Sulayman Nar, back to his court as hostages to insure the loyalty of their father. After Mansa Musa's death in 1332, the two princes escaped back home to Gao. There a new dynasty, the dynasty of the Sonnis, was established in 1335 with Ali Kolen as king. The new ruler took the title *sonni*, which meant liberator. Ali Kolen led a successful rebellion that resulted in Gao regaining her independence from Mali. However, Mali still continued to dominate other Songhay territories.

In 1375 Songhay freed herself from Mali domination and regained most of her territory. The Songhay ruler at that time was Sulayman Nar, the second sonni of the Sonni dynasty. To prevent being reconquered, Songhay had to defend her territory from attacks by neighboring groups of people such as the Mossi, Mandingo, and Tuareg. In the process of defending her territory, Songhay built up an army that was not only strong enough to defend her territory but was also able to conquer other states. Songhay was now ready for the future conquests of the remarkable Sonni Ali.

In 1464 Sonni Ali, one of the greatest Songhay kings, came to power. Through conquest, he expanded Songhay from a small state to a large and powerful empire. He first defeated the Mossi of Yatenga and drove them out of Songhay territory. The Mossi had raided Songhay territory for a long time. In 1468 Sonni Ali captured the city of Timbuktu and forced the Tuaregs, who had earlier conquered the city, to leave. He also killed many of the inhabitants of the city for collaborating with the Tuaregs, his bitter enemies. The Songhai towns and villages, including Timbuktu, had from very early times been the constant prey of the nomadic Tuaregs.[38]

After his conquest of Timbuktu, Sonni Ali decided to bring the city of Jenne into his realm. The problem, however, was that Jenne had never been captured. The city had withstood at least ninety-nine sieges in its history. Sonni Ali, believing that he could succeed where others had failed, put a siege on the city of Jenne. The city resisted for seven years, seven months, and seven days before it surrendered to Sonni Ali. Unlike what had happened at Timbuktu, Sonni Ali did not harm the citizens of Jenne. As a result of this conquest, Sonni Ali now controlled the three major trading centers in the area—Jenne, Gao, and Timbuktu.

The following is a description of Jenne, an important trading and cultural center that became a part of the Songhay Empire.

> Jenne was a valuable prize to the Songhay, since it was a prosperous trading center, containing buildings of attractive design, and surrounded by great scenic beauty. It was also the home of advanced culture, being the seat of a noted university, which employed a staff of thousands of teachers who gave courses of lectures and conducted researches on a variety of subjects. Their medical school trained physicians and surgeons of great skill. Among the difficult surgical operations performed successfully by doctors in Jenne was the removal of cataracts from the human eye.[39]

About 1480 Sonni Ali decided to dig a canal that would connect the town of Walata to the Niger River. The job was started but it was never finished because of raids into the area by the Mossi of Yatenga. Sonni Ali retaliated against the Mossi and defeated them in 1483. Afterwards, Songhay forces raided Mossi territory but were unable to bring the Mossi States into the Songhay Empire.

Sonni Ali's death came in 1492. He drowned "while returning from a successful [military] expedition against the Fulani of Gurma."[40] He had ruled Songhay for twenty-eight years, 1464 to 1492. During his reign the small and insignificant state of Songhay grew into an empire and replaced Mali as the supreme power in the western Sudan.

Sonni Ali was a great conqueror and general. In addition, "he was a military genius, ambitious and ruthless."[41] He never lost a battle. His superb cavalry was the backbone of his conquering army. Through conquest he transformed Songhay from a small state into a wealthy and powerful empire. At the time of his death he had conquered a vast area, including a large part of the old Mali Empire. Sonni Ali was also a great ruler. He was able to unite the Songhay people by gaining the support of both the Muslims who lived in the towns and cities and the non-Muslims who lived out in the rural areas. His strongest support, however, came from the common people who lived in the rural areas and who practiced the indigenous African religion. It was said he was a Muslim by name and a pagan at heart. He was wise enough politically, however, to yield to Islam when necessary in order to maintain the support of the Muslims.

Sonni Ali's successor to the throne was his son Sonni Baru. Sonni Baru declared his loyalty to the traditional African religion and refused to accept Islam. This was not a wise move politically because it cost him the support of the Muslims, who were powerful in the towns and cities. The Muslims then organized against him and began to plot his removal from power. After a year or less on the throne, Sonni Baru was dethroned by the ambitious and clever Muhammad Ture, who had been Sonni Ali's ablest general and chief minister. Muhammad Ture was a devout Muslim. He mounted the Songhay throne in 1493 and took the title Askia. Thus the Askia dynasty was born with Askia Muhammad I as its first ruler.

Askia Muhammad I became known as Askia the Great. He had a long reign as king of Songhay, ruling from 1493 to 1528. He was a wise and inspiring leader, a great general, and a brilliant administrator. His strongest support came from the Muslims who lived in the towns and cities. He made the pilgrimage to Mecca from 1495 through 1497. On this trip he was appointed the caliph, or Muslim spiritual leader, of West Africa. He also pushed the spread of Islam in West Africa.

Askia the Great had much admiration and respect for scholars. He encouraged scholarship and learning throughout the empire. The cities of Gao, Timbuktu, Walata, and Jenne thrived as centers of learning. The University of Sankore, located at Timbuktu, became world renowned for its excellent scholarship. It attracted scholars from all over the Islamic world.

Like Sonni Ali before him, Askia the Great expanded the Songhay Empire through conquest. In 1498 he raided the territory of the Mossi but was unable to conquer them. This military campaign, however, prevented the Mossi from raiding Songhay territory for a long time. About 1513 Askia the Great attacked the Hausa States and brought them into the Songhay fold. Next he conquered the nomadic Tuaregs of Air, adding their territory to his empire, including the commercial center of Agades. Askia the Great also added other territories to his empire through conquest. As a result, he became the ruler of a vast empire that extended far and wide. It stretched from the Hausa States of Northern Nigeria in the east to the Atlantic Ocean in the west; northward it extended into the Sahara Desert, including the Taghaza salt mines; southward it reached to the territories of the Mossi and Mandingo.

Askia the Great was a man who possessed many skills. His greatest skill, however, was administrating. He was considered one of the greatest, if not the greatest, administrator of his time. He reorganized the Songhay government into a strong, centralized one. He divided his vast empire, an area larger than the continental United States, into provinces with a governor in control of each. He established a council of ministers to head various departments of government, similar to present-day governments. The most important ministerial posts were the chief tax collector; the chief of the navy; the chiefs of forests, woodcutters, and fishermen; and, last but not least, the treasurer.[42] He established a strong army to defend the empire both internally and externally. The Songhay Empire was at its zenith during Askia the Great's reign. It was characterized by peace and prosperity, law and order, and justice for Muslims and non-Muslims alike. Trade, agriculture, and learning flourished within the empire.

For an eyewitness account of life in the Songhay Empire during the reign of Askia the Great, we turn to the writings of Leo Africanus. He was a well-educated and well-traveled Moor who was born in Spain. He visited the Songhay Empire about 1513. In his book, *The History and Description of Africa*, he described his visit to West Africa. Leo Africanus was impressed with much of what he saw in Songhay. He described the many shops that he saw. Some contained "linen and cotton cloth" that had been woven by the people. He also saw many wealthy people, especially the foreign merchants. He observed the abundance of food and the many wells that had been dug. He described King Askia the Great's palace at Timbuktu as being "magnificent and well-furnished." He also described the king as being rich and having in his possession "many plates and scepters of gold, some weighing as much as thirteen hundred pounds each." Still in the same city, Timbuktu, he saw many priests, judges, doctors, and learned men. All were supported by the king. Also at Timbuktu, Leo Africanus wrote "that books were sold there for more money than any other item." This is important because "only an intellectually oriented society places that kind of value on books."[43] Leo Africanus described the citizens of Timbuktu as being "gentle and cheerful."

Timbuktu was a great multipurpose city in the Songhay Empire. It was a well-known learning and religious center as well as an important commercial and administrative center. Located at Timbuktu was the famous University of Sankore. During the sixteenth century it became one of the top universities in the world for Islamic scholarship. It attracted students and scholars from near and far—Africa, Asia, and Europe. At the University of Sankore one could study medicine and surgery, law, geography, grammar, literature, mathematics, astronomy, and other subjects.

There were a number of scholars in West Africa during the sixteenth century. The most celebrated was Professor Ahmed Baba. He was born in 1556 in Timbuktu. He was the last chancellor of the University of Sankore before it was occupied by the Moors. This outstanding scholar and educator authored over forty books, almost all of which had different subjects. Basil Davidson, a British author, says "thirteen of Ahmed Baba's writings, of varying length and value, are at present known; two of these were discovered recently in Northern Nigeria...."[44] Ahmed Baba was also the author of a biographical dictionary of Muslim scholars. In addition, he had an excellent library that contained sixteen hundred volumes.

The continent of Africa has lost an uncountable amount of knowledge due to the destructive impact of invasions. The works of many African scholars as well as their names have been lost forever. In West Africa, fortunately, the names and works of a few African scholars have survived. In addition to Ahmed Baba, we know of works by three other scholars: Mahmud Kati, Abderrahman es Sadi, and an unknown author. Like Ahmed Baba, these men were all scholars of Timbuktu and each left to posterity an important account of West African history.

Mahmud Kati was born in 1468. He was a member of Askia the Great's personal following; he made the pilgrimage to Mecca with him. In 1519 he started writing *Tarikh al-Fettash* (History of the Seeker after Knowledge), a history of the western Sudan. He died in 1593 at the age of 125. However, "a grandson later worked on his notes and on the notes of his children (scholars, as he had been), and brought the story down to 1665."[45]

Abderrahaman es Sadi was born in 1596 in Timbuktu. In addition to being an author, he also during his life worked "as a notary ...[and a] government secretary."[46] His book is called *Tarikh es–Sudan* (*History of the Sudan*). He died about 1655.

The name "of the third author"[47] is unknown. He authored the book, *Tedzkiret en–Nisian*. This book deals with the history of Songhay in general and Timbuktu in particular. The time period of this book is roughly 1655 to 1750.

Askia the Great later grew old and feeble. He eventually went blind. He was able to hide this condition for quite some time. Finally, however, the truth became known.

In 1528 his oldest son, Askia Musa, rose up against him and forced him from power. This brought the eighty-five-year-old ruler's glorious reign to an end. Askia Musa treated his blind father badly during his short and ineffective reign of three years. In 1531 Askia Musa was assassinated. His death brought Muhammad Bengan to the throne. Muhammad Began treated Askia the Great worse than Askia Musa had; he exiled him "to a small mosquito-infested island on the Niger...."[48] There, Askia the Great lived in agony and humiliation. In 1537 his son Ismail dethroned Muhammad Began and took over as king. Ismail then brought his aged and feeble father back home to the royal palace, where Askia the great died in 1538 at the age of about ninety-five.

Ismail's reign ended with his death in 1539. He was followed to the throne by Askia Ishak I, who ruled from 1539 to 1548. During Askia Ishak I's reign, signs of future trouble with the Moors manifested. The ruler of Morocco began to eye the important Taghaza salt mines, which were a part of the Songhay Empire, enviously. In 1546 he asked Askia Ishak I to surrender them. Askia Ishak I responded to this insult by sending 2,000 Tuareg Desert-warriors to raid southern Morocco. Askia Ishak I's reign ended with his death in 1548. Askia Duad, another son of Askia the Great, was his successor.

Askia Duad reigned as the Songhay emperor from 1548 to 1582. He stabilized the Songhay government and became its most effective ruler since his father, Askia the Great. During his reign, forces from Morocco attacked the Taghaza salt mine area and forced the survivors to move to another location, where they opened up another salt mine in 1557. Askia Duad did much to help Songhay recapture some of the glory of the past. He encouraged learning and the construction of buildings. He also had some successful military campaigns. He died in 1582. After his death the Songhay Empire began to have serious problems: the capture of the precious Taghaza salt mines by the Moors in 1582, internal conflicts, rebellions by vassal states, and attacks by the Tuaregs and the Mossi. In 1591 the Moors invaded the Songhay Empire and dealt it such a devastating blow that it was never able to recover.

We turn now to the circumstances that led to the Moroccan invasion of the Songhay Empire. In 1578 there was a power struggle in Morocco. This power struggle brought a ruler to power in Morocco who decided to invade Songhay and take her wealth. Morocco, for a long time, had envied the wealth of Songhay.

"Early in 1578, Sultan Mohammed XI, sometimes called the Black Sultan because of his...[color], appealed to Dom Sebastian, king of Portugal, to help him recover the throne which his uncle, Abdul Malek, had usurped."[49] The king of Portugal gladly accepted the offer. This was a chance to get even with the Moors, who had occupied Spain and Portugal for hundreds of years. Also as an added incentive, "Sultan Mohammed XI had promised Dom Sebastian a permanent foothold on the Moroccan coast; and it was this promise which made Europe more than usually interested in the campaign."[50] That same year Dom Sebastian invaded Morocco with an army of about twenty-five thousand men, including Portuguese, Englishmen, Germans, and Italians. At the Battle of El Ksar el Kebir, the Portuguese and their European allies were overwhelmingly beaten by the Moors. The battle took the lives of the Black Sultan, Dom Sebastian, and Abdul Malek, the uncle of the Black Sultan. The people of Morocco were now without a ruler. The man selected as the new ruler of Morocco was twenty-nine-year-old Mulay Ahmed El Mansur, the younger brother of Abdul Malek.

El Mansur, the young sultan of Morocco, became increasingly interested in the wealth of Songhay. In 1582 his troops took the Taghaza salt mines from Songhay. Next he decided to make a very bold move, to invade the Songhay Empire and take control of her gold and other wealth. The Moroccan Council of War, however, found the idea of marching an army across the desert to attack Songhay very unwise, a case of very poor judgment. However, by skillfully challenging their courage, El Mansur was finally able to enlist their support. He then began to make preparations for the military campaign to West Africa. When the news of the proposed venture reached Europe, certain countries found it very interesting—so interesting, in fact, that they willingly provided Morocco with soldiers and firearms. If the Moors directed their military interests toward West Africa, their threat to Europe would diminish. The chance of obtaining gold also lured the Europeans—Englishmen, Portuguese, and Spanish. Queen Elizabeth of England provided firearms, cannonballs, and ammunition to the war effort.

The four thousand-man, well-equipped Moroccan army left Morocco for West Africa in October 1590. It was led by Judar Pasha, a Spanish eunuch who had been reared in Morocco. When the Moroccan army reached Songhay in 1591, its size had been reduced by the difficult march across the desert.

"The actual arrival of Moroccan forces in the western Sudan clearly demonstrated the decline in the political condition of Songhai. Messengers...[dispatched] by Askia Ishak II to block the water holes along the desert routes were waylaid by robbers and failed in their mission."[51] If these messengers had been successful, the Moroccan soldiers probably would have died of thirst in the desert and never reached West Africa.

The two armies met at the historic Battle of Tondibi in 1591. The Moroccan army, smaller than the Songhay army, was armed with guns and cannons. The Songhay army, led by Askia Ishak II, consisted of nine thousand infantry and eighteen thousand cavalry. They were armed with bows and arrows, spears, and battle-axes. The Songhay forces, most of whom were undisciplined, fought bravely. The veteran Songhay soldiers chose death over running away. Many were shot down as they fired their arrows. But in the end, the Songhay forces were routed. Bows and arrows and spears were no match for guns and cannons.

Judar Pasha and his Moroccan forces went on to capture, loot, and burn the Songhay cities of Gao, Timbuktu, and Jenne. They brought ruin and desolation to an area that was characterized by "peace and prosperity."[52] To quell the people and break their spirit, the Moroccans filled in the wells and destroyed the cultivated fields.[53]

Although he was able to win battles and ravage the land, Judar Pasha was unable to get the large amounts of gold that the sultan of Morocco, El Mansur, desired. He also sent a message to the sultan asking him for permission to negotiate a peace treaty with Songhay when large numbers of his soldiers began to die from tropical diseases. This talk of negotiation with Songhay did not please the sultan. So El Mansur replaced Judar Pasha with another leader who he hoped would be able to get the gold from Songhay. His name was Mahmud ben Zergun. The sultan sent Mahmud to West Africa, accompanied by a force of Arab soldiers. These reinforcements, however, were unable to bring the whole empire under their control, despite their use of treachery.

When Askia Nuh came to power in Songhay, he fired up the spirit of the people. Instead of fighting the invaders in the savannahs, he carried the fighting to the dense forests, where he engaged them in guerrilla warfare. Askia Nuh won a number of battles against the Moors using guerrilla tactics, which neutralized the superiority of their weapons. Malaria, dysentery, and the tsetse fly also killed off men and horses, and the Moroccans were unable to advance further south.[54]

Askia Nuh's guerrilla tactics so frustrated the Moors that they began to mistreat the people in the towns and cities, especially the scholars at Timbuktu. They marched them in chains across the desert to Morocco. Included in this group of captives was the famous scholar Ahmed Baba. He "was not released from his Moroccan prison until 1607, and in that same year he returned to Timbuktu to die."[55]

The struggle between the Moroccans and the people of Songhay continued for years. The Moroccans were never able, however, to gain control of the whole empire. It would have taken a much larger force of Moroccan soldiers to accomplish that. Neither were the Moroccans able to obtain the fabulous wealth that they had sought. Eventually, "the Moroccan soldiers became haughty, insolent, and unruly; and in due course they took to electing their own commanders."[56] By 1660 they had broken ties with the sultan of Morocco altogether and declared independence. By 1737 they no longer counted politically in West African affairs and were forced to pay tribute. The Moroccan soldiers remained in West Africa, marrying West African women, and their offspring were eventually absorbed into the West African population.

The historic Battle of Tondibi, between Morocco and Songhay, which ended in a victory for the Moors, was probably the most significant battle in West African history. After this battle, the Moors began their disastrous occupation of Songhay, and conditions in West Africa changed. The Moors robbed the Songhay

Empire of what gold and other wealth they could find; they destroyed the important learning centers along with their priceless libraries and manuscripts; they turned peace and prosperity in the land into ruin, insecurity, decline; and they disrupted the important trans-Saharan trade of the western Sudan. They destroyed the political cohesiveness of the Songhay Empire, which disintegrated into a group of small states, each fighting to control the others. As a result of the Moroccan occupation, the Songhay Empire was never able to recover. Like Ghana and Mali before her, she passed into history.

The collapse of the Songhay Empire impacted the future of the western Sudan. When the Europeans arrived in the western Sudan, they faced a group of small, disorganized states instead of a united empire. It was much easier for them to control a group of small, disorganized states than a strong, united empire.

Other States of West Africa

The great trading empires of Ghana, Mali, and Songhay were not the only states in West Africa. The Mossi States, the Hausa States, and the Kanem-Bornu Empire were among the smaller states known for their cultural achievements.

The Mossi States consisted of a union of five states, each independent of one another and at the same time dependent upon one another. The five states were Wagadugu, Yatenga, Fada-Gurma, Mamprusi, and Dagomba. Wagadugu was founded about 1050 and Yatenga was founded about 1170. The other states were founded prior to 1500. The Mossi States, or Mossi Empire, comprised the modern West African countries of Upper Volta (Burkina Faso) and northern Ghana.

The Mossi had a highly organized and efficient political system. At the top of the government were the supreme king, or Mogho Naba, and his council. Next came the state king (governor) and his council, followed by the district chief and his council, and finally the village chief and his council. The five governors of the states were also chief ministers of the king. In addition, there were eleven other ministers, each heading a department, for a total of sixteen ministers.

The Mossi were farmers, traders, and craftsmen. They raised a variety of crops, including cotton, yams, rice, kola nuts, millet, and wheat. They also raised horses of an excellent quality, known for their speed. These fast horses were a vital part of their dashing cavalry. The Mossi made leather, iron, cloth, baskets, hats, pots and jars, and other goods. The Mossi exported cotton and cotton cloth, horses and donkeys, and other products.

The Mossi were a very interesting African people. They all had the same traditional African religion and all were members of the same ethnic group. They rejected things that they thought would divide them. They were determined to keep their religion, ethnic identity, and their independence. They held on firmly to their traditional African religion and refused to accept Islam. They were aware of the possibility of conflict between those who would embrace Islam and those who would not. They allowed Muslims into their country to trade, but they were carefully watched to prevent the spread of their religion. They had a special minister whose job was to carefully watch all outsiders when they came into their country. The Mossi protected their women. They did not allow them to marry outside the nation. When the Mossi were attacked by outsiders, they all came together to defend their territory. In fact, their unity was strongest when they felt threatened. The larger and more powerful states such as Mali and Songhay were unable to conquer them. Europeans were not allowed to enter Mossi territory for many years. They tried various ways to enter but were unsuccessful.

From the earliest times, Africans had welcomed strangers to their continent with their traditional hospitality. The Mossi were a little different from Africans in general, however, when it came to strangers. They did not put blind trust in strangers and they treated them with caution. The Mossi had learned an important lesson from the history of foreigners in Africa. They had learned that foreigners did not always come directly when attempting conquest. Instead of attacking directly, foreigners sometimes attacked indirectly, using the tactics of deception and manipulation to divide and weaken a people before moving in to conquer them. For example, instead of coming in with an army, foreigners sometimes came in with gifts and smiles to gain a people's trust before setting them up for conquest. Unfortunately, many other African states did not have the Mossi's alertness and caution, and they, therefore, walked blindly into traps and pitfalls. The Mossi thought tactically and defensively. They were probably the most alert and cautious of all African people. Because of their alertness and caution, it was difficult to divide and conquer them. The Mossi were able to hold onto their independence until the end of the nineteenth century, when they were finally defeated by the French. Because of their alertness, unity, and wisdom, the Mossi States survived longer than the larger and wealthier empires of Ghana, Mali, and Songhay.

The Hausa States were located in present-day northern Nigeria. According to tradition, the Hausa States all shared a common ancestor, whose name was Bayajidda. He came to the area about 1000. His descendants created the seven states of Gobir, Rano, Kano, Zaria, Katsina, Daura, and Biram, known collectively as the Hausa States. These seven city-states never formed a centralized government; each remained independent of the other. However, they sometimes came together for a common purpose. The states of Kano, Katsina, and Zaria were the most prominent of the seven. The state of Zaria was sometimes governed by women. A couple of them were among Zaria's best rulers.

About 1400 the Hausa kings began to embrace Islam. The people out in the countryside, however, continued to practice the traditional African religion. In the 1500s Islamic scholarship and trade flourished in Kano and Katsina. Scholars, students, and traders were attracted to them. Kano and Katsina each had a university, similar to the one at Timbuktu, where students were taught grammar, mathematics, religion, philosophy, ethics, and other subjects. The Moroccan invasion of Songhay caused many scholars and merchants to leave the cities of Timbuktu, Jenne, and Gao and settle in the peaceful Hausa city-states.

Because they were not strongly united, the Hausa States had problems with invasions from neighboring states. About 1513 they were conquered by the Songhay Empire of Askia Muhammad and forced to pay tribute. There were also periods in the seventeenth and eighteenth centuries when they were forced to pay tribute to the Kanem-Bornu Empire. In 1804 the zealous Fulani went on a *jihad* or holy war, to conquer the Hausa States and to convert the people to Islam. They were led by Usman dan Fodio. Within four years the Fulani had conquered the Hausa States. They went on to conquer other states as well. The Fulani controlled the Hausa States and other territories they had conquered until the early 1900s, when their land came under British rule.

The Kanem-Bornu Empire was centered in the Lake Chad area. Kanem and Bornu were separate states before they became a joint empire. The history of Kanem-Bornu goes far back into the distant past. The early inhabitants of the area around Lake Chad were a people called the So. They were farmers, fishermen, and craftsmen. The So had developed a culture of their own before a nomadic people known as the Zaghawa came to settle among them in the seventh and eighth centuries. About 700, a small group of Zaghawa people settled east of Lake Chad among the So. They were led by a man named Sef (Saif), who founded the state of Kanem and started the Sefewa dynasty, which lasted over a thousand years. The first Kanem ruler to embrace Islam was Mai Umme, who reigned from 1085 to 1097. The word *mai* was a title for the king. Islam brought about contact between Kanem and the Muslim traders and scholars of North Africa. As time passed, Kanem grew wealthy and powerful from trade. It began to expand southward and westward, around Lake Chad, into Bornu territory. By 1250 Kanem had taken control of Bornu. The state of Kanem had now expanded into an empire. This empire completely encircled Lake Chad and in the north extended far into the desert. "The empire of Kanem-Bornu flourished between the fourteenth and eighteenth centuries. Trade was the basis of its strength during these centuries of greatness."[57]

During Kanem-Bornu's long history, both as separate states and as an empire, a number of mais rose to prominence. The most celebrated of these mais was Idris Alooma. He was the mai of Kanem-Bornu for thirty-seven years, 1580 to 1617. He was a brilliant administrator and a great general. The empire of Kanem-Bornu reached its peak during his rule.

The empire's power began to decline in the last half of the seventeenth century. Military struggles with the Tuareg of Air and forces from Jukan contributed to its decline. In 1808 the fanatical Fulani attempted to conquer Bornu. Despite their early victories against Bornu, the Fulani were eventually defeated. In 1846 the long-lasting Sefewa Dynasty came to a close when Shaikh Amin came to power. It had lasted for over a thousand years, making it one of the longest-lasting dynasties in world history. The Kanem-Bornu Empire came under British and French colonial rule about 1900.

▲▲▲

This chapter has shown that West Africa reached a high level of civilization well before the colonial era. The viewpoint that West Africa lacked a history and culture before the arrival of Europeans has been proved inaccurate. The three great trading empires of Ghana, Mali, and Songhay flourished in West Africa from 700 to 1600. These empires "achieved a level of culture comparable to any in the world"[58]during this period. Historian John G. Jackson calls this period "the Golden Age of West Africa."

West Africa (the western Sudan) began to decline after the Moroccan invasion. The defeat of Songhay forces by the Moors at the historic Battle of Tondibi in 1591 was a turning point in West African history. British historian Basil Davidson discusses the impact of the Moroccan invasion on West Africa.

> Today we can assign perfectly clear historical reasons for the social and political disintegration which had overcome a large part of Africa by the middle of the nineteenth century. The great systems of the Western Sudan had never recovered from the shock of the Moroccan invasion of the Songhay empire at the end of the sixteenth century, accompanied and followed as this had been by the political and economic decline of North African civilization when the trans-Saharan trade gave way, increasingly, to a seaborne trade between West Africa and Europe. A brave effort was indeed put forth by Western Sudanese leaders during the nineteenth century to restore the systems of the past, but it came too late and was swept away by European invasion.[59]

Before closing this chapter, let us examine a very fascinating African people known as the Dogon. They reside in the present-day West African nation of Mali. Their "complex knowledge of astronomy"[60] is amazing. Knowledge about the universe and the solar system, which has just recently become known to modern scientists, their priests have known for centuries. Scholar

Ivan Van Sertima comments on the knowledge of the Dogon:

> They knew that the moon was a barren world. They said it was "dry and dead, like dried blood." They knew also of things far in advance of their time, intricate details about a star [Sirius B] which no one can see except with the most powerful of telescopes. They not only saw it. They observed or intuited its mass and its nature. They plotted its orbit almost up until the year 2,000. And they did all this between five and seven hundred years ago.[61]

Van Sertima continues about the Dogon:

> The Dogon were studied very closely and over a considerable period of time by two French anthropologists, Marcel Griaule and Germaine Dieterlen. From 1931 to 1956—a whole generation—the two lived and worked with these people, looked at and listened to everything, wrote down all they could find out, even drew diagrams of the evocative architecture of the Dogon village, which is patterned after the form of the human body. Griaule and Dieterlen sank their roots into the people so deep that they became Dogon. They were initiated into the tribe. Griaule became so loved and trusted that, when he died, [a] quarter of a million Africans turned up at his funeral. And yet, in spite of this intimacy, they had to pass through stage after stage of initiation—"the word at face value"—"the word on the side"—"the word from behind" before the Dogon allowed them to enter the inner sanctum of their most secret knowledge. Their education lasted longer than the American student's passage from high school to Ph.D. Not until the sixteenth year...did the Dogon call together a conference to reveal to these Europeans the first level in an eight-level stage on the highest ladder of their knowledge. This stage was known as "the clear word."[62]

The eight-level clear word stage of the Dogon reveals their "most sacred knowledge...,from the creation of stars and spiraling galaxies to the creation of plants...,[to] the purpose of human existence."[63] Van Sertima comments on "the clear word" stage of the Dogon:

> Among the revelations that emerged at this stage was the Dogon's intimate knowledge of, and concern with, a star within the Sirius star system. They had a ceremony to Sirius every sixty years, when the orbits of Jupiter and Saturn converge. But the odd thing about it was that, although Sirius is the brightest star in the sky, the ceremony was not to Sirius at all but to its companion, Sirius B, a star so small, so dense, so difficult to perceive, it is truly amazing that any medieval science was aware of it. It turned out that the Dogon were not only aware of it but saw it as the basis of that star system while Sirius A, the big, bright star we know so well, was simply the point around which this unusual little star orbited. To the Dogon this dwarf was the most important star in the sky. To them, it was "the egg of the world."[64]

The Dogon have a detailed knowledge of Sirius B. For example, they "knew that this star, although invisible to the naked eye, had an elliptical orbit around Sirius A that took fifty years to complete,"[65] which has been confirmed by modern science.

> The Dogon drew a diagram...showing the course and trajectory of...[Sirius B] up unto the year 1990. Modern astronomical projections are identical with this. The Dogon say this tiny star is composed of a metal brighter than iron and that if all the men on earth were a single lifting force they could not budge it. Modern science confirms that this is the nature of that type of star—"a white dwarf"—a star so compacted that its mass may be many times greater than a star which appears many times larger. But the

Dogon go even farther than that in their observations about this star, beyond what we know now. They say it has an orbit of one year around its own axis. They were so certain of this that they held a special celebration—the bado celebration—to honor that orbit. Modern science has not yet been able to confirm or deny that observation.[66]

The Dogon's detailed knowledge of Sirius B has astounded modern scientists. One scientist, Kenneth Brecher of the Massachusetts Institute of Technology, found their knowledge of astronomy unbelievable. He said, with a bit of arrogance, "They [the Dogon] have no business knowing any of this."[67]

Chapter 9

The Enslavement of the African

They had eyes but they couldn't see;
they had ears but they couldn't hear;
they had mouths but they couldn't speak.

It is so natural for people in today's world to think of Africans or people of African descent whenever the word *slavery* is mentioned. Why? It is because of our recent enslavement.

This is most unfortunate.

The institution of slavery existed long before Europeans began transporting enslaved Africans to the New World in the sixteenth century. The origin of slavery goes back into prehistoric times. Slavery began when war captives were enslaved rather than killed. In time it became very profitable to exploit the cheap labor of enslaved war captives. The enslavement of war captives was the main source of slaves in the ancient world. Other sources of slaves were criminals, people who were kidnapped, and people who were unable to pay their debts. In the ancient world slavery was not based on race. Anyone—yellow, brown, white, or black—could have become a slave if misfortune befell him or her. In this remote period Europeans, Africans, and Asians were all enslaved.

Slavery existed in the ancient civilizations of Egypt, Sumeria, Babylonia, Greece, and Rome. The ancient Egyptians enslaved various people. They enslaved people from western Asia, people from around the Mediterranean, and fellow Africans from Nubia to the south. The Sumerians enslaved people they captured in warfare. In ancient Babylonia the *Code of Hammurabi* indicates that slavery existed there. The Greeks enslaved fellow Europeans as well as people from North Africa and western Asia. The Romans did likewise.

Slaves in ancient times were used in a variety of ways. They were used as house servants, as laborers in fields and mines, as concubines, as soldiers, and also to build public projects. Some slaves in ancient times were able to rise to such positions of importance in society as public officials, doctors, and priests. For example, Joseph in the Bible was sold into slavery in Egypt, but he eventually rose to the position of viceroy of Egypt. Also in ancient times when a people were conquered and enslaved, they were sometimes more cultured than the people who enslaved them. In this situation, the conquerors gained valuable knowledge from the people they enslaved.

Slavery existed in Africa long before Europeans began the transatlantic slave trade in the sixteenth century. Slavery in Africa goes back into ancient times. Africans enslaved one another just as Europeans, Asians, and American Indians enslaved one another. Prisoners captured in warfare were the main source of slaves in Africa. These prisoners of war did not always remain with their captors, however. Sometimes it was more profitable for their captors to sell them. Criminals and people who were unable to pay their debts were also enslaved in Africa.

The African system of slavery differed sharply from the system of chattel slavery practiced in the New World by Europeans. In Africa slaves were considered human beings; therefore, they had certain basic rights. In contrast, in the New World slaves were considered items of personal property, like cattle or horses, and were therefore often cruelly treated as if they were nonhumans.

The African system of slavery was actually a type of servitude. In some ways it was similar to *serfdom*, which existed in Europe during the Middle Ages. Under African slavery, slaves had most of the rights that their owners had. For example, in some societies they could take an oath; they could hold positions of authority; they could marry and own property; they could even own slaves of their own. Another right slaves had in Africa was that an owner could not sell the children of his slaves. In addition, slaves became a part of the village or community in which they lived; they also became a part of their owner's family and could marry into it. Sometimes a slave would marry into his owner's family and in time become the head of that family. In short, African slavery was a kind of servitude in which the slaves (servants) were protected by rights.

The coming of the Arabs to Africa had a big impact on African culture and history, including the institution of slavery. The Arabs invaded North Africa in 639 A.D. They soon realized that the buying and selling of Africans was a quick way to gain wealth. The Arabs obtained African slaves by conquest and by purchase. Some African kings and chiefs were partners with the Arabs in the slave trade. The Arabs' desire for more and more slaves contributed to the expansion of "slavery and slave raiding"[1] in Africa. Wars began to be waged specifically for the capture of prisoners to be sold into slavery. The Arabs exported African slaves to Iraq, Turkey, Arabia, and other places in the Islamic world. In 869 there was a revolt by African slaves at Basra, Iraq. This large revolt "was undoubtedly the greatest slave rebellion in history, including even that of Haiti."[2] It was called the Zenj or Zengh (Blacks from Africa) Rebellion. The Zenghs killed more than half a million of their oppressors, an enormous number for that day.[3] The Zenghs founded an independent state of their own in Iraq that lasted until 883.

The Arabs began their slave trade in Africa over 700 years before the Europeans began their slave trade in Africa. The Arab slave trade, like the European slave trade, brought pain and suffering to African people. The Arab slave trade lasted much longer in Africa than the European slave trade. However, in terms of volume, the European slave trade was much larger. The number of Africans exported to Islamic lands by the Arabs was without a doubt in the millions, but a true figure can't be given because the records don't exist. The Arab slave trade in Africa reached its peak during the nineteenth century. The stronghold of the Arab slave trade was "the island of Zanzibar...[located] twenty-four miles off the"[4] East African coast. By 1840 Zanzibar had become the world's greatest slaving emporium.[5] There, slaves of all kinds were sold, including blacks from different parts of Africa and even white Circassian women slaves. One of the cruelties of the Arab slave trade was the castration of black males for use as eunuchs in harems. Many didn't survive this operation. The Arabs also marched enslaved Africans across the Sahara Desert to slave markets in North Africa.

Compared to European chattel slavery, however, Arab slavery was more humane. The Arabs used African female slaves mainly as concubines in their harems and African male slaves as craftsmen, as eunuchs, as domestic servants, and as soldiers in the military. African soldiers were a vital part of Islamic armies. Africans conquered and held Muslim Spain for Islam during the Middle Ages. Some Africans became generals in Islamic armies.

When a searchlight is turned on a people's history, it will more than likely reveal that at some period in their history they were slaves. In fact this applies to almost everyone. Blacks are generally associated with slavery, but the searchlight of history reveals that whites also have been slaves in their history. White slaves were common in the empires of Greece and

Rome. Large numbers of white slaves, including Gauls, Britons, Celts, Spaniards, Slavs, and Teutons, were sold daily in the slave markets of ancient Rome.

With the fall of the Western Roman Empire in the fifth century, the strong central government that the Romans had provided in Europe disintegrated. By the 800s a new system of government called feudalism had emerged in Europe. Feudalism was a political, economic, and military system whereby the strong exploited the weak. "The king was at the top of the feudal pyramid...."[6] He had men under him called vassals, who had pledged to serve him in exchange for a piece of land called a fief. The king's vassals generally had their own vassals (knights) who had pledged loyalty to them in exchange for a piece of land. When a person had vassals under him, he became their lord. The medieval lord was generally powerful and wealthy, ruling over a large manor. The lord's knights protected his land, while his serfs (peasants) tilled his land.

The serfs of medieval Europe were a large group. They were exploited by the lords. The serfs were not free; they had given up their freedom for protection by a lord. The serfs were worked hard and sometimes barely had enough to eat. The serfs had a hard life. In some ways they were just a little better off than slaves. They were also tied to the land, meaning that if the land was sold they remained with the land because they were considered property. In return for their labor the lord provided the serfs with protection and a plot of land they worked to feed themselves.

During the Middle Ages, from 1096 to 1270, European Christians went on military expeditions (Crusades) to recover the Holy Land from the Muslims. Children led one of these crusades. In 1212, thousands of European children—boys and girls—set out on the Children's Crusade. They believed that because of their strong faith in God, they would miraculously be able to recover the city of Jerusalem from the Muslims. However, they were ill prepared for the long and dangerous march southward, down through Europe to the Mediterranean Sea. Along the way a large number of them died from starvation and exposure to the bitter cold. Others were fortunate enough to reach the Mediterranean Sea. But being innocent and naïve, like most children are, some were persuaded to climb aboard ships that were supposedly going to the Holy Land. Instead the ship owners took them to seaports where they were sold to Arab slave traders.

Although it is not a well-known fact, whites were once sold in the slave markets of North Africa. During the intense rivalry between European Christians and Muslims in the Middle Ages, Christians enslaved Muslims and Muslims enslaved Christians. For centuries Muslim seamen from North Africa raided the coasts of Europe and also European ships in the Mediterranean for slaves. Generally these European captives were held for ransom by the Muslims. Organizations were created in Europe to raise money for their ransom. For example, "the Catholic Church founded two orders for the purpose of ransoming Christians enslaved by Muslims: the Trinitarians in 1198 and the Mercedarians in 1218."[7] White captives were sold in the slave markets at Tripoli (Libya), Tunis (Tunisia), Tangier and Salee (Morocco), and Algiers (Algeria). European slaves were used as domestic servants, concubines, eunuchs, and in other ways. The Arabs had a white slave army in Egypt known as the Mamelukes, who later revolted and established their own rule in Egypt.

Europeans also sold other Europeans during the Middle Ages. North Africa was one of the places they sold them. British historian Basil Davidson says:

All the great city-states of medieval Italy appear to have dealt in Christian slaves. The Venetians and the Genoese were deep in the trade as early as the tenth and eleventh centuries. They continued in it, together with the Pisans and the Florentines and the merchants and mariners of ports as far apart as Lucca and Amalfi, until as late as the middle of the fifteenth century. Throughout the thirteenth century, European slaves were being carried in European ships to the Sultanate of Egypt despite all ecclesiastical rebukes and threats.[8]

The word *slave* comes from the word *Slav*. The Slavs are a white people of Eastern and Central Europe. The word slave was first used to denote Slavs who had been captured and enslaved by the Germans. The sultans in Muslim Spain were the primary buyers of Slav captives from Greek and Venetian slave traders. These Slavs, usually purchased as children, were used as bodyguards and as eunuchs in harems by the Muslims in Spain.

Europeans Make Contact with Africa and America

After the collapse of the Western Roman Empire in the fifth century, Europe went into the *Dark Ages*. This term once referred to the whole period from the fall of the Roman Empire to the 1500s, a period of over a thousand years. Now it has come to mean the period from the fifth century to the tenth century. During this five hundred-year period, Europe declined economically, politically, intellectually, and population-wise.

However, by the eleventh century, Europe was beginning to undergo a political and economic recovery. It became safer for traders to travel the land and water routes of Europe. As a result there was an increase in trade. This led to the founding of new towns and the development of a merchant class. During the 1300s Europe witnessed wars, plagues, and famines. There were peasant revolts against oppressive feudal lords in England, France, Germany, and Italy. Between 1337 and 1453, England and France fought the Hundred Years War. In this long and destructive conflict, England attempted to gain control of France but was unsuccessful. In 1347 a deadly disease called the bubonic plague, or Black Death, hit Europe. It had a devastating effect on the continent. Before it ended in 1352, it wiped out a third or more of Europe's population.

The Europe of the Middle Ages was much different from the Europe of today. Europe during the Middle Ages was stagnant, poor in resources, and had large numbers of poor people, unlike the wealthy, powerful, and technological advance Europe of today. Scholar E. Jefferson Murphy describes the Europe of the Middle Ages:

> Europe itself had not been a well-developed continent [before the age of exploration]. Its peoples, despite the civilizing influences of Rome, progressed with snail-like slowness for nearly a thousand years after the decay of Roman civilization. Northern Europe was especially backward; southern Europe, bordering the Mediterranean, not only retained more of the Roman and Greek heritage, but benefited from close contact with Islamic civilization after Rome's decline. Between the fifth and fifteenth centuries, while northern Europe was in a state of near stagnation, the Mediterranean countries had at least a small share of the enlightenment that Islam brought.[9]

The hard times of the Middle Ages created in Europeans a desire to trade with distant lands such as Asia and Africa for precious metals, spices, and other products so they could improve their living conditions and stimulate their depressed economies. This desire for trade with distant lands set the stage for the future age of exploration, which brought much wealth and prosperity to Europe, as we shall see.

With the emergence of the Renaissance, Europe began to move out of the long and stagnant period of the Middle Ages into modern times. During the Renaissance, a period of about three hundred years, Europe witnessed a revival in art, literature, and learning. The Renaissance began in Italy in the fourteenth century and spread to other parts of Europe in the fifteenth and sixteenth centuries.

The Crusades (1096-1270) also helped to move Europe out of the Middle Ages. There were eight crusades in all. They affected Europe in a number of ways. For example, the Crusades exposed Europeans to new foods and products, new military tactics and machines, new lands and people, and new ideas. Perhaps most importantly, the Crusades stimulated in Europeans an interest in distant lands such as China, the East Indies, and Africa. These distant lands contained valuable gems, precious metals such as gold and silver, precious spices such as nutmeg and cloves that could be used to season dried and salted meat, and other products that Europe desperately wanted. But the Muslim control of the trade routes across North Africa and southwest Asia prevented Europe from trading directly with these distant lands. The Muslims served as middlemen, controlling the products coming into Europe, and as a result made most of the profit. Europe, at this time, did not have the military muscle to defeat the Muslims and take control of the overland trade routes to Asia and Africa.

Europeans knew very little about Africa before the age of exploration and discovery, which began in the 1400s. Nevertheless, they were fascinated by the names of two legendary figures identified with Africa. These two figures were Mansa Musa and Prester John. Both had been on the minds of Europeans for years. Mansa Musa, the legendary king of the Mali Empire, had made an extravagant pilgrimage to Mecca in 1324-25. The news of his dazzling display of tons of gold on his famous pilgrimage had reached Europe, where it created much excitement among European kings, noblemen, and merchants. Maps were drawn in Europe showing Mansa Musa's kingdom in Africa, where gold was so plentiful that it made him the richest king in all the land. The legend of Prester John had been circulating in Europe for centuries. In 1170 a letter was sent to the Pope in Rome and to the emperor in Byzantium asking for help in warfare against the infidels.[10] Europeans believed that Prester John was the source of this letter requesting their help. However, they didn't know exactly where to find him. The letter purported to come from a powerful and wealthy Christian ruler located somewhere in the East.[11] But where in the East? At first Europeans thought his kingdom was located in China or India, but by the 1300s it was thought to be in Ethiopia. According to the legend, Prester John was a very religious Christian priest-king. He was also rich and powerful, with a number of subordinate kings under him. He lived in a magnificent palace, where hospitality was always shown to travelers or pilgrims. It was said that Prester John was over 500 years old but he had kept from growing old by bathing in the Fountain of Life. Europeans wanted very much to find this Christian king of Ethiopia so they could join forces with him. The idea was to unite the Christian forces of Europe with those of Africa in an all-out war against the Arabs.[12] Europeans thought this strong Christian alliance might break the power of Islam.

By the early 1400s, Europe was becoming more and more impatient with Muslim control of the overland trade routes to Africa and Asia. Europe needed a way around the Islamic Empire to make direct contact with the wealth of Asia and Africa. Since the land routes were blocked, the only other alternative was to reach Asia and Africa by sea.

Portugal took the initiative in searching for a way around the Islamic Empire, thus leading Europe into the age of exploration. Portugal, along with Spain, had been under Moorish domination since the 700s. Both countries had benefited from their contact with the science and culture of the Islamic Moors. By 1179 Portugal had freed herself from Moorish rule and was established as a country. In 1415 the Portuguese, led by Prince Henry, captured the Muslim citadel of Ceuta on the Moroccan coast. This was not a major military victory, but it boosted the self-confidence of the Portuguese. They had taken the struggle against the Moors to Africa, something they had wanted to do for centuries. The Portuguese had built up a strong dislike for the Moors, and the capture of Ceuta was a way of getting revenge. Some scholars consider the Portuguese capture of Ceuta as the beginning of European overseas expansion.

During his stay in Ceuta, Prince Henry of Portugal learned about the trans-Sahara trade that brought gold, slaves, and other products to Morocco from the Guinea coast of West Africa. Prince Henry then became interested in making contact with Guinea by ship. He believed Portugal could profit from trading with this rich region. "In 1418 Prince Henry"[13] founded a cartography and navigation school in Portugal at Sagres. He brought to Sagres scholars of all faiths from all around the Mediterranean: geographers, cartographers, mathematicians, astronomers, and experts in the reading of manuscripts in many languages.[14] Skilled shipbuilders were also brought here. The purpose was to improve and teach the methods of navigation to Portugal's sea captains, to teach the new decimal mathematics, and to sift the evidence from documents and maps concerning the possibility of sailing southward along the African coast and thence to the Spice Islands.[15]

Meanwhile, Prince Henry began to send ships out to sea every year on exploratory voyages. His captains soon reached the Canary Islands, located "less than one hundred miles off the African coast."[16] In 1420 the Portuguese reached the Madeira Islands, which were located farther out in the Atlantic Ocean. By 1432 the Portuguese had reached the Azores Islands, which were located even farther out in the Atlantic Ocean. Despite their successes in reaching these islands, the Portuguese encountered much opposition from their sailors when they attempted to sail down the African coast beyond Cape Bojador. Portuguese sailors thought that if they sailed beyond Cape Bojador they would encounter serpents lurking in the water, a boiling sea, and a scorching sun so hot that it would turn them black. In 1433 a Portuguese captain named Gil Eannes attempted "to sail around [Cape] Bojador"[17] but was forced to turn back when his crew rebelled. The following year, 1434, he attempted the feat again. This time he used a little trick to fool his fearful crew, and he was successful. The trick was to pass the dreaded Cape Bojador without the fearful crew knowing it. So, when Gil Eannes reached the Canary Islands, he turned westward and "sailed boldly out to sea, far out of sight of land."[18] Then he turned his ships southward and sailed past the latitude of the dreaded Cape Bojador, but his fearful crew didn't know it because they were far away from land. After passing Cape Bojador, he turned his ships eastward and sailed toward the African coast. Once they reached the African coast nothing dreadful happened to them. The Portuguese had finally sailed beyond Cape Bojador and had hurdled a major obstacle.

The Portuguese continued to send ships of exploration down the west coast of Africa. In 1441 a Portuguese crew under Captain Antam Gonçalvez, arrived on the coast of what is now Mauritania. Wanting to please Prince Henry, Gonçalvez decided to kidnap some of the people of the area and bring them back to Portugal. Gonçalvez and his men then went ashore, where they ambushed and captured two Moors, a man and a woman. Soon afterwards, Gonçalvez teamed up with another Portuguese captain, Nuno Tristao. This band of Portuguese surprised and captured ten Moors. These twelve Moorish captives (Africans) were taken to Portugal, along with some gold. The arrival of these enslaved Africans created much excitement in Portugal. Prince Henry was pleased with the accomplishment of his captains. He then sent word to the Pope, requesting his support in future enslavement ventures and conquest in Africa. The Pope assured Prince Henry his support, granting the Portuguese permission to enslave Africans so they could be converted from their traditional religion to Christianity. The Pope also granted the Portuguese the permission to conquer and claim African territory.

One of the enslaved Africans brought back to Portugal desperately wanted his freedom. He told the Portuguese that he was of royal birth and if he was returned home, he could be exchanged for five or six slaves. Subsequently, the Portuguese took him and one of the other slaves back to West Africa and exchanged them for ten other slaves. The number of enslaved Africans brought back to Portugal had now grown to twenty. The number grew to forty-nine when a third voyage brought twenty-nine captives back to Portugal.

In 1444 Portugal sent Eannes and Lancarote (a Portuguese captain) down the African coast on a raiding expedition that consisted of six ships. Some inhabitants were killed resisting the Portuguese in these raids. This raiding expedition returned to Portugal with 235 Moorish captives. News of this human cargo of men, women, and children spread quickly in Portugal, where it created much interest in profiting from slaving.

As the Portuguese pushed farther south, they began to make contact with the Africans along the coast, and trade developed. The Portuguese then began to obtain slaves by trading instead of relying primarily on kidnapping and raids. They also traded for other African products such as gold, ivory, nuts, fruits, and skins. With each passing year the number of African slaves brought back to Portugal increased. By 1456 about a thousand slaves a year were being shipped back to Portugal. The Portuguese continued to push southward along the West African coast. By 1460, the year of Prince Henry's death, they had sailed far enough southward to reach Sierra Leone on the

Guinea Coast. Prince Henry the Navigator, although he never went to sea as a navigator, was probably more responsible than anyone else for beginning Europe's overseas expansion. The Portuguese continued his work, and by 1473 they had sailed down the West African coast beyond the equator.

Meanwhile, the Portuguese had been benefiting from the lucrative gold trade at Elmina (the Mine) on the Gold Coast of West Africa since about 1471. In December 1481 King John II of Portugal sent an expedition to Elmina to build a fort. A knight of the royal court named Diego da Azambuja was put in charge of the operation. He was skilled in the art of diplomacy. After arriving on the Gold Coast in January 1482, Azambuja immediately met with the local African king, Kwame Ansa. Azambuja pleaded with Kwame Ansa "for land on which to build a house for the storing of merchandise."[19] After much hesitation Kwame Ansa finally consented to the building of the *house*. However, Kwame Ansa "was surprised to find the Portuguese erecting what was obviously much more than a house, and that they were building it, moreover, on a piece of land traditionally held as sacred."[20] A conflict then broke out between the Africans and the Portuguese. However, "Azambuja...managed to buy himself out of the fighting...."[21] Afterward the Portuguese hurriedly erected the castle and fortifications. This fortified castle that the Portuguese built in 1482 is still standing; the country of Ghana has made it a historical monument.

Motivated by a desire for bigger profits, the Portuguese continued their voyages of exploration. In 1488 Portuguese navigator Bartolomew Dias sailed around the southern tip of Africa into the Indian Ocean. The Portuguese were now confident that India could be reached by sailing around Africa. In 1497 the king of Portugal sent Vasco da Gama on a sea voyage to India. Da Gama left Portugal on July 8, 1497. After sailing around the Cape of Good Hope, he turned northward and sailed up the coast of East Africa. He stopped at seaports along the coast that would now be located in present-day Mozambique and Kenya. He found a thriving and splendid Swahili civilization along the coast. At the port city of Malindi, the Portuguese asked for a pilot to lead them to India. They were given one by the ruler of Malindi. This African pilot, Ibn Madjid, guided the Portuguese on to India. Prince Henry's dream of finding a sea route to India had finally been achieved. Vasco da Gama returned to Portugal in September 1499 after having been gone over two years. During this long voyage he lost over two-thirds of his crew; many died from scurvy.

The Portuguese went to sea (1) to find a route around the Islamic Empire, which was blocking their path and keeping them from making direct contact with the wealth of Asia and Africa and (2) to make contact with Prester John, the legendary king of Ethiopia. By 1500 the Portuguese had accomplished the first objective but they were never able to make contact with Prester John, because he didn't exist. However, they did eventually meet the king of Ethiopia, who was just an ordinary king. Prester John was a myth. Nevertheless, the legend was a powerful motivating force for the Portuguese. It was one of the factors that inspired them to send out voyages of exploration in the 1400s. The Portuguese had hoped to join forces with the legendary Christian king in a major war against the Muslims, aiming to destroy their power and their control of the overland trade routes.

It is interesting that the Portuguese, during their early voyages along the coast of West Africa in the 1400s, called the Africans they enslaved Moors. Also when the Portuguese stopped along the coast of East Africa during the late 1400s and early 1500s, their accounts indicate that they called the Africans they encountered Moors. However, the ambiguous word Negro [meaning black in Portuguese and Spanish] would eventually come into general use.

Meanwhile, Spain became the second European country to become involved in exploration when Queen Isabella agreed to finance Christopher Columbus' voyage to Asia. Columbus believed that the earth was round and that he could reach Asia by sailing westward. Columbus' thinking had been influenced by geography and navigation books he had read and by contact with scholars and mariners of his time. Columbus and his three ships left Spain on August 3, 1492. After being at sea for over two months, the sailors became restless and talked of mutiny. This trouble was avoided, however, when a sailor sighted land at 2:00 A.M. on October 12, 1492. That morning Columbus and his crew stepped on the beach of a small island, where they saw red men for the first time. While exploring the Caribbean waters, Columbus saw a big island that he named Hispaniola (present-day Haiti and the Dominican Republic). Columbus, unknowingly, had made contact with a New World instead of Asia. Pedro Alonzo Niño, the captain of the *Santa Maria*, one of Columbus' three ships, is said to have been a black man, an African Moor. This contact by Columbus with the island of Hispaniola was not the first meeting between the Old World and the New World. The Vikings, Chinese, Africans, and perhaps others had made contact with the New World before Columbus.

There is ample evidence of an African contact with America before Columbus. In his work, *Africa and the Discovery of America*, German-American Leo Wiener argues that there was an African presence in the Americas before Columbus and he offers much evidence to prove it. Wiener points out "the presence of an African and Arabic influence on some medieval Mexican and South American languages before the European contact period."[22] He mentions the representation of Africans in American-Indian sculpture and design that predates Columbus. He cites evidence of Africans trading with American-Indians before the arrival of Europeans. For example Wiener "found that these Negro traders travelled as far north as New England. Their relics have been found in graves there, most notably a pipe with a Negro face."[23] This Harvard professor's three-volume work was published between 1920-1922. In 1926 Wiener published another work, *Mayan and Mexican Origins*, which investigates an African influence on Mayan and Mexican cultures. Many of Wiener's colleagues at that time considered his books ridiculous. However, the passing of time has validated his claims. Another German-American, Professor Alexander von Wuthenau of the University of the Americas in Mexico City, has also done work in this field. His excavations have unearthed numerous Negroid heads that were sculptured in clay and other materials. This African presence in pre-Columbian art is an indicator of an African presence in pre-Columbian history. In 1976 Ivan Van Sertima, a black scholar, published *They Came Before Columbus*. Van Sertima's book is well documented and provides overwhelming evidence of African contact with America before Columbus.

Despite the overwhelming evidence, many scholars today do not accept the view that there was an African presence in America before Columbus. The image of the African as a slave or servant is deeply rooted in the minds of people in today's world. They can very easily visualize the forced bringing of Africans to America in slave ships, naked and in chains. But it is very difficult for them to visualize Africans having the knowledge to sail to America on their own, trading and making other contacts with the American Indians. Nevertheless, documents reveal that the Spanish saw Africans in the New World. The Spanish explorer Vasco Nuñez de Balboa is reported to have seen Africans on the Isthmus of Panama (Darien). The Indians on the island of Hispaniola told the Spanish that they had traded with black men who came to their shores from across the sea. Also the statues of gods with Negroid features found in Central America cannot be ignored. But to reveal that Africans were worshiped as gods in ancient times by the American Indians is probably too much for the modern mind to deal with, because in modern times the African has always been portrayed as a slave, servant, or an inferior. However, these statues of gods with Negroid features can't be explained away by saying that they are statues of slaves. People do not erect monuments to slaves or servants, "but only to gods, kings, and heroes."[24]

The image of the African has not always been as a slave, servant, or an inferior. Only in the last five hundred years has this been so. The image of the African as a primitive and an inferior being was created during the slave trade to justify the enslavement and exploitation of Africans. But before the age of conquest and slavery, the African was not looked upon as an inferior being in the eyes of the world. For example, before the age of exploration, during the 1300s and early 1400s, when European kings and merchants talked about making contact with Africa, they thought of two legendary African figures: King Prester John of Ethiopia and Mansa Musa of Mali. Both of these African figures represented power and wealth. Europeans wanted to join forces with the wealthy and powerful Christian king, Prester John of Ethiopia, in a war against the Muslims. Maps displaying a drawing of Mansa Musa and the location of his gold-rich African kingdom were published by European cartographers. The powerful and wealthy Mansa Musa was seated on a golden throne, holding a gold nugget in one hand and a scepter in the other. Before the age of slavery and conquest, Europeans visualized Africans having power and wealth. And in ancient times the same was true. Only in modern times has the image of the African been as a slave or servant or an inferior. Many scholars carry the prejudices of this five hundred-year period back to the past, applying them to medieval and ancient history. They make the African an eternal slave whenever and wherever he appears in history.

Columbus returned to Spain in March 1493, where he received a hero's welcome. News of his contact with a strange land across the sea spread quickly in Europe. The Spanish knew that they would have to move fast to prevent Portugal from trying to claim the new lands with which Columbus had made contact. So they went to the Pope in Rome and told him about the problem with Portugal. Pope Alexander VI agreed to arbitrate the dispute between Spain and Portugal. In May 1493 he drew the Line of Demarcation, which divided the world between the two countries. This imaginary north-south line was located one hundred leagues (about three hundred miles) west of the Azores and Cape Verde Islands in the Atlantic Ocean. Spain was allowed to claim all the land west of the line, while Portugal was allowed to claim all the land east of it. The Treaty of Tordesillas made the following year, 1494, moved the line farther west in Portugal's favor. In this treaty the line was set at 370 leagues (about twelve hundred miles) west of the Cape Verde Islands.

Besides settling the land rights between Spain and Portugal, Pope Alexander VI also granted both countries the right to colonize all new lands with which they made contact. In addition, he granted them the right to convert the indigenous people of these lands to Christianity.

Columbus' contact with America opened up a New World for European expansion. This New World contained seemingly unlimited resources and was inhabited by indigenous people whose weapons of war were inferior to those of Europe. Europeans saw the New World as a paradise on earth waiting to be exploited for its wealth. But to exploit this new land for its wealth, cheap labor was needed.

Fifteen hundred settlers accompanied Columbus on his second voyage to America in 1493. This expedition founded the town of Isabella on the island of Hispaniola. The settlers Columbus brought to Hispaniola were unfit for heavy labor in the tropical climate. Many became ill and died. Columbus then turned to the Indians for labor. The Indians were not used to toiling in fields and spending long hours panning for gold. Having had enough of Spanish cruelty, the Indians revolted against them in 1495. However, the revolt was ruthlessly put down and many Indians were killed. Columbus' poor administrative ability as governor of Hispaniola led to his replacement in 1499 by Francisco de Bobadilla. When the new governor arrived on the island he was so upset with the conditions there that he sent Columbus and his brother back to Spain in chains. Columbus was set free, however, by Queen Isabella.

In the early 1500s Spanish indentured servants and some slaves were shipped to Hispaniola from Spain to provide additional labor. The slaves were (1) Moors, some of whom still remained in Spain and (2) Africans, who had been brought to Europe from West Africa by the Portuguese.

The Spanish were dissatisfied with the African slaves because they resisted slavery and frequently escaped. The Spanish also found that when the African slaves ran away to the Indians, they encouraged the Indians to rebel. In 1503 the governor of Hispaniola, Nicolás de Ovando, asked Queen Isabella not to send any more Africans over to the colony. She agreed. A shortage of labor, however, forced Ovando to reconsider his thinking about African slaves. In 1505 Spain sent seventeen African slaves to Hispaniola to provide labor. In 1510 a group of two hundred enslaved Africans arrived in the West Indies from Seville, Spain.

Despite the increase of African slaves, the Spanish were still depending heavily upon Indian slave labor to work their fields and mines. For example, in 1514 the Spanish had about twenty thousand Indians in forced labor camps in Hispaniola. The harsh labor of the mines and fields, European diseases such as smallpox and measles, and deaths in rebellions all combined to sharply reduce the Indian population in the West Indies.

Bishop Bartolomé de Las Casas became tired of seeing the Indians in Hispaniola being treated so cruelly and decided to do something about it. In 1517 he went to Spain, where he made an emotional plea before King Charles V, begging him to save the Indians. Las Casas had observed both Indians and Africans doing hard labor and had concluded that the Africans could withstand hard labor much better than the Indians. As an alternative to Indian labor, Las Casas suggested to King Charles V that each Spaniard be allowed to import twelve African slaves. Las Casas' suggestion was approved by King Charles V. The king then "issued a patent to one of his friends giving him the authority to import four thousand black slaves annually to Cuba, Hispaniola, Jamaica, and Puerto Rico."[25]

The Atlantic Slave Trade

The "yoke of bondage" had now been placed on the African, meaning that he had been selected by Europeans to provide the labor for the development and exploitation of the New World. The Portuguese had begun the European enslavement of the African when they captured and brought back to Portugal twelve Africans, called Moors, in 1441. The Portuguese quickly saw the profit in the buying and selling of Africans and began to bring more and more of them back to Portugal. By 1506 about thirty-five hundred slaves were being shipped back to Portugal annually from West Africa. Although African slaves were arriving in Europe, there was never a big demand for them there. Large amounts of slave labor would have taken jobs away from Europeans who needed employment. The New World was where large amounts of cheap labor were needed. If the New World hadn't opened up and created a market for slaves, there would have been no need for a slave trade.

In 1518 a cargo of slaves was shipped to the West Indies directly from the Guinea Coast, bypassing the slave markets in Portugal. The Atlantic slave trade had now begun in earnest. Before it ended over three centuries later, millions of blacks would be uprooted from their native land in Africa and shipped across the Atlantic Ocean to the Americas. The right to transport African slaves to the Spanish colonies required a royal permit or license known as the *asiento*. Charles V of Spain had first granted this permit to a friend in 1517. The king's friend, not realizing "the value of the asiento," sold it "for 25,000 ducats...to a syndicate of Genoese merchants...."[26] In 1528 the asiento was sold again, this time to two German merchants at a big price. For more than two centuries the asiento was to be a prize in European wars.[27] The scramble for it would be furious. Thousands of Dutchmen, Frenchmen, and Englishmen would die so that each of their nations in turn could possess that valuable piece of paper.[28]

Portugal was the first European nation to become involved in the selling of Africans. The Line of Demarcation, drawn by Pope Alexander VI in 1493, permitted Portugal the right to claim the entire African continent. Portugal dominated the slave trade between 1450 and 1600. However, by the mid-1500s other European countries were beginning to compete with Portugal for a share in the riches of the Atlantic slave trade. These new competitors were the French, English, Dutch, Swedes, Danes, and later the Prussians and Americans. These rivals fought bitter wars with one another over the riches of the slave trade.

As the demand for labor increased in the New World, so did the demand for African slaves. Trading was one way in which Europeans obtained slaves in Africa, but there were other ways.

Kidnapping was another way Europeans obtained slaves in Africa. It was common and widespread throughout the history of the slave trade. Victims were kidnapped either by surprise or by deception. On his expedition to the West African coast in 1443-44, Portuguese captain Nuno Tristao surprised and took captive twenty-nine Africans—men and women—while they were paddling in boats along the shore. The aim of kidnapping by deception was to lure the victims into a trap and then capture them. For example, a captain of a slave ship might lay out goods such as brandy, tobacco, or beads on deck and then persuade the Africans to come aboard and get them; once the Africans were on the ship they would be captured and the ship would sail away. In another example, two black slave traders were enticed to come aboard Captain Strangeways' ship in the Sierra Leone River. Once they became dead drunk from drinking the captain's brandy, the ship sailed away. These black slave traders who had sold other blacks into slavery were now slaves themselves. Kidnapping by deception was not always successful. Sometimes the Africans would see the trap and jump overboard, avoiding capture. Another example of kidnapping by deception involved an American black man named Charlie Smith. Before his death about the age of one hundred twenty, Smith was the "last known living slave brought to America."[29] When he was a kid living in Africa, he was lured down to a slave ship by the offer of candy; then he was captured and brought to America and sold. The author listened to Charlie Smith on audio-tape in a history class at Tennessee State University back in the early 1970s. A professor there, Dr. Ed Cullen, had gone down to Florida where Charlie was living and taped a conversation with him. Charlie told some very interesting stories.

A second way Europeans obtained slaves in Africa was by raiding villages or towns and selling the captured survivors into slavery. One of the most notorious slave raiders was Englishman John Hawkins. Sailing along the African coast, Hawkins attacked villages and towns, capturing men, women, and children and selling them into slavery. Hawkins was born in 1532 to a merchant-captain father who had visited the Guinea Coast of West Africa. When Hawkins was a kid, his father had told him fascinating tales about the Guinea Coast and the Blackamoors he had traded with there. In 1562 Hawkins, aiming to capture some of those Blackamoors and sell them, made his first voyage to the Guinea Coast in a little fleet of ships. He raided the Guinea coast and obtained three hundred Africans partly by the sword and partly by other means. He then sold his captives illegally in Spanish Hispaniola and made a huge profit. When the news of his slaving voyage reached Queen Elizabeth, she found it repugnant. But when she saw a sheet showing his huge profits she changed her mind and "became a shareholder in his second slaving voyage."[30] This second slaving voyage occurred in 1564. Once Hawkins and his little fleet reached the Guinea Coast they began looking for Africans to enslave. His first group of captives came from the Sambula Island, located off the coast of Sierra Leone. Hawkins captured the inhabitants of the island, two tribes, after looting and burning their towns. Continuing on down the coast, Hawkins stopped at a town called Bymba. He and his men looted the town but because of the fierce resistance of the inhabitants, they only managed to capture ten Africans, while losing seven of their own. Continuing southward along the coast, Hawkins captured more Africans. After filling the holds of his ships with captives, Hawkins took his cargo to Venezuela, where he forced the governor there to buy it. The profit from his second slaving voyage made Hawkins a financially well-off man.

A third way Europeans obtained slaves in Africa was by warlike alliance. They entered into an alliance with one group of Africans which was fighting another group and then enslaved the Africans they captured. In some instances African kings and chiefs asked the Europeans for help against another group of Africans.

In other instances the Europeans volunteered to help one group fight another. On his third voyage to the Guinea Coast in 1567, John Hawkins obtained a group of African captives by warlike alliance. He was asked to help in an African family feud and he gladly accepted. Hawkins aligned himself with two African kings against two other African kings. The aim of their alliance was to capture a town that had a population of about "eight to ten thousand inhabitants."[31] After a difficult battle, the town was finally captured and burned. This attack resulted in the death of many of the town's inhabitants. For his efforts Hawkins came away with 470 captives to be sold into slavery.

A fourth way Europeans obtained slaves in Africa was by meddling in the internal affairs of the Africans. For example, a European slave trader would marry into an African chief's family and thereby gain some say in the tribe's political affairs. Then the slave trader would provoke a war between this chief and another chief and sell the captives from the war into slavery. In another example, Europeans would use gifts and promises to win over the friendship of African kings and chiefs, then become advisors in their internal affairs. These advisors were supposed to help the Africans settle their internal disputes. However, their real objective was to provoke warfare among the Africans. Increased warfare among the blacks meant more captives for slavery.

The Africans used poor judgement when they allowed the Europeans to become involved in their family disputes. Outsiders should never be allowed to settle family disputes. Only members inside the family should be allowed to do this. The Europeans took advantage of the Africans' political naïveté, setting one group against the other. When the Africans were weakened from internal blows, the Europeans conquered both groups.

The fifth way Europeans obtained slaves in Africa was by trading. Africans would sell other Africans to

Europeans for goods such as guns, beads, liquor, and cotton textiles. In all fairness to the Africans, however, when they began selling one another to the Portuguese in the 1440s, they were not engaging in a practice that was unique to Africans. Peoples on other continents had sold one another also. For example, medieval European slave traders had sold other Europeans abroad to countries in North Africa. Moreover, when Africans sold one another to Europeans, they were not engaging in a practice contrary to African laws and customs. Africans had bought and sold one another long before the Portuguese arrived on the coast of West Africa in the fifteenth century. So when the Africans sold one another to the Portuguese, they thought that they were providing laborers needed overseas. They were not aware of the Europeans' inhumane concept of chattel slavery. In African culture slaves were considered human beings and they had rights. As the years passed, the African slave traders eventually learned of the cruelty of the slave trade, yet they continued to sell their people for profit.

When Africans sold other Africans into slavery, usually they sold members of another tribe, not their own people. They could sell members of another tribe because they did not share a common loyalty and oneness with them. Historian Chancellor Williams emphasizes this point.

> According to African tradition leader and people were one and the same, sharing a common lot. This sense of oneness, however, applied only to the members of one's tribe, and not to Africans outside of it—another tragic fact of Black history. This is why the chiefs and kings would secure prisoners of war by attacking other states.[32]

The inability of the African states and tribes to settle their differences and come together against a common foe was their undoing. The Europeans saw this weakness of disunity and took advantage of it by playing one group of Africans against the other. Feuds and rivalries between Africans were often manipulated and turned into warfare, pitting Africans against Africans. The game was to provoke warfare between the blacks, which meant more war captives to be sold into slavery.

The use of guns heightened the intensity of the wars between the blacks, making the conflicts more deadly and at the same time greatly increasing the number of war captives for slavery. Many European slave traders quickly saw this and exploited the situation by providing guns to certain chiefs and kings who would aggressively attack other black kingdoms to secure large numbers of captives, which meant big profits for themselves. More and more captives also meant bigger and bigger profits for the European slave traders. With the Africans divided and fighting among themselves, the Europeans, from a position of power, could demand that the chiefs and kings bring them a certain number of captives or be sold into slavery themselves.

As European slave traders brought more guns to Africa, it became a matter of survival for African states to obtain them. A state armed with guns was more likely to defeat a state armed with shields and spears. In some instances the only way a state could obtain guns was by trading slaves for them. This catch, "only slaves in exchange for guns," could force a state into the slave trade even though it didn't want to participate in it. This happened to a number of African states. British historian Basil Davidson describes how the African state of Dahomey was pushed into the slave trade because it needed guns to keep from being enslaved by other states.

> But the new state of Dahomey could defend itself effectively only if it could lay hold on adequate supplies of firearms and ammunition. And these it could obtain only by trade...and, of course, only in exchange for slaves. Hence, Dahomey's power to resist Oyo (itself in turn subjected to the same pressure) depended on deliv-

ering slaves to the coast; the drastic but inescapable alternative was to enslave others—in order to buy firearms—or risk enslavement oneself. This indeed was the inner dynamic of the slaving connection with Europe; and it pushed Dahomey, as it pushed other states, into wholesale participation in slaving.[33]

As a result of this catch, "only slaves in exchange for guns," many Africans were forced into participating in the slave trade. However, most modern history books that discuss the slave trade fail to point out this important fact.

Eventually a tragic psychology emerged among many blacks: every man for himself. This fateful psychology meant that many stopped trying to come together in brotherhood to resist the common European threat. Rather, they turned on their neighbors and enslaved them before their neighbors could do the same. It became a matter of survival: enslave or be enslaved.

In all fairness to the African chiefs and kings, they lacked experience at the international level, a highly competitive and dog-eat-dog world, which was much different from the humane African world in which they were used to operating. The international level is filled with danger, intrigue, and trickery. At the international level one meets some of the cleverest of the clever, people who can make things look one way when they are another way. To operate successfully at the international level, one has to be cautious and alert and also understand how to look beneath the surface of things for hidden meanings. Something false can be made to look genuine. African culture hadn't prepared the chiefs and kings to operate at the tricky, dog-eat-dog international level. They weren't prepared psychologically to deal with it. They would have had to make a psychological adjustment to deal with it, and it seems they had difficulties doing this. As a result, with their blind trust in strangers and excessive generosity, they became easy prey to shrewd European slave traders.

After their capture by kidnapping, raids, or through warfare, Africans were forcibly marched to the coast where they were sold, put on ships, and taken to distant lands to serve as slaves. These slavers could be Europeans or Arabs. The march to the coast could be short or long, depending upon the distance from the coast. A large slave coffer, which contained hundreds of captives marching one behind the other, could be miles in length. The captives suffered tremendously during their march to the coast. They were forced to march mile after mile with their necks tied to a heavy, forked pole. To make matters worse, the men's hands or ankles were also bound. The women were often forced to carry heavy burdens on their heads. The whip was used to help slow-moving captives keep pace with the others. Some captives poisoned themselves with poison they had secretly brought along, preferring death to a life as a slave. Captives who tried to commit suicide and failed were severely beaten. Sometimes healthy-looking Africans suddenly dropped dead for no apparent reason. Only the strong among the captives were able to survive the brutal march to the coast. The weak and injured who couldn't go on were left to die along the trail.

When a European slave trader arrived at a trading post or factory on the African coast to buy Africans from other Africans, it was customary for him to first obtain the king's permission. The trader could usually get the king's permission to trade by giving him gifts. Some kings demanded more gifts than others. Guns, hats, beads, and liquor were some of the items given to the African Kings. Once the king was satisfied with his gifts and had granted the trader permission to trade, negotiations over the price of the slaves began. Sometimes, however, the king demanded more goods than the trader was willing to pay for each slave. As a result, the negotiations might continue for a week or longer before an agreement was finally reached. One trick the traders used to help them in their bargaining with a king, especially one skillful in trading, was to give him brandy and get him drunk. A drunken king could be more easily manipulated than a sober one. This trick didn't work on an alert king, however.

Africans who sold other Africans to European slave traders were usually paid in trade goods. The trading posts located along the African coast contained a variety of trade goods: fancy hats, guns and ammunition, knives, beads, metal utensils, textiles, iron bars, whiskey, brandy, and rum. The trade goods were generally made cheaply and were of poor quality. It was a common practice to mix the liquor with water. The trading guns were usually of poor quality; some were of such poor quality that they exploded "after the first few shots."[34] After buying the enslaved Africans with cheap trade goods, the slavers generally made a handsome profit when they sold them.

Following the agreement between the king and the trader over the prices of the captives, it was time for the trading to begin. The captives were brought to the trader's physician so that they could be examined. The African who brought the captives to the physician was called the *caboceer*; he was the king's main assistant. The trader wanted only the best Africans for slaves—the healthiest, the strongest, and the youngest. Africans over thirty-five, diseased, or with some kind of defect were rejected. Frequently, the prospective slaves had been so cleanly shaven and soaked in palm oil that it was most difficult to ascertain their ages or physical condition.[35] To try to determine their age or physical condition, the physician thoroughly examined the naked bodies of the Africans. They were forced to jump, stretch, and run in order to test their stamina and the condition of their limbs. The Africans' teeth were checked to determine their age; decaying teeth were equated with old age. The physician also carefully checked every other part of the captives' bodies, including their genitals, eyes, and lips. After the physician thoroughly examined the captives, he put aside the rejected ones and kept the best ones for branding. African men, women, and children were branded like cattle with a red-hot iron. The mark of the European slaving company was put on them for identification purposes. Examples of some of these slaving companies were the British Royal African Company, the Dutch West India Company, the Portuguese Company Cacheo, and the French Company of the West Indies.

Following their branding, the Africans were either put on a slave ship for transport to the Americas or put into a slave pen at the trading post to await the arrival of a slave ship. More than likely they would be put into the slave pen to wait until a ship arrived at the trading post. Sometimes a slave ship would have to stop at a lot of trading posts before it could obtain enough slaves to fill its hold. Some captains would pack six or seven hundred Africans on one small ship. The European in charge of the slave pen at the trading post was called a *factor*. Enslaved Africans were treated like cattle inside the slave pen, where they experienced much degradation and suffering. The men were attached to "a long chain,"[36] which was held in place by two stakes driven into the ground, one at each end. "The women and children"[37] could usually move freely around the pen. The enslaved Africans were carefully watched by an armed guard. They were generally fed only one time per day. Driven by hunger, they would fight over the food thrown to them. The strongest among them would get enough food to survive, while the weaker ones often starved to death.

When a slave ship arrived at the trading post, the Africans were brought out of the slave pen and forcibly marched down to the beach, where boats were waiting to carry them out to the ship. Once they were on the slave ship they would begin the infamous voyage to the Americas known as the Middle Passage.

Getting the Africans on the slave ship was a difficult job for the slavers. The Africans were terrified at the thought of leaving their homeland and going across the sea into the unknown. Some "flung themselves on the beach, clutching handfuls of sand in a desperate effort to remain in Africa."[38] Others attempted to commit suicide by putting their chains around their necks and strangling themselves. Despite the resistance of the Africans, the slavers were determined to put them in the boats and row them out to the waiting ship. As a result, the Africans "were beaten, pushed, dragged, and even carried to the"[39] boats.

Some Africans regretted leaving their homeland so much that they jumped out of the boats and ships into the sea, preferring to be drowned or eaten by sharks than to be carried across the sea to be slaves in a strange land. Sharks often followed the slave ships; sometimes they followed the ships all the way across the Atlantic to the Americas, anticipating bodies being thrown overboard.

Aboard the slave ship, the naked Africans were chained together "two by two, the right wrist and ankle of one to the left wrist and ankle of another."[40] The part of the ship they were taken to was called the hold. The Africans were packed in the hold very tightly with hardly enough room to move, "like books on a shelf." The profits from selling the Africans were so big that "few traders could resist the temptation to wedge in a few more."[41] Often six to seven hundred slaves were crowded into a ship built for carrying a cargo of 450. On one voyage a captain left Africa with seven hundred slaves but upon reaching Barbados, he had a human cargo of only 372. A law was passed to prevent overcrowding on the ships, but it was generally ignored by the captains.

The notorious Middle Passage was a living hell. Overcrowding and unsanitary living conditions made the slave ship a haven for diseases. The two most deadly diseases were the bloody flux (an intense diarrhea) and smallpox. The bloody flux could wreak havoc on a ship and cause a heavy death toll. Smallpox, against which the Africans had no immunity, was probably more feared than the bloody flux. A single individual with this disease could infect many others on the ship. Sometimes a captain lost half of his cargo from smallpox. Sick and weak Africans who looked like they were not going to live were generally tossed overboard to the sharks, along with the dead ones. On some ships each morning the slaves were brought up on deck out of the filthy hold so that it could be washed. But on other ships the hold was rarely cleaned at all. Some captains even travelled the entire voyage without having the hold washed, forcing the slaves to wallow around in filth. Some Africans were overwhelmed by the stench and heat in the hold and died from suffocation. Also the women slaves on the ship were fair game to the captain and his crew. The women who refused to submit risked being beaten to death.

The Africans naturally rebelled against the cruel treatment they received on the ships during the voyages to the Americas. There were many mutinies on slave ships during the long history of the slave trade. In the successful mutinies sometimes whole crews were killed and the ships were destroyed. Most mutinies occurred when a ship was anchored near the African coast. If the ship was anchored near the shore and the Africans aboard the ship "managed to kill the crew, as they did in perhaps one mutiny out of ten, they could cut the anchor cable and let the vessel drift ashore."[42] Once ashore the Africans had a chance to escape to freedom. The records indicate that the Africans did not submit to the Middle Passage docilely; rather, many died fighting bravely for their freedom. In one incident in 1790, an English sailor named William Richardson described how his ship went to the aid of a French slaver on which the Africans had rebelled. Even though the mutiny was finally suppressed, the Africans fought bravely against the crew armed with guns. The sailor admired the bravery of one young African in particular; he was armed with only a wooden stick, yet he refused to surrender and fought heroically to his death by gunfire. The captains of the ships were fearful of mutinies and took precautions to prevent them. For example, they tried to avoid putting Africans together who could speak the same language. If they unknowingly filled the hold of their ship with a group of Africans from a single tribe, they were probably headed for trouble.

The most famous mutiny aboard a slave ship was the *Amistad* mutiny, which occurred in 1839. It has recently been made into a movie. Historian Stanlake Samkange describes the *Amistad* mutiny and its results.

> On board the slave ship *Amistad*, Cinque successfully led a revolt, killed all except one of the crew, and ordered the lone white man to steer the ship back to Africa. During the day, the white man sailed, keeping the sun on his right as he had been instructed to do but turned the ship at night so that, eventually, it was found off the New England coast, where Cinque and his friends were arrested. A group of American citizens organized a committee which, in spite of strong opposition from the southern states, successfully fought the Africans' case in American courts. Cinque and his friends were freed and returned to their homeland.[43]

Africans sometimes rebelled by going on hunger strikes. Ship captains used different methods to try to force them to eat. One method was to put a shovel of red-hot coals from a fire near a slave's mouth to try to frighten him into opening it so he could be fed. A second method was to whip the slave unmercifully until he would eat. A third method was to use a device called a mouth opener, which would forcefully "open the slave's mouth"[44] so food could be poured down his throat. Sometimes nothing could make the Africans open their mouths. They would eventually starve to death and be tossed overboard the ship. Also the Africans would sometimes will themselves to death; they would die "for no apparent reason."[45] This baffling condition was known as fixed melancholy.

Sometimes the harsh conditions the Africans had to deal with on the slave ships drove them insane. Slaves who went insane were of little value to the slavers. "Men who went insane might be flogged to death, to make sure that they were not malingering. Some were simply clubbed on the head and thrown overboard."[46] The women who went insane might be treated a little better.

After being at sea from five weeks to three months, the slave ship finally reached the Americas. The Africans who survived the Middle Passage were sold at slave markets in Jamaica, Santo Domingo, Cuba, and elsewhere. The slavers generally made a big profit from the sale of their human cargo. However, getting their human cargo to the slave markets in the New World hadn't been without risks. They had risked: being attacked by revengeful Africans on the Guinea Coast, the crew catching tropical diseases, being attacked by pirates or another European vessel, and slave mutinies on the ships. Despite the risks the slave trade continued to flourish. The slavers figured that the great profits made from the sale of the Africans were well worth the risks.

Why the captains of the ships were so unnecessarily cruel to the enslaved Africans is difficult to understand. After all, the enslaved Africans were the source of the wealth the slavers were seeking. It would have benefited them more commercially if they had treated the enslaved Africans better. The Africans would not have died in such large numbers and they would have been in better condition when they arrived at the slave markets in the New World. The slave trade seemed to have numbed the feelings of the ship captains and created in them a disregard for human life. Profits became the motivating force among the slavers. If an African had some kind of defect that made him worthless at the slave market, then he was of no value to the slavers and he was subsequently thrown overboard.

When African chiefs and kings began selling other Africans to the Portuguese in the 1440s, little did they realize that they were setting in motion a practice that would eventually devastate the continent. In "the first stages of the slave trade many African chiefs and kings actually thought they were supplying workers needed abroad—and at a great profit to themselves."[47] They were unfamiliar with the European system of slavery, which was equated with race. However, as the time passed, they eventually became aware of the brutal European slavery, which was much different from the African slavery. Therefore, it was very cruel of them to sell their people into chattel slavery. Historian Chancellor Williams makes the following comments about the African chiefs and kings who sold other Africans into slavery: "So, I am saying that while at first the African slave sellers may not have known the fate to which they were consigning their brothers, in time they did learn. And for this reason these Blacks will stand condemned forever before the bar of history...."[48]

The point here is some African chiefs and kings willingly participated in the slave trade to enrich themselves. Yet other African states and tribes, as we have seen, were forced into the slave trade by ruthless European slave traders. The catch "only slaves in exchange for guns" forced many Africans into the slave trade against their will. They had to enslave or else be enslaved themselves.

The African chiefs and kings who sold their people into slavery were generally paid in trade goods. These goods included guns, liquor, textiles, beads, fancy hats, and metal utensils. By selling their people for trade goods, these kings and chiefs didn't get anything of real value from the Europeans. If they were going to sell their people, then they should have gotten something that could have helped to raise their nations to greater heights technologically and economically. For example, they should have gotten European science and technology. But when they sold their people for trade goods, they didn't get anything that could really benefit them or their people. Unfortunately, some of today's blacks have the same mind-set. These blacks, just like the chiefs and kings during the slave trade, sell their people out and turn their backs on their suffering. They sell their people out for promotions, high positions, bribes, and other gifts.

The African slave sellers failed to see the future devastating impact of the slave trade on Africa. Their vision was blurred by their desire for European trade goods, especially guns and liquor. European slave traders had generated in them a desire for these goods and they were unable to resist the temptation to buy them. The chiefs and kings were focused on the small picture, buying European trade goods, but there was a much larger picture on which to focus: the destiny of African people at stake as a whole, which was more important than the wealth of states or the personal riches and glory of kings. The slave trade brought ruin, death, and pain to African people. The lack of foresight by African chiefs and kings proved costly to the future of black people.

To the clear-eyed, the slave trade was a deadly trap. The trade goods served as the bait that lured participants into the trap. The slave trade, like any trap, was easy to get into but hard to get out of. By the time many African chiefs and kings saw and understood the true nature of the slave trade, how it cleverly lured its participants, it was too late. They had already become trapped in the trade.

The slave trade was disastrous to Africa in a number of ways. The slave trade depopulated whole towns, villages, and provinces in Africa. Millions of the best young Africans—the cream of the crop—were transported to the Americas for their labor. This forced removal of the cream of the crop left a void that could not be filled. The slave trade created many destructive wars in Africa, bringing ruin and decay to many of Africa's states and kingdoms and large coastal towns. Europeans fought one another over the control of the slave trade. War between Dutch, Portuguese, English, and even Yankee slave traders destroyed the large coastal towns.[49] The Portuguese and the Dutch in particular fought some fierce battles up and down the African coast. Intense wars erupted when African tribes and states tried to enslave one another. This warfare between Africans was often provoked by European slave traders in order to increase the supply of slaves. The slave trade also caused bitter wars between Africans and Europeans. The slave trade brought about a decline in Africa's economy. Her agriculture, metal-working, textile, and other industries were ruined. The slave trade brought disunity and decline to states and kingdoms in Africa where there had once been peace, prosperity, unity, and organization. Finally, the slave trade created animosity, mistrust, fear, and suspicion among Africans, making it very difficult for them to achieve unity.

We turn our attention now to the Africans who opposed the slave trade. The common people in Africa did not benefit from the slave trade; only the ruling groups benefited. The common people were the ones who were generally enslaved, but in some instances the royalty were enslaved also. Africans in general were opposed to the slave trade; they would have stopped it had they been able to do so. The supporters of the slave trade were the chiefs and kings and their followers who participated in it. Historians have highlighted the role of African chiefs and kings in the slave trade; little is said about the general African opposition to the trade or about the kings and chiefs who led the fight against it.[50] Many Africans died fighting against enslavement. They chose to die free men rather than to be slaves. Sometimes whole groups of Africans died resisting the enslavers to the end.

There were African groups who refused to participate in the slave trade. Historian W.E.F. Ward says, "Some peoples, such as the Lozi and the Nguni, would never touch the slave trade." The Lozi people (southern Zambia) and the Nguni people (southern Africa) wouldn't participate in the Arab slave trade of the 1800s.

Some African people couldn't be enslaved. The Mossi people of West Africa couldn't be enslaved. The Mossi united to defend their country and would not let anyone divide them. They were also very alert, cautious, and wise. It was difficult to divide or trick them. The Krumen were another African people who couldn't be enslaved. The Krumen were big and strong, with very dark skins. The Wacamba people of East Africa also could not be enslaved. Some African people didn't trust Europeans. They wouldn't trade with them, nor would they allow them to build trading posts on their land. These distrustful Africans were generally labeled hostile, warlike, savage, and the like by European slave traders.

The quick riches obtained from selling Africans made the slave trade very attractive. It has been said that once the slave trade began in earnest in Africa, it spread like wild fire. The kingdom of Congo is a classic example of how rapid the slave trade could spread in a country. The king of Congo tried to check the spread of the slave trade in his country but was unable to do so. The Portuguese-Congo story began in 1483 when Portuguese mariner Diogo Cão became the first European to see the mouth of the mighty Congo River, where it empties into the Atlantic Ocean. Four years later, the Portuguese met the king of Congo at his capital, Mbanza. The Portuguese presented themselves as men of goodwill who wanted to establish a partnership with the kingdom of Congo. The Portuguese, using skillful diplomacy, described to the king how both countries could benefit from such a partnership. Trusting the Portuguese, the king of Congo agreed to become their trading partner. Within a few years of this visit to Mbanza, *the royal brothers* of Portugal and Congo were writing letters to each other that were couched in terms of complete equality of status.[51]

The Congo kingdom of West Africa was a highly advanced state when the Portuguese arrived there in the 1480s. It was prosperous and well organized, both politically and economically. The Congo's political organization was the equal of Portugal, but it lagged behind Portugal technologically. For example, it did not have a knowledge of firearms like Portugal. Both Spain and Portugal had benefited from their contact with the science and culture of the Islamic Moors. The Congo king hoped to further advance his state by acquiring the new Christian civilization that the Portuguese had offered him—education, religion, and trade. Nzinga Kuwu was the Congolese king when the Portuguese first arrived in the Congo kingdom. About 1492 he embraced Christianity and was given "the Portuguese name...João I."[52] His successor, Nzinga Mbemba, did likewise and took the Portuguese name Affonso. Other African chiefs and ministers also became Christians.

The partnership between Portugal and the Congo kingdom started off friendly and brotherly. But it began to unravel when the Portuguese changed their course and began to pursue their own interests. In 1512 King Manuel of Portugal sent Affonso, the Congo king, a document called the *regimento*. This historical document was sugarcoated with charming words of brotherly love and friendship. But removing the flowery words of disguise, revealed the *regimento* to be a detailed plan for the eventual Portuguese control of the Congo kingdom. It called for the reorganization of Congo, which would put the Portuguese in a position to better control the administration of the country. It also required that Affonso send shiploads of ivory, copper, and slaves to Portugal to pay for the cost of Portuguese operations in the Congo kingdom. The real intentions of the Portuguese were becoming clearer to

Affonso. He saw that they wanted to exploit Congo for its riches rather than provide him with the teachers needed to educate and train his people. Affonso was now in a very unfavorable political position. His allies the Portuguese, who had helped him militarily to come to power in 1506, were moving to undermine his rule. However, he could not afford to cut ties with them because they would encourage his vassals to rebel against him. Things quickly got out of hand.[53] The Portuguese became more and more interested in exploiting the Congo kingdom for slaves. It seemed like everyone sent over from Portugal, including priests, settlers, laborers, craftsmen, and sailors, became involved in the slave trade. They all became slavers, one way or the other. Some had their quotas of slave girls to serve them.

Affonso tried to stop the spread of the slave trade in the Congo kingdom, but he tried too late. By the time he saw and understood the Portuguese real intentions (to exploit the Congo kingdom for slaves and other wealth) it was too late; he was already in the trap. He had mistakenly let the Portuguese take sides in the Congo kingdom's family disputes. As a result, they were in a position to play one side against the other. Affonso had been unable to see, in time, that the Portuguese offer of education and material benefits was just bait.

Although he was trapped in the slave trade, Affonso still tried to stop its spread. He resisted the Portuguese in ways that he could. He also wrote letters to his royal brother, the king of Portugal, describing how the slave trade was depopulating and creating chaos in his country. He was ignored, however.

There were other African rulers besides Affonso who opposed the slave trade and tried to stop its spread. "A firsthand Swedish report of 1787 tells of...[a] king of Senegal in the far west of Africa who, 'very much to his honour, enacted a law that no slave whatever should be marched through his territories."[54] The French responded to this defiance by having the king's country attacked. In another example, the king of Dahomey, Agaja, took control of a stretch of land along the Slave Coast in 1727. As a result, he was able to reduce the number of slaves being exported from the ports along the Slave Coast. During the history of the slave trade, roughly 1441 to 1888, there were no doubt a number of African rulers who tried to stop or contain it. Unfortunately, historians have concentrated on the Africans who sold their people rather than the ones who tried to stop or contain it.

The most famous African abolitionist of slavery was the great Queen (Ann) Nzinga of Angola. This brave and determined queen fought the Portuguese invaders for over forty years. She was a great leader as well as a master military strategist. Queen Nzinga came to power in 1623. Before continuing with the story of her reign, it is necessary to examine the events that led to her coming to power.

The riches from the slave trade in the Congo kingdom whetted the Portuguese appetite for more and more slaves. As a result, they began to expand the slave trade into regions around Congo. The African ruler of Ndongo, a tributary state of Congo, helped the Portuguese in their slave expansion operations. This ruler's title was the *Ngola*, a word from which the territorial name Angola soon derived.[55] In 1556 the Ngola of Ndongo broke away from the Congo kingdom and declared his state's independence. A war followed as the king of Congo moved to regain control over his former tributary state. The Portuguese royal forces backed the king of Congo, while the Portuguese slave trader forces backed the Ngola of Ndongo. Actually, the Portuguese did very little fighting; it was really a war between Africans. The side of the Ngola of Ndongo and the slave traders defeated the side of Congo and the royal forces. After the war the Portuguese—the slave traders and the royalty—settled their differences and came together in a new alliance. The Portuguese had encouraged the war. It was part of their divide-and-conquer strategy. This war weakened both Congo and Ndongo (Angola), whereas it worked to the Portuguese advantage, enabling them to gain "a foothold on the"[56] coast. They now planned to conquer Angola and use the country as a source for much-needed slaves. There was a growing market for slaves in Brazil.

In 1575 the Portuguese began their attempt to conquer Angola. Their strategy was to divide the Africans and have them fight among themselves. The Portuguese used various ways to accomplish this. One way was to get involved in African family feuds and play one side against the other. Another way was to encourage a king or chief to extend his power over other tribes and states and then provide him with guns to do it. Guns would intensify the warfare between Africans, forcing the spear-and-shield-armed groups to raid for slaves so they could buy guns to defend themselves against the gun-armed groups. The aggressive and ruthless Portuguese strategy of divide and conquer in Angola swelled the number of war captives to be sold into slavery. Also, "Portuguese gangs roved the countryside, seizing captives wherever they could."[57]

The slave trade was ruining Angola. Conditions worsened when the Jaga, a fierce raiding tribe, joined forces with the Portuguese. The deteriorating conditions finally caused the king of Angola to realize what the slave trade was doing to his country. The king had been profiting from the slave trade and had been in complicity with the Portuguese slave traders; now they were squeezing his profits and tremendously depopulating his country. To counter this threat, the king began a war of resistance against the Portuguese. The Angolan war of resistance was successful in halting the growing momentum of the Portuguese and Jaga alliance. The war between the two sides continued on, however.

The Portuguese sent a new governor to Angola in 1622, although they didn't have control of the country.

This governor's aim was to establish peace between Angola and Portugal. The king's sister, Ann Nzinga, was sent to the conference at Luanda (the Portuguese stronghold on the coast) to negotiate with the Portuguese. Ann Nzinga was "the woman power behind a weak king, and the one responsible for inspiring the people to continue the war of resistance...."[58]

The Portuguese governor had a little surprise waiting for Ann Nzinga at the peace conference. He had decided on a studied insult at the outset by providing chairs in the conference room only for himself and his councilors, with the idea of forcing the black princess to stand humbly before his noble presence.[59] When the princess came into the room, the arrogant governor remained in his chair, looking at her with a sneer on his face. The princess, always alert, immediately understood the governor's little game to humble her. She, therefore, kept her emotions under control and "did not make a scene."[60] Her attendants "quickly rolled out the beautifully designed royal carpet they had brought before Nzinga, after which one of them went down on all-fours and expertly formed himself into a 'royal throne' upon which the princess sat easily without being a strain on her devoted follower."[61] The princess stood up once in a while so her attendant wouldn't get tired. Ann Nzinga had cleverly eluded the governor's little trap to insult and humble her. At the peace conference, she tried to get the best possible terms for her country and she succeeded.

In 1623, a year after the peace conference at Luanda, Ann Nzinga's brother died. Her brother had been a weak king and a slave trader. Ann Nzinga had been the inspiration behind the war of resistance against the Portuguese, not her brother.

With the death of her brother, the inspirational Ann Nzinga was now the ruler of Angola. Queen Nzinga immediately began to put pressure on the Portuguese, demanding that they carry out the terms of the Treaty of 1622 or else prepare for war. Suddenly, a Dutch fleet arrived on the scene. The Dutch hadn't come to help the Africans free themselves from the Portuguese, however. Instead they had come to challenge the Portuguese domination of the slave trade in Africa. The Dutch wanted to profit from the slave trade just like the Portuguese. To help their cause, the Dutch aligned themselves with the king of Congo, who was also fighting the Portuguese. The Dutch situation worked in Queen Nzinga's favor, giving her more time to get ready for the war against the Portuguese.

Queen Nzinga was a strong and brave military leader with a very alert mind. She understood the Portuguese strategies and tactics. She could read their clever cat-and-mouse games. She also devised strategies and tactics of her own to counter theirs. In short, she saw that the confrontation with the Portuguese was like a checkers game, a battle between minds, a game of moves and countermoves.

In 1624 Queen Nzinga made a move that made her the greatest African slave abolitionist. That year "she declared [that] all territory in Angola over which she had control was free country; all slaves reaching it from whatever quarter were forever free."[62]

After this act of defiance, Queen Nzinga made another bold move. She had observed that African troops were a vital part of the Portuguese army used to fight other Africans. She therefore devised a strategy to attack this source of Portuguese strength. Queen Nzinga "carefully selected groups of her own soldiers to infiltrate the Portuguese Black armies, first separating and spreading out individually into Portuguese held territory and allowing themselves to be 'induced' by Portuguese recruiting agents to join their forces."[63] Once they had infiltrated the Portuguese armies, the Queen's secret agents went to work on the black soldiers, inducing them to rebel. Queen Nzinga's strategy was successful. "...Whole companies rebelled and deserted to the colors of the black queen, taking with them the much needed guns and ammunition which she had been unable to secure except by swiftly moving surprise attacks on enemy units."[64] Escaped slaves also continued to come into Queen Nzinga's camp, increasing the size of her forces. Queen Nzinga was even able to get a number of vassal chiefs to desert the Portuguese and come over to her side. The Portuguese had had enough of Queen Nzinga; she was uniting the Africans against them. She had become too smart and bold. She had to be dealt with.

The Portuguese responded to Queen Nzinga's bold moves by sending her a message demanding that she send back all escaped slaves, soldiers, and chiefs or else war would be declared. Actually the two sides were already at war because the Portuguese had ignored the terms of the Treaty of 1622. The Portuguese next announced that Queen Nzinga was not the legitimate ruler of Angola. They made a vassal chief named Kiluanji the ruler of Angola. But of course the people didn't recognize this Portuguese puppet king.

The Portuguese, becoming more and more irritated with Queen Nzinga, decided to deliver her a knockout blow. They put together a powerful military force, including riverboats, to accomplish this. Queen Nzinga began the fighting by attacking the Portuguese puppet king, Kiluanji, and his troops. The Portuguese responded to Queen Nzinga's offensive move. They "captured her principal island stronghold in the Cuanza River in July 1626, thus dividing her forces and, by a swift encircling movement designed to capture the Queen, cut off her main supporting regiments and forced her not only to retreat but to withdraw from her country."[65] The Portuguese were happy. They had finally gotten rid of that terrible Queen Nzinga. So they thought.

Meanwhile Queen Nzinga was busy gathering her forces and strengthening her army. Her devoted followers were aware of what she was doing. The next year, 1627, she came back into her country leading a powerful army. She retook her island stronghold in the

Cuanza River and defeated the Portuguese puppet king Philip I (formerly Kiluanji). The fury of Queen Nzinga's army forced the Portuguese back to their coastal strongholds.

The Portuguese were now busy plotting how to destroy Queen Nzinga. They decided to offer "a big reward for her capture, dead or alive." Queen Nzinga, knowing that her people would fight to the finish to prevent her capture and that many of her people might be killed in such an all-out war, decided to trick the Portuguese by leaving the country. She therefore told "her lieutenants to spread the word everywhere that she had fled the country, mistakenly entered the territory of an enemy, and had been killed."[66] The people in her country actually thought she had been killed. There was sadness everywhere in Angola. The Portuguese, too, thought she had been killed.

Suddenly in 1629 Queen Nzinga appeared on the scene, terrifying the Portuguese. The fierce Jaga warriors were now fighting on her side. She had been able to convince even the unpredictable Jaga warriors that her cause was just. Queen Nzinga's forces overwhelmed the Portuguese. She had not only retaken her own country but had, meanwhile, become Queen of Matamba also, having replaced the weak queen there.[67] This made her the queen of two states, Angola (Ndonga) and Matamba. Queen Nzinga also increased her effort against slavery. She made both countries a refuge for escaped slaves.

The Portuguese now began to plan another strategy to overcome Queen Nzinga—the peace route. Ambassadors arrived in Angola in 1639 to negotiate peace between the two sides. Queen Nzinga listened to their talks of peace and friendship, but she was wary and distrustful of them. With the failure of the peace talks, the Portuguese resumed the war against the queen.

Queen Nzinga's success against the Portuguese continued. The Dutch war against the Portuguese also worked in her favor. The Dutch, aided by Africans, captured the important Portuguese stronghold of Luanda in 1641. In 1648 the Africans, helped by the Dutch, seized the Portuguese citadel of Masangano. That same year the Portuguese retook Luanda when additional forces from Brazil arrived to help them. The Africans had been left to defend the city of Luanda alone because the Dutch, disliking the odds, had pulled out. The Africans fought bravely at Luanda but were dealt a crushing defeat by the Portuguese. Despite the victory at Luanda, the Portuguese were unable to bring Queen Nzinga's two countries of Angola and Matamba under their control.

Having failed to conquer Queen Nzinga on the battlefield, the Portuguese again decided to try to conquer her through peace negotiations. The Portuguese were at their very best when they devised the treaty for Queen Nzinga to sign; it was a work of art in high-level deception. The treaty was written in flowery language but in a very ambiguous way, meaning that it could have two or more interpretations. The Portuguese could interpret it one way one day at a peace conference and another way at a peace conference later. For example, the treaty could be interpreted in a way to give the impression that the Portuguese were submitting themselves to the Africans, but later it could be interpreted to mean that the Africans had submitted to the Portuguese. The Portuguese knew from experience that Queen Nzinga had a sharp mind. They didn't believe, however, that her mind was sharp enough, functioning on a high enough level, to "see through" the clever disguise covering their treaty. "But, stripping away all the glittering verbiage, [Queen] Nzinga saw at a glance...what it all meant...she was to be a vassal of the Portuguese king, and...paying him a big annual tribute."[68] This was unacceptable to Queen Nzinga; she refused to sign the treaty. Queen Nzinga knew that if she signed the treaty, she would be signing her freedom away and also the freedom of her people. They had fought too long and hard for that to happen. She therefore waited six years, thinking and planning, before she decided to sign it. "Finally...in 1656—tired and weary from four decades of relentless struggles—she signed a treaty that was revised and made acceptable to her."[69]

Queen Nzinga spent the last years of her life getting her people properly prepared to continue on after her death. She passed away in 1663, at the ripe old age of eighty-one. Her people continued to resist Portuguese domination. Angola finally won its independence from Portugal in 1975, 312 years after her death.

Queen Nzinga was an extraordinary person. She had a sharp mind and was very alert. She observed things with hindsight, insight, and foresight. She could read the abstract, being able to see through clever disguises and smoke screens. She saw and understood how the game was played at the international level. She was also a brilliant military strategist, a strong leader who united and inspired her people, and Africa's greatest slave abolitionist. She was a thorn in the side of the Portuguese, resisting their invasion for many years. She could not be conquered; she could not be tricked; she could not be frightened; she could not be corrupted. She is one of the greatest leaders that the black race has ever produced. British historian Basil Davidson reflects on the Portuguese invasion of the Congo states and the great Queen Nzinga's determined resistance.

> Little by little, the Portuguese undermined the feudal order of the Congo states and inserted their own vacillating but destructive power. The story of their intervention and penetration is too long and complicated for rehearsal here. It was slow, erratic, and seldom successful except in ruining the social fabric they had found. Many of its wars and adventures, and many of the personalities associated with them on either side, have remained warm in African memory; none more so, perhaps, than that famous Queen Zhinga of Matamba who held the invad-

ers at bay for year after year. Fighting from her rock-bound strongholds in Matamba, Zhinga held out even when the Portuguese had defeated, at least for the time being, her allied armies of the Mani-Congo and the Ngola.[70]

Queen Nzinga's life is an excellent example of how important black women have been to the liberation and survival of black people. Black women have been leaders and generals in African history, just like men.

The slave trade could have been stopped in Africa in its early stages if the African states could have settled their differences and formed a united front against the European slave traders. But this didn't happen. The African states were unable to settle their differences and unite against a common threat. Also they were unable to see, in time, that it didn't matter who helped to put the raging fire out, just that it was put out. The slave trade was that raging fire, which eventually engulfed them all.

The period 1475 to 1675 was a critical time in history for black people. It was during this period that the great noose of encirclement was completed and fixed, and the Blacks of Africa found themselves hemmed in and threatened from all directions—from the north, from the east, from the west, and, finally, from the south.[71]

Once the slave traders had established permanent strongholds along the coasts and had succeeded in dividing the African coastal states against one another, it was too late to stop the slave trade. The Africans were trapped in it.

Europeans were concentrated in forts and towns near the coasts of Africa until the nineteenth century, when they began to penetrate the interior of the continent. For centuries they had been discouraged from penetrating the interior by mosquitoes, the hot and humid climate, and diseases like malaria and yellow fever. However, the main factor that discouraged European penetration of the interior was African military resistance.

> Writers of the colonial period have sometimes explained this fact of successful African resistance by reference to the climate and the mosquito. Certainly, malaria and the sun were grim discouragers of foreign invasion. Yet the early records indicate another and more persuasive safeguard against conquest. They point to the striking-power of African armies. They show that it was the military factor, time and again, which proved decisive.[72]

European military expeditions attempted to penetrate the interior from the coast but were discouraged by the strong resistance of African armies. So, the fighting skill of African armies was the main reason Africa was able to resist conquest up until the last half of the nineteenth century. In the end, however, Europeans eventually won because of their superior weapons. Spears and shields were no match for firearms.

The historic Berlin Conference of 1884-85 didn't begin the scramble to conquer Africa. This had begun much earlier. What the Berlin Conference did was to accelerate the conquest of large parts of Africa not yet under European control. By 1912 the whole African continent except Ethiopia and Liberia had been conquered by Europeans. (The United States was a protector of Liberia's independence.) The Italians tried to conquer Ethiopia but were decisively beaten by the Ethiopians at the Battle of Adowa in 1896. In this historic battle, the Ethiopians were led by the great Menelik II. So, Ethiopia was able to maintain its independence when the rest of Africa was conquered.

Chapter 10

Blacks in the United States and Latin America: Bondage to Freedom

After being at sea for weeks or even months, the slave ship finally arrived in the New World. Many Africans didn't survive the horrors and cruelties of the Middle Passage. The ones who did survive were generally sold by the slavers for large profits.

Slave markets, where Africans were sold, were located both on the Caribbean Islands and on the mainland. The island of Jamaica was a big slave-trading center. Slaves were also sold in Cuba, Barbados, and Hispaniola. Charleston, South Carolina was a famous mainland port for selling slaves in North America. Famous mainland ports for selling slaves in Latin America were Porto Bello, Panama; Cartagena, Colombia; Bahia, Brazil; and Caracas, Venezuela.

Once a slave ship arrived in a port, arrangements were made for the sale of the Africans aboard the ship. But sometimes before they were displayed for sale, the Africans were marched through the streets in the town so prospective buyers could look at them. Africans were sold to the buyers in several different ways: by public auction, by scramble, and by private negotiation. Selling by auction meant that the slave was sold to the person bidding the highest price. In port cities such as Charleston, South Carolina, and Savannah, Georgia, the slaves were generally sold by auction. However, in the West Indies the selling of Africans was a bit different. In the West Indies the maimed or dis-eased Africans called *refuse slaves* were sold by auc-tion at a place such as a tavern, while the healthy Afri-cans were sold by scramble. "There were some slaves who could not be sold...and they were often left to die on the wharfs without food or water."[1] Selling Africans by scramble meant that the buyers rushed in a disor-derly manner to select the Africans they wanted to purchase. "The healthy slaves...were sold by 'scram-ble,' that is, at standard prices for each man, each woman, each boy, and each girl in the cargo."[2] The time, date, and place of the scramble were announced in advance. The scramble could take place on the deck of the ship or in a slave yard. At the firing of a gun or some other kind of signal, the buyers rushed in like madmen and seized the slaves they wanted to buy. Sometimes quarrels among the buyers turned violent. Some Africans, not knowing what to think of all this commotion, were so terrified that they jumped from the ship into the water. Still another way of selling Af-ricans was by private negotiation. For example, a ship captain would meet with a wealthy plantation owner and discuss the selling of the slaves that were aboard the ship. Needing laborers, the plantation owner would agree to buy the whole shipload of Africans.

The Africans who were sold into slavery in the New World came mostly from West Africa, but some came from other parts of the continent. For example, the Xhosa people of South Africa and Africans from Mozambique in East Africa were brought to the Ameri-cas. There were cases in which Africans were captured in the interior of the continent and forcibly marched five or six hundred miles to the factories on the West Coast, where they were sold to European slave traders. Records indicate that captives from as far away as Mo-zambique were sometimes sold on the West African coast. Blacks from the island of Madagascar, located off the coast of East Africa, were also brought to the Americas. However, no matter what part of Africa the

Africans came from or what religion they were (indigenous African religion, Muslim, or Hebrew) or how they
differed in appearance, once they were enslaved and
put on a slave ship they became Negroes.

The coastline of the slaving area in West Africa
stretched from Senegal in the north to Angola in the
south. Geographers have divided this slaving area into
three regions: "Senegambia, Upper Guinea, and Lower
Guinea."[3]

Senegambia, the first region, comprised land
stretching from the Senegal River to the Gambia River.
The main African groups living in this region were the
Mandingos, Fulani, Serer, Felup, and Wolof. The Felup
were the only Africans from this region considered by
the slavers to be appropriate for hard labor in the
fields. The others were considered to be more suitable
as house slaves. In addition to their use as house servants, the Mandingos were also widely used as plantation coopers and blacksmiths.[4]

Upper Guinea, the second region, was located be-
tween the Gambia River and the Bight of Biafra. Upper
Guinea was subdivided into six areas: (1) Rivers of the
South, (2) the Grain Coast, (3) the Ivory Coast, (4) the
Gold Coast, (5) the Slave Coast, and (6) the Bight of
Biafra.

The Rivers of the South area comprised the present-day African countries of Guinea-Bissau, Guinea,
and Sierra Leone. This area was characterized by its
numerous rivers and islands. The Susu, Baga, and
Chamba were some of the African groups in this area.
The slaves from the Rivers of the South area "brought
fairly high prices in the New World markets."[5]

The Grain Coast comprised present-day Liberia.
Large amounts of rice and malaguetta pepper were
grown on the Grain Coast. Slave ships purchased rice
and malaguetta pepper there for use on their voyages
to the New World. The slave traders also bought slaves
on the Grain Coast. However, the harbors on the Grain
Coast were considered less than adequate, for the un-

derwater rocks could wreck ships. The Krumen people were the best known of the Africans on the Grain Coast. They were fishermen and boatmen, very dark skinned, of great size, and muscular. The Krumen couldn't be enslaved but would sometimes sell their criminals to the slave traders.

The Ivory Coast (present-day nation of Ivory Coast) got its name from the large amounts of elephant ivory that were collected for sale there. The Africans on the Ivory Coast were suspicious of white people and wouldn't allow them to build forts or trading posts along their shores. The Africans from the Ivory Coast were labeled a savage and hostile people and were regarded as the least hospitable of all Africans on the African coast by the slavers. Nevertheless, some Africans from the Ivory Coast were brought to the Americas and sold.

The Gold Coast comprised the present-day nation of Ghana. The Gold Coast got its name from the abundance of gold found in the area. Europeans were allowed to establish dozens of trading posts and forts on the Gold Coast. Among them was the well-known fort of Elmina, which still stands today. The Africans who inhabited the Gold Coast were the Fanti people and the Ashanti people. The Fanti occupied the land along the coast, while the Ashanti occupied the land behind the coast. Slaves from the Gold Coast were highly regarded by the English and usually sold at a higher price than those from other regions.[6] They were also frequently the subject of conversation among slavers and planters. In the West Indies they were called *Coromantees* (a name spelled in various fashions) after the port of Cormantine, from which many of them had been exported.[7] The Coromantees (Fanti and Ashanti) were feared and disliked by some slavers and planters because they encouraged other slaves to revolt against their masters. They were often the leaders of slave mutinies.[8] Records from Jamaica in the mid-1700s indicate that the Coromantees were the leaders of "a series of slave revolts"[9] that occurred there. The Coromantees were looked upon favorably by others. Their great courage was held in high regard. They were also said to be faithful to their owners. Some admirers thought the Coromantees possessed the kind of traits that heroes were made of. One observer who had particularly high praise for the Coromantees was Christopher Codrington, governor of the Leeward Islands. Writing about the Coromantees in 1701, he noted:

> They are not only the best and most faithful of our slaves, but are really all born Heroes. There is a difference between them and all other negroes beyond what 'tis possible for your Lordship to conceive. There never was a raskal or coward of...[that] nation.... My father, who had studied the genius and temper of all kinds of negroes [for] 45 years with a very nice observation, would say, Noe man deserved a Coramantoe that would not treat him like a friend rather than a slave....[10]

The Slave Coast was the area between the Volta River and the Niger River, roughly what is now Togo, Benin (Dahomey), and part of Nigeria. The Slave Coast was the busiest slave trade center on the African coast. The Yoruba and the Dakotans were the main African nations on the Slave Coast. In the Caribbean Islands both nations of people brought a good price on the market but not as high as the Africans from the Gold Coast.

The Bight of Biafra was the swampy area between the Niger Delta and the present-day nation of Cameroon, roughly eastern Nigeria. The Ibo were the main African people there. The Ibo slaves were considered docile and prone to suicide by the slavers. Some plantation owners in the New World were hesitant about buying them, whereas others liked their gentle temperament and preferred them.

Lower Guinea, the third region, comprised the present-day nations of Cameroon, Equatorial Guinea, Gabon, Congo, and Angola. The slavers considered the

Africans from Lower Guinea not as advanced and hardworking as the Africans from Upper Guinea. As a result, they were sold in the Americas at a lesser price.

From their penetrating observations, the slave traders and planters gained valuable knowledge about the physical appearance, temperament, and psychology of various Africans. They learned which Africans could be trusted as house servants and which ones were better suited for the fields. They learned to be more cautious and alert with certain African groups because they were more inclined to rebel. They learned which Africans were more likely to be loyal to their masters and which ones were not. They learned which Africans could be trained to do the bidding of their masters and which ones could not. By studying various African nations and groups, the slave traders and planters greatly improved their understanding of them. And the better they understood Africans the better they could control them.

The following examples show why the slave traders and planters realized that Africans differed in physical appearance and temperament. The Wolof were described as being very dark-skinned, very tall in stature, and having large chests and thin legs. The Fulani were Muslims; they had light copper-colored skin and long hair. The Krumen were very dark-skinned, large, and very well built. The Ashanti were a very proud people who would fight for their freedom. It was said that the Mandingos didn't make good field slaves, instead they made good house slaves and craftsmen. The Ibo were considered gentle and prone to suicide. The Ivory Coast Africans had a reputation for being distrustful of white people.

Like the Africans, the various Europeans who came to America also differed in physical appearance, temperament, and psychology. However, despite their differences, the English, French, Germans, Italians and other Europeans have fused over time to become white Americans. The same is true of the various Africans who were brought to America such as the Wolof, Ashanti, Fulani, and Mandingos; they have fused over time to become black Americans. "But ancestral traits of physique or temperament may reappear in unexpected fashions, and one is tempted to recognize...the Wolof in an immensely tall and slender-legged basketball player, and the Ashanti in a boxer."[11] For example it is possible that the celebrated former NBA basketball player Michael Jordan could be a descendant of the Wolof of Senegal, West Africa. He is six feet six inches tall, has slender legs and wide shoulders, and is dark skinned. If his roots could be traced like Alex Haley's were, they might lead back to the Wolof people of Senegal. It is also possible that the famous former heavyweight champion of the world "Smoking" Joe Frazier could be a descendant of the Ashanti of Ghana. He showed a tremendous amount of pride and fighting ability in his fights with the legendary boxer Muhammad Ali. They fought three times. "Smoking" Joe won the first fight, and Muhammad Ali won the last two. In the last fight, even thought he was taking a lot of punishment, "Smoking" Joe's pride would not let him quit. His corner had to finally throw in the towel to stop the fight. If his roots were traced, they might lead back to the Ashanti people of present-day Ghana. The Ashanti were a very proud people; they were also great warriors.

The accurate round number of Africans brought to the New World during the four-hundred-year Atlantic slave trade is not known. And it will never be known "because the necessary records either are lost or were never made."[12] One thing is certain: the number of Africans brought to the Americas was in the millions. Some historians estimate that about fifteen million Africans were brought to the Americas. Others believe this figure is too low. The best estimate is probably about fifty million. Still others believe the figure fifty million is much too low. In addition to the millions of Africans who landed alive in the New World, many millions died during slave raids and voyages across the Atlantic. One source says, "For every slave that came to the slave markets in Havana, Bahia, or Jamaica, perhaps two had died in the process of capture and shipment."[13] So, then, if fifty million Africans were brought to the slave markets in the Americas, then at least one hundred million must have died before they reached the slave markets of the Americas.

Blacks in the Caribbean

Christopher Columbus, sailing for the Spanish crown, first made contact with the Caribbean Islands in 1492. On his second voyage to the New World in 1493, Columbus brought fifteen hundred settlers with him to colonize Hispaniola. The settlers Columbus brought with him failed to satisfy the labor needs of the new colony. Some died from tropical diseases. Others wouldn't work. Columbus then forced the Indians of Hispaniola to do the heavy labor such as panning the streams for gold and working in the fields. The Indians rebelled against the harsh treatment in 1495. Their rebellion, however, was crushed by the Spanish.

The need for cheap labor steadily increased in the new colony. To help fill this need, the Spanish shipped laborers from Spain to Hispaniola in the early 1500s. These laborers were white indentured servants, enslaved Moors, and enslaved Africans. The newly arrived African slaves quickly developed a reputation for being rebellious and hard to handle. Some escaped to the Indians and encouraged them to rebel against the Spanish. Their rebelliousness caused Governor Ovando of Hispaniola to not want any more of them shipped to the colony. However, the critical need for cheap labor forced the Spanish to rethink the situation and decide against stopping the African trade. As a result, African slaves continued to come into the West Indies, but not in large numbers.

Meanwhile, the need for large amounts of cheap labor continued to present a problem for the Spanish.

They had tried to solve their labor problem with white indentured servants and Indians, but neither group had been the answer. The Indians had died in large numbers; the white laborers had died from tropical diseases and had run away to the hills. Also, "the church and the crown were reluctant to permit widespread use of Christian European labor in the harsh conditions of the New World mines...."[14]

In 1517 the labor problem of the New World was solved. That year Bishop Bartolomé de Las Casas suggested to King Charles V of Spain that he replace the Indian slaves working in the mines and fields in the West Indies with African slaves. The bishop had observed how cruelly the Spanish had treated the Indians in the Caribbean and also how they had died in large numbers. He wanted to keep the rest from being destroyed. The Spanish king adopted the bishop's suggestion. Four thousand Africans were shipped from the Guinea Coast to the Caribbean Islands in 1518. The infamous Atlantic slave trade had formally begun. African people had been chosen to provide the labor for the development and exploitation of the New World. A time of great troubles lay ahead for black people.

According to historians, in later life Bishop Las Casas regretted what his suggestion had done to Africans. He saw how they were suffering from the brutal Spanish slavery. However, his regret came too late to help Africans. The slave trade was steadily gaining momentum, and the large profits made it practically impossible to stop.

Africans were brought to the Caribbean in increasing numbers. By 1540 the annual importation had reached approximately ten thousand.[15] The second half of the 1500s witnessed the arrival of still more Africans in the Caribbean. They were needed to work the mines and to cultivate crops on the plantations. Some of the crops grown on the Caribbean Islands were sugar cane, tobacco, ginger, cotton, and coffee. Sugar cane cultivation became widespread. Large numbers of slaves were brought in to cultivate this important and profitable crop. Many blacks worked in the mills, processing the sugar cane into sugar. Africans provided the labor for the cultivation of other crops such as yams, manioc, and bananas. Cattle and other animals were also raised in the Caribbean.

The process by which newly arrived Africans were prepared to be slaves was called *seasoning*. It was a time of much pain and suffering. As a result, Africans died in large numbers, "with estimates of deaths running to as much as 30 per cent in a seasoning period of three or four years."[16] Some of the major causes of the death among the newly arrived Africans were "old and new diseases, change of climate and food, exposure incurred in running away, suicide, and excessive flogging...."[17]

Some Africans resisted the attempt to make them into slaves. It was the duty of an overseer or a slave-breaking specialist to make the newly arrived Africans humble and obedient. The slave breakers devised cruel ways to put fear into the slaves and to break their spirit. One common way of punishing a slave was with a long whip. Hard lashes from an overseer's whip could cause a slave to bleed profusely. "Another favorite type of punishment was to suspend the slave to a tree by ropes and tie iron weights around his neck and waist. Still another was to crop the slave's ears and to break the bones of his limbs."[18] The aim was to create in them a slave mentality. Once they had been indoctrinated with a slave mentality, the Africans would naturally obey their masters, know their place in society, and perform their duties.

Life on the sugar cane plantations in the Caribbean was one of toil and uncertainty for the slaves because they could be sold at any time. The slaves on the plantations were divided into three groups: field slaves, house servants, and skilled artisans.

The field slaves did the hard, backbreaking labor on the plantation. They cleared the land of trees and weeds; they planted, weeded, and harvested the sugar-cane crop; they worked in the sugar mill, processing the sugar cane; they also planted and harvested other crops. Slaves working in the boiling house of the sugar mill had to endure severe heat. The heat often caused them to suffer from dropsy, a condition in which the body swells. Many died. Only the strongest and health-iest slaves could survive the intense heat of the boiling house without becoming sick.

When the sleeping slaves heard the sound of the plantation bell tolling, they knew it was time to get up and begin another day's work. The slaves worked long hours, from day-break to dark, or as was said "from can see to can't see." It wasn't unusual for the slaves to work up to eighteen hours a day. Slaves who were late coming to the field or mill were given lashes by the overseer with his long whip. About nine o'clock the slaves stopped working to eat breakfast, which lasted about thirty minutes. At noon they took a two-hour break to eat their dinner and to do light jobs such as feeding the chickens or hogs. About two o'clock in the afternoon they began working again and worked until it became too dark to see.

The overseer with his long whip drove the slaves hard to get the maximum amount of work out of them. Men and women both had to work hard, and if they neglected their duties, they were lashed with a whip. "The investigations made by the British Parliament in 1790-91 brought out the fact that pregnant women were forced to labor up to the time of childbirth and that a month was the maximum amount of time al-lowed for recovery from childbearing. Pregnant women were lashed severely when they were unable to keep pace with the other workers."[19]

The house slaves and skilled artisans had a some-what better life than the field slaves. Yet if they fell out of favor with the slave master, they could be sold or demoted to work in the fields. House slaves worked as coachmen, footmen, butlers, valets, cooks, maids, and hairdressers. The female house servants, girls and young women, were at the mercy and whim of their slave masters. It was common for slave masters to have black or mulatto mistresses. The children born from these black-white sexual unions were called mulattoes or coloreds. The mulatto children took the status of their slave mothers. Therefore, they were slaves at birth. As time passed, a large mulatto slave population emerged in the Caribbean.

Africans did not come to the New World without skills and knowledge. Many were skilled artisans. The skilled artisans on the plantations included blacksmiths, coopers, carpenters, and brick masons. Some skilled artisans were hired out to work for other people. The money they made usually went to their masters. However, some masters let their slaves keep some of their earnings. Africans "were also skilled in tropical farming and in mining, being in these respects far superior not only to the Amer-Indians but often to the Europeans as well."[20]

Besides working on the plantations, black slaves also worked in the urban areas of the Caribbean as laborers, domestic servants, and skilled artisans.

Although they were worked hard, the slaves were generally inadequately fed. Their slave masters provided them with a basic diet of dried fish and cornmeal, which was issued to them in meager amounts. This basic diet lacked the necessary calories to sustain a person working hard in the fields and mills. On one plantation each adult slave was given a pint of grain and half of a herring (not infrequently rotten) for twenty-four hours.[21] On some plantations the blacks were allowed to have small gardens where they grew fruits and vegetables to supplement their poor diets. They generally cultivated their gardens on Sundays, their day off to rest.

The overseer's job was to get the maximum amount of productivity out of the slaves. The productivity of a slave was more important than his health. If a slave was worked to death, the planter could always buy another slave to take his place.

The institution of slavery revolved around economics. Big profits were made from slave labor and from the sale of slaves. The drive for profits took precedence over the welfare of the slaves. As a result, the mistreatment of slaves was common in the Caribbean. Many planters thought it was cheaper to buy slaves than to breed them. In the Caribbean the death rates of blacks exceeded the birth rates. So, slaves had to be constantly brought in from Africa to replace the ones who had died.

Slave laws were put into effect to control the black population of the Caribbean Islands and to maintain the institution of slavery there. The British, French, Spanish, Danish, and Dutch all had slave laws in their colonies. The French enacted the Black Code or *Code Noir* in 1685. The Code Noir was supposed to improve the living conditions of the slaves and protect them against cruel masters. But in reality this didn't happen because the laws were not enforced. The slave laws of the Caribbean Islands became more harsh as the black population increased and blacks began to outnumber whites. There was a relatively large number of slave laws enacted in the Caribbean Islands. Slaves were not allowed to gather in groups; they were not allowed to carry firearms or other weapons; they were required to have written passes if they left the plantations. According to slave law, children took the status of their mothers. Slaves were severely punished for stealing and running away. Slaves could be harshly whipped, branded with a hot iron, or have the bones of their limbs broken for these offenses. Also if found guilty of stealing and destroying horses or cattle the slaves could be hanged. The law punished slaves for insulting, striking, or killing a white person. They could be severely beaten, have their bodies mutilated, branded with a hot iron, or be put to death for an offense against a white person. On the other hand, slave masters often went unpunished for killing slaves. In some instances slave masters were fined for killing or abusing slaves. By law slaves were considered the property of their masters. This put slaves at the mercy of cruel slave masters. Also slaves were not allowed to beat drums or blow horns. The slave masters feared that these forms of communication could be used to start rebellions.

Denied their freedom, the blacks of the Caribbean Islands still found ways to resist the evil institution of slavery.

One way slaves retaliated against a cruel slave master was to poison him. Certain blacks brought to the Caribbean Islands from Africa were skilled in food poisoning. They possessed knowledge of plants that looked harmless but were lethal. Leaves or roots from these plants, put into a slave master's food, would slowly poison him over a period of time. A death from food poisoning was hard to detect.

A second way slaves retaliated against a slave master was by destroying his property. They killed or maimed the slave master's horses, cattle, hogs, and other animals. They destroyed tools belonging to the slave master. They sometimes destroyed the slave master's house, barn, and other buildings. Fire was probably the most common way of destroying buildings.

A third way slaves resisted slavery was by theft. They devised clever ways to steal from the slave master. They grabbed food from the master's table when his head was turned. They took a ham or shoulder from the smokehouse when the master or his snitches weren't watching. They learned to skillfully conceal the food they took under their clothes and hats. They had to be careful not to get caught because stealing was a serious offense.

A fourth way the slaves resisted slavery was by running away. Africans began running away from their slave masters soon after they first arrived in the Caribbean Islands in 1501. In 1503 the Spanish Crown received a complaint about African runaway slaves in Hispaniola. Some slaves there had run away from their masters to live among the Indians. These runaway slaves became known as *maroons*. They established communities in places where they could hide and defend themselves, such as in mountains and forests. In their communities the maroons lived a free life but they had to always be on the lookout for slave masters and military forces trying to recapture them. The maroons were an irritant to the whites. They constantly raided the plantations, carrying away cattle and other loot. They attacked travelers and other isolated people. They encouraged slaves to escape from their masters and join them. They also encouraged slaves to rebel. The authorities in the Caribbean Islands sent out military forces again and again to solve the maroon problem, but they were never able to wipe them out. The maroons in Jamaica fought a successful guerrilla war against the British. In 1739 a peace treaty was signed recognizing their freedom. The maroons also signed peace treaties with the authorities in Haiti, Cuba, and Suriname, which recognized their freedom.

A fifth way slaves resisted slavery was by rebellion. They rose up in armed warfare against their masters to obtain their freedom. A rebellion was the most feared form of resistance. Slave rebellions started soon after Africans began to arrive in the Caribbean Islands in relatively large numbers. Four thousand Africans were brought to the Caribbean Islands in 1518. Four years later, in 1522, the Caribbean Islands witnessed their first slave revolt, which took place in Hispaniola. In 1527 there was a slave revolt in Puerto Rico. Slave revolts continued to occur in the Caribbean Islands throughout the long history of slavery there. Slave revolts occurred in Jamaica, Barbados, Haiti, the Virgin Islands, and elsewhere in the Caribbean.

The slaves in Jamaica displayed a strong resistance to slavery. They often rebelled against their masters;

they ran away in large numbers and established their own maroon communities. The frequent rebellions and the maroons' long, heroic struggle against the British reflect the Jamaican slaves' rebellious spirit. The slaves in Jamaica were probably more active against slavery than slaves elsewhere.

Caribbean slave records indicate that the Coromantee Africans played a dominant role in the slave revolts that occurred in Jamaica. The Coromantees, Ashanti and Fula, were from the Gold Coast (present-day Ghana). After 1655 the Coromantees were brought into Jamaica in increasing numbers. Records show that some planters in the Caribbean believed the Coromantees differed from other Africans. They were described as courageous and having a rebellious spirit. The Coromantees were known to be leaders and participants in slave revolts. For example, the slave rebellion that occurred in Jamaica in 1760 was led by a Coromantee named Tacky. During this rebellion the slaves burned homes and fields, destroyed property, and killed whites. However, the rebellion was finally put down and its leaders ended up killed. "Tacky...was killed in the forests; of the three other ringleaders two were hung up in irons and left to die, whilst another was forced to sit upon the ground, chained to an iron stake, and slowly burned alive, beginning with his legs."[22]

The system of slavery in Haiti was the worst in the Americas. The slaves in Haiti were over-worked and cruelly treated. As a result, they died in large numbers. "In fact, slavery in Haiti was so vicious that slaves had to be replaced by fresh African imports...every four years rather than every seven or eight as in the other sugar-producing islands."[23] Treated so cruelly, it is not surprising that the slaves in Haiti rose up in arms to free themselves.

Before it declared independence, Haiti was known as Saint Domingue. It lies on the western part of the island of Hispaniola. The Spanish colony of Santo Domingo was located on the eastern part of the island.

In 1789, two years before the outbreak of its revolution, Saint Domingue was a flourishing French colony. It exported sugar, cotton, coffee, indigo, and other items. It was "the wealthiest colony in the Caribbean" and was important to France.

The inhabitants of Saint Domingue were divided into three groups: (1) whites, (2) free coloreds and free blacks, and (3) slaves. According to a 1789 population estimate, the colony had forty thousand whites, thirty thousand free coloreds, and 450,000 slaves. The whites were at the top of the caste. There were large numbers of wealthy white people in Saint Domingue, including planters, merchants, and lawyers. Many sugar and coffee planters had amassed large fortunes. The wealthy enjoyed the luxuries of life—big and spacious homes, large numbers of slaves and servants, the best foods and liquors, sparkling jewelry, fine clothes, feasts, balls, and trips. The poor whites held positions such as overseers, craftsmen, farmers, and shopkeepers. The free coloreds or mulattoes were in the middle of the caste system. They served as a buffer between the whites and the slaves. The free coloreds were not allowed to hold public office or practice the professions. They held positions such as craftsmen, tenant farmers, and petty traders. They also worked on the rural police force catching slaves. Some free coloreds were wealthy, having inherited property and other wealth from their white fathers. Some were also educated. They had been sent to France to be educated. The coloreds or mulattoes generally thought that they were better than the blacks. They had been taught that they were better because of their white blood. The manifestation of this superior attitude created friction between the coloreds and the blacks. On the other hand, many mulattoes were bitter toward the whites for discriminating against them. The slaves were at the bottom of the caste. They performed the backbreaking labor to produce wealth for the colony. The slave population was composed of both blacks and coloreds. Most of the slave population had been born in Africa. The slaves had to be constantly replaced because of their high death rates. The death rates were higher than the birth rates.

The very cruel slavery in Saint Domingue caused the slaves to run away in increasing numbers. These maroons established communities in inaccessible areas in the mountains and forests. The maroons remained in contact with their brothers still in bondage and encouraged many to run away or rebel. The maroons often attacked plantations to get food, weapons, and other items. Their hit-and-run tactics were troublesome to the planters and hard to defend against.

The maroons became a serious threat when a charismatic leader emerged among them about 1750. His name was Macandal, an African-born black. Macandal's "six-year rebellion (1751-57) left an estimated 6,000 dead."[24] The terror he created in Saint Domingue made him famous. Macandal was said to be a sorcerer, skilled in the use of magic and charms. He used "traditional African religions to inspire and unite his followers." Macandal "announced that he was the Black Messiah, sent to drive the whites from the island."[25]

About 1758 Macandal devised a plan to take over the island. He would begin by poisoning the water supply of the city of Le Cap. Once the whites were very sick from drinking the poisoned water, he and his followers would lead the blacks on the island in a great rebellion, which would result in a black takeover of the island. By accident, the plot was discovered, and the fear-stricken planters hunted down Macandal and executed him.[26] Yet even in death he left behind a legacy of unrest, for he prophesied that he would one day return, more terrible than before.[27] Many Negroes, and perhaps some whites, were later to believe that

Toussaint L'Ouverture was the reincarnation of Macandal.[28]

In 1789 there was much discontent in Saint Domingue. The whites wanted to be independent from France; the free coloreds wanted equality with the whites, and the slaves wanted their freedom. Saint Domingue was a powder keg ready to explode. Only a spark was needed to ignite it. The French Revolution provided that spark.

The French Revolution of 1789 began in earnest with the attack on the Bastille, a state prison in Paris. The storming of the Bastille on July 14 felled the government of the king, the night of August 4 destroyed the power of the French nobility, and on August 20, the "Declaration of the Rights of Man" committed the National Assembly to principles which condemned the very bases of colonial society.[29]

When news of the political upheaval in France reached Saint Domingue, it raised the hopes of the people for social and political changes. The poor whites desired political power, and the free coloreds desired equal rights. The free coloreds were also encouraged by the activities of an antislavery society in France called the Amis des Noirs. This society advocated the stopping of the slave trade and the granting of equal rights to the free coloreds. The whites in Saint Domingue, however, were opposed to the granting of equal rights to the free coloreds. As a result, tensions developed between the free coloreds and the whites. In October 1790 a colored named Vincent Orge led a group of 300 coloreds in a revolt against the authorities in Saint Domingue. Orge's revolt was put down and he was brutally executed. The National Assembly in France responded to Orge's brutal execution by passing a decree in the mulattoes' favor on May 15, 1791. The decree gave equal rights to free coloreds born legitimately of free parents. This decree affected only a small group of free coloreds. Yet the whites were opposed to it. They were determined not to yield an inch to the decree. The whites' firm stand made the coloreds even more impatient. A civil war between the two groups seemed inevitable.

Meanwhile, the slaves were watching the growing hostility between the whites and the free coloreds. They too felt the winds of change blowing in the air. Some knew about the French Revolution and its philosophy of "Liberty, Equality, and Fraternity." Others had listened to the whites discuss equality and liberty around the supper tables. Taking advantage of the growing hostility between the whites and the free coloreds, the slaves decided to rebel.

The leader of the plot to rebel was a man named Boukman. Boukman was a maroon and a voodoo priest. He had sworn many slaves into his secret cult. The voodoo ritual bound the initiates together in brotherhood. The voodoo religion was very important to the blacks in their fight for freedom in Saint Domingue. It gave them faith and courage while at the same time uniting and inspiring them. It inspired them to continue fighting despite numerous setbacks and hardships. On the night of August 14, 1791, an important voodoo ceremony was held. At the ceremony directed by Boukman, it was announced that the revolt would begin.

On August 22, 1791, Boukman and his followers began the rebellion, which erupted with great fury. The blacks burned plantations, factories, fields, and other property. They also killed planters and their families. The rebellion increased in size and momentum as it spread. The well-armed whites retaliated against the blacks. There were acts of extreme cruelty on both sides. The rebellion left an estimated ten thousand blacks and two thousand whites dead and more than one thousand plantations sacked and razed.[30] Boukman was killed early in the fighting. The rebellion had begun so suddenly that it had taken the whites by surprise.

The devastating slave rebellion in the north was followed by free colored rebellions in the west and south. The free coloreds were fighting the whites for equal rights. There was bitter fighting between the two groups and heavy losses on both sides. In some instances the planters armed their slaves to fight against the free coloreds. In the north the blacks and the free coloreds united against the whites.

In late November three civil commissioners arrived in Saint Domingue from France. They had come to bring peace to the troubled colony. They got their chance on December 10 when the black insurgent leaders Jean-François and Biassou offered to negotiate with the planters for peace. The terms of the black leaders were as follows: they and their main followers would be allowed to remain free, but the rest of the blacks would be forced back into slavery. The planters scoffed at these terms. They thought the black leaders and their main followers deserved punishment rather than pardon. The negotiations ended in failure. The black insurgents responded to the peace failures by renewing their attacks on the planters. Meanwhile, the conflict between the free coloreds and the whites was raging.

On April 4, 1792, France passed a law that gave the free coloreds equality with the whites. The free coloreds (mulattoes and blacks) were very happy with the news, but the whites were in a state of despair. Given equal rights, the free coloreds began to acquire political power in Saint Domingue. They were aided by the French Republicans. "With the white colonists eclipsed and the slave revolt close to suppression, the spring of 1793...[was] the high point of mulatto control in Saint Domingue."[31]

In June 1793, Le Cap was a city ready to explode. The white colonists had been enraged by the actions of the civil commissioners, who had been sent from France with six thousand troops to insure the enforcement of the law giving equal rights to the free coloreds.

They had quickly angered the whites with their arrogance and manipulative tactics. Commissioner Sonthonax in particular had caused the whites much pain. He had put free coloreds in office and had also recruited large numbers of them for soldiery. On June 20, a fight erupted between the commissioners and their forces and the newly arrived Governor-General Galbaud and his forces. The battle raged fiercely but as the day closed it was clear that the commissioners were losing. If they didn't get help by the next day, they would be defeated. Their help came from black insurgents. "During the night the Commissioners, knowing that they would be beaten on the morrow, had offered plunder and liberty to the"[32] blacks in exchange for their support. The next day thousands of blacks swept into the city of Le Cap. They sacked and burned it. Following the destruction of Le Cap, 10,000 whites left the colony in a fleet of ships for refuge in the United States.

Meanwhile, the situation in Saint Domingue had changed dramatically when Spain and Britain went to war against France in the spring of 1793. The outbreak of war made the French colony of Saint Domingue prey for the Spanish and English. The Spanish made contact with the black insurgents in Saint Domingue and were able to buy the services of the black leaders Jean-François and Biassou. To rally large numbers of blacks to the French cause, Commissioner Sonthonax decided to issue a proclamation abolishing slavery. On August 29, 1793, the proclamation was issued. The strategy backfired on Commissioner Sonthonax, however, as it failed to attract large numbers of blacks to the French cause. After the proclamation was issued, the blacks also became unruly and insubordinate. They no longer wanted to follow orders. Many refused to work in the fields again.

Both the Spanish and the British intervened in the fighting in Saint Domingue. They recruited large numbers of blacks to fight on their side against the French

Republicans. However, the Spanish and English had-n't come to liberate the blacks; rather, their aim was to take control of the colony once the unrest was put down. They wanted to maintain slavery and the plan-tation system in Saint Domingue, which would benefit them greatly economically.

If the blacks in Saint Domingue were to gain their freedom, they would have to fight for it. It wasn't going to be given to them by the Spanish, British, or French. The figure who emerged to lead them to freedom was Toussaint L'Ouverture, soon to be internationally known.

Toussaint L'Ouverture was born about 1743 near the city of Le Cap in the northern part of Saint Domingue. His father had been born in Africa. His master was impressed with his intelligence and trained him as a coachman. He was also taught to read and write. Toussaint possessed the kind of social skills and personality that enabled him to gain various peoples' trust and make them feel at ease with him. The blacks, both free and slave, held him in high regard. He had a good reputation among the white planters; they felt comfortable with him. When the big slave revolt broke out in August 1791, he was in his late forties. In the fall of 1791 Toussaint joined the troops of the black leaders Jean-François and Biassou. His intelligence and natural leadership ability enabled him to immedi-ately rise to a position of high rank within their forces.

When Spain and England went to war against France in the spring of 1793, Toussaint joined the Spanish forces. He was now in command of six hundred black soldiers of his own; he wasn't under Jean-François and Biassou's leadership anymore. Toussaint quickly distinguished himself as a master tactician, skillful at using the terrain to his advantage. "In the great jumble of mountains of the North Prov-ince, he immediately won a series of startling military victories against the French and free coloreds. These early campaigns reveal at once a leader of acute intelligence, who was adept at ambush and at totally confusing his opponents."[33] Toussaint's exploits attracted soldiers to his command. Within a year his forces had increased to four thousand.

In the spring of 1794, Toussaint switched his loyalty from the Spanish to the French Republic. The alert Toussaint had realized that neither the Spanish nor the British intended to emancipate the blacks from slavery. Although the Spanish had promised emancipation, they showed no signs of keeping their word in the territories that they controlled, and the British had reinstated slavery in the areas they occupied.[34] On the other hand, the French had issued a proclamation in February 1794 that emancipated all slaves throughout her colonies. It was a smart move for Toussaint to change sides and fight for the French if the blacks were going to gain their freedom.

Toussaint's decision to desert the Spanish and support the French thrust the Haitian Revolution into high gear. The blacks, led by the brilliant Toussaint, were now fighting for their own cause of self-liberation. This idea of self-liberation gave them direction and a common purpose. It was also a force that drew and bound them together.

Toussaint's game of deception completely caught the Spanish off guard. He had pretended to be loyal right up to the last moment before defecting to the French cause. The Spanish weren't prepared psychologically for this sudden move; it demoralized their forces.

With his growing army, Toussaint attacked the Spanish forces in the north and began to take control of the territory they had conquered. By the beginning of 1795, Toussaint had most of the north under his control and the Spanish were no longer a threat. In the summer of 1795 Spain quit the war against France. According to the Treaty of Bale, the Spanish had to give up Santo Domingo, the other part of Hispaniola, to France. The black leaders Jean-François and

Biassou, who had been fighting for the Spanish, retired from fighting and left the island. Many of their
former soldiers joined Toussaint's army. The departure
of the black leaders worked in Toussaint's favor,
strengthening his army and making him the supreme
black commander.

Toussaint now commanded a good-sized army of
experienced soldiers. In addition to having fought in
Saint Domingue, many of his troops had been soldiers
back in Africa. They had been captured as prisoners of
war in Africa and shipped to Saint Domingue to be
slaves.

Toussaint was unsure of the intentions of the
French Republic concerning the issue of slavery in
Saint Domingue. Although they had abolished slavery,
he knew the French could still restore it if they regained control over the colony. Toussaint believed that
if the blacks were going to be liberated, they would
have to do it themselves. He therefore began to maneuver for power. He was already the main black leader. In
March 1796 his power increased some more. That
month the mulattoes in Le Cap led a coup to rid themselves of Governor Laveaux. However, Toussaint intervened in the coup and forced the mulattoes to release
the governor from prison. The governor was so thankful to Toussaint that he made him lieutenant governor
of Saint Domingue.

Toussaint was now maneuvering to increase his
power in Saint Domingue. In the fall of 1796, he and
Commissioner Sonthonax, who was also maneuvering
for power, decided that Governor Laveaux had to go.
Laveaux was then tricked into being elected deputy for
Saint Domingue and was sent to Paris, out of the way.
Although he wasn't aware of it, the ambitious Commissioner Sonthonax was also in Toussaint's way. In the
summer of 1797, Toussaint suddenly accused him of
plotting to make Saint Domingue independent.[35] Commissioner Sonthonax wasn't ready to leave, but
Toussaint and his soldiers forced him to return to

France. In the spring of 1798, General Hedouville arrived in Saint Domingue to negotiate with Toussaint and to try to check his growing power. Toussaint saw through General Hedouville's game of trying to use the mulattoes to neutralize him. By fall General Hedouville had worn out his welcome in Saint Domingue. The word was spread that he wanted to reinstate slavery. This news aroused strong emotions among the blacks, and they rose up in revolt. General Hedouville was forced to leave for France.

Toussaint's strategy had worked. His double game of pretending to be loyal to France while at the same time maneuvering for power had eliminated the French officials. The Spanish and British also had been expelled from Saint Domingue. The British had held on as long as they could. The British had sent seven thousand additional soldiers to Saint Domingue in the fall of 1795 in an attempt to conquer the colony, but their strong push had ended in failure. The British had been unable to defeat Toussaint and the mulatto leader André Rigaud. Yellow fever had also wreaked havoc on the British soldiers, killing many of them. As a result, the British had been forced to evacuate Saint Domingue in the spring of 1798.

With the Spanish and British driven out and the French officials expelled, Toussaint now controlled the north and west of Saint Domingue. The south was controlled by the mulatto leader Rigaud, the only rival left to compete with Toussaint for control of the colony.

Toussaint and Rigaud were unable to settle their differences. Both men wanted to rule Saint Domingue, but there could be only one ruler. The French had a hand in preventing the two leaders from settling their differences. The French had stirred up the animosity that existed between the mulattoes and the blacks. Their strategy was to pit the mulatto Rigaud against the black Toussaint. When they came to blows, the French would take advantage of it or simply divide and rule. The coming struggle between the blacks and the mulattoes was inevitable; emotions were rising on both sides. In the summer of 1799, a very bitter struggle broke out between Toussaint and Rigaud. The conflict was called the War Between the Castes, pitting the light-skinned blacks against the dark-skinned blacks. The conflict raged on into the next year. In July 1800 Rigaud's forces suffered a devastating defeat at Acquin, and he fled the island soon afterwards. Toussaint was now the one and only ruler of Saint Domingue.

As ruler of Saint Domingue, Toussaint did his best to rebuild a war-torn land. He encouraged the production of sugar, coffee, and other crops for use at home and for export. He tried to heal the deep wounds that the internal fighting had created. He tried to be fair to everyone, yet he had to be firm to command the people's respect.

In January 1801 Toussaint and his forces invaded the former Spanish colony of Santo Domingo and conquered it. This put the whole island of Hispaniola in Toussaint's hands. The invasion and capture of Santo Domingo was a strategic move on Toussaint's part. But to the French it was an act of defiance because Santo Domingo belonged to France as part of the Treaty of Bale. Napoleon Bonaparte, who had just come to power in France, was very angry when he learned of Toussaint's capture of Santo Domingo. This black ex-slave had the audacity to disrespect France in the eyes of the world. This act of defiance was too much for Napoleon. He was now convinced that he would have to send troops to Saint Domingue to restore French rule and teach Toussaint a lesson.

In the summer of 1801 a new constitution was drawn up for Saint Domingue. It formally recognized Toussaint as master of the colony. He was proclaimed governor-general for life with the authority to select his successor. The new constitution also made Saint Domingue an independent state in practice, but not officially. The new constitution was another act of defiance by Toussaint, and it increased Napoleon's anger.

Napoleon was now anxious to begin the invasion of Saint Domingue, but before he could begin it, he first needed British approval for his ships to cross the Atlantic Ocean. British approval came in October 1801, when the two countries signed the Peace of Preliminaries of Amiens.

Napoleon gathered twenty thousand of his best troops for the invasion of Saint Domingue. He put his brother-in-law, General Charles Leclerc, in charge of the expedition. The troops didn't all arrive in Saint Domingue at the same time. Twelve thousand arrived in late January 1802. Two weeks later, in mid-February 4,500 more arrived. The rest came later. Leclerc and his forces faced the black general Toussaint L'Ouverture and his twenty thousand seasoned troops.

Napoleon's plan to conquer the colony was divided into three phases. In the first phase Toussaint and his generals were to be flattered and treated very well as a strategy to gain their trust and confidence. Once Leclerc had gained the trust of Toussaint and his generals and had established his troops in the colony, it was time for the next phase. In the second phase resistance was to be put down and the island seized. In the third and final phase, Toussaint and his officers were to be sent to France and the whole black population was to be disarmed. The removal of the leadership would "break the spirit of the black masses."

Leclerc, the French general, decided to begin the fighting immediately. Toussaint had observed the large French fleet from a distance. His strategy was to draw Leclerc into the mountains, his stronghold, and fight him there. The French soon gained control over the port towns. The town of Le Cap was burned by Henri Christophe, one of Toussaint's generals, and the town of Leogane was burned by Jean-Jacques Dessalines, another of Toussaint's generals. Toussaint's policy was to burn and destroy so the French couldn't live off the land. The heavy fighting began when Leclerc and his troops reached the mountains, where Toussaint and his troops were lodged. The fighting was fierce, and large numbers of soldiers were killed on both sides. The black generals Toussaint, Christophe, and Dessalines put up a brave resistance but in the end the tide turned in the favor of the French and their allies—the mulattoes and white colonists. In late March the French took Toussaint's stronghold of Crete-a-Pierrot, which was a big blow to the blacks. In early April Toussaint's general, Christophe, surrendered to the French and became an officer in their army. In May Toussaint and Dessalines also surrendered to the French. Dessalines became an officer in the French army, whereas Toussaint went home to live on his plantation. However, "the French believed and many modern historians say that the cagey general [Toussaint] was waiting for yellow fever to decimate the ranks of his enemies."[36] Then he was going to strike them.

Although Leclerc, had successfully put down resistance in Saint Dominque, he had lost half of his troops in the process of doing so. With an army at half strength, he didn't have the muscle to carry out Napoleon's orders of disarming the blacks and sending the black officers to France. If he attempted Napoleon's orders, there would surely be much resistance. Leclerc was now in an unfavorable position. Things got worse when the dreaded yellow fever hit his camp around the middle of May and his troops began to die by the hundreds.

In June, with the yellow fever situation getting worse, Leclerc decided that Toussaint was too dangerous a man to be left alone on his plantation. He believed that Toussaint was planning a rebellion against the French. A clever trap was then set to capture Toussaint. The bait for the clever trap was a charming letter, skillfully written, to disarm Toussaint and lure him to his enemies. African-American historian Lerone Bennett describes the charming letter:

> Like most conquerors, Toussaint was vain. There came to his plantation one day a letter calculated to appeal to his vanity. The letter, couched in deferential, respectful terms, was from General Brunet, one of Leclerc's aides. Could Toussaint come to Brunet's headquarters for an important conference? He would not find all the comforts Brunet would like to put at his disposal, but he would find, the letter said, a "frank and honest man, whose only ambition is to promote the welfare of the colony and your happiness."[37]

The charming letter was a work of art in deception. It completely won over Toussaint and made him drop his guard. Toussaint, unarmed and not suspecting trickery, walked into the trap. He was subsequently put in chains and taken to France by ship. In France, "Napoleon refused to see him, and sent him to a bleak prison in the Alps, where he died of tuberculosis."[38]

After Toussaint's departure, Leclerc decided to try to disarm the black population of Saint Domingue. He was successful in the south and west but encountered much difficulty in the north. Suddenly word came that France had restored slavery in her colony of Guadeloupe. The blacks of Saint Domingue, thinking they would suffer the same fate, rebelled against Leclerc. As the weeks passed Leclerc's position grew worse. His soldiers continued to die daily from yellow fever, and the black rebellion grew stronger. In October Leclerc suffered a big blow when the colored general Clervaux deserted the French and took his soldiers with him. The coloreds had become uneasy when they learned about the situation in Guadeloupe. There the French had taken away equal rights from the coloreds, which they had earlier granted to them. The coloreds in Saint Domingue believed the French would do the same to them. Within a week of Clervaux's desertion, the black general Christophe also deserted the French.

Next other black officers deserted the French, including Dessalines. On November 2, 1802, Leclerc, died from yellow fever. He was replaced by the ruthless General Rochambeau, who was brutal in his war with the blacks.

In May 1803 the French and British began to fight again. This forced Napoleon to focus his attention on the war with Britain in Europe. His attempt to conquer the blacks in Saint Domingue had failed. Meanwhile, the energetic black general Dessalines, known as "The Tiger," had become the leader of the black and colored forces. He led them in driving the French from the colony. In November 1803 General Rochambeau surrendered, ending France's attempt to restore her rule in Saint Domingue. On January 1, 1804, General Dessalines proclaimed Saint Domingue independent and gave it the name *Haiti*, an Indian name.

The Haitian Revolution was one of the greatest in world history. It began as a slave revolt and emerged as a successful revolution. The Haitian Revolution was an inspiration to slaves in the Americas, but it frightened slave owners everywhere. The blacks' struggle for freedom in Haiti was filled with adversity and setbacks, yet in the end they were victorious. Their self-liberation was a remarkable achievement.

The Haitian Revolution also contributed to the growth of the United States. The story begins with Napoleon. Napoleon had a "plan to create a great French empire in the New World."[39] The Louisiana Territory was already in his hands. He was going to use it to supply Haiti with food and other goods. Haiti was going to be his all-important base of operations and the center of his empire. But before he could get started creating his empire, he first needed to recapture Haiti from the rebellious blacks. President Thomas Jefferson, realizing the threat to the United States if Napoleon retook Haiti and established a base there, allowed guns and ammunition to be shipped to the blacks. The French were unable to recapture Haiti from the blacks and were defeated. This defeat was a major factor in spoiling Napoleon's plans of creating a large empire in the New World. As a result, he sold the Louisiana Territory to the United States for about fifteen million dollars in April 1803. The Louisiana Purchase nearly doubled the size of the United States, expanding its area westward to the Rocky Mountains. But if French forces had conquered Haiti, Napoleon wouldn't have sold the Louisiana Territory to the United States. From his base in Haiti, he would have begun the conquest of the Caribbean Islands and would have attempted to expand the Louisiana Territory in North America. If French forces had been able to conquer Haiti, Napoleon might have grown into a monster. Under those threatening circumstances, the United States might not have been able to expand westward, grow in size, and develop into the world's most powerful and wealthiest nation.

The Haitian Revolution was an inspiration to blacks throughout the Caribbean Islands. It made them desire their freedom more and more. It also inspired them to revolt. In 1816 a large slave rebellion erupted in Barbados. In 1831 another big slave rebellion erupted, this time in Jamaica. These serious slave revolts caused many people to believe that slavery had to be abolished in the Caribbean. In 1833 slavery was abolished in Jamaica and in the following year, 1834, it was abolished in Barbados. The following countries abolished slavery in all their Caribbean territories: Britain in 1838, France and Denmark in 1848, and the Netherlands in 1863. The slaves in Puerto Rico were freed in 1873, and in Cuba the slaves were freed in 1886.

In summary, Africans were brought to the Caribbean in 1501 to provide labor for the plantations and mines. The life of African slaves in the Caribbean was filled with pain, suffering, and indignities. Despite all the adversity, blacks adjusted to the institution of slavery and survived it. In addition to contributing to the economic prosperity of the Caribbean with their hard labor, the blacks also contributed to the culture of the Caribbean Islands with their music, religion, dance, poetry, art, and language. The descendants of African slaves live throughout the Caribbean Islands today.

Blacks in Mexico, Central America, and South America

Africans accompanied Europeans in the exploration of Mexico, Central America, and South America. During these ventures with Europeans, they were soldiers, slaves, servants, and explorers. There were thirty Africans in the expedition of the Spanish explorer, Vasco Nuñez de Balboa, when he marched across the Isthmus of Panama and saw the Pacific Ocean for the first time in 1513. One African in Balboa's expedition was a nobleman, Nuflo de Olano. Africans were also in other Spanish expeditions. Two hundred Africans were with Hernando Cortés when he went to Mexico. One African in this expedition, Juan Garrido, "planted and harvested the first wheat crop in the New World."[40] In South America, Sebastián Benalcázar, the founder of Quito, listed three black men as his companions and co-founders of the city, and their names are carved in stone in the original plaza there.[41] Africans were also in Francisco Pizarro's expedition to Peru and Diego de Almagro's expedition to Chile.

The colonizing of Mexico, Central America, and South America created a huge demand for labor. Large numbers of workers were needed to work in the mines and in agriculture. The Spanish and the Portuguese first used Indian slaves to do their hard labor. But when the Indians died in large numbers, they began to bring in thousands of Africans to do the heavy labor. During the course of slavery, millions of Africans were uprooted from their homes in Africa and brought to Mexico, Central America, and South America. Africans provided slave labor in Mexico, Panama, Guatemala,

Chile, Argentina, Brazil, Peru, and other countries of mainland Latin America.

Cortés invaded the Aztec Empire of Mexico in 1519. Two years later, in 1521, he had conquered the Aztecs and was in control of the country. After the conquest, the Spanish established settlements and began to exploit the land for its wealth. Needing large numbers of laborers to work in the mines and in agriculture, the Spanish began to import Africans to Mexico in large numbers. About 1550, Africans outnumbered Spaniards in Mexico. And by the end of the sixteenth century, over sixty thousand Africans had been brought to Mexico. In the seventeenth century thousands of Africans continued to be imported. In all, at least two hundred thousand Africans were brought to Mexico during its slave period. In addition, Mexico was a major market for selling African slaves.

In Mexico African slaves did hard and often dangerous work for their masters. They performed backbreaking labor in the silver mines. They worked on the haciendas herding livestock, often under harsh conditions. They worked long and hard on the sugar cane and cacao plantations, reaping wealth for their owners. In the urban areas they worked as domestic servants and as skilled craftsmen.

There was heavy race mixing among the Indians, blacks, and whites in Mexico. The black-white mixtures were called *mulattoes*, the black-Indian mixtures were called *chinos* or *zambos*, and the Indian-white mixtures were called *mestizos*.

Due to their heavy intermixing with the Indians and whites, blacks are no longer identifiable as a distinct group in Mexico. Today, Mexicans are generally identified racially as mestizos and Indians, but if their roots were traced, some of them would have African ancestry. "This is especially true...[in] the states of Guerrero and Oaxaca; the warm regions of the Gulf, [such] as the city of Veracruz; and parts of the Pacific coast."[42]

Presently in Mexico there exist communities whose inhabitants are of African-mestizo descent. Authors Michael Conniff and Thomas Davis comment on Afro-Mexicans:

> Until recently, Mexican authorities chose to ignore this small Afro-mestizo presence. Today, however, local officials have begun to organize carnivals to celebrate the foundations of such towns, playing up African vestiges in attempts to attract tourists from Africa. Afro-mestizo artisans, musicians, dancers, and storytellers have gained deserved recognition, for both their talents and the history they have preserved. One contingent even participated in the Smithsonian Institution's Quincentenary Folklife Program in 1992, joining other maroon groups from the Americas in celebrating the lives of Africans and their descendants in the hemisphere.[43]

The Central American country of Panama was colonized by the Spanish in 1510. The Spanish in Panama first used Indians to do their slave labor. But when European diseases and the cruelty of enslavement caused the Indian population to decrease rapidly, the Spanish turned to Africans for their slave labor. By the 1520s there was a fairly large number of Africans in Panama. As the decades passed, the demand for African slave labor steadily increased. As a result, Africans were brought to Panama in larger numbers.

African slaves in Panama worked in various jobs. They drove pack trains of mules loaded down with goods across the Isthmus. Slaves who performed this difficult and dangerous job usually died within seven years and new imports from Africa were brought in to replace them. Slaves also worked as domestics in Panama. In addition, slaves built and repaired ships for the trade along the Pacific coast; they worked in furniture factories that produced goods for West Coast Spanish settlements; and they mined gold in the region throughout the colonial period.[44]

In present-day Panama blacks and mulattoes comprise about a third of the country's population. Many of these Afro-Panamanians are descended from slaves who were brought to Panama from Africa. Some Afro-Panamanians, however, are descended from black West Indians who came to Panama to build the Panama Canal. Carlos Mendoza, a past president of Panama, was "a dark mulatto."

Africans were also brought to Guatemala, Honduras, Nicaragua, El Salvador, and Costa Rica, but in smaller numbers. In these Central American countries, black slaves worked on ranches and farms, in gold mines, and as domestic servants.

People of African descent live in the present-day countries of Guatemala, Honduras, Costa Rica, and Nicaragua, mainly along the Caribbean coast. Blacks comprise about 2 percent of the population of Costa Rica. In Honduras blacks comprise a very small percentage of the population. In Nicaragua blacks and mulattoes comprise about 11 percent of the population. A small number of blacks also live in Guatemala and El Salvador.

Large numbers of Africans were brought to South America. Their slave labor was very important to the development and economic prosperity of the continent.

Pedro Cabral, a Portuguese mariner, made contact with Brazil in 1500. In 1531 the Portuguese began the colonization of Brazil. The Portuguese first used Indian labor but in 1538 they started to bring in enslaved Africans to help meet their growing labor demands. As the decades passed, more Africans were brought to Brazil to provide labor for the expanding sugar industry. A population count in 1585 listed fifty-seven thousand inhabitants in the colony, and of these fourteen thousand were Africans. In the 1600s, 1700s, and 1800s millions of enslaved Africans were brought to Brazil. While the Brazilian historian, Calogeras, insists that at least eighteen million were brought into the country, his fellow countryman, Ramos, asserts that not more than five million Negroes actually arrived in Brazil.[45]

The African slaves in Brazil worked as laborers in the fields and mines, as domestic servants, and as skilled craftsmen. Many Africans brought to Brazil already possessed knowledge of agriculture, mining, metalworking, and weaving. The field slaves in Brazil had the most difficult time. They were required to work long, hard hours. If they neglected their duties they were whipped or tortured by an overseer. The field slaves worked on plantations that grew sugar, cacao, coffee, and other crops. Large numbers of slaves worked in the gold mines, a hard and risky job. A slave would be very tired after a long day's work in the mines, laboring with a pick and shovel. Domestic servants on the plantations had somewhat easier jobs than the field slaves. They were cooks, maids, butlers, and coachmen. The women and girls were often sexually exploited by their slave masters. Sometimes the slave masters' wives became so jealous of their husbands' attractive black and mulatto mistresses that they had the women whipped or tortured. Some slaves were skilled craftsmen: carpenters, masons, coopers, and jewelers. Slaves who lived in urban areas were generally "allowed more freedom of movement" than slaves who worked on rural plantations. Slaves in urban areas worked as domestic servants, skilled craftsmen, laborers, and in other ways. Some were hired out by their masters to work for other people. The slave masters received the income, of course, but in some instances they shared the money with their slaves. A skilled slave such as a craftsman might make enough money over a period of time to buy his freedom.

From the beginning of Portuguese colonization in Brazil, there was widespread mixing of the races. With white women in short supply, the Portuguese men mated with the Indian women, producing the *mestizo*. African male slaves, lacking African women to mate with, mated with the Indian women; their offspring were called *zambos*. The Portuguese men also mixed with African women, producing the mulatto. In addition, the mulattoes, zambos, and meztizos also mixed among themselves.

The racial policy adopted by Brazil for the classification of the mulatto is the direct opposite of the policy adopted by the United States. In Brazil a mulatto can officially pass as white, whereas in the United States a mulatto is considered black. Passing as white enables light-skinned blacks in Brazil today to get better treatment than dark-skinned blacks. However, Brazil's racial policy in effect encourages many mulattoes to reject their African ancestry.

Africans were brought to Brazil in such great numbers that they eventually comprised the majority of the population. According to a 1798 survey, there were 1,010,000 whites, 1,582,000 slaves, 406,000 free blacks, and 250,000 civilized Indians in Brazil. A population estimate in 1822 listed a little over one million whites, around two million blacks, and about a half-million mulattoes.

Beginning in the 1850s European immigrants came to Brazil in increasing numbers. A population count in 1872 listed 3,787,289 whites, 1,954,542 blacks, and 4,188,737 *pardos* (mulattoes). As a result of whitening campaigns, the white population in Brazil increased rapidly. By 1940, whites were in the majority in Brazil, comprising about 63 percent of the population. The whitening campaigns encouraged Europeans to migrate to Brazil. They also resulted in mulattoes and blacks whitening themselves; mulattoes classified themselves as white, and blacks classified themselves as mulattoes. A 1950 census count in Brazil listed 30,027,661 whites, 5,692,657 blacks, and 13,786,742 pardos.

The immigration of Europeans to Brazil, blacks whitening themselves, and the intermixing of the races have led to a decline in the percentage of blacks in the Brazilian population. However, people of African descent still comprise a sizable portion of the population of present-day Brazil. There are an estimated 60 million people in Brazil of African descent, making them the largest concentration of African people outside Africa.

The Golden Law freed blacks in Brazil in 1888. Although they were freed, very little was done to help them adjust to life as freedmen. They still faced injustice and inequality. As a result, they were forced to accept menial jobs in order to survive. In the twentieth century they remained at the bottom of the social ladder. In 1931 Afro-Brazilians founded an organization called the Brazilian Black Front. The purpose of this organization was to fight for equality and justice for Afro-Brazilians. The successes of the organization enabled it to attract new members. However, it was seen as a potential threat and banned by the government in 1937.

Brazilian sociologist Gilberto Freyre, writing in the 1930s, described Brazil as a *racial democracy*. According to Freye, race didn't determine a person's status in Brazilian society. Visitors who go to Brazil expecting to see pure democracy at work in this regard are disappointed to note few very dark-skinned people among the well-to-do or the professional classes and to watch the heavy menial labor done by markedly Negroid and Indian types.[46] Brazilians explain away this situation by saying it is based on class rather than race. Racial democracy does not exist in Brazil; blacks there still experience prejudice and injustice. The term racial democracy has been used to disguise a subtle, confusing, elusive type of racism in Brazil, which is hard to fight because it is not open and clear. Being subtle and elusive, this type of racism can always be denied.

Africans contributed much to Brazil. They participated in the exploration, conquest, and defense of the country. Their slave labor was vital to the survival of colonial Brazil. Africans also influenced the music, religion, dance, folklore, language, dress, and cuisine of

Brazil. The Portuguese language as spoken in Brazil, the largest and most important Portuguese-speaking nation, is said to have softer sounds, less harsh consonants because of the African influence.[47] The *samba*, the famous Brazilian dance, is of African origin. African slaves from Angola brought a form of martial arts to Brazil called *capoeira*. With its kicks and punches, capoeira was so deadly that it had to be outlawed by the authorities. It was subsequently turned into a dance. Today, however, blacks are allowed to perform capoeira. Also some of them practice a religion of African origin called Candomble. The blacks in Brazil were able to retain more of their African culture than blacks in the United States. The outstanding artist of colonial Brazil, Aleijandinho, and the one outstanding classical composer, Jose Mauricio, were both of African blood.[48]

African soldiers participated in Francisco Pizzaro's conquest of Peru in the early 1530s. After the conquest many Spaniards came to Peru. Some brought enslaved Africans with them. These Africans were used as soldiers and as laborers. As the decades passed, more and more Africans were brought to Peru. Their labor became essential to the growing Spanish colony. They worked on the plantations producing sugar, grain, wine, and other products. They also worked in the silver mines in the Andes Mountains. A population estimate in 1622 listed thirty thousand Africans in Peru, with twenty-two thousand living in the city of Lima. A population count in 1791 listed forty thousand blacks in Peru of a total population of approximately 1,250,000.

Today in Peru blacks comprise less than 2 percent of the population. After the abolition of slavery, no more Africans were imported into the country. The ones who remained have practically been absorbed into the general population.

One hundred fifty Africans accompanied Diego de Almagro in the conquest of Chile in 1535. An African named Juan Valiento was awarded land and Indian servants for his bravery in warfare against the Indians. Other Africans also received land and Indian servants for their bravery in battle.

The Spanish imported large numbers of Africans into Chile. African slaves worked on the plantations growing crops, on the ranches herding livestock, in the gold mines, and as domestic servants in the towns. A population count about 1791 listed thirty thousand blacks and mulattoes out of a population of five hundred thousand in Chile.

The abolition of slavery in Chile stopped the importation of Africans. Today population data do not list blacks as part of the Chilean population. They have been absorbed into the general population.

In colonial times Bolivia was called Upper Peru. African slaves were brought to Bolivia but not in large numbers. They worked as laborers on the ranches, as laborers in the silver mines, and as domestic servants. There was much race mixing between the blacks and the native Indian population in Bolivia. Blacks exist in present-day Bolivia but in small numbers.

Large numbers of Africans were brought into Venezuela by the Spanish. They worked on the coastal plantations growing indigo, cacao, and other crops; they herded livestock on the ranches; they worked in the gold mines. Caracas was a large slave-trading market. A population count in 1810 recorded nine hundred thousand people living in Venezuela, of whom 493,000 were blacks and mulattoes. A number of Venezuelans of African blood distinguished themselves in Venezuela's war of independence from Spain, including Pedro Camejo, known as *El Negro Primero*, and General Manuel Piar, a brilliant military strategist. Venezuela has also had four mulatto presidents.

The percentage of blacks in Venezuela has declined since the abolition of slavery in 1854. In 1929 blacks were barred from migrating to the country. Today people of African descent comprise 10 percent of the population of Venezuela; they live mostly near the coast.

The Spanish brought large numbers of Africans to Colombia and Ecuador. These Africans provided slave labor for agriculture, logging, loading and unloading ships, and gold mining. They also worked as domestic servants. Cartagena was a large and well-known slave-trading market. In 1810 there were 1.4 million people in Colombia (including Panama also), of whom 210,000 were blacks and mulattoes. A population count in 1810 listed 600,000 inhabitants in Ecuador, of whom fifty thousand were black

The people of African descent in present-day Colombia and Ecuador live mainly along the coast. Colombia's population is about "32 percent...[black and] mulatto."[49] Ecuador's population is about 10 percent black.

In the 1500s the Spanish began bringing enslaved Africans to Argentina. Over the centuries large numbers of Africans were imported to Argentina, where they worked in the fields cultivating crops, on ranches herding livestock, and as domestic servants. In 1778 the city of Buenos Aires was populated by 24,363 people, of whom 7,256 were black (30 percent). A population count in 1852 listed about 800,000 people living in Argentina: twenty-two thousand whites, fifteen thousand blacks and 110,000 mulattoes, and the remainder mestizo and Indian.

White campaigns in the late 1800s and early 1900s encouraged the migration of millions of Europeans to Argentina. As a result, Argentina changed from a non-white nation into a mainly white one.

Although blacks once comprised a significant portion of the population of Argentina, they now exist in very small numbers there. They are found mainly in the city of Buenos Aires, the capital. "Throughout the twentieth century...Buenos Aires blacks have maintained a separate identity. Their organizations staged carnival parades, and they have continued to publish an African American newspaper."[50] Presently, it is estimated that about three or four thousand blacks live in the city of Buenos Aires, which has a population of over eleven million.

People of African descent have practically disappeared in Argentina because of the heavy influx of European immigrants and being absorbed through race mixing. Also large numbers of black soldiers died fighting in Argentina's wars, which created a shortage of black men with whom black women could mate. General José San Martín, the liberator, had numerous blacks in his army. Black slaves could gain their freedom by fighting in the army. One of the most spectacular figures of the Argentine wars was an unmixed Negro, Antonio Ruiz, "El Negro Falucho," who on the night of February 3, 1810, was surprised by the rebels while on guard, and died rather than pull down the flag.[51] He is "Argentina's black hero." "A monument stands...[in] his honor in Buenos Aires."[52]

Large numbers of Africans were imported into Uruguay and Paraguay during the slave era. They provided labor for the cultivation of crops, for livestock raising, and for domestic service. Montevideo, the capital of Uruguay, had a population of 4,726 inhabitants in 1803, of which 1,040 were black. Today people of African descent comprise less than 4 percent of the country's population. Several factors have contributed to their disappearance: large numbers of Europeans migrating to Uruguay, large numbers of black soldiers killed in Uruguay's wars, and absorption through race mixing. In Paraguay, the blacks who were once there have been absorbed into the general population.

The country of Suriname was once called Dutch Guiana. The Dutch began bringing enslaved Africans to Suriname in the 1600s. Their labor was needed to cultivate crops on the plantations. In present-day Suriname blacks comprise 10 percent of the population and Creoles (mulattoes are called Creoles there) comprise 35 percent of the population. Suriname also has a large Asian population, about 34 percent.

French Guiana was colonized by France about 1604. Later in the 1600s, Africans began to be imported into the colony to labor on the plantations. Today people of African descent, blacks and Creoles (mulattoes), comprise 90 percent of French Guiana's population.

Guyana was formerly called British Guiana, but it was first colonized by the Dutch in the 1620s. Africans were brought to the colony to work on the sugar plantations in the latter 1600s. In present-day Guyana blacks and Creoles (mulattoes) comprise about 40 percent of the total population. Also descendants of indentured servants from Asia (East Indians) comprise about half of Guyana's population.

The slave laws of mainland Latin America (Mexico, Central America, and South America) were devised to control the Africans. They were similar to the slave laws of the Caribbean. Slaves were punished for running away and stealing, two serious offenses. For these offenses they could be seriously whipped or their bodies could be mutilated. Examples of punishment by mutilation were slashing of the ears, breaking a leg, and branding the face. In some cities slaves were required to be with their masters when walking the streets at night, and if they weren't, they were punished by whippings or having their bodies mutilated. Disobedient slaves were punished. A slave considered dangerous was harshly dealt with. If he couldn't be captured alive, the authorities would give a bounty for his head. Slaves were punished for insulting, striking, or killing a white person. The punishment could be a hundred lashes, body mutilation, or death, depending on the severity of the offense. Blacks were forbidden to wear certain clothes or jewelry. There were laws for protecting the slaves but enforcing them was the problem.

Historians have generally described slavery in Latin America as mild compared to slavery in the United States. This is a misconception. Slaves were at the mercy of a cruel slave master in Latin America just as they were in the United States and the Caribbean. In Latin America, slave women were sexually exploited just as they were in other parts of the New World. Probably the main reason why slavery has been described as relatively mild in Latin America is that the Spanish and Portuguese readily mixed their blood with the Africans. This has been seen by some as a "showing of greater respect to blacks as human beings." But the real reason why the Spanish and Portuguese intermixed so freely with African and Indian women was that they didn't bring many white women with them. On the other hand, in the United States, the English brought more of their women with them and there was less race mixing.

One way Africans resisted slavery in mainland Latin America was by running away. These runaway slaves established maroon communities in dense forests, mountains, and other inaccessible places where they could defend themselves. The maroons raided plantations and attacked travelers. Maroons were also called *cimarrons.*

There is a very interesting story about a runaway slave in Panama. His name was King Bayamo. Taking to the mountains with a number of other slaves, Bayamo set up a kingdom of his own, from where he descended on the pack-trains of the Spaniards, capturing a great quantity of gold, silver, and precious stones.[53] After much difficulty, the Spanish were eventually able to defeat the elusive Bayamo and his men. Finally captured, Bayamo was taken before the Spanish viceroy, who not only received him with honors for his bravery and resourcefulness but sent him a free man to Spain where he lived in luxury from the loot he had captured.[54]

In northeastern Brazil, Africans established a large runaway community called the Republic of Palmares. The name Palmares was derived from the many palm trees in the area. The Palmares story began about

1595, when a small group of runaway slaves fled to the dense forests. As time passed more and more runaway slaves joined them. The community these runaway slaves founded eventually grew into the black state of Palmares, which at its peak had over twenty thousand inhabitants. The blacks of Palmares grew vegetables, fruit, cotton, corn, and other products for themselves and for trade. They traded with whites and Indians living in towns and villages near them. The capital of the black state was at Cerca Real do Macaco. The king lived there and was assisted by a minister of justice, guards, and many military and civil servants.[55] Zumbi, the king of Palmares at its peak, ruled over thousands of subjects and commanded a guard reported to number five thousand.[56] These blacks of Palmares "were very effectively organized, both socially and politically, in their African manner and tradition, and were highly skilled in the art of war."[57]

The blacks of Palmares were determined to live as free men and women. Their communities were well fortified to thwart invasions. They successfully resisted twenty-seven Dutch and Portuguese invasions over a period of sixty years. But the Portuguese were determined to destroy Palmares. In 1696 they sent out a well-organized army to lay siege to the city. The battle for the city was long and hard, as the blacks fought heroically. The audacity, resourcefulness, and courage of the defenders have caused the siege to be described as the "Black Troy."[58] But in the end the city was taken. The king and his main followers jumped from a promontory to their deaths rather than surrender to the Portuguese.

Palmares was a remarkable political and economic achievement for the fugitive slaves of Brazil.[59] They developed a small runaway community into a well-organized free black state with over twenty thousand inhabitants. Their defense of Palmares against invasions was a remarkable display of courage and determination.

Another way Africans resisted slavery in mainland Latin America was by rebellion. A few of the slave revolts will be mentioned here. There was a slave revolt in Panama in 1531. In 1537 a group of black and Indian slaves plotted to take over Mexico City. The plot failed, however, when a slave among them revealed the plot. As a result, twenty-four of them were put to death. There were also slave revolts in Mexico in 1669 and 1735. There were violent slave rebellions in Colombia in 1550 and 1555. There were numerous slave rebellions in Brazil. In 1772 blacks and Indians there united against the whites. The rebellion was put down after much difficulty. In the state of Bahia, Brazil, African Muslim slaves carried out a series of deadly revolts against the whites. In 1807, 1809, 1813, and 1816 there were outbreaks in Bahia.[60] In 1835 Muslim blacks carried out a large rebellion in Bahia. The uprising was not put down until after the entire city of Bahia had been thoroughly terrified and many persons killed and wounded.[61] These Islamized Hausa Africans from the Sudan were engaging in holy wars against their slave masters. Some of them were literate in Arabic, and they possessed numerous skills, not the least appreciated of which were gold-mining techniques.[62]

Slavery ended at different times in mainland Latin America. In Mexico slavery was ended by its president of African descent, Vicente Guerrero, in 1829. Guerrero was a mulatto. Slavery was abolished in Central America in 1824. Slavery was abolished in the other countries as follows: Colombia, 1851; Ecuador, 1852; Uruguay and Argentina, 1853; Venezuela and Peru, 1854; Bolivia, 1861; and Paraguay 1869. Brazil was the last country in the Americas to emancipate its slaves in 1888.

Africans first came to mainland Latin America with the early Spanish explorers. They participated in the exploration and conquest of mainland Latin America, serving as aides, servants, slaves, soldiers, and explorers. Later, millions of enslaved Africans were brought to mainland Latin America to work on the plantations and ranches, and in the mines. After slavery they had to adjust to life as freedmen, which wasn't easy. As freedmen they faced inequality and prejudice, often so subtle that they were hard to fight. In the United States blacks have struggled against prejudice and discrimination, but in mainland Latin America those obstacles haven't been blacks main fight, rather their main fight has been to survive as a distinct black people and to prevent themselves from being assimilated.

Blacks in the United States

The year 1619 is generally given in history books as the date blacks first arrived in what is now the United States. Blacks, however, first arrived in what is now the United States over a century earlier.

Blacks accompanied the Spanish explorers and colonizers when they first came to what is now the United States in the 1500s. The explorer Ponce de Leon arrived in Florida in 1513. There he searched for the mythical Fountain of Youth but, of course, didn't find it. "One of the leaders of...[his expedition] was"[63] of African descent. This mulatto's name was Pedro Mexia. There were Africans with Hernando de Soto when he explored the southeastern United States from 1539 to 1542, searching for gold and other riches. One African in his expedition became ill and was left behind in present-day Alabama among the Native Americans. They were amazed at his dark skin and wooly hair and wanted him to stay with them. Dark-skinned Indians found later in this area are thought to have been his descendants. Africans participated in the expedition of the explorer Francisco Coronado. Coronado searched parts of the southwest (present-day Arizona, New Mexico, Texas, and Kansas) from 1540 to 1542, looking for the "fabulous Seven Cities" rumored to be filled with gold. He came up empty in his search, however. Africans, serving as soldiers and slaves, were with Lucas de Ayllon when he founded a Spanish colony in what is now Virginia or North Carolina in 1526. Harsh treatment caused the African slaves with Ayllon to rebel. The colony failed and the Spanish abandoned it. The Spanish also used African slaves to help build the town of St. Augustine, Florida, in 1565. Today, St. Augustine has the distinction of being the oldest city in the United States.

The best-known black explorer with the Spanish was a giant Moor named Estevanico, who was a servant of the Spaniard Andres Dorantes. Estevanico was "born in Azamore, Morocco."[64] He was described as being "very black with thick lips." Estevanico and his master were members of Pánfilo de Narváez's expedition that reached Florida in 1528. Narváez, believing that great riches were in Florida, began searching for it with his men. However, they failed to find the gold that they were looking for. They then returned to the Florida coast and discovered that the expedition's ships had abandoned them. The stranded crew, needing ships, "killed their horses on the beach and from the horsehides constructed five small ships."[65] The crew's goal was to sail to Mexico. The small, crude ships didn't hold up in the rough sea, however, and "by the time they arrived at Galveston Island all the boats were wrecked...[and] there were only eighty survivors...."[66] Hardships during the winter reduced the eighty to fifteen. The fifteen survivors were captured by the Indians and enslaved. Four survived "six years of"[67] Indian enslavement before finally escaping. The four survivors were Estevanico, an officer named Álvar Núñez Cabeza de Vaca, and two others. These four disguised themselves as medicine men to hoodwink the Indians and began wandering aimlessly from place to place. They traveled through present-day New Mexico, Arizona, and perhaps California before reaching a town in northern Mexico called Culiacán in 1536. Cabeza de Vaca, writing of this long journey, had nothing but praise of Estevanico as an equal.[68]

In 1538 Estevanico led an expedition that "opened up New Mexico and Arizona for the Spaniards."[69] The expedition started in Mexico and proceeded northward into the present-day southwestern United States. Traveling in front of his party, Estevanico eventually arrived at a large Pueblo town, thought to be one of the "fabulous Seven Cities." The Indians had been watching Estevanico's approach, and when he "entered the city, the Indians killed him, believing him to be an imposter when he said that he was the emissary of two white men."[70] However, Estevanico's exploits as a trailblazer paved the way for Spanish settlement in what is now the southwestern United States.

The first permanent English settlement in the United States was established at Jamestown, Virginia in 1607. Twelve years later, in 1619, a Dutch ship with a cargo of twenty Africans arrived in the Virginia colony. The captain of the ship exchanged the Africans for food. The names of three of these Africans were Pedro, Anthony, and Isabella. In 1624 a child was born to the union of Anthony and Isabella; he was named William Tucker.

The first Africans brought into the Virginia colony were classified as servants, not slaves. A 1624 census lists the Africans in the colony as servants. Their status was similar to the poor whites who had been brought into the colony as indentured servants. The white indentured servants labored for a number of years, after which they were set free and given land. These first Africans in the colony were also given their freedom when their tenure was complete. African-American historian John Hope Franklin says, "The records of Virginia contain many indentures of Negro servants during the forty-year period following their introduction; and during the same period there are records of free Negroes in the colony."[71]

As the colony grew so did the demand for cheap labor. Workers were needed to clear the land of trees and weeds, to plant and harvest crops, and to do other hard labor. The pressing demand for cheap labor caused the authorities to rethink the African situation and decide that the Africans brought into Virginia should be slaves for life rather than indentured servants. A law in 1661 put this into effect, formally making it legal to enslave Africans for life in Virginia.

After 1675 enslaved Africans were brought into Virginia in increasing numbers to labor in the tobacco fields. A population count in 1715 listed twenty-three thousand blacks and 72,500 whites in Virginia. A little over four decades later the black population had increased to 120,156 compared to a white population of 173,316.

The increasing black population in the Virginia colony aroused fear among the whites. They were afraid the slaves would rise up against them. In 1687 a serious slave rebellion was thwarted in the colony because the authorities had learned of the plot beforehand. To control the blacks in the colony, the authorities passed strict and harsh slave laws.

Besides Virginia, Africans were also brought to the southern colonies of Maryland, North and South Carolina, and Georgia.

Africans were first brought to Maryland in small numbers. In 1663 a law was passed recognizing slavery in Maryland. As the decades passed, Africans were imported into Maryland in increasing numbers to cultivate tobacco and other crops. A population count in 1750 listed approximately forty thousand blacks and one hundred thousand whites in Maryland. Whites in Maryland, fearful of slave rebellions, subsequently passed laws to keep blacks under control. Punishments such as whippings, brandings, and executions were carried out on blacks who disobeyed the slave laws. The blacks in Maryland resisted slavery by burning buildings, taking food and other items, killing their masters, and in other ways.

It had already been decided that slave labor would be used in the Carolina colony before it was settled. Africans were imported into Carolina in large numbers to cultivate tobacco, rice, and indigo. A population count in 1708 listed 4,100 blacks and 4,080 whites in Carolina. Seven years later blacks outnumbered whites in Carolina 10,500 to 6,250. By 1765 the black population of Carolina numbered ninety thousand, compared to forty thousand whites.

The Carolina colony separated into two parts in 1729 creating a North and a South. The large number of slaves residing in South Carolina caused the whites to become fearful of slave revolts. Strict and severe slave laws were devised to control this large and growing black population. A series of slave revolts occurred in South Carolina between 1720 and 1740. The blacks in colonial North Carolina were not as active against slavery as the blacks in South Carolina, probably due to their smaller numbers.

The colony of Georgia was founded by James Oglethorpe in 1733. The first settlers in this colony were convicts and prostitutes. Also, this colony was to have no slaves. This policy didn't work out, however. As time passed the settlers began to want to import Africans to do their hard labor. The sentiment for slavery in Georgia grew so strong that in 1750 a law was passed formally allowing the importation of African slaves. Within ten years, three thousand blacks had been brought into Georgia. A population count in 1766 listed eight thousand blacks and ten thousand whites. The slave code of Georgia was adopted as a whole in 1755.[72] It was designed to control the blacks, like elsewhere. Colonial Georgia was relatively free of slave revolts. Although the blacks in colonial Georgia didn't revolt, they manifested their dissatisfaction with slavery in another way, by escaping to freedom in Spanish-controlled Florida.

Africans were first brought to the Middle colonies in the 1620s. The Middle colonies of New York, New Jersey, Pennsylvania, and Delaware imported fewer Africans than the Southern colonies.

New Netherland (New York) was founded by the Dutch in 1624. The exact year Africans were first introduced into New Netherland is not known, but it is certain that they were in the colony by 1628. The West India Company, a Dutch slave trading company, imported enslaved Africans into New Netherland. The Dutch used the Africans to grow crops on their farms. Dutch laws to control the blacks of New Netherland were not very strict or harsh; as a result, blacks seem to have been treated fairly well under their slavery. For example, blacks were sometimes given their freedom for years of hard work. Things began to change for the blacks, however, when the English took New Netherland from the Dutch in 1664 and gave the colony another name, New York. The English installed a stricter and harsher slave system than the Dutch and also imported larger numbers of blacks into New York.

In April 1712 a serious slave revolt erupted in New York City. It was organized and carried out by Coromantees, "known to be leaders of slave revolts." The Coromantees were armed with hatchets, guns, and swords. They began the revolt by setting fires to buildings. When the whites tried to escape from the burning buildings, the Coromantees either killed or injured them. The authorities captured twenty-one of the blacks; six others killed themselves. The ones captured were brutally put to death by hangings, burnings, and being broken on the wheel. Fear of slave revolts continued to plague New York throughout the colonial period.

The Dutch and Swedes brought small numbers of Africans into the colony of New Jersey. When the English took control of New Jersey in 1664, an increasing number of Africans were imported into the colony. The English also made the slave laws harsher. A population count in 1726 listed 2,581 blacks in New Jersey. By 1750 there were 5,354 blacks in New Jersey out of a total population of 71,393. The blacks in New Jersey were not very active against slavery during the colonial period. There was some resistance such as burning of property and theft, but no serious revolts.

Africans were brought to Pennsylvania and Delaware in small numbers. Africans were laboring in these colonies as early as the 1630s. In 1750 there were 2,872 blacks in Pennsylvania out of a total population of 119,666. In Delaware the same year there were 1,496 blacks out of a total population of 28,704. There were Quakers in Pennsylvania who wanted slavery abolished. There were also Germans in Pennsylvania who wanted slavery abolished. The strong opposition to slavery that existed in Pennsylvania didn't exist in Delaware, however. As a result, Delaware's attitude toward slavery became increasingly like that in the colonies of the South.

Africans might have been first introduced into New England during the 1620s, but it is certain that they were there by 1638. Africans were brought to New England in small numbers during the 1600s. Their importation increased, however, in the 1700s. A population count in 1715 listed approximately two thousand blacks in Massachusetts. Twenty years later, in 1735, the black population had increased to twenty-six hundred, compared to 141,400 whites. By 1776 the black population of Massachusetts had grown to 5,249, compared to 343,845 whites. A population count in 1715 listed approximately fifteen hundred blacks in Connecticut. By 1774 the colony had 6,464 blacks and 191,392 whites. A population count in 1708 listed 426 blacks and 6,755 whites in Rhode Island. In 1774 Rhode Island had 54,435 whites and 3,761 blacks. Population data in 1700 listed 150 blacks in New Hampshire. In 1773 New Hampshire had 674 blacks and 71,418 whites.

The New England colonies imported fewer African laborers than the Middle and Southern colonies. New England's thin, rocky soil and short growing season was not suitable for the growing of plantation crops such as tobacco and rice that needed slave labor in large numbers. It was more profitable for New England to buy and sell Africans than to use them as laborers on her small farms and in her factories. As a result, slave trading became very important to New England's economy. At first, "it was difficult for the New England slave traders, with fewer ships and smaller resources to compete with the powerful trading companies of Europe."[73] But as time passed they were able to compete, and by the early 1700s they had entered "the golden age of the New England slave trade,"[74] which lasted about fifty years.

On a map, the shipping routes of the New England slave trade were shaped like a triangle having three sides. This three-way trade was known as the Triangular Trade. The three chief items of the Triangular Trade were rum, slaves, and molasses. On the first leg, Yankee ships left New England loaded with cargoes of rum bound for West Africa. Once they reached West Africa, the ship captains traded their rum for enslaved Africans. On the second leg, called the Middle Passage, the enslaved Africans were transported to the West Indies, where they were sold for big profits. On the third leg from the West Indies to New England, the ships returned home loaded with molasses that had been purchased in the West Indies with money from selling the slaves. The molasses would then be distilled into rum, and the three-way voyage would start over again.

The slave trade was very important to the economy of colonial New England. It generated employment for seamen, shipbuilders, coopers, longshoremen, tanners, and farmers. Much wealth was accumulated from the New England slave trade. A lot of this money was invested in industries such as distilleries, mills, weapons making, and shipbuilding that made still more money.

In 1763 England began to change her economic and political policies toward her thirteen American colonies. She wanted to exert more control over them and she also wanted more revenue from them. England had defeated France in the French and Indian War (1754-63) but it had been costly to her financially. One way England could bring money into her depleted treasury was by taxing her colonies. In April 1764 Parliament passed the Sugar Act, which put a tax of three pence (pennies) on each gallon of foreign molasses bought by the colonies. England then "sent out twenty-seven warships to patrol the New England coasts and soldiers and revenue agents to enforce the act."[75] The New England slave merchants reacted angrily to the Sugar Act because the tax on molasses would deprive them of profits from the very lucrative slave trade. The colonists were further angered when Parliament passed the Quartering and Stamp Acts in 1765. The colonists protested these injustices and the words "taxation without representation" became their rallying cry.

The citizens of Boston, Massachusetts were particularly active against the British. Protests in Boston often turned into street fights between British soldiers and the townspeople. In March 1770 a street fight between British soldiers and Boston citizens turned ugly when the soldiers fired on the citizens, killing three of them and wounding two others, who later died. The first person the British soldiers killed in this incident was a black patriot named Crispus Attucks. Attucks was a tall mulatto who had been one of the leaders of the crowd that had confronted the British. This shooting of Boston citizens in the streets became known as the Boston Massacre. News of it spread throughout the colonies.

After the Boston Massacre, tension between Britain and her thirteen colonies continued to increase until by 1775 it was at a peak level. Fighting erupted in 1775 when the British decided to march to Concord, Massachusetts to capture patriot weapons. This fighting at Lexington and Concord, Massachusetts, on April 19, 1775 began the American Revolution. Black minutemen fought at Lexington and Concord. Patriots such as Lemuel Haynes, Pomp Blackman, and Peter Salem were there. In June 1775 black soldiers, free and slave, participated in the Battle of Bunker Hill. Two black soldiers distinguished themselves in this battle. Peter Salem shot and killed the British Major John Pitcairn. The other black soldier who fought heroically at Bunker Hill was Salem Poor. Poor's bravery and fighting ability impressed his commander and other officers. They said that Poor "behaved like an experienced officer as well as an excellent soldier."

Despite their heroic efforts, a decision was made by General George Washington and others on November 12, 1775, to prohibit blacks (slave and free) from fighting in the Continental Army. However, when Lord Dunmore attracted thousands of slaves to the British army with a proclamation giving freedom to those who fought for the British, Washington was forced to rethink the situation. Washington was well aware of the danger of slaves going over to the British and fighting against their former masters. He said, "Dunmore's strength will increase like a snowball by rolling and faster if some expedient cannot be hit upon to convince the slaves and servants of the impotency of his designs."[76] Washington, therefore, changed his mind and decided to allow free blacks to fight. His decision was approved by Congress in January 1776. Eventually slaves were also allowed to fight. For example, "in 1778 both Rhode Island and Massachusetts permitted slaves to serve as soldiers."[77]

Thousands of blacks fought in the Continental Army during the Revolutionary War. Most fought in regiments with white soldiers. But there were some all-black units also, such as the ones from Massachusetts, Connecticut, and Rhode Island. Black soldiers fought bravely and skillfully in the American Revolution. They participated in most of the battles of the war, including Ticonderoga, Trenton, Red Bank, Princeton, Saratoga, Monmouth, Brandywine, Savannah, and Yorktown. Blacks also served in the navy as sailors and pilots.

Some blacks became famous as a result of their service in the American Revolution. A few are mentioned here. Pompey, a slave, served as a spy who helped General Anthony Wayne capture Stony Point in 1779. Pompey, playing the role of a grinning and submissive slave selling strawberries, was able to gain entrance to the British fort. The British officers felt so comfortable with this happy and seemingly harmless slave that they allowed him to return. Pompey then learned the password for night entrance to the fort and helped General Wayne capture it. For this extraordinary feat, Pompey "was given a horse and excused from all work for the rest of his life."[78] Another black soldier who became famous was Oliver Cromwell. He was with George Washington when he crossed the Delaware River. Cromwell fought in such battles as Yorktown, Monmouth, Brandywine, Trenton, and Princeton. This brave and able soldier was held in high regard by George Washington. The famous black minuteman Lemuel Haynes distinguished himself at the Battle of Ticonderoga. Haynes later became a well-known minister.

The Revolutionary War formally ended on September 3, 1783, with the signing of a peace treaty in Paris that recognized the United States as an independent nation. As a result of the war, large numbers of blacks gained their freedom. Some were freed because of their military service in the war. Most, however, gained their freedom by running away. Thousands of blacks took advantage of the disruption the war created in the land and escaped to freedom. Many ran away to freedom in Canada and Florida. Many others ran away to live in the swamps among the Indians. They also ran away to the British. Despite the large numbers of blacks who gained their freedom from the War of Independence, the institution of slavery remained in the new nation. Many thousands of blacks were still slaves.

After the war, a movement against slavery spread in the North. People spoke out against it and anti-slavery societies were formed. Still, this wasn't enough to eradicate the institution of slavery because the Southern states were so firmly for it.

When the Constitutional Convention was held in Philadelphia in 1787, disputes arose over slavery. Southern delegates wanted the importation of slaves to continue, whereas Northern delegates wanted the importation of slaves to end. Also, Southern delegates wanted slaves to be part of the state's population count, which determined a state's representation in Congress. On the other hand, most delegates from the North didn't want slaves to be part of the state's population count. Two compromises finally settled the disputes. First, the importation of slaves would continue until 1808. Second, a slave was to be counted as three-fifths of a person in determining a state's representation in Congress. The constitution that the delegates signed on September 17, 1787 formally recognized slavery. As a result, slavery would continue in the United States for almost eighty years.

Some of the famous blacks in the United States during the last half of the eighteenth century were Phillis Wheatley, Benjamin Banneker, Richard Allen, and Prince Hall. Phillis Wheatley was brought to Boston, Massachusetts, from Africa in 1761 when she was about seven or eight years old. She was purchased by the wealthy John Wheatley of Boston. John Wheatley made the young girl his wife's servant. The shy and intelligent girl quickly learned to read and write, and by the time she was fourteen she had written her first poem. Phillis eventually became a famous poet who was known internationally. In 1773 Phillis traveled to England, where she made a big impression on the people there. She also sent General George Washington a poem she had written especially for him. Phillis died in 1784. Benjamin Banneker was born in colonial Maryland in 1731. He became a brilliant astronomer, surveyor, and mathematician. He published his own almanac and helped to lay out the city of Washington, D.C. He also had the courage to condemn slavery and racism. In a letter to Thomas Jefferson, he pointed out Jefferson's hypocrisy of wanting liberty from British rule while at the same time denying it to his slaves. He also told Jefferson that his abilities as a mathematician and astronomer were proof that Africans were not inferior. Richard Allen was born in 1760. He was a religious leader who founded the Bethel African Methodist Episcopal Church in Philadelphia in 1794. Prince Hall was born in 1748. He was a minister and a black leader of his day. He also was the organizer of the black Masons in America. Through his leadership, the first Black Grand Lodge was organized in Boston in the year 1792. Hall was appointed Grand Master of that lodge.

We turn now to the gradual ending of slavery in the Northern states. From the beginning, slavery wasn't very profitable on New England farmland because of her short growing season and rocky soil. In the 1780s and 1790s, northern states such as Connecticut, Rhode Island, Massachusetts, Pennsylvania, and New York passed legislation that called for the immediate or the gradual abolition of slavery. As a result, slavery eventually died out in the northern states.

In the 1780s the future of slavery didn't look very promising to many Southern slaveholders. Tobacco, indigo, and rice, all of which required large numbers of slaves to cultivate, were no longer as profitable as they once were. Also, the continuous growing of tobacco crops had exhausted the soil on many plantations. The planters of the South needed a new crop to make it profitable to own large numbers of slaves. The new crop the planters experimented with was cotton. There were two varieties of cotton, long staple and short staple. The long-staple cotton could only be grown in certain areas such as along the South Carolina and Georgia coast, whereas the short-staple cotton could be grown in many areas of the South. However, for the short-staple variety to be profitable, a faster way was needed to separate the seeds from the fiber. In 1793 Eli Whitney solved that problem with the invention of the cotton gin. This machine saved time and money. A slave could seed about one pound of cotton per day, whereas a cotton gin could seed about fifty pounds per day. The cotton gin led to the expansion of both cotton cultivation and slavery in the South. Without cotton and the new technology that made cotton production profitable, the institution of slavery might have died out in the South. Of course, the rich probably would have kept slaves as a status symbol.

In 1808 the importation of slaves was prohibited in the United States. This law was supposed to stop the importation of enslaved Africans, but it was weakly enforced. The slavers devised ways to bring slaves into the country illegally. Thousands of slaves were smuggled into the coastal states of Florida, Alabama, Louisiana, and Texas. Slave smuggling was a very profitable activity. Famous men such as the pirate Jean Laffite and Jim Bowie, inventor of the famed Bowie knife, engaged in slave smuggling.

The prohibition of the foreign slave trade made the domestic slave trade a thriving economic activity. A number of people were involved in the domestic slave trade, including planters, businessmen, auctioneers, newspapermen, slave traders, and slave breeders. Planters often sold their slaves along with their plantations. Slave traders traveled throughout the South searching for slaves to buy cheaply and then sold them at the highest price they could. Major slave-trading markets were in Memphis, New Orleans, Montgomery, Norfolk, Charleston, Richmond, Baltimore, and Washington, D.C. These and other cities had slave pens, auction blocks, and slave jails. Another aspect of the domestic slave trade was slave breeding. Many historians deny that it occurred, but it did. In 1832 Thomas R. Dew admitted that Virginia was a "Negro-raising state" and that she was able to export six thousand per year because of breeding.[79] Slave women were often encouraged to have as many children as possible. Slave breeding was very profitable. At twenty, some young women had given birth to as many as five children.[80]

After the War of 1812, settlers began to move westward in increasing numbers. Thousands of them poured into the rich lands of Alabama and Mississippi. They also migrated to Tennessee, Arkansas, Louisiana, Missouri, and Texas. Many brought their slaves along with them.

Cotton production spread rapidly in the South, becoming the region's main crop. The area of the South where much cotton was grown became known as the Cotton Kingdom. The crop itself became known as King Cotton. Southern planters produced millions of bales of cotton and made huge fortunes. Large numbers of slaves were used in the production of cotton. Large numbers of slaves were also used in the cultivation of sugar cane in Louisiana.

The black population of the United States grew tremendously from 1790 to 1860. A population count in 1790 listed 757,181 blacks in the United States. Of these 697,624 were slaves and 59,557 were free. Seventy years later, in 1860, there were 4,441,830 blacks in the United States, of whom 3,953,760 were slaves and 488,070 were free.

Slavery in the American South has been called the *peculiar institution*. This peculiar institution had a number of characteristics, including immorality, cruelty, greed, and corruption.

Slavery was deeply embedded in the southern way of life. Although the majority of whites in the South didn't own slaves, they were still affected by the institution of slavery—politically, economically, and socially. Many non-slaveholding whites defended slavery. They occupied a higher caste than the blacks because they were white. They thought they were better than the blacks because they were white. Also many non-slaveholding whites desired to be wealthy and have large cotton plantations and slaves of their own.

The large cotton plantation was a village and factory in one. The planter or owner lived in a spacious home called the *big house*. Other buildings on the plantation included the house or cabin of the overseer, the rude cabins of the slaves, barns, stables, sheds, and a cotton gin. On a large plantation the planter generally hired an overseer to manage his land. The overseer's job was to get the maximum amount of work out of the slaves. To do this, the overseer often had to use his long whip on the slaves. Sometimes the overseer was assisted in his duties by a slave called a *driver*. The driver was in charge of the other blacks in the fields and saw to it that they did their work. If they didn't, he punished them. This was another way of dividing the slaves: turning one of their own against them.

On a typical cotton plantation there were three groups of slaves: field slaves, house servants, and skilled craftsmen.

The hard labor on the plantation was done by the field gangs. They cultivated crops, cut down trees, cleared the land of weeds and underbrush, repaired fences, etc. The field slaves lived in small, poorly built cabins, usually without windows. These dilapidated cabins usually had dirt floors and little or no furniture. Clothing and food for the field slaves were generally inadequate. They were issued just enough to get by. They wore simple shirts, pants, and dresses made of cotton, wool, and other materials. They wore crude and uncomfortable shoes called *Negro brogans*. Slaves were generally issued a peck of cornmeal and three or four pounds of salt pork each week. Some slaves, if allowed to, supplemented their diets by growing vegetables in their own little gardens. Some were also allowed to hunt and fish, but this depended upon their slave master. The slaves worked long and hard in the cotton fields from sunup to sundown. Slaves who were late coming to the field or didn't work to the overseer's satisfaction were whipped. Slaves worked the longest and hardest during harvest time, sometimes as many as eighteen or twenty hours a day.

House servants, skilled craftsmen, and drivers didn't have it as hard as the field gangs. House servants included butlers, cooks, valets, and coachmen. They often ate the same food as the slave master and were sometimes given the slave master's second-hand clothes to wear. Skilled craftsmen on the plantation included blacksmiths, carpenters, coopers, brick masons, and millers. The slave driver on the plantation assisted the overseer in forcing the other slaves to work. He was generally disliked by his fellow slaves.

Young black women and girls on the plantation were often taken advantage of sexually by the slave master, his sons, and house guests. Those who offered resistance could be severely whipped or beaten. Black men and white women also had sexual relations, but not as often as the white men and black women. Children born from these relationships were identified as coloreds or mulattoes. But by American standards they were classified as blacks. Some white men cared for and sometimes freed their colored children, while others ignored and sold them. A large mulatto population grew out of this race mixing. In 1860 there were 3,953,760 slaves in the United States, of which 411,000, about ten percent, were colored or mulatto.

Slaves also lived and worked in the towns and cities, where they labored as domestic servants, factory workers, and skilled craftsmen. Some of the skilled craftsmen built mansions and other grand structures. "Most famous of the structures built by slave labor were the White House and the Capitol at Washington. It was a Negro slave, a highly skilled mechanic, who performed the delicate and difficult task of fitting the Statue of Freedom on the dome of the Capitol."[81]

Slave codes or *Black Codes* were enacted by state legislatures to control slaves and also to perpetuate the institution of slavery. Slaves who violated these laws were punished with whippings, body mutilations, brandings, and even execution. The more severe the violation, the greater the punishment. The slave codes were designed to keep the slaves ignorant, to make them fear and respect white people, to make them feel powerless and inferior. Slaves were not to be taught to read or write. Children born of slave mothers were slaves. Slaves were punished for stealing and running away. Slaves were not allowed to possess guns or own property. Slaves were not allowed to blow horns or beat drums. Slaves were the property of their masters. Slaves were not allowed to gather in groups of three or more outside the plantation on which they lived. (This varied, depending upon the state and the situation.) Not more than seven slaves were allowed to be out together unless some white person was with them.[82] Slaves could not leave the plantation without authorization, and any white person, finding a slave [who was] out without permission, could take him up and turn him over to the public officials.[83] Slaves were punished for insulting, striking, or killing a white person. Slaves also had to show their respect for authority and all white people in general. For example, if a white person approached, slaves had to rise from their seats. They could not sit down in the white person's presence. Slaves couldn't remain on a sidewalk if a white person wanted to pass. In certain instances slaves had to remove their hats when talking to a white person. Slaves had to address the master and his wife as "Massa" and "Missus" and say, "yes, sir" and "no, ma'am." Slaves were punished for not acting humble and for disrespecting white people.

One of the devices set up to enforce the Black Codes was the patrol, which has been aptly described as an adaptation of the militia to maintain the institution of slavery.[84] These patrols watched the slaves.

They were on the lookout for runaways; they were on the alert for slave revolts; they observed slaves gathered in groups such as for religious meetings. These patrols also occasionally searched slave cabins for weapons.

The slave system was designed to exploit the labor of the slaves. Slaves were driven hard by the overseers to get the maximum amount of work out of them. The harder a slave worked the more his slave master benefited economically. Because the slave system existed for economic benefits, it is not surprising that acts of cruelty to the slaves were common.

Many slaves didn't passively accept the cruel institution of slavery. They resisted it in a number of ways.

Avoiding work and taking items from the slave master were two ways slaves showed their discontent. Some avoided work by pretending to be ill. Others worked as slowly as they could or just enough to keep from being punished. Still others got revenge by taking personal items, food, clothing, cotton and corn, and tools from slave masters.

A third way slaves resisted slavery was by performing acts of violence against their cruel slave masters and overseers. One woman, after being whipped by an overseer, picked up her hoe and chopped him to death. The slave of William Pearce of Florida killed his master with an axe when Pearce sought to punish him.[85] Some slaves poisoned their slave masters by "mixing ground glass in gravy," by putting "beaten up spiders in buttermilk," with arsenic, and in other ways.

Some slaves earned reputations as "bad Negroes" or "crazy Negroes." These slaves were proud and defiant. They talked back to overseers. They would not allow anyone to whip them. Their spirits could not be broken. Some of these bad Negroes were able to escape the plantation to freedom. But most, if they stayed around, were eventually killed. Bad Negroes included both men and women.

A fourth way slaves resisted slavery was by destroying property. They burned homes, crops, sheds, barns, and cotton gins. They broke tools and machines. They also sometimes killed or maimed animals or worked them extra hard.

A fifth way slaves resisted slavery was by running away. From the beginning of slavery in the United States, thousands of blacks ran away to freedom. Like those in the Caribbean, runaway slaves in the United States established maroon communities in inaccessible areas in swamps, forests, and mountains. A slave might run away alone or with a partner or a group. Both blacks and mulattoes ran away; men, women, and children ran away; all three classes—field slaves, house slaves, and skilled artisans—ran away. A slave who was literate might write a free pass to help another slave escape. Slaves often risked punishment to take food to runaways who were hiding. Sympathetic whites in both the North and South also helped slaves to escape. They provided runaways with hiding places, clothing, and food.

Many blacks escaped to freedom on the Underground Railroad, a secret network of escape routes that began in the Southern states and ended in the Northern states and Canada. The term Underground Railroad came into use in the early 1830s. Both blacks and whites worked on the Underground Railroad, helping fugitive slaves move from one hiding place to another on their journey to freedom. The best-known black person to work on the Underground Railroad was Harriet Tubman. Harriet was born into slavery about 1820 but escaped to freedom in 1849. Not satisfied with just her own freedom, Harriet became a conductor on the Underground Railroad and led over three hundred other slaves to freedom. She made nineteen dangerous trips to the South and on each journey successfully led a group of slaves to freedom. She carried a gun with her and threatened to shoot any slave who tried to turn back. Though small in stature and unable to read or write, Harriet was highly intelligent, very brave, and quick of wit. Harriet possessed an uncanny ability to sense danger before it closed in on her. As a result, she was able to avoid capture on a number of occasions. Harriet's exploits on the Underground Railroad made her famous. At one time a bounty of forty thousand dollars was offered for her capture. Yet she was never captured, and she never lost a passenger on the Underground Railroad.

Harriet Tubman was also skillful at disguising herself and her intentions. For example, when Harriet reached a plantation in the South where she was going to help some slaves escape, she might disguise herself as an old singing peddler to hoodwink the overseer. While she walked along the road on the plantation, she might be singing the old spiritual "Steal Away to Jesus," which had a double meaning. The slaves and overseer in the fields on the plantation who didn't know her would think that she was just a simple old lady singing about escaping her earthly pains to go live with Jesus, but to the alert and aware slaves, she was singing about escaping up North to freedom. Harriet and the aware slaves would meet that night at a prearranged spot and then head North to freedom.

Slaves also ran away from their masters to live among the Indians. They lived with the Seminoles, Creeks, Cherokees, Choctaws, Shawnee, and others. While living with the Indians, blacks were either free or slave. Indian slavery was generally a mild type of slavery. A number of blacks rose to positions of leadership among the Indians. Black Abraham was an interpreter and leader among the Seminoles. Jim Beckwourth, a black scout, trapper, and frontiersman, became a Crow chief.

A sixth way slaves resisted slavery was by rebellion. During the slave period in the United States there were a number of revolts and plots to revolt. A few are discussed here. In 1687 slaves in Virginia plotted a violent uprising but before it could happen the plot was discovered. In 1712 a group of blacks revolted in New York City. Nine whites were killed and perhaps six were wounded. The authorities captured twenty-one of the participants alive and put them to death. In 1741 trouble struck again in New York City. That year a big plot was uncovered. Blacks and oppressed whites had conspired to burn the city of New York and kill its white inhabitants. Afterwards they planned to take control of the city. The discovery of "the Great Negro Plot" filled the city with fear. Both blacks and whites were brought to trial for their alleged participation in the conspiracy. Four whites and eighteen blacks were hanged, fourteen blacks were burned alive, and seventy-one blacks were sent into exile in the West Indies.

The two best-known plots to revolt were led by Gabriel Prosser, a slave, and Denmark Vesey, a freeman.

Gabriel Prosser's plot to revolt occurred in 1800. For almost half a year, Gabriel and his followers carefully planned an attack on the town of Richmond, Virginia, where large numbers of weapons were stored. After Gabriel seized the weapons, he planned to attack other towns in Virginia. Gabriel had convinced thousands of slaves (some estimate between two thousand and fifty thousand) to assist him in the attack. The date for the attack on Richmond was set for August 30, 1800. But before the attack could occur, two slaves told their master about the plot and he alerted the authorities. Despite the betrayal, the attack on Richmond probably would have been successful if heavy rain from a violent storm hadn't destroyed bridges and flooded roads leading into the city, causing Gabriel to postpone the attack. Before Gabriel and his men could regroup and reorganize, the Virginia militia moved in on them, arresting a number of the insurgents. In the end, Gabriel and thirty-four of his followers were put to death by hanging.

Denmark Vesey was a slave before he bought his own freedom in 1800. As a free man, Vesey was a carpenter, earning a good living. Yet he was dissatisfied because many of his brethren were suffering in bondage. Inspired by the success of the Haitian Revolution, Vesey began thinking about liberating his brethren. The best way to liberate them, he concluded, was by armed revolt. Vesey recruited about nine thousand blacks in and around Charleston, South Carolina, to help him carry out a large revolt. The date chosen for the revolt was July 16, 1822. But before the uprising could take place, a house servant told his master about it and he alerted the mayor. Vesey responded by changing the date of the revolt from July 16 to June 16. However, just before June 16 arrived, another slave warned the authorities, who notified the militia. This led to the arrest of Vesey, his five aides, and others. The judiciary system convicted Vesey and his aides of conspiring to revolt and sentenced them to death by hanging. Other blacks were also arrested, found guilty, and hanged.

Nat Turner, a slave, was the leader of the deadliest slave revolt in U.S. history. He was born in Southampton County, Virginia in 1800. Nat easily learned to read and write and was very intelligent. Other slaves looked up to him and considered him a leader. Nat was also a very religious man who saw visions. He often preached to his fellow slaves at religious meetings. Nat's fellow slaves called him "the Prophet." Nat felt that he was divinely inspired, that God had chosen him to lead his people in a revolt against slavery. When it was time for the revolt to begin, God would show him through a sign. When Nat saw an eclipse of the sun in February 1831, he believed this was the sign he had been looking for. On August 21, 1831, Nat and his followers struck without warning, killing about sixty whites in less than thirty-six hours. The infuriated whites organized quickly, and a coalition of volunteer groups and the militia put down the revolt. Many innocent blacks were killed. Nat escaped but was eventually captured and hanged. Sixteen other blacks were also hanged.

News of Nat Turner's revolt spread like wildfire, creating widespread fear in the South. In response, slave laws were made stiffer and harsher; blacks, both freemen and slaves, were watched more carefully. Also, since this deadly revolt had been led by a preacher, whites began to pay more attention to the type of message that black preachers were delivering to the slaves. They didn't want black preachers delivering a liberation message to the slaves, but rather a message that would help the slaves cope with their suffering.

Slavery was a time of great troubles for black people. Many ex-slaves told their descendants about their experiences in slavery. These oral accounts have been handed down from generation to generation. Ex-slaves such as abolitionist Frederick Douglass and novelist William Wells Brown wrote narratives about their experiences in slavery.

Slaves found many ways to cope with the pain and suffering of slavery. One way they coped with slavery was by helping and comforting one another. Slaves would share food and other items. They would also help one another escape. The slave masters generally tried to set the slave groups against one another—field slaves against house slaves, field slaves against skilled craftsmen, house slaves against skilled craftsmen. Despite these attempts the slave groups helped and sympathized with one another. For example, the cook in the big house would sometimes slip food to the field slaves.

Another way slaves coped with slavery was by escaping through dancing. Dances were held on Saturday nights and on special holidays. Christmas was the main holiday and slaves looked forward to it. Slaves held dances in cabins, barns, and fields. At these dances, slaves had a merry time singing, dancing, and drinking liquor. They danced to the music of banjos and fiddles. They danced to the rhythms of hand-clapping, feet-stomping, and rattling of bones.

They did dances such as the juba and the *set de flo*. They also did jigs and shuffles.

Still another way slaves coped with slavery was through religion. The slaves took a European-style Christianity, modified it somewhat, and used it to escape the pain and suffering of slavery. For example, spirituals like "Steal Away to Jesus," "Old Ship of Zion," and "Swing Low, Sweet Chariot" enabled the slaves to transcend their earthly plane of pain and suffering to a spiritual plane of eternal peace and happiness, where every day was Sabbath and one could walk around heaven all day and do nothing but sing and shout. In addition, this slave Christianity also helped the slaves to keep hope and faith alive. Many related their slavery in the United States to the biblical Hebrew slavery in Egypt. Just as God had delivered the Hebrews from bondage, they believed that God would someday deliver them too. This slave Christianity helped blacks to survive slavery. Its creation is a testimony of the African genius.

Slaves would sometimes steal away to the fields, woods, and swamps and secretly hold religious meetings. At these religious meetings, the slaves would release their emotions. They would tell God all about their pain and suffering. The singing, praying, testifying, and preaching would arouse the slaves to a state of spiritual ecstasy and euphoria. The religious meeting was a type of group therapy for the slaves. It was a way for them to escape their troubles, release tension, and comfort one another. The religious meetings helped to keep the slaves from going mad by providing them with an escape from their pain and suffering.

We turn now to the controversy over slavery. By 1815, many people in the Northern states believed that slavery was evil and immoral and were opposed to it. Northern opponents of slavery used newspapers and public speeches to attack it. Most Southerners, however, were in favor of slavery. They believed slavery was necessary, profitable, and not immoral.

Beginning in the 1820s, abolitionists launched strong attacks on slavery. In the *Genius of Universal Emancipation*, white abolitionist Benjamin Lundy called for the emancipation and colonization of blacks. In 1831 white abolitionist William Lloyd Garrison, an antislavery zealot, began publishing a newspaper called the *Liberator*. In his newspaper Garrison demanded in forceful language that blacks be freed immediately. Black abolitionists also wrote publications attacking slavery. In 1829 a defiant black abolitionist named David Walker published his antislavery pamphlet *Walker's Appeal*, denouncing slavery and calling for blacks to rise up and liberate themselves. Also in 1829 another defiant black abolitionist Robert A. Young, published his *Ethiopian Manifesto* denouncing slavery. In 1847 famous black abolitionist Frederick Douglass began an antislavery newspaper called the *North Star*. Other well-known black abolitionists were Henry Highland Garnet, William Wells Brown, Samuel Ward, Charles Remond, and Sojourner Truth.

Many Southerners came to the defense of slavery. They argued that since blacks were naturally inferior to whites, it was only proper that they be enslaved. They also argued that since blacks were an uncivilized, pagan people in Africa, whites had done them a favor by bringing them to America and introducing them to a higher Christian civilization.

The expansion of slavery bitterly divided the North and South. Southern states supported the expansion of slavery into new territories, whereas Northern states were against it. The issue was revolved around power. Southerners feared their power in Congress would decrease with the admission of new free states. Northerners feared the admission of new slave states would increase the Southerners' power in Congress.

When the territory of Missouri applied to join the Union in 1818, bitter arguments erupted in Congress over whether Missouri should be admitted as a free state or as a slave state. The dispute was eventually settled by the Missouri Compromise of 1820-21, which admitted Missouri into the Union as a slave state and Maine as a free state.

Following the Mexican War (1846-1848) the United States gained territories from Mexico. Bitter debates arose in Congress over the prospect of slavery in the new territories. Tensions between the North and the South were eased somewhat with the Compromise of 1850. California was allowed to enter the Union as a free state while the people of the new territories could decide for themselves whether to allow slavery. Slave trading was made unlawful in Washington, D.C. Texas was compensated ten million dollars to withdraw her claim to the territory of New Mexico. The Compromise of 1850 also enacted a strict fugitive slave law.

The 1850s brought about increased tension between the North and South. In 1852 Harriet Beecher Stowe published the antislavery novel, *Uncle Tom's Cabin*. The book was very popular and it sold very well. It brought sympathy to the slaves and it won support for abolitionists. However, it aroused anger in Southerners, thereby further straining the relations between the North and South. In 1854 the Kansas-Nebraska Act was passed. This act divided an area west of Missouri into the territories of Kansas and Nebraska. In both territories the inhabitants had the right to decide whether they wanted slavery. The people of Nebraska were generally against slavery. But in Kansas, violence erupted as proslavery groups clashed with antislavery groups.

In 1857 the Supreme Court handed down the infamous Dred Scott Decision. Dred Scott was a slave of John Emerson in Missouri. When his master left Missouri and moved first to the free state of Illinois and then to a free territory, Scott was with him. Upon his return to Missouri, Scott sued for his freedom on the ground that residence on free soil had liberated him.[86] The Supreme Court ruled against Scott, however, saying roughly that "living in a free area for a time didn't make a slave free." This decision angered Northerners.

In 1859 white abolitionist John Brown decided to put into action his plan to liberate enslaved blacks through warfare. On October 16 Brown and a small group of men, including five blacks, captured the town of Harper's Ferry, Virginia, along with its federal arsenal. After he captured the arsenal, Brown had hoped large numbers of slaves would join him in a gigantic slave rebellion. However, this didn't happen. Meanwhile, federal troops led by Col. Robert E. Lee moved in and overpowered Brown and his men. Brown was subsequently arrested by the troops and imprisoned. The court convicted Brown of treason and on December 2, 1859, he was hanged. John Brown's raid further strained the relationship between the North and the South and brought both sides closer to war. The North and South were now on a dangerous collision course. It was only a matter of time before they came to blows.

The year 1860 ushered in an important election. The Democratic Party was divided over the spread of slavery. The Republicans were mostly against the spread of slavery. As the November election approached, the nation was deeply divided. Some Southern leaders had even threatened to secede from the Union if Abraham Lincoln, the Republican candidate, was elected president of the United States. The South's nightmare came true when Lincoln won the November presidential election, defeating the divided Democratic Party's two candidates, Stephen John Douglas and John Breckinridge, and John Bell of the Constitutional Union Party. The state of South Carolina responded to Lincoln's victory by seceding from the Union in December 1860. In January 1861 five more Southern states seceded from the Union. These six seceded states formed the Confederate States of America and chose Jefferson Davis as their president. In March the Confederacy grew by one when Texas seceded. On April 12, 1861, Confederate troops fired on Fort Sumter, a federal military base in Charleston, South Carolina. This attack ignited the Civil War.

When the Civil War began, Lincoln's objective was to save the Union rather than to free the slaves. If he could have saved the Union without ending slavery he would have done so.

At the beginning of the Civil War, Lincoln rejected offers by blacks to fight for the North. He feared that if he used black troops, it would anger the border slave states, which might then join the Confederacy. Lincoln was also aware of the many prejudiced Northern whites who were opposed to black soldiers fighting in the Union army.

As the war continued, more pressure was put on Lincoln to use black troops. White abolitionists such as William Lloyd Garrison and Wendell Phillips were critical of Lincoln for not using black troops. Black leaders and black abolitionist Frederick Douglass demanded that blacks be allowed to fight in the Union army. Other abolitionists also advocated the use of black troops.

From the beginning of the war, the Confederacy was using black manpower to build fortifications, lay railroad tracks, cook food, and to do other military chores. This slave labor was important to the Confederacy because it freed large numbers of white men to fight on the battlefields.

Although reluctant to allow blacks to fight for the Union, Lincoln was eventually forced to do so. The Southern rebels were giving the Yankees all they could handle on the battlefield. Lincoln realized that the North was fighting for its life and needed all the support it could get. By the fall of 1862, he had made up his mind to allow blacks to fight. Lincoln's strategy was to use blacks as a weapon against the South.

On January 1, 1863, Lincoln issued his famous Emancipation Proclamation, which freed all slaves residing in areas fighting against the Union. The Emancipation Proclamation formally allowed black troops to fight for the Union. In addition, it clearly defined the Civil War for the Union, "making it a war against slavery." The Emancipation Proclamation was a war measure designed to weaken the South. It pulled away slave manpower that was valuable to the South. Thousands of slaves ran away from their masters to support the Union army, serving as soldiers, laborers, cooks, etc. The Emancipation Proclamation also created fear and disorder in the South as whites became fearful of slave uprisings and slaves became insubordinate, refusing to work and to take punishments.

Once they were allowed to fight, blacks made an important contribution to the Union army. About 186,000 black troops served in the Union army during the Civil War. Approximately thirty-eight thousand lost their lives. Black soldiers fought in all-black regiments, mostly commanded by white officers. However, some blacks became officers. The highest-ranking of the seventy to one hundred black officers was Lt. Col. Alexander T. Augustana, a surgeon.[87] "Black soldiers participated in 410 military engagements and 39 major battles...."[88] They fought at Nashville in Tennessee, Port Hudson in Louisiana, Tupelo in Mississippi, Richmond in Virginia, and many other places. Black soldiers and white soldiers were not treated equally. For example, black soldiers received seven dollars a month in pay as compared to thirteen dollars a month for white soldiers. Blacks also served as spies and scouts. Familiar with the Southern terrain, they were invaluable to the Union army. John Scobell was a skilled spy for the Union. He disguised himself as a happy, singing black man who loved to eat and have a good time. Southern whites didn't suspect that he was a spy. Alfred Wood did valuable spy work in the state of Mississippi. He was a master of deception. "Once, when captured by the enemy, he said he was a runaway slave and told such a convincing tale of the cruelties he had suffered...[that] he was permitted to join the Confederates, to whom he gave much false information."[89] The most famous black spy was the daring Harriet Tubman of Underground Railroad fame. She "was a spy for Union troops at many points on the eastern seaboard." [90] Besides being soldiers, scouts, and spies, blacks also worked as laborers, cooks, and nurses for the Union army.

It was thought by many that once blacks got the chance to fight for their freedom, they would perform poorly in battle. However, the bravery and skill of black soldiers proved them wrong. For example, black soldiers displayed much courage when they attacked Fort Wagner, a Confederate fort near Charleston, South Carolina. This battle silenced a lot of Northern critics who had doubts about the fighting skill of black soldiers. Blacks also distinguished themselves at places like Milliken's Bend, Port Hudson, and Petersburg. For their valor in the Civil War, twenty-three blacks were awarded Medals of Honor.

The use of black soldiers by the Union angered the Confederates. They were outraged at the sight of their former slaves in Yankee blue, fighting against them. Some black soldiers were killed when they were captured by the Confederates. Perhaps the low point of the Civil War was the massacre at Fort Pillow, Tennessee, in April 1864. The leader of the massacre was Confederate General Nathan Bedford Forrest. A congressional investigating committee said Forrest's men murdered three hundred soldiers and civilians after the fort surrendered.[91] Killed in the massacre were black soldiers and their white officers and also black women and children. However, during the Civil War not all black soldiers were killed by the Confederates when captured; instead, they became Confederate prisoners of war.

Nearly thirty thousand blacks served in the Union's navy during the Civil War. They made an important contribution to the navy's war effort. Five black sailors won Medals of Honor for their Civil War efforts.

In the spring of 1865 the Confederacy surrendered to the Union, bringing the bitter and bloody Civil War to an end. In December 1865 the Thirteenth Amendment, which formally ended slavery in the United States, was ratified. Blacks were no longer the property of slave masters. They were free. This new freedom evoked shouts of joy and tears of happiness from many black people.

Ex-slaves reacted in different ways to their new freedom. Some remained on the plantations with their former slave masters. Others went to live in towns and cities. Still others walked the roads from place to place searching for relatives who had been sold away from them during slavery. Some found their lost relatives; others did not.

After the Civil War the United States went through a controversial twelve-year period known as Reconstruction, which began in 1865 and ended in 1877. Reconstruction witnessed the rebuilding of the war-ravaged South and its readmission to the Union.

During Reconstruction blacks tried to adjust from slavery to freedom. Most freed slaves were poor, uneducated, and homeless. In 1865 an agency called the Freedmen's Bureau was established to assist freed slaves and also poor whites. The Freedmen's Bureau helped large numbers of blacks. It provided them with food, clothing, jobs, schools, and hospitals. Still, blacks needed something else to make them more economically independent. What they needed was land. Thaddeus Stevens, a radical congressman and friend of blacks, advocated giving each black adult forty acres of land and a mule. This didn't happen, of course.

Without land, without tools, without capital or access to credit facilities, the freedmen drifted into a form of peonage: the sharecropping system.[92] Black sharecroppers were often exploited. White landowners provided the tools, mules, seeds, and land for farming, while the blacks provided the labor. The benefits were supposed to be shared equally, but this didn't often happen. Typically, white landowners took more than their share, often leaving blacks with hardly enough to survive on.

While blacks were trying to adjust to a life of freedom, Southern whites were trying to adjust to blacks being free. Many whites reacted angrily at the sight of their former slaves living a life of freedom. Throughout the South, Black Codes were passed to "keep blacks in their place." In response, the Civil Rights Act was passed in April 1866, giving blacks full citizenship. Many Southern whites resented freedmen having civil rights, including the right to vote and hold office. As a result, they turned to violence to intimidate blacks. In May 1866 a race riot broke out in Memphis, Tennessee. This riot was led by city policemen, who teamed with other whites in attacking blacks. Forty-six blacks were killed during the riot and many others were wounded. The rioters also raped black women and burned churches and schools. In July 1866 another race riot broke out in a southern city. This time it was in New Orleans. Again the riot was led by policemen. The rioters killed thirty-four blacks and three whites and injured over a hundred blacks. Terrorist groups such as the Ku Klux Klan also committed acts of violence against blacks. The Ku Klux Klan was organized by Nathan Bedford Forrest, the infamous leader of the brutal Fort Pillow Massacre.

The rejection of the Fourteenth Amendment by the Southern states, their enactment of Black Codes, the widespread disorder in the South, and President [Andrew] Johnson's growing obstinacy persuaded many people that the South had to be dealt with harshly.[93] As a result, Congress enacted the Reconstruction Act in 1867, which paved the way for Radical Republican control of the South.

Who were the Radical Republicans in the U.S. Congress; what was their aim; and where did they come from? They were a group of radical Republican Congressmen who took control of the Republican

Party. Their aim was to punish and humiliate the arrogant South for its rebellion against the Union and continuous denial of equal rights to freedmen. Principal members of the Radical Republicans were: Benjamin Butler (Massachusetts), Charles Sumner (Massachusetts), Benjamin Wade (Ohio), Oliver Morton (Indiana), Zachariah Chandler (Michigan), George Boutwell (Massachusetts), James Ashley (Ohio), Richard Yates (Illinois), and James Wilson (Iowa). The leader of this group of radicals was sharp-tongued Thaddeus Stevens of Pennsylvania, the architect of the Radical Reconstruction program and a main supporter of equal rights for blacks.

The Reconstruction Act of 1867 was passed over President Johnson's vetoes. One measure of the Reconstruction Act was to divide the ex-Confederate states, except Tennessee, into five military districts; each district was to be occupied by federal troops. Another measure was that each state had to adopt a new constitution, which included allowing blacks to vote. Also the ex-Confederate states had to ratify the Fourteenth Amendment, which gave blacks citizenship, in order to be allowed back in the Union.

The Reconstruction Act enabled the Radical Republicans to take control of the South. The Republicans rewrote the constitutions of the Southern states and formed new state governments. The three groups that comprised the Republicans in the South were *scalawags, carpetbaggers*, and blacks.

Scalawags were white Southerners who were generally poor and resided in hilly areas. They hoped to benefit both educationally and economically from the new state governments. Some held political offices and were despised by many Southern whites for supporting radical reconstruction governments.

Carpetbaggers were Northern whites who came South, supposedly carrying their belongings in carpetbags. They were comprised mostly of ex-Union soldiers seeking economic opportunities, teachers, and missionaries. The carpetbaggers, whatever their intentions, aroused much anger in Southern whites. They were generally looked upon by Southern whites as exploiters and opportunists. Some carpetbaggers became politicians and businessmen; others such as teachers and missionaries helped blacks.

Blacks were the largest of the three groups. Black voters helped the Republicans to establish radical governments throughout the South. Blacks also held political offices during Reconstruction, both at the state level and the national level. Blacks, being in the majority, were able to dominate the state legislature in South Carolina. There were two black U.S. senators from the state of Mississippi, Hiram Revels and Blanche K. Bruce. In all seventeen blacks were elected at the national level—two in the U.S. Senate and fifteen Representatives in the House.

In the early 1870s Republican power began to wane in the South. White Southerners used violence and intimidation to keep both black and white Republicans away from the polls. As a result, Southern Democrats began taking control of the state governments. By 1876 the Democrats controlled all Southern states except Florida, Louisiana, and South Carolina. In the presidential election of 1876 Rutherford B. Hayes, the Republican candidate, made a deal with the South. He promised to withdraw federal troops from the South and also let the South control its own affairs if Southerners helped him win the controversial election against Democrat Samuel J. Tilden. The Southern Democrats responded by ending their "filibuster that prevented the orderly counting of the electoral votes,"[94] and Hayes was elected president. Federal troops were then withdrawn from the South, ending Reconstruction.

The end of Reconstruction restored *home rule* in the South. Southern whites were now back in power. They immediately began the business of reestablishing their control over blacks and putting them back into a subordinate status. They used violence and intimidation to discourage blacks from voting. They also used clever schemes to keep blacks from voting. For example, they located polling places where blacks couldn't reach them or changed the location of polling places without telling black voters. In 1883 the Supreme Court ruled that the Civil Rights Act of 1875 "was unconstitutional." This ruling by a conservative Supreme Court denied blacks the use of public accommodations which had been guaranteed to them in 1875. It set in motion the segregation of blacks in hotels, theaters, trains, etc. In the 1890s a strong push was made to *disfranchise* blacks in the South, to take away their right to vote. Ingenious devices were used to keep them from voting. One device was the poll tax. Blacks had to pay a poll tax before being allowed to vote. Another device used was the grandfather clause. If a person's father or grandfather had voted before 1867, then he could vote. However, blacks forefathers weren't allowed to vote before 1867, so they couldn't vote either. Other devices to keep blacks from voting were literacy and understanding tests. By 1910 the voting rights of blacks had been practically taken away in the South. The 1890s was also a decade of widespread lynching of blacks. Lynching actually became a source of entertainment. In 1896 the Supreme Court ruled in favor of racial segregation in *Plessy v. Ferguson*. This ruling officially recognized the "separate but equal" doctrine.

A year before *Plessy v. Ferguson*, Booker T. Washington emerged as the new black leader, replacing the great warrior Frederick Douglass who had just passed away. Washington was the epitome of hard work and determination. He had built Tuskegee Institute in Alabama from scratch, having very little to work with in the hostile Southern environment. Washington's famous speech at the 1895 Atlanta Exposition thrust him into the national spotlight. In this speech he urged blacks to "Cast down your bucket where you are," meaning to be patient about acquiring equality and to develop "friendly relations" with white people. Some blacks disagreed with Washington's compromising stance. They wanted him to attack racism openly and to demand equality for blacks.

Chief among Booker T. Washington's critics was William E.B. Du Bois. Du Bois was a proud, passionate, Harvard-educated and outspoken black man. He opposed Washington's doctrine of vocational education and submissiveness toward whites. Du Bois advocated an educational program of arts and sciences that would produce men with "manhood and knowledge of the world," men who would work to change the conditions of the world for the betterment of black people, rather than a vocational education that would produce skilled carpenters and bricklayers "but not necessarily men." Rejecting Washington's conciliatory and apologist attitude, Du Bois advocated a direct attack on inequality and prejudice in society. In addition, Du Bois "favored immediate social and political integration and the higher education of a Talented Tenth of the black population."[95] Du Bois was the leader of the Niagara Movement, which was started in Niagara Falls, Canada in 1905 to gain equal rights for blacks. He was also a founding member of the NAACP. Despite Du Bois and others such as William Monroe Trotter, who also attacked Booker T. Washington's philosophy, Washington remained the main black leader until his death in 1915.

Another black leader who rose to prominence during this period was Jamaican Marcus Garvey. In 1914 Garvey founded an organization in Jamaica that became known as the Universal Negro Improvement Association (UNIA). In 1916 he arrived in the United States and began a movement to unite and awaken blacks all over the world. His headquarters was located in Harlem, a black section of New York City. He used his newspaper, the *Negro World*, to spread his ideas. Garvey preached a message of black pride and self-determination, which had a magnetic appeal to the black masses. At the peak of his popularity, Garvey had an estimated 6 million followers worldwide. They were in places such as Africa, the Caribbean, Central and South America, Europe, and the United States. Garvey urged the masses to accompany him back to Africa to establish a nation of their own since they were mistreated and not welcome in the Diaspora. However, not everyone accepted Garvey's message. No doubt some of them were jealous of his success and his appeal to the masses. Garvey's main critic was W.E.B. Du Bois. Du Bois believed that Garvey's back-to-Africa movement was impractical and undermined the fight for justice and equality in the United States.

In retrospect all three black leaders—Washington, Du Bois, and Garvey—had something of value to offer black people. Washington's doctrine of self-reliance and vocational education was needed then and is needed now. Blacks need to know how to repair cars, make shoes, and build houses. Dubois' program of acquiring a higher education in the arts and sciences and his policy of fighting against racial prejudice and injustice was needed then and is needed now. The black community needs doctors, lawyers, and teachers. It also needs people who are not afraid to speak out against injustice and inequality. Garvey's philosophy of self-reliance and black pride was needed then and is needed now. Nothing can substitute for a people doing for themselves and being proud of their heritage. Blacks would have benefited more if there could have been less friction between Washington and Du Bois and Garvey and Du Bois. All three men were trying to do the same thing, uplift the race.

About 1910 blacks began migrating from the South to the North in large numbers. They left the farms and plantations and towns and cities of the South to relocate in the North, mostly in large cities such as New York, Philadelphia, Boston, Detroit, Milwaukee, Chicago, and St. Louis. They hoped to leave racism behind in the South, and sought better job opportunities and living conditions in the North. Many found good paying jobs working in factories and wartime industries, and improved their lives. But on the other hand, many didn't find the North to be the Promised Land they had hoped for. They found racism in the North just as they had in the South. Lacking skills and education, they had to accept jobs as common laborers and servants in order to survive. Many could find housing only in crowded all-black neighborhoods with run-down apartments and houses. Despite the negative circumstances they found in the North, many Southern blacks still thought they could find a better life in the North than the South and they, therefore, continued to migrate to the North. This movement of large numbers of blacks from the South to the North became known as the Great Migration. "The first wave (300,000) came between 1910 and 1920, followed by a second wave (1,300,000) between 1920 and 1930. The third and fourth waves, even larger, came in the thirties (1,500,000) and the forties (2,500,000)."[96]

World War I broke out in Europe in 1914 and ended in 1918. "According to official records, approximately 370,000 black soldiers and 1,400 commissioned officers served in the armed forces [during World War I]."[97] These soldiers were in all-black units. Black soldiers frequently complained of the racism they encountered in the military from degrading names by white officers to discrimination in promotions. Poor race relations led to fights between black and white soldiers. Despite the racism, black soldiers generally fought well. Large numbers of blacks fought in France. The U.S. Military didn't award any medals to blacks; but the French *Croix de Guerre* (Medal of Honor) was awarded to each soldier in three black regiments. Historian Lerone Bennett says, "Four of the outstanding American regiments were composed entirely of black enlisted men—the 369th, the 370th, the

371st, and the 372nd. Three of these regiments—the 369th, the 371st, and the 372nd—received the Croix de Guerre for valor and the fourth covered itself with distinction in battles in Argonne Forest."[98]

The exciting 1920s, the heyday of the Garvey movement, also witnessed the *Harlem Renaissance*. The Harlem Renaissance, or *Black Renaissance*, was a consciousness awakening period in which black writers produced large volumes of literature about the experiences of black people in America. Many of these writers protested injustice and inequality in America through their writings. They wrote essays, plays, poems, novels, and musical compositions. The Renaissance was centered in Harlem, but blacks in other cities such as Washington, D.C., Chicago, and Boston also wrote during this period. Some of the famous writers of the Harlem Renaissance were James Weldon Johnson, Claude McKay, Jean Toomer, Countee Cullen, and Langston Hughes.

James Weldon Johnson (1871-1938) was born in Jacksonville, Florida. He authored and edited a number of works. In public life he served as a newspaper editor, lawyer, school principal, and as field secretary of the NAACP (1916 to 1920). He was an important part of the Harlem Renaissance and played a key role in its rise to international attention. He is perhaps best remembered today for writing the beautiful and powerful song "Lift Every Voice and Sing" (1900), which is known as the black national anthem. In 1917 he published *Fifty Years and Other Poems*. "The title poem [in this work], written on the anniversary of the signing of the Emancipation Proclamation, made it clear that Negroes were determined to remain here in America and to enjoy the full fruits of their labors."[99] In 1927 there appeared his *God's Trombones*, Negro sermons in verse, and in 1930 his *Saint Peter Relates an Incident of the Resurrection Day*, a burning indictment of the current discrimination against Negro Gold Star mothers.[100]

Claude McKay (1890-1948) was born in Jamaica. He won widespread fame as a poet and novelist. He was the most militant, the most defiant, and the most important of the Harlem Renaissance writers. "He published poems in several magazines, including *The Seven Arts*, *The Liberator*, and *The Messenger*, but it was the appearance of his volume, *Harlem Shadows*, in 1922 that placed him in the front ranks of post-war America. In "The Lynching," "If We Must Die," and "To the White Fiends" there is expressed in eloquent verse a proud defiance and bitter contempt that became one of the salient characteristics of the Harlem Renaissance."[101] McKay's novels include *Home to Harlem*, (1928), which tells of black life in New York, and *Banjo*, (1929).

The following lines from "If We Must Die" capture McKay's defiant spirit:

> If we must die, let it not be like hogs,
> Hunted and penned in an inglorious spot,
> While round us bark the mad and hungry dogs,
> Making their mock of our accursed lot.
> If we must die, O let us nobly die.[102]

Jean Toomer (1894-1967) was born in Washington, D.C. He was a talented poet and short story writer. He is considered one of the most important writers of the Harlem Renaissance. Historian John Hope Franklin paints a vivid picture of Toomer's work, *Cane*, and his eloquent writing style:

> In 1923 he published *Cane*, which ranked with McKay's *Harlem Shadows* in its significance for the literary movement. This only contribution of Toomer to the Renaissance was a series of realistic stories on Negro life, together with a number of extraordinary moving lyrics of great beauty. Both the poetry and prose of *Cane* reflected the capacity for self-revelation which Toomer had developed in France. His writings were unrestrained, yet objective, passionate, but proud. They are full of love and pride of

race, and they revealed the inner yearnings as well as the joys and hurts of the New Negro.[103]

Countee Cullen (1903-1946) was born in New York City. He earned a bachelor's degree from New York University and an M.A. degree from Harvard University. He was a gifted poet and novelist, and one of the important writers of the Harlem Renaissance. In 1925 he burst upon the literary scene with his work, *Color*, a book of poems. In 1927 he published *The Ballad of the Brown Girl* and *Copper Sun*, both books of poetry. In 1929 he published *The Black Christ*, a volume of poetry. In 1932 his novel, *One Way to Heaven*, appeared, satirizing bourgeois blacks of Harlem. Franklin describes Cullen and his beautiful writing style:

> He doubtless felt as keenly about the problem of the Negro as McKay or his other contemporaries, but his protests were couched in some of the most delicate, gentle lyrics that the post-war period witnessed. There was a finesse about his lines that distinguished him from the others, and at times his protests were so subtle as almost to escape detection. He was at his best when writing verse dealing with aspects of the race problem, but the beauty and effectiveness of his lines did not depend on the use of the experience of race. The lyric quality, rich imagination, and intellectual content of his works make him one of the major poets of twentieth century America.[104]

Langston Hughes (1902-1967) was born in Joplin, Missouri, and was educated at Lincoln University in Pennsylvania. He was a gifted and versatile writer; he wrote poems, plays, short stories, a novel, and an autobiography. Franklin paints a vivid portrait of Hughes and his writings:

> During the Renaissance, New York attracted from Missouri via Mexico, Africa, and Europe its most cosmopolitan as well as its most prolific writer, Langston Hughes. Few writers in America have had such rich and varied experiences,

and few are so indiscriminate in selecting materials for their writings. While Hughes is a true rebel poet, writing in the best traditions of the New Negro, he did not cry or moan. Frequently he laughed....He could pen deeply moving verses full of pride of race, such as "The Negro Speaks of Rivers," or he could write of the most lowly walks of life...such as "Brass Spittons." In 1926 his *Weary Blues* appeared, followed the next year by *Fine Clothes to the Jew*. He demonstrated his versatility by bringing out a novel, *Not Without Laughter*, in 1930 and a volume of short stories, *The Ways of White Folks*, in 1934. At a later time he experimented with pieces for the theater, and in 1940 his autobiography, *The Big Sea*, appeared. Numerous smaller works of his were published, and as he moved about the country ever broadening the scope of his art and continuously experimenting with new forms of expression, there appeared to be some justification for regarding him as "Shakespeare in Harlem."[105]

During the 1930s and 1940s blacks experienced a depression, a war, and economic and social gains. In October 1929 the stock market crashed, bringing on the Great Depression, which caused many blacks to lose their jobs. There was widespread suffering among blacks during the Depression. They suffered discrimination in employment and in obtaining public relief. Many blacks held Republican President Herbert Hoover accountable for the Great Depression. As a result some of them switched their loyalty from the Republican Party, the party of Abraham Lincoln, to the Democratic Party in the 1932 election, in which Democrat Franklin D. Roosevelt was elected president. Roosevelt called his program of recovery and relief from the Great Depression the New Deal, which helped blacks. Roosevelt was able to attract large numbers of blacks to the Democratic Party. In the 1936 election a majority of blacks cast their votes for Roosevelt and he was reelected. In 1941 the United States entered World

War II. During World War II thousands of blacks worked in industries that made weapons and materials for the war effort. They worked in the aircraft, iron and steel, and shipbuilding industries to name a few. Also during World War II nearly one million blacks (men and women) were members of the armed forces. Following World War II black organizations such as the NAACP began to put more pressure on the federal government to end discrimination and inequality in society. In 1947 Jackie Robinson desegregated major league baseball when he began playing for the Brooklyn Dodgers baseball team. The next year, 1948, the U.S. government began the desegregation of the armed forces.

In the *Brown v. Board of Education of Topeka* [Kansas] case of 1954, "the Supreme Court ruled that segregation in public schools was unconstitutional." The winning of this case was an important victory for the NAACP because it showed them that through struggle changes could be made. Also, this victory gave blacks in general the self-confidence to attack discrimination elsewhere.

In December 1955 in Montgomery, Alabama, a courageous black woman named Rosa Parks, tired from a long day at work, remained seated when she was required by law to yield her seat on a bus to a white man. Parks was subsequently arrested for disobeying the law. In protest, blacks in Montgomery decided to organize a bus boycott. The bus boycott was led by a dynamic young black minister named Martin Luther King, Jr. After 382 days of economic pressure, the city of Montgomery yielded to the bus boycott and allowed blacks to ride on the city buses on a first-come, first-served basis.

The successful Montgomery bus boycott of 1955-56 ignited the Civil Rights Movement by lifting the spirits of blacks throughout the nation and inspiring them to push forward. It also made Dr. King a nationally known figure.

In the late 1950s and 1960s blacks in America, oppressed for centuries, confronted racism head-on for the first time in a determined effort to gain their civil rights. In 1957 blacks attempted to desegregate Central High School of Little Rock, Arkansas, but were resisted strongly by enraged whites. Federal troops had to be called in before the school could be integrated. Also in 1957 Dr. King and others established a civil rights organization called the Southern Christian Leadership Conference (SCLC). In February 1960 four students from North Carolina A&T University in Greensboro staged a sit-in at a Woolworth's store there to protest segregation and discrimination. The sit-in became an effective weapon of protest and its use spread throughout the South. Other tactics civil rights workers used to combat segregation and discrimination were marches, boycotts, and freedom rides. In the early 1960s civil rights groups such as the SCLC, CORE, SNCC, and the NAACP used these tactics of protest to successfully desegregate theaters, stores, libraries, hotels, and other public places throughout the South.

The year 1963 marked the pinnacle of the Civil Rights Movement. Early that year Dr. King decided to desegregate Birmingham, Alabama, called by some "the most thoroughly segregated city in America." Birmingham was a stronghold of white supremacy. Dr. King was aware that it would be a bold move to attempt to desegregate Birmingham. He was also aware that if he could succeed in desegregating Birmingham, the back of segregation would be broken in the South. In April 1963 the battle to desegregate Birmingham began. Opposing King and his demonstrators was a force of police and firemen commanded by Police Commissioner Eugene "Bull" Conner, a tough, chunky segregationist who had become a national symbol of Southern intransigence.[106] Throughout the month of April the demonstrators protested using the nonviolent tactics of sit-ins and marches, and the only reaction from

Birmingham officials was to arrest large numbers of them, but on May 3 the situation turned ugly. That day Bull Conner ordered the use of billy clubs, high-powered water hoses, and dogs on the demonstrators, some of whom were children under twelve. News of this brutality spread quickly over the nation, evoking sympathy from many people. On May 10 an agreement was reached between the two sides. The agreement called for the city of Birmingham to begin desegregating its facilities and implementing an employment program of job hiring and job upgrading for blacks. The battle for Birmingham had been won. The showdown in Birmingham might have been Dr. King's finest hour as a civil rights leader. There he showed great boldness, courage, and poise under fire, and also brilliant tactical and strategic skills. The year 1963 also witnessed the historic March on Washington where Dr. King delivered his famous "I Have a Dream" speech. But the year 1963 also witnessed the murder of civil rights leader Medgar Evers in his home state of Mississippi.

The year 1964 saw Dr. King win the Nobel Peace Prize; race riots break out in New York City, Philadelphia, Chicago, and Jersey City, New Jersey; and passage of the Civil Rights Act of 1964.

The years 1965 through 1968 were turbulent years in the United States, marked by white backlash, black unrest and militancy, and assassinations. When Dr. King attempted to help blacks register to vote in Selma, Alabama, in January of 1965, he met strong white opposition. Law enforcement in Selma arrested large numbers of blacks who tried to register to vote. The voter registration drive was marred by violence, including the killing of Jimmy Lee Jackson, a black civil rights worker; the beating to death of the Reverend James Reeb, a white Boston, Massachusetts, minister; and the shooting to death by Klansmen of Viola Liuzzo, a white civil rights worker. During a march from Selma to Montgomery on March 7, 1965, led by Dr. King, marchers were beaten with billy clubs and whips by law enforcement officers. The violence-marred Selma, Alabama, voter registration drive influenced the passing of the Voting Rights Act of 1965. Earlier, in February 1965, Malcolm X, the charismatic and fiery spokesman for the Nation of Islam (Black Muslims), was assassinated in New York City. Malcolm had preached a message of self-reliance, racial pride, and separation. In August 1965 a serious riot erupted in Watts, a black section of Los Angeles, California. Its intensity and fury shocked the nation. The cry of many of the rioters was "Burn, Baby, Burn." The riot left thirty-four people dead and did about forty million dollars in damage. In 1966 Stokely Carmichael, the leader of the civil rights organization SNCC, used the term *Black Power* to describe what blacks must aim for in America. Whites had power; blacks needed to acquire power. The term black power also became associated with racial pride. Blacks used the phrase "Black Is Beautiful," and wore a new hairstyle called the *natural* or *Afro*. Blacks identified themselves as Afro-Americans or blacks rather than as Negroes or colored people. The Black Panther Party was also formed in 1966. In 1967 riots broke out in cities across the nation, during the long, hot summer. The riots in Newark, New Jersey, and Detroit, Michigan, were the most devastating. On the political side, the year 1967 witnessed the election of Richard Hatcher as the first black mayor of Gary, Indiana, and Carl Stokes as the first black mayor of Cleveland, Ohio. Also in 1967 a black person was appointed to the Supreme Court for the first time. The new justice was Thurgood Marshall, a veteran civil rights lawyer.

The year 1968 was marked by the tragic assassination of Dr. King in Memphis, Tennessee. Dr. King had gone to Memphis in March to aid black sanitation workers who were on strike. Dr. King had been the principal leader of the Civil Rights Movement from 1955 to 1968.

Thousands of people worked in the Civil Rights Movement. Most were black, but there were some whites also. The efforts and sacrifices of these courageous civil rights workers haven't been forgotten. Some of them lost their lives in the struggle; many others were arrested, beaten, or jailed. Still others lost their jobs, homes, careers, and money in the struggle.

In the 1970s blacks progressed economically, socially, and politically. Affirmative action programs helped blacks to combat discrimination in employment. As a result, they were able to get higher-paying jobs in private industry and in government that had been previously denied to them because of racism, even though they were qualified. Employment gains among blacks in the 1970s helped the black middle class to grow. Also in the 1970s black ownership of businesses increased. There was a substantial increase in the number of blacks attending college in the 1970s, both at historically black institutions and white institutions. The availability of financial aid (grants, loans, and work-study) and affirmative action programs contributed greatly to the increased enrollment of blacks in college. In the 1970s blacks made gains in sports, entertainment, and in literature. Athletes such as O.J. Simpson, Kareem Abdul Jabbar, and Reggie Jackson became famous and signed lucrative sport contracts. In 1977 author Alex Haley won a Pulitzer Prize for his famous work, *Roots*. Blacks made big gains politically in the 1970s. Having gained the right to vote, they elected black mayors in Los Angeles (Tom Bradley in 1973) and in Atlanta (Maynard Jackson in 1973). They also elected blacks to the U.S. House of Representatives and had a major impact on national, state, and local elections.

In the 1980s blacks continued to progress politically, but socioeconomically their progress was stifled by the conservative administration of Republican President Ronald Reagan. The conservative Reagan administration cut back a number of social programs designed to help blacks and the poor climb out of poverty. For example, it cut back financial aid for higher learning and job training programs. It was also against affirmative action. In the 1980s the median income for blacks continued to be much lower than that of whites. For example, in 1988 the median black income was 58 percent of the median white income. During the 1980s blacks elected for the first time black mayors in Chicago and New York City, Harold Washington and David Dinkins. Also during this period black membership in the U.S. House of Representatives increased. They made gains at the state and local levels as well.

The conservative trend in the 1980s continued to the 1990s. In 1991 Republican President George Bush appointed Clarence Thomas, a very conservative black Republican, to the Supreme Court. In November 1992 George Bush was defeated by the moderate Democrat Bill Clinton in the presidential election. Clinton's Democratic administration was met by strong opposition from conservatives in Congress. Job bills and programs that would have helped the poor were unable to pass through Congress. In the mid-term election of 1994 the Republicans regained control of the U.S. Senate, making it even more conservative. In 1995 affirmative action came under strong attack as many conservatives across the nation claimed it was reverse discrimination against whites. That same year affirmative action was dealt a devastating blow by the Supreme Court, which ruled that it was unconstitutional for federal programs to be set aside for certain individuals based on their race. The assault on affirmative action by a conservative Supreme Court wiped out hard-earned gains of blacks that were made possible by the Civil Rights Movement of the 1960s. And the irony of ironies was that a black man on the Supreme Court, Clarence Thomas, helped to lead the attack to reverse the Civil Rights gains of the 1960s and to set the clock back.

In November 1996 Bill Clinton was reelected, beating Republican candidate Robert Dole. The black vote was important to Clinton's victory. Blacks gave 83 percent of their vote to Clinton and only 12 percent of their vote to Dole. In contrast, whites gave 43 percent of their vote to Clinton and 46 percent of their vote to Dole.

In the mid-term election of November 1998, a Democratic disaster was predicted because of Clinton's sex scandal with former White House intern Monica Lewinsky. However, a heavy black turnout at the polls helped the Democrats avoid the predicted disaster. In fact, the Democrats not only dodged the predicted disaster, but they also picked up five seats in the U.S. House of Representatives and held their own in the U.S. Senate. In this election blacks voted 88 percent for the Democrats and 11 percent for the Republicans. Among ethnic groups, blacks were the Democrats' biggest supporters by far. A disappointment in the mid-term election of 1998 for blacks was the defeat of Democratic Senator Carol Moseley-Braun of Illinois. She was the only black in the U.S. Senate.

Also during the 1990s, African-Americans were the center of some dramatic events that captured national headlines in newspapers and brought much attention to Black America.

In March 1991, four white policemen in Los Angeles, California, stopped black motorist Rodney King for speeding, and then beat him. This beating was video-taped by a witness who released it to the media. When the videotape of the beating was shown on national television, it created an emotional outburst of shock and anger among millions of people. In April 1992 an all-white jury found the white policemen not guilty in the beating of Rodney King. The acquittal reaffirmed the belief in the minds of many blacks that they could not get justice in American courts. The acquittal of the white policemen also sent shock waves of emotion through many blacks, triggering a riot in Los

Angeles. Federal troops had to be called in to stop the looting and burning and unrest in South Central Los Angeles. This echo of the 1965 Watts riot was devastating to the city; it took fifty-eight lives and did millions of dollars in damage.

On October 16, 1995, over a million black men came together in Washington, D.C., in a spirit of love, peace, and brotherhood. They came together to atone for their irresponsibility, divisiveness, and disrespectful behavior toward their families and the black community, and to make a new start. They also came together to implement an agenda that would work toward improving the condition of black people politically, economically, socially, and spiritually. The historic event was called the *Million Man March*. It was spearheaded by Minister Louis Farrakhan, the charismatic and very outspoken leader of the Nation of Islam. The day of the event was called "A Day of Atonement." The Million Man March drew together black men from different faiths, different areas of the country, and different socioeconomic backgrounds.

During 1995 and 1996 a number of black churches were burned to the ground in mostly Southern states, including Tennessee, South Carolina, Louisiana, Kentucky, Alabama, Georgia, and Oklahoma. The burnings were thought to be the work of white supremacist groups such as the Ku Klux Klan. At a convention in St. Louis, Missouri, in June 1996, black ministers discussed the problem. One minister said thirty-two burnings of black churches had occurred over the last eighteen months.

In June 1998 three white men dragged a black man named James Byrd, Jr. to death behind a pickup truck. This heinous crime in Jasper, Texas, shocked the nation. Byrd, forty-nine, had accepted a ride from these white men and was subsequently driven to an isolated spot in the backwoods, chained to the truck, and dragged to death. In March 1999 a trial was held for John King, one of the three men accused of murdering Byrd. The jury selected for the trial in Jasper consisted of eleven whites and one black. To the surprise of many people, the jury found John King guilty of first-degree murder and sentenced him to death by lethal injection. It was the first time since slavery ended that a white person in the state of Texas had been sentenced to death for the murder of a black person. In September of 1999 a jury found the second man, Lawrence Russell Brewer, guilty of murder and gave him the death penalty. In November of 1999 a jury found the third man, Shawn Berry, guilty of murder and gave him life in prison.

On October 16, 2000, hundreds of thousands of Americans gathered in Washington, D.C. to celebrate family unity and religious faith. The gathering consisted of mostly African-Americans, but whites, Hispanics, Asians, and Native-Americans were also present. This event, called the *Million Family March*, was led by Nation of Islam's leader, Minister Louis Farrakhan. In his speech, Farrakhan said, "The family is the basic unit of civilization; therefore, everything must be done to care for the family unit." Other speakers at the march also stressed the importance of the family, pointing out how important strong families were to the well-being of a society. One concern of many march participants was the eroding of family values in society. They thought more emphasis should be put on the implementation of strong family values.

The march radiated a spirit of hope, joy, and unity. The atmosphere of the march was described as that of a huge family picnic. Many people who attended, said, "They were energized by the singers, musicians, and speakers."

The organizers of the Million Family March called for increased voter registration, Social Security reform, improvements in education and health care, substance abuse prevention, the right of families to live in crime-free communities, the establishment of an Economic Development Fund to rebuild deteriorated cities and other issues.

On November 7, 2000, African-Americans went to the polls in large numbers to cast their votes. In the Congressional races, their votes helped to reelect all thirty-nine black U.S. Congressmen. In the very close presidential race, blacks voted overwhelmingly for Democratic candidate Al Gore, giving him 90 percent of their votes, although Republican candidate George W. Bush was the winner.

The presidential race between Gore and Bush was marked by bitter controversy. After the election results were in, Gore challenged Bush's close victory in Florida, alleging voting irregularities, and demanded a hand recount of votes in certain Florida counties. Eventually, the Florida Supreme Court ruled in Gore's favor, demanding a hand recount of certain counties in Florida. However, a conservative U.S. Supreme Court, voting five-to-four, overturned the Florida ruling and decided in Bush's favor, stopping any further recounting of votes in Florida. This ruling by the U.S. Supreme Court sealed Bush's disputed victory in Florida, giving him that state's twenty-five electoral votes and the presidency of the United States. Gore, then conceded defeat ending thirty-six days of controversy.

▲▲▲

Blacks first came to what is now the United States with the Spanish in the 1500s. They arrived in the English settlement of Jamestown, Virginia, in 1619. A 1624 census classified blacks in the early Virginia colony as servants rather than slaves, but by 1661 a law had been put into effect formally recognizing slavery in Virginia. Enslaved Africans were also brought into the other American colonies. The increasing demand for cheap labor eventually brought millions of enslaved Africans to the United States. Slaves endured much pain, suffering, and dehumanization. However, they survived these adverse conditions with their remarkable strength and will, their great resiliency, their strong faith, and their ingenuity.

Blacks have contributed much to the development of the United States into the most powerful and wealthiest nation on earth. They have fought in all the nation's wars, from the Revolutionary War to Desert Storm. Blacks have also contributed to American music, dance, religion, cuisine, language, literature, and science. For example, black music such as jazz, blues, and gospel is famous the world over. Words used in everyday American language such as OK from *yaw kay*, hip from *hipi*, and dig from *dega* are of African origin. OK or okay means to approve, hip means to know what's happening, and dig means to understand.

Chapter 11

Psychological Effects of Slavery on Black People

For over three hundred long years European slave traders transported enslaved Africans to the Americas, where they were forced to labor in a brutal system of chattel slavery. This period of enslavement was a time of much pain and suffering for blacks. It seemed like they would be trapped in bondage forever and deliverance would never come. But in the nineteenth century slavery in the Americas began to end. Blacks in the French colony of Saint Domingue rose up against their oppressive slave masters, fought a revolution, won their freedom, and established the nation of Haiti in 1804. The Thirteenth Amendment abolished slavery in the United States in 1865. Slavery was abolished in Brazil in 1888.

Although slavery has been over for more than a century, blacks still are haunted psychologically by its legacy. The slave experience was cruel, destructive, humiliating, dehumanizing, and unnatural. The trauma of the slave experience has left psychological scars on blacks today, even though we are over a century removed from it.

During slavery, blacks were conditioned to have a *slave mentality*, to be loyal, submissive, respectful, and obedient to their slave masters. Slaves were expected to accept their subordinate roles in society and behave accordingly. Slaves who got out of their place were punished, generally with a whip. Fear was a weapon used by the slave masters and overseers to keep the slaves in their place. Fear was put into the slaves at an early age. Slaves were conditioned to feel unimportant and inferior so they would more readily accept their status and look up to their slave masters. Slaves were also set against one another, which was another way of controlling them.

Although it has been six generations since blacks were slaves in the United States, the legacy of slavery is still alive today. The alert observer who has knowledge of the history of slavery in America and knowledge of psychology can recognize attitudes and behavior patterns in present-day black Americans that are rooted in slavery.

Some might argue, however, that slavery occurred too long ago to affect present-day blacks psychologically. Yet we must understand that the slaves passed their attitudes and behaviors on to their children, who in turn passed these same attitudes and behaviors on to their children, and so on. The slaves were conditioned to feel inferior, to be submissive, to be divisive, and to disrespect one another. In short, the slaves were conditioned to self-destruct. Present-day blacks have inherited many of these destructive attitudes and behaviors.

Whites, like blacks, have also been haunted by slavery. The alert observer can detect many of their attitudes and behaviors toward blacks that are rooted in slavery. For example, whites are always concerned about blacks gathering in groups. Whites seem to think that blacks are conspiring against them when they gather in groups. This is a carry over from slavery, when their forefathers were concerned about slave rebellions.

Many books have been written about the history of blacks in slavery. However, very few books have been written about how this painful experience still affects African-Americans psychologically. More work needs to be done on this important but neglected subject.

Na'im Akbar, a black psychologist, has written a book that deals with the devastating psychological impact of slavery on African-Americans. Akbar's scholarly work, *Chains and Images of Psychological Slavery*, was first published in 1984. In his book, Akbar stresses the impact of slavery on blacks today.

> Slavery was "legally" ended in excess of 100 years ago, but...its brutality and unnaturalness constituted a severe psychological and social shock to the minds of African-Americans. This shock was so destructive to natural life processes that the current generation of African-Americans, though we are 5-6 generations removed from the actual experience of slavery, still carry the scars of this experience in both our social and mental lives.[1]

Another black psychologist who has done research in this field is Amos Wilson. His knowledge of the psychological impact of slavery on black people is reflected in his lectures, audiotapes, and written works. In his book, *The Developmental Psychology of the Black Child*, Wilson observes the impact of slavery on black people: "Enslavement of black people was not just physical but more importantly it was mental. Blacks suffer from a 'slave mentality' which is the result of the most massive and successful behavioral modification and brainwashing program in history."[2]

A number of African-American historians have known for some time about the psychological impact of slavery on black people, including Carter G. Woodson, Chancellor Williams, John Henrik Clarke, and Josef ben-Jochannan.

Woodson, in his book, *The Mis-education of the Negro* (1933), explains why blacks have problems with a black person in charge. "This refusal of Negroes to take orders from one another is due largely to the fact that slaveholders taught their bondsmen that they were as good as or better than any others and, therefore, should not be subjected to any member of their race."[3]

Williams is well acquainted with the psychological impact of slavery on black people. His understanding of the psychological scars that blacks carry from slavery is reflected in his book, *The Destruction of Black Civilization*. The scar that seems to concern him most is the lack of respect blacks show one another. Williams observes:

> This one concerns an inheritance from slavery. It is the attitude of indifference and disrespect of Blacks toward Blacks. To the average Black another Black is not as important as someone—anyone—of another race. Therefore, Black clerks or salespersons will serve whites more quickly and politely than they will serve members of their own race. This evil spirit from slavery pervades all "classes"—whether lawyers, carpenters, doctors, painters, nurses, shop owners, school heads, teachers, repairmen, garbage and trash men, paperhangers, taxi drivers, movers and haulers, employees in homes et al.[4]

Lack of respect is a "major obstacle to unity and progress...[yet it] is hardly ever openly discussed"[5] by black people. Williams says it "must not only be discussed but attacked in a nation-wide program in the home."[6]

Clarke has a great understanding of the impact of slavery on the black mind. One shackle from slavery that concerns him is blacks' lack of self-confidence. He says, "In slavery and in colonialism African people lost their self-confidence."[7] Clarke continues his discussion of self-confidence:

> When you want to lose a people from history, you first destroy their self-confidence and historical memory. This is the basis of our dilemma: Our...[oppressor] wants us to forget who we were so we will not know what we still can be. This statement is really about conflict in culture and self-confidence. Culture, conflict, and self-confidence are reoccurring themes in our lives and in the lives of all people.

With our people, these themes take on a special meaning. We created the world's oldest culture, and we act as if we are not aware of this fact...If we had confidence in our culture, the second rate cultures of other people would not fascinate us. [8]

This lack of self-confidence hurts us in many ways. It makes us doubt our ability to lead and manage; it makes us doubt our ability to compete in fields such as math and science, business and manufacturing, and law and medicine. It also causes us to doubt our ability to act independently; we often need other ethnic groups to verify things before we feel they are valid. But on the other hand, we have much self-confidence in our ability to compete in sports and entertainment.

Another shackle from slavery that concerns Clarke is blacks' lack of self-love. He is well aware that how you feel about yourself influences what you will do for yourself. If you don't love yourself, then you will destroy yourself rather than save yourself. Clarke says, "Psychologically, you cannot save yourself until you love yourself. And you begin with the mirror. You stand in front of the mirror until you like what's staring back at you."[9]

Ben-Jochannan (Dr. Ben) is very knowledgeable about the psychological impact of slavery on black people. In his book, *Africa: Mother of Western Civilization* he explains that slavery made black people believe that they were inferior, "even to the point of believing that...they never produced any history."[10]

The shackle from slavery and colonialism that seems to concern Dr. Ben the most is dependency. He is well aware that some black scholars follow in the footsteps of their white professors, teaching and quoting their biased history of black people, instead of doing independent thinking and analysis, and reaching their own conclusions about black history. Dr. Ben wishes these black scholars would be more independent in their works. He is a dedicated scholar with a lot of pride, and it hurts him to see black scholars writing the same biased literature as their former professors.

Sometimes it is necessary to return to the past in order to understand the present. To understand how mental shackles were put on the minds of blacks during slavery, and to understand how blacks today have inherited these destructive mental shackles, we must return to the past and investigate. The past has much to tell.

Still, many people, both black and white, are hesitant to revisit the past and discuss this emotional subject. It often arouses feelings of anger, guilt, shame, and shock. They believe discussing slavery, an event that occurred over a century ago, will reopen old wounds and stir up animosity between blacks and whites. Some say, "We can't undo what has been already been done. The past is over. Let's bury it and forget about it." Others say, "We are not responsible for what happened in the past, so don't bring it up." However, the aim of this psycho-historical analysis is neither to stir up animosity nor to reopen old wounds but rather to seek a better understanding of slavery and how its legacy still affects blacks psychologically. Armed with a better understanding of slavery and its psychological effects on black people, we may begin to break the shackles of mental slavery.

Black Inferiority

The view that black people are inferior is a myth. This myth is a modern creation. It was created to justify the slave trade, slavery, and the exploitation of black people.

The myth of black inferiority didn't exist in ancient times. The ancient Ethiopians and Egyptians developed great cultures. These Africans were well known in the ancient world for their knowledge and wisdom. Ethiopia was the mother of Egypt. The great civilization of Egypt dazzled the ancient world for thousands of years. The ancient Greeks borrowed much knowledge from ancient Egypt—philosophy, religion, science, and the arts. The modern world has inherited much knowledge that originated in Africa.

The myth of black inferiority also didn't exist in medieval times. During the Middle Ages (roughly 500 to 1500), while Europe was experiencing decline and stagnation, the West African empires of Ghana, Mali, and Songhay were witnessing a period of high cultural achievements. The University of Sankore, located at Timbuktu in the Songhay Empire, became famous as a center of learning. Also during the Middle Ages the African Moors were in power in Spain; they were part of the learned Islamic civilization that had spread over parts of Africa, Asia, and Europe.

In the 1300s and early 1400s, two African figures were on the minds of Europeans: King Mansa Musa of the Mali Empire, who made the extravagant pilgrimage to Mecca, and Prester John, the wealthy and powerful Christian king of Ethiopia. Mansa Musa was identified with the fabulous gold of West Africa, a region Europeans wanted very much to trade with. Europeans wanted to join forces with the legendary Christian king Prester John in a major war against the Muslims, aiming to break their power and their control of the trade routes to Africa and Western Asia. Both of these African figures reflected an image of power and wealth.

The Portuguese, directed by Prince Henry, began sailing down the coast of West Africa in the 1400s. The Portuguese made contact with the Africans and relationships soon developed between the two groups. These early relationships were between equals and were marked by mutual respect. The Portuguese were keenly aware that to establish successful trading relations and alliances with the Africans, they first had to gain their trust and confidence. Therefore, the Portuguese treated the Africans with respect, gave them gifts, and made promises to them. Had the Portuguese disrespected the Africans and angered them, they would have ruined their chance to develop successful trading relationships.

An example of the Portuguese making contact with an African ruler will be given here. In 1482 the Portuguese arrived on the Gold Coast to build a fort. But they first had to get permission from the king of the area, Kwame Ansa. The king was hesitant about giving the Portuguese permission to build a fort on his territory. In a beautiful speech, showing his foresight and alertness, King Ansa said that he noticed a difference in the Portuguese, that they now wore "rich-looking" clothes and wanted to be granted permission to erect buildings and remain in Africa, whereas before they dressed more modestly and were eager to return to Portugal when they finished trading. King Ansa thought it would be better if things continued as they had in the past. He could foresee conflict developing between the Portuguese and Africans if the Portuguese were allowed to build the fort and stay permanently on the Gold Coast. The Portuguese, however, with pleas, gifts, and promises were finally able to get his consent to build the fort.

The year 1517 is one of the most significant dates in the history of black people because it's the date when Africans were selected to be the slaves of the New World. That year Bishop Bartolomé de Las Casas went to Spain to plead the case of the Indians before King Charles V. Las Casas had seen the Indians in Hispaniola die in large numbers from brutal Spanish slavery. He pleaded to the king to spare the rest of them. He then suggested to King Charles V to use Africans to do the slave labor in the New World rather than the Indians. King Charles V agreed with Las Casas' suggestion and authorized the transport of four thousand Africans to the West Indies.

Africa had now been selected as the source of the cheap labor needed to develop and exploit the New World. The riches obtained from buying and selling Africans caused slaving to spread like wildfire in Africa. As a result, Africa became a big hunting ground for slaves.

As the years passed, European attitudes toward Africans began to change. Several factors caused them to look at Africans in a negative way. Europeans grew accustomed to seeing blacks not as free men, but as slaves, owned by whites. Slavery became so firmly entrenched in the Americas that it became institutionalized, a way of life. Africa became the source for slaves, a huge hunting ground, causing the continent and its people to be looked upon unfavorably in the eyes of the world. From allies, the Africans had sunk in European eyes to contemptible providers of slaves.[11] By the 1600s Europeans had begun to treat Africans as less than equals.

The literature written about Africa and African people has been mostly negative in the last four hundred years, reflecting the effects of the slave trade and slavery on the minds of the peoples of the world. This negative literature, unfortunately, contributed to blacks being labeled an inferior people and the race being identified with slavery. In the 1500s negative literature written about Africans was scarce, but beginning in the 1600s it became more common. For example, John Barbot, a slave trader, wrote a book about Africa about 1682 called *Description of the Coasts of North and South Guinea*. In this book Africans are described in a negative way. He makes it appear that the slave traders were doing the poor Africans a favor by bringing them to the Americas to serve as slaves. Barbot, of course, was trying to justify the transatlantic trade, by which he earned his living.[12] In the 1700s negative literature written about blacks became more widespread. Large numbers of books were written about Africa. These books used race to justify slavery, describing Africans as lazy, ignorant, and childlike. In the 1800s still more negative literature appeared. This literature was used to justify slavery, the scramble for Africa, and colonialism. Africa was called the *Dark Continent*, a primitive land where time had stood still, filled with murky swamps and dense jungles, inhabited by a people with no history and culture. In the 1900s large numbers of books, films, magazines, comic books, and newspaper articles appeared about Africa, describing it in a negative way. For example, in the jungle movies, Africans were portrayed as ignorant, cowardly, and primitive; whereas Europeans were portrayed as intelligent, courageous, and advanced. The jungle movies were anti-Africa propaganda; they did irreparable damage to Africa's image in the eyes of the world. Today this negative literature about Africa continues. For over four hundred years most literature written about Africa has conveyed one simple message: The African is inferior. This message has taken root and is very deeply embedded in the minds of the people of the world, like a religion.

We now turn to how the Africans were made to feel inferior. The slave masters were aware that Africans were a proud people. They were also aware that a proud people would rather die as free men than live as slaves. The slave masters, therefore, devised a system of inferiorization to deprive the Africans of their self-respect so they would more easily accept slavery and not resist. A number of dehumanizing and humiliating things were done to the slaves to deprive them of their self-respect. Slaves who didn't respect or submit to their slave masters were punished. For example, sometimes all the slaves on a plantation were forced to watch a slave who had disrespected his master be brutally lashed. This was also a warning to the other slaves not to step out of line or the same thing would happen to them. At the slave markets, slaves were examined like horses; buyers made them stretch, jump, and run. The slaves were kept ignorant. They were punished if they were caught trying to learn to read or write. The light of knowledge was not to be allowed to enter their minds. The slaves were constantly shown that they were helpless and powerless. For example, families were sometimes broken up and sold. A father might never see his wife again; a mother might never see her children again; a brother might never see his sister again. The men were unable to protect their families, which shattered their pride. In addition, the Africans were stripped of their culture—name, language, religion—and forced to adopt a European one. Stripped of their culture, subject to constant humiliation and dehumanization, and trapped in a powerless position, it is easy to understand how slaves could lose their self-respect and come to feel that they were inferior and whites were superior.

This feeling of inferiority is probably the most damaging scar that blacks have inherited from slavery. This evil spirit from the past continues to affect blacks in many different ways. The lack of respect for one another's abilities and knowledge stems from a feeling of inferiority. For example, a black man ran for mayor of a large city some years ago and was opposed by a white candidate. The black man possessed a bachelor's degree and a law degree in comparison to the white man's bachelor's degree. Yet some blacks thought the black man wasn't qualified to be mayor of the city. They said, "You can't vote for a man just because he is black. He has to be qualified." The question is, how qualified does a black candidate have to be? African-Americans not being comfortable with their blackness comes from a feeling of inferiority. Some blacks use chemicals to lighten their dark skins and straighten their kinky hair. Blacks who equate intelligence with being white and ignorance with being black reflect a feeling of inferiority. For example, some black kids in schools have been led to believe that speaking correct English and making good grades is *acting white.* These misguided kids, unfortunately, will sometimes tease and taunt other black kids who strive to make good grades and speak correct English, accusing them of acting white.

It is very painful to see African-American kids associate intelligence with whites and ignorance with blacks. However, you can't put all the blame on them. They have been programmed since birth to feel inferior about themselves. Throughout their young lives their color has been associated with things negative. They have no doubt watched many hours of television where blacks are portrayed as clowns, criminals, servants, and subordinates. They have no doubt listened to countless hours of disrespectful music on the radio that degrades black people, women in particular. In their environment, they probably never meet black lawyers, doctors, managers, scholars, and other professionals who could serve as role models; instead they interact with hustlers, high school dropouts, drug addicts, and gang members. On the other hand, when these kids see whites, they are mostly seen in a positive light, reflecting intelligence, leadership, power, and wealth. Through the power of suggestion these kids have been programmed to associate blacks with things negative, including ignorance, and whites with things positive, including intelligence. In other words, through the power of negative images the black kids have been unconsciously programmed to feel inferior.

The feeling of inferiority among blacks is perpetuated by their continuous appearance in a negative light. Blacks quickly make the front page of newspapers if they commit a sensational crime. They continue to be portrayed as criminals, clowns, menaces, and hustlers in movies. These negative portrayals are a continuation of the humiliations of slavery. During slavery blacks were humiliated by being sold naked at slave markets and by being whipped with an audience watching. Today they are humiliated by being shown in negative ways on the big screen. The constant humiliations diminish self-respect, making blacks feel inferior.

The feeling of inferiority hinders the progress of blacks, making them falsely believe that they can't achieve their aspirations and dreams because of their color. Therefore, blacks look at many things in a negative way rather than in a positive way. Their color becomes a handicap. Negative thinking, caused by negative programming, can make a person give up trying and say, "I can't accomplish this because I am black; the odds are too much against me." Negative programming causes blacks to direct their energy into destructive behaviors. For example, a young black man with a sharp mind and quick wit who has the potential to become a brilliant courtroom lawyer instead becomes a street hustler like a character in a movie, applying his smarts on the streets, where he makes quick money hustling—selling drugs and stolen items, gambling with loaded dice, and playing con games on people. However, this flashy but dangerous career in the underworld might lead him to prison or to an early death.

Blacks can overcome the feeling of inferiority. But they must turn away from the negative images of self and create positive images that will help them regain their self-respect. The music to which they listen should lift their spirits rather than ridicule them. The movies they watch should increase their self-esteem rather than mock and degrade them. The clothes they wear, their conversations with each other, the homes they live in, and their neighborhoods should reflect a positive image of themselves. Their children need to be taught to identify with *brothers and sisters* who respect themselves and bring dignity to African-Americans. Their children need to be taught about African-Americans who tried to uplift blacks as a people. Their children must be taught to strive for excellence and to respect themselves. Their children must be encouraged to stand tall and be strong. Their children must be encouraged to struggle against adversity and not surrender to it. These positive images of self will help blacks regain their self-respect and overcome the destructive feeling of inferiority.

Self-Hatred

In today's world the color black is generally associated with things negative or harmful. When the stock market crashes it is referred to as a *black day*. To get something from someone by threatening to embarrass him or her is known as *blackmail*. At the movies, bad guys dress in black and good guys wear white. However, the color black has not always been associated with things negative or harmful.

In ancient times the color black was associated with the divine. It symbolized being in touch with God. In the Old Testament, God often spoke to the Hebrews from thick, dark clouds. In ancient Egypt the color black was considered sacred. Egypt's greatest goddess was Isis; she was black, having African features. Her husband was Osiris, god of the underworld and the dead; he was black also. Their son was the god Horus, also black.

In medieval Europe some artists and writers associated the color black with evil and the devil. The black Moors, who were of the Muslim faith, were sometimes depicted in European paintings as being in complicity with the antichrist. The Moors had gotten on the bad side of European Christians because of the constant warfare in Spain. The European Christians were trying to drive the Moors back into Africa and, therefore, saw them mostly in a negative light.

Before the arrival of Europeans in Africa, many African societies associated the color white with evil spirits and things harmful. Dancers put white chalk on their bodies and performed dances to drive away evil spirits that were white.

The point here is, Africans and Europeans saw things differently in their respective cultures. Their different perceptions of the colors black and white at this juncture in history reflect this difference. In indigenous African cultures the color white was generally associated with things bad and the color black with things good. On the other hand, in European culture black was associated with things bad and white with things good.

Beginning in the 1500s, large numbers of enslaved Africans were brought to the New World by Europeans to help meet the growing demand for cheap labor.

Made to feel inferior, the enslaved Africans began to identify their pain and suffering with their black skin color. They began to think if they didn't have a black skin, they wouldn't be slaves and have to suffer. The enslaved Africans observed that people with white skins were free in society and didn't have to experience the suffering of slavery; they observed that their slave masters who had the power of life and death over them were white; they also observed that a white skin was equated with positive things such as wealth, knowledge, and power. Now a strange thing occurred in the minds of the enslaved Africans, call it magic if you want to. The strange thing was this: their psychology about the colors black and white were reversed. White was no longer associated with things evil or bad with the enslaved Africans; instead it was now associated with positive things such as happiness, good, power, and wealth. On the other hand, the color black had changed its meaning with the enslaved Africans; they now associated black with negative things such as evil, bad, sorrow, and suffering. People wore black to funerals and white to weddings.

Associating his pain and suffering with his black skin, the slave came to hate his blackness. He wanted to escape from it. He therefore concluded that to escape from his blackness he would have to change the color of his skin. The color to which he desired to change his skin was white. If he had white skin, he would be free in society and would be able to enjoy the benefits that it provided. In short, the slave had developed self-hatred and wanted to escape from his blackness by changing the color of his skin.

During slavery sexual unions between white slave masters and black female slaves produced mixed offspring called mulattoes or coloreds. The colored slaves were taught that they were better than the dark-skinned slaves because their skins were lighter. In many instances the light-skinned slaves were the skilled craftsmen and the house servants on the plantation. They had it easier than the dark-skinned slaves who toiled in the fields from sunup to sundown. Some mulatto slaves, because of their white blood, looked down on the dark-skinned slaves. Friction sometimes developed between the light-skinned slaves and the dark-skinned slaves, causing ill feelings between the two castes. The color hierarchy on the plantation gave rise to a well-known saying: "If you are white, you are all right; if you are yellow, you are mellow; if you are brown, you can stick around; but if you are black, get back."

The ending of slavery didn't destroy self-hate or rejection of self in the black community. Since slavery many blacks have continued to try to escape their blackness because of the pain and suffering associated with a black skin—conditions such as injustice, inequality, prejudice, and discrimination.

During the days of segregation many light-skinned blacks escaped their blackness by passing for white. In his book, *Sex and Race* (Vol. II), first published in 1942, J.A. Rogers cites a number of cases in which light-skinned blacks crossed the color line and passed for white. Many were able to get good jobs and marry into white families without their true racial identity being discovered. Some even rose to positions of prominence in society.

In addition to passing for white, some blacks have used chemicals to lightened their skin and straighten their kinky hair as a way to escape their blackness.

Unfortunately, when blacks attempt to escape their African identity, they are cutting the very roots that anchor them. And without their roots, the source of their strength and inspiration, they become more open to exploitation and manipulation. Blacks spend huge amounts of money to enhance or modify their African features, including money spent to buy beauty products and chemicals and money spent on surgery to alter their thick lips and wide noses. Blacks spend millions of dollars on alcohol each year to escape the pain and suffering of being black in society. However, this money could be better used for education, starting businesses, and rebuilding homes. When blacks attempt to escape their African identity, their true self, they also become vulnerable to taking on a *sub-planted identity*. A popular sub-planted identity among blacks is fads and fashions. For example, many young blacks today identify with particular brands of sneakers and sport jackets and, unfortunately, buy these items at "grossly inflated prices." Also, many young black males are currently wearing earrings, the latest fad, and are being economically exploited. In short, when blacks attempt to escape their blackness, they become vulnerable to manipulation and exploitation.

Self-hatred is a destructive mental shackle from slavery. Its vicious cycle is maintained by the continuous association of blackness with things negative. It lowers the self-esteem of its victims, causing them to be deficient in such valuable qualities as racial pride, self-confidence, self-love, self-capability, and knowledge of self. It may also cause its victims to desire to escape their true selves or to be on the defensive against negative experiences that a black skin may cause them in society. In the process, the victim spends valuable time and energy.

Back in the early 1960s when I was in elementary school, I remember a twelve- or thirteen-year-old girl who was very sensitive about her pronounced African features. She was very dark skinned and had very short hair on her head. By the standards of beauty then, she was considered very unattractive. This was before the *black is beautiful* movement of the late 1960s. If this girl were called *black* by another student, she would become very angry and challenge that student (boy or girl) to a fight. And she had a reputation for being able to fight very well. She was sort of tomboyish; I once saw her throw around a boy who wasn't a pushover. However, I thought she was kind of cute; she was just very dark skinned. A relative of mine told me some years ago that she had turned out all right. She had married and was raising a family with her husband.

Despite the pain and suffering and negativity associated with their blackness, there have always been blacks who were proud of their African identity, even during the time of slavery. In the 1790s blacks named the church they founded in Philadelphia, Pennsylvania, the African Methodist Episcopal Church, in reference to the motherland from which they had been uprooted. In 1829 David Walker, a free black abolitionist, published his antislavery pamphlet, *Walker's Appeal*. In this pamphlet Walker launched a bitter attack on slavery and stated that blacks didn't wish to be white, even though they were mired in bondage. In the 1920s Jamaican-born Marcus Garvey preached a message of black pride and self-determination. His message appealed to the black masses, who for such a long time had been taught that the color of their skin was a curse. In 1966 the black is beautiful movement began. It was highlighted by blacks wearing Afro hairdos and an African garment called a *dashiki*. This movement helped large numbers of blacks to become comfortable with their blackness. They were no longer ashamed to be called black or to identify with Africa.

This brings us to the old saying, "blacker the berry, sweeter the juice," which has been around for a long time. This old saying speaks to the everlasting pride that some blacks have maintained about their color down through the centuries, even during slavery. No matter how badly they were abused and scorned, they never wished to change the color of their skin. They desired to remain the way God had made them.

African-Americans can reverse the damaging effects of self-hatred by associating their blackness with positive things rather than negative things. Blacks need to learn more about American history and world history in general, and black history in particular. With a better knowledge of history, they can successfully combat the negative misconceptions and myths about black people and put them to rest. They need to create movies, music, and stories that reflect a positive image of black people. Their schools and neighborhoods should reflect a positive environment. By associating blackness with positive things—achievements, contributions, heroes, and wholesome environments—black self-esteem will grow. And with increased self-esteem comes increased pride, self-respect, and self-confidence. With these positive qualities, blacks will begin to feel that a black skin is not a handicap and that they can compete with any other ethnic group in society.

Dependency

Although they had been self-reliant in Africa, the enslaved Africans became totally dependent upon their slave masters for survival. In Africa the Africans had produced their own food, made their own clothing, built their own communities, and governed themselves. But on the plantation they had to rely on their slave masters for food, clothing, and shelter. The slave masters made the slaves dependent upon them as a way of maintaining control over them.

Over time the slaves developed a strong sense of dependency. Many came to believe that they couldn't make it on their own and, therefore, were afraid to run away from the plantation. They feared leaving *Old Massa*. Even when freedom came in 1865, many ex-slaves remained on the plantation with Old Massa rather than striking out on their own. They were reluctant to leave the plantation because they hadn't been prepared to make it on their own. The plantation was the only world the ex-slaves had known, so they remained on the plantation as sharecroppers, another form of servitude.

The shackle of dependency among many of today's blacks is a carryover from slavery that has been handed down from generation to generation. This shackle hampers the progress of the black community because it checks independent thinking and action, which are critical ingredients for the uplifting of a people. If blacks are going to uplift themselves in society, they must learn to have more confidence in their ability to solve their own problems. Many blacks rely on white people to do things for them that they should be doing for themselves. And if they do a task for themselves, they often need white people's stamp of approval on it.

Many blacks have become defiant and comfortable in their state of dependency. They say, "Let the white people do it for us." If you try to talk to them about self-reliance, they say, "We don't want to hear that old black stuff." They are more interested in watching NBA superstar Michael Jordan play basketball or boxer Mike Tyson fight than going to a PTA meeting to help plan the future of their kids or organizing to clean up their community. They don't believe that blacks are capable of doing independent research, independent planning, independent analyzing, and independent organizing. They have no confidence in blacks doing things by themselves. They feel that whites have to be there to assist them. These blacks feel more comfortable being consumers than business owners and producers; they feel more comfortable being followers than leaders. However, to be treated as equals and to be respected in the world, *blacks must stand on their own feet.*

Many black leaders have advocated self-reliance. Booker T. Washington founded Tuskegee Institute in Alabama, where students were taught vocational skills instead of the liberal arts. He was teaching them how to construct buildings, how to cook, how to farm and produce your own food, and how to be a skillful mechanic. These are survival skills. The liberal arts are important, but vocational skills are important too. Washington also urged blacks to own land, the base for all wealth. Marcus Garvey admired Washington's program of acquiring vocational skills. Garvey was a printer by trade, and "he too believed in education for self-reliance."[13] Garvey urged blacks to be more independent. He wanted them to be businessmen and manufacturers instead of consumers. Unlike Washington, Garvey believed in political agitation and speaking his mind. Elijah Muhammad was an admirer of Marcus Garvey and became a Garveyite. He became the leader of the Black Muslims (Nation of Islam) in 1933. Muhammad was a firm believer in self-reliance and urged his followers "to do for self." He wanted his followers to open businesses and become more independent.

The state of dependency in which blacks are now makes it difficult for many modern scholars and scientists to deal objectively with African cultural achievements in ancient and medieval history. These scholars and scientists seem to think that blacks have always been in a state of dependency.

Great Zimbabwe is an example of a great African architectural feat that was constructed during the Middle Ages, a time period when blacks were not in a state of dependency. Many modern writers have been unable to accept the fact that this stone city was constructed by indigenous Africans. The stone ruins are located in the southern part of the African nation of Zimbabwe. It is "the most immense construction site found in Africa outside of the pyramids of Egypt."[14] Great Zimbabwe was the capital of Monomotapa, a black empire that rose in the southern part of Africa in the 1400s. A German treasure hunter named Karl Mauch saw the great stone ruins of Great Zimbabwe in 1871. The finding of Great Zimbabwe created much controversy among European scholars and scientists. Many didn't believe that Africans were capable of building on such a grand scale. As a result, they attributed the construction of Great Zimbabwe to outsiders such as Arabs, Chinese, Portuguese, and others. However, recent work done by scientists using radiocarbon dating has determined that indigenous Africans built Great Zimbabwe.

Blacks can break the shackle of dependency by striving to stand on their own feet. Trying to do things by one's self is a confidence builder. Nothing builds confidence better than accomplishing a task or goal by one's self. For example, a student can gain more confidence solving five difficult math problems by himself than solving a hundred difficult math problems with the help of a teacher. Black people can gain valuable confidence in their own abilities by doing things for themselves. For example, the Million Man March of October 16, 1995, which attracted over a million black men to the nation's capital, was organized and financed by the black community. This Day of Atonement by black men helped to raise the self-esteem of millions of black people. Black Americans need to organize and do more things to help solve their own problems. They could organize to clean up and rebuild their neighborhoods and raise funds for education and self-development. Successful projects like these would help to raise self-confidence in black people. And with self-confidence to boost their spirit, black people would begin more and more to stand on their own feet.

Divisiveness

Slavers were aware that they had to keep the enslaved Africans divided so they couldn't come together against them. Slavers tried never to fill the hold of a ship with a group of Africans from the same tribe. Speaking the same language, Africans from the same tribe had united against slavers and had mutinied on ships. Planters had made the mistake of purchasing a group of Africans from the same tribe who then rebelled. Slavers were keenly aware that they had to keep the enslaved Africans divided or it could mean trouble.

On the plantations the slave master was aware that he needed to keep the slaves divided so they couldn't come together against him. He, therefore, used various tricks to manipulate the slaves into fighting among themselves so he could control them. The house slaves were divided against the field slaves. The house slaves generally had it easier than the field slaves and were allowed more privileges. A house slave might be allowed to go hunting or to town with the master, whereas the field slave had to stay behind and work on the plantation. On some big, prestigious plantations the house slaves were allowed to eat the same kind of food the master ate, wear the same kind of clothes the master wore, and live in the big house. Given better treatment, some of the house slaves developed an air of superiority over the field slaves. With one group receiving better treatment than the other, rivalries and jealousies, which worked in the master's favor naturally emerged. He could use one group to control the other. For example, if the master suspected a rebellion, he could use the loyal butler to visit the slave quarters and report back to him what the field slaves were plotting.

The skilled craftsmen were also divided against the field slaves. The carpenters, coopers, and brick masons had skills that the other slaves on the plantation didn't have. Having special skills, the craftsmen were led to believe that they were a notch better than the field slaves.

The slaves were also divided by skin color. The slaves who were the illegitimate off-spring of the master were usually given greater privileges.[15] These mulatto slaves, having white blood, were led to believe that they were better than the dark-skinned slaves. In many instances they worked in the big house, occupying positions such as butlers, coachmen, maids, and concubines. Because their lighter skin generally gave them more privileges and a higher caste, many mulatto slaves came to feel that they were superior to the darker-skinned slaves. This feeling of superiority sometimes created bad blood between the two groups. For example, during the Haitian Revolution the French manipulated the animosity between the mulattoes and blacks and caused them to go to war. This bitter struggle between the dark-skinned blacks and the light-skinned blacks became known as the *War between the Castes.*

The slave master's strategy of pitting the slaves against one another prevented unity from developing. His game of manipulation kept their attention focused away from the real problem—slavery itself.

Divisiveness is one of the most destructive shackles African-Americans have inherited from slavery. It continues to haunt the black community. The number of things that divide the black community have increased since slavery. Blacks are divided over such things as religions (Christianity, Islam, and Judaism), political parties (Democrats and Republicans), ideologies, (liberals, conservatives, integrationists, and separatists), identities (black, African-Americans, Black Muslims, Black Hebrews, mixed, colorless, and Americans), and occupations (managers, production workers, maintenance workers, professionals, and entertainers).

The old division of house against field is still alive today; however, it has taken on a more sophisticated form. For example, the house Negro may now be a manager in an industry wearing a suit and tie, but he is still stabbing and pulling rank on the field slave who is now the production worker.

The old divisiveness that existed on the plantation still manifests itself among blacks. For example, when blacks come together for a unity summit they all want to help solve the problems of Black America, but they generally disagree on how to do it. Instead of finding common ground among themselves, they focus on their differences such as ideology, religion, and political party. Their differences often cause the unity summit to come to a standstill.

Blacks can overcome the destructive shackle of divisiveness by striving to find common ground with one another, rather than spending so much time and energy debating about how they differ with one another. The Civil Rights Movement of the 1950s and 1960s is an example of a successful group effort by blacks working toward a common goal. Blacks who worked in the movement came from different political, social, and economic backgrounds, but they were able to transcend their differences and successfully combat discrimination, injustice, segregation, and inequality. The success of this movement against racism is an indication of what blacks can accomplish when they put aside their differences and work toward a common goal.

Over the years numerous black leaders have made fiery speeches urging blacks to unite or suffer the consequences. However, unity will be achieved only when people come together and work toward common goals. Historian Chancellor Williams emphasizes this point.

> Actual unity will be achieved, not by preaching, pleading or exhortations, but almost unconsciously as people work together for mutual benefits to each other and the advancement of the race as a whole. Meaningful, practical activities which involve even children in attacking the problems of their race will be the cement which we call unity.[16]

Mind Control

Rather than pay armed guards to watch the slaves, the slave owners devised a system of mind control to keep blacks in slavery.

The slave makers knew that in order to make the Africans into slaves they first had to break their spirit and then train them to be humble and obedient. One way of gaining control over the slaves' behavior was by punishment. If the slaves were not humble, obedient, and respectful to their masters they were punished. The slaves, therefore, tried to avoid doing things that would get them punished. So, by threat of punishment, the masters could control the thinking of the slaves, making them do things the masters wanted them to do.

On the other hand, a few masters gave rewards to influence their slaves' behavior. For example, a master might tell the slaves on the plantation that they could have a big dance at the end of the harvest season if they worked hard and were good slaves. To the slaves this meant a great deal because they generally had only two social periods a year, Christmas and *summer lay-by*; the rest of their time was spent doing monotonous labor.

The aim of the slave masters was to convince the blacks that they were supposed to be slaves. Therefore, things were done to slaves to make them feel helpless, powerless, and inferior. In time the blacks came to believe that they were inferior and were fit only to be slaves.

The slave owners knew that once they gained control of the thinking of the slaves, they would be in control of their minds and wouldn't have to be so concerned about their actions. The slaves would do what they had been programmed to do, even if the slave master wasn't around watching or even if it was to their detriment.

Back during slavery time on a bitterly cold winter night, a military officer told his slave to hold the reins of his horse while he went inside the officer's club for a moment. Inside the officer's club the military officer saw some of his old friends and began talking and drinking with them. Having such a good time, he forgot about his slave outside in the bitter cold and remained in the officer's club for hours. When he finally thought about his slave outside in the bitter cold, he rushed out the door and found his slave frozen to death. The military officer observed that his slave, even in death, was still holding the horse's reins in his hands. The point here is the slave had done what he had been programmed to do. That was to obey his master, although obeying his master cost him his life. This story shows how effective mind control could be on a slave.

However, some slaves couldn't be brainwashed. They never were convinced that they should be slaves. They were always looking for the chance to escape to freedom. Many did escape to freedom.

On the other hand, some slaves had been so successfully programmed that they identified with their slave master. They became upset when he became upset; they disliked something because he disliked it; they watched his plantation more carefully than he did, as if it belonged to them. Some slaves also told their slave master everything that they knew.

It has been over a century since slavery, but many present-day blacks still manifest a slave mentality. They still lack self-esteem and see themselves as inferior to whites. They still display a subservient attitude toward their boss. The slave mentality shouldn't come as a surprise, however, since the minds of blacks were shackled during slavery and haven't been unbound.

Over sixty years ago Carter G. Woodson observed that many of his people had a slave mentality. He was a very alert historian and had a great understanding of the psychology of black people. He was aware that education was one of the ways in which their minds were being controlled. He saw that through history and other subjects they were being subliminally taught (meaning their minds were being influenced unconsciously, without them knowing it) to admire and respect whites while at the same time they were being taught to look down upon themselves. He therefore initiated Negro History Week to counter this negative influence. Woodson has been called by some the "Father of Black History." His book, *The Mis-education of the Negro*, is probably his best work. In this book he explains how blacks were being educated to serve others instead of being educated to serve themselves. This great work is still relevant for black people today. In the following passage Woodson talks about blacks' shackled minds:

...The Negro's mind has been brought under the control of his oppressor. The problem of holding the Negro down, therefore, is easily solved. When you control a man's thinking you do not have to worry about his actions. You do not have to tell him not to stand here or go yonder. He will find his "proper place" and will stay in it. You do not need to send him to the back door. He will go without being told. In fact, if there is no back door, he will cut one for his special benefit.[17]

Freeing our shackled minds will be a difficult task. It will not be accomplished overnight, but it can be done. Slavery cut us off from our roots, the source from which a people draws strength and inspiration. We were forced to adopt a new culture. We were taught new ideas and new things, many of which worked to our disadvantage. For example, we were taught that we had no history or culture, which caused us to feel inferior to other people. The Jews have also been an oppressed people in history, but unlike us, they have never been completely cut off from their history and culture.

Cut off from our history, we have become a confused, frustrated, and dependent people. Proper education can help us clear up many things that we are confused about. For example, it can clear up who we are and what we have done in history. Education for self-reliance can train us to do for ourselves what we depend on others to do for us. The association of positive images with ourselves can help us to increase our pride and self-respect. Proper education and positive images are keys to freeing our shackled minds.

The Buffoon

During slavery one way a slave could get on the good side of a slave master was to entertain him. The funny slave who could make the slave master laugh with his joking, singing, and dancing was generally favored by the slave master. He was allowed to go to events that other slaves on the plantation were never allowed to go to. For example, the slave master might take the clowning slave with him to foxhunts and horse races, where he would show him off to his friends. The funny slave often could go unpunished for doing little things for which other slaves would be punished. The funny slave was less likely to be sold than one who wasn't favored by the slave master.

The art of buffoonery was used as a survival tactic by slaves. They mastered how to be funny, using this skill to shield themselves against the slave master's anger. Even a cruel slave master could be relaxed or disarmed by a funny slave who was a master of buffoonery. Clowning and buffoonery became one of the primary ways that the violent and abusive slave master could be controlled and manipulated.[18]

In having the slave entertain him, the slave master was reinforcing in his mind the idea that he was superior to the slave. Writers have long pointed to the jester, the clown, or the fool, as the inferior one who was responsible for making his superior laugh.[19] By being the object of laughter, the slave was being subtly mocked. Mockery is one of the more sophisticated forms of humiliation.[20]

We now turn to the present-day African-American buffoon, a throwback to the slavery buffoon.

The actor Lincoln Perry, who was better known as Stepin Fetchit, played the buffoon character in a number of movies. Fetchit was the first adult major black film personality whose career lasted beyond one or two movies, and during the 1930s, [he] became the best known film actor of his race.[21] He acted in such films as *Hearts in Dixie* (1929), *The Prodigal* (1931), *Charlie Chan in Egypt* (1935), and *Zenobia* (1939). In these movies Fetchit played a stereotyped character who was simple minded, lazy, scared, servile, and did everything in a slow manner, but if some imaginary danger such as a ghost threatened him, he suddenly came to life and started moving in a hurry. The stereotyped character that Fetchit played in these movies was a mockery to black manhood. Some conscious blacks pleaded with Fetchit to quit playing those stereotyped roles that degraded the race. It is said that he was defiant in his response and wouldn't admit that his roles in films were harmful to his people. Although he started out in 1927 earning seventy-five dollars a day, Fetchit probably earned over one million dollars before he went bankrupt in the 1940s.[22]

Movies and television comedies today still portray blacks as clowns and buffoons. These stereotyped presentations are a continuation of the Stepin Fetchit era films of the 1930s and 1940s.

It is often said that laughing is good for the soul, and just about everyone likes a good laugh. However, too much laughing can hinder one's development and progress. If a people's time is occupied mostly with comedy, it will distract them from doing more serious things such as pursuing academic excellence, delving into the secrets and mysteries of the universe, and seeking to advance mankind.

Blacks as a people spend too much of their time and energy with entertainment, which causes them to neglect more serious endeavors. They stay at home and watch the Chicago Bulls play basketball on television rather than attend their children's African-American history program at school. They go out and socialize when they should be at home helping their children with their homework. Young black males spend more time developing basketball skills than trying to master geometry and algebra. Because blacks spend so much time and energy with entertainment, their children's heroes and role models inevitably become mostly athletes, comedians, and singers rather than scientists, leaders, and scholars. And since black children's heroes and role models are mostly athletes, comedians, and singers they in turn strive to become athletes, comedians, and singers instead of leaders, scientists, and scholars.

Blacks are generally an optimistic and a fun-loving people. They love to laugh and have fun. Laughing is vital to people's well-being because it relaxes them and helps to soothe their nerves. There is nothing wrong with comedy as long as it doesn't reach the point where it degrades and mocks a people. On television programs and in movies we play buffoon roles that mock our leaders, our history, our religion, and our manhood and womanhood.

The continuous portrayal of blacks on television and at movie theaters as clowns, buffoons, and undesirables demean them in the eyes of the world. Many peoples of the world who have little or no contact with blacks see movies and television comedies in which blacks are clowning, and they are influenced by them. They come to believe that blacks are good at entertaining but when they attempt to do serious things such as leading and problem solving they are out of their league. This negative portrayal of blacks also reinforces the belief in peoples' minds that they are an inferior people. However, some blacks are blind to this hidden message of inferiority. They see blacks clowning in these movies and television comedies and they enjoy what they see, expressing their satisfaction with laughter and applause. But they fail to understand that while these negative images are entertaining them, they are also subliminally teaching their subconscious minds how to think negatively about themselves.

Some blacks justify African-Americans playing roles as buffoons on the grounds that they make a lot of money. They say, "You can talk that dignity stuff, but look at the millions of dollars these black actors and actresses are making."

We have to remember, however, that money can buy many things, but it can't buy true friends and dignity. These two things have to be earned. There have been many cases where people had an abundance of friends as long as they had an abundance of money to share with them, but when they lost their money they also lost most of their friends. Their so-called friends deserted them once the friendship was no longer profitable, whereas their few true friends remained with them, benefits or not.

There is a story about a famous boxer who had earned millions of dollars in the ring, but due to circumstances beyond his control he went bankrupt. Although he had lost all his money, he hadn't lost his dignity. Since his dignity was still intact, his friends and many admirers still respected him. And because they respected him, they helped him to become wealthier than he had been before. However, if he had lost his dignity, his friends and many admirers probably would have lost respect for him and wouldn't have wanted to be associated with him. And without his friends and many admirers to help him, he would have remained broke. The same thing is true for a people. If they lose their dignity, people won't respect them. If we as a people want other ethnic groups to respect us, we first must respect ourselves.

If a people sell their dignity for money, they have lost a priceless thing. Dignity can't be bought; it has to be earned.

The old slavery buffoon continues to haunt us. Hopefully, it can be overcome with time. Taking life more seriously can help us to overcome it. We must remember that if we don't take ourselves seriously, others won't take us seriously either. Laughter is good for the soul, but too much laughter is a distraction.

Rebelling

In defense of slavery, slave owners tried to present a favorable image. Their books, pamphlets, and pictures portrayed slaves as passive, docile, and happy. Contrary to this propaganda, however, the slaves were generally not happy in slavery and resisted it. Some slaves resisted by running away and by organizing slave revolts. Others resisted by destroying the slave master's property and avoiding work.

The slaves were forced to work for their slave master. They were his property. The slaves worked long hours, from sunup to sundown. The work cycle of the slaves began when they were small children, five or six, and lasted until they died or became totally disabled. No matter how hard the slaves worked, they didn't reap the fruits of their labor; instead their labor benefited their slave master.

Work in a natural society is looked upon with pride, both because it permits a man to express himself and because it supplies his survival needs.[23] However, in an unnatural environment such as slavery, where work is forced, it can become something a person hates and tries to avoid.

In his book, *Chains and Images of Psychological Slavery*, psychologist Na'im Akbar elaborates on how blacks, in the unnatural environment of slavery, came to hate and despise work.

> During slavery, work was used as a punishment. The need for workers was the most identifiable cause of the African-American's enslavement. Work came to be despised as any punishment is despised. Work became hated as does any activity which accomplishes no reward for the doer. Work became identified with slavery. Even today, the African-American slang expres-

sion which refers to a job as a "slave" communicates this painful connection.[24]

Avoiding work was a subtle and indirect way slaves rebelled against slavery. Probably the favorite method slaves used to avoid work was to pretend that they were ill or disabled. Some clever slaves devised ingenious ways to trick their masters into believing that they were ill or disabled. For many years a slave on a Mississippi plantation escaped work by persuading his master that he was nearly blind.[25] Another convinced his owner that he was totally disabled by rheumatism, until one day he was discovered vigorously rowing a boat.[26]

One can easily understand why slaves developed a negative attitude toward work and sought to avoid it when possible. Their labor benefited their slave master rather than them. A lifetime of hard work benefited neither the slaves nor their children.

Many blacks today have a negative attitude toward work, a mental shackle they have inherited from slavery. Although there are millions of blacks who work in society and many more who want to work but can't find employment, there are others who avoid work. Many African-Americans have developed a variety of habits to avoid work, such as reliance upon gambling, and other get-rich-quick schemes.[27]

Because work was forced during slavery, many slaves came to associate work with punishment and enslavement rather than something to enjoy and take pride in doing.

This negative attitude toward work often hurts blacks when they attempt to establish successful businesses. Some blacks don't want to invest the proper amount of time and effort that is required to establish a successful business. They are too shortsighted. They want overnight success, whereas it might take a few years before a business begins returning a good profit.

This same negative attitude causes some blacks not to take pride in their work. Lack of pride in their work can cost blacks promotions and, even worse, their jobs. In addition, some black businesses are hurt by their owners' lack of pride in their work. When the operation of these black businesses is not satisfactory, their customers sometimes never patronize them again or don't recommend their services to other people. Blacks need to take more pride in their work and also need to strive for excellence in whatever they do.

Destroying the slave master's property was another indirect way slaves rebelled. Slaves burned cotton gins, houses, crops, and barns. They broke tools and machines. They maimed or killed farm animals.

In today's society some blacks are still rebelling against the master by destroying his property. This negative attitude toward property is particularly evident in housing projects and tenement buildings, both of which are often seen by blacks as belonging to the white man but not to them. Therefore, some blacks vandalize and abuse these buildings. They kick in doors and knock out windows in abandoned apartments in these buildings. They also write on building walls. These blacks are indirectly getting back at the white man for racism against them. Vandalism is unconsciously gratifying in that it acts out that long-present resentment of the master's property.[28]

Although destroying the master's property was an indirect way of rebelling against slavery, it now works to our disadvantage. We need to make our neighborhoods clean, beautiful, safe, and strong rather than contributing to their destruction. Some black leaders have been known to say, "You can take the person out of the ghetto, but it is much more difficult to take the ghetto out of the person." Hopefully by understanding how this rebellious state of mind evolved we can begin to overcome it.

In his book, *Manchild in the Promised Land* (1965), Claude Brown says that he was "rebelling" when he was a juvenile delinquent youth in Harlem in the 1940s and 1950s. His early life of stealing, selling drugs, staying away from home at night, gang fighting, and truancy from school landed him in juvenile delinquent homes like Wiltwyck and Warwick. At Warwick a woman named Mrs. Cohen gave him books to read. These books were generally about famous people like Sugar Ray Robinson, Jackie Robinson, and Albert Einstein. Brown enjoyed these books, and he soon began to expand his mind beyond that of a hustler in the ghetto. Brown eventually returned to school, attending at night, and after a difficult struggle with the books he finally graduated. He then went on to attend law school at Columbia University in New York.

Brown was able to turn his young life around by redirecting his energy from negative things to positive things. At first he was rebelling against the system—stealing, playing hooky from school, and selling drugs. But in time he woke up and realized that his rebellious ways were self-destructive. He then channeled his anger and frustration into positive things—reading to develop and expand his mind, going to school to become a lawyer. The positive direction Brown chose put him in a position to save himself rather than destroy himself. It also put him in a position to help his people rather than contribute to their destruction.

A *brother* who works in a prison in Atlanta, Georgia, says, "Many young black men tell me the reason they are in prison is because they are rebelling." However turning to crime to vent their frustrations and anger is self-destructive. Instead it would be better if they channeled their energy into more positive things such as earning an education, learning a skill, participating in sports, and developing a better understanding of the world. These things can help them, their families, and their communities. On the other hand, directing their energy into such rebellious activities as gang fighting, dropping out of school, and selling drugs can destroy them and their communities. Young black men need to arm themselves with knowledge and thinking minds rather than with guns.

The Black Family

Slavery was very destructive to the black family. It did not respect the institution of marriage among slaves. It did not respect the black man's role as a father to his children. It did not respect the black woman's role as a mother to her children. This unnatural and inhuman treatment destabilized and weakened the black family. Black men and women in America today still carry scars from slavery's devastating effects on the black family.

Slaves were chattels like cattle or horses. They had no rights. Therefore, the law did not consider their marriages legally binding. Slave owners could break up slave marriages whenever they desired. Sometimes a slave master sold a man away from his wife and a woman away from her husband. A slave master could tie the knot between slaves by simply saying, "George, you and Betsy are now married."

The slave maker made the black male and female into reliable slaves by breaking their will to resist and by reversing their minds. The following is a procedure by which blacks were made into slaves. The slave maker, using a strong whip, often beat the most defiant and aggressive male slave in the presence of other male slaves and a female slave. This traumatic step served to break the male slave's will to resist and also put fear into the other slaves. The next step involved testing the resistance of the female slave. The slave maker tested the will of the female slave and if she resisted, she would be whipped into complete submission. The slave maker knew that once the female slave's will to resist had been broken, and she was in a state of mind whereby she would completely submit to her slave master's will, she would then, out of fear, raise her children to submit to his will also. Breaking the female slave's will to resist was a key step in the slave making process. We will now proceed further. In a natural environment the female depends upon the male for protection, and she also raises her female children to be dependent upon the male for protection, but she raises her male children to be independent like their father. However, the slave making process reversed the natural order of things. It convinced the female slave that the male slave was helpless and she could no longer rely upon him for protection; it also convinced her that she was all alone, standing by herself. As a result of the slave making process, the female slave was transformed from a natural *psychologically dependent state of mind* to an unnatural *frozen psychological independent state of mind*. The female slave, in a frozen psychological state of independence, would reverse the way she trained her male and female children. She would raise her female children to be psychologically independent like her. However, fearing that if she raised her male children to be psychologically independent, they would be killed, she became over-protective of them; and she therefore raised them to be psychologically dependent, and timid, but strong physically.

Through the slave making process the female slave was trained to reverse the roles of the raising of her male and female children. The male slave became a good worker in the fields but was submissive and psychologically dependent. The female slave became psychologically independent. This male-female slave role reversal led to the following scenario: the woman was now leading the man.

Slavery stripped away the black man's role as a true father to his children. It didn't allow him to be a provider, protector, and supporter of his children. Men who attempted to be true fathers to their children were generally punished or put to death. After several generations of such unnatural treatment, the African-American man adapted and began to avoid the role of a true father.[29]

During slavery the black man's manhood was measured in terms of the number of babies he could produce and his ability to do hard work. His ability to breed produced more slaves for his slave master, thereby increasing his slave master's wealth. His ability to do hard work produced bigger crops for his slave master, which in turn increased his slave master's profit. Qualities such as leadership and true fatherhood were not measures of a black man's manhood during slavery. In essence, slavery programmed the black man to be mentally and psychologically weak, but strong physically.

Black women were used as breeders and as workers during slavery. Slave women, who were good breeders were prized by slave masters because they could make them large profits. Indeed, breeding was so profitable that many slave girls became mothers at thirteen and fourteen years of age.[30] The state of Virginia became well known for its slave-breeding activities. In addition, female slaves were sexually exploited by slave masters, overseers, and other white men. Those who resisted were punished. Black women also worked in the fields and as house servants. Their hard work benefited their slave masters.

The physical and mental abuse of the black woman damaged the bonding between her and her children. On many occasions the black woman was sexually exploited and, as a result, conceived children because of forced pleasure or to bring profits to the slave master, not because of love and emotions for her mate. Conceiving children in such a negative manner impacted the way the black woman felt about her children. For example, if a slave woman had a love child and a rape child, she probably felt differently toward them. Looking at the love child no doubt brought sweet memories back to her, but looking at the rape child no doubt brought painful memories back to her. The harsh environment in which the female slave lived was not supportive of childbearing and child rearing. Many women either became abusive to their children or over-protective of them in response to such inhuman conditions.[31]

We turn now to the destructive legacy that slavery passed down to today's black family. Many black men and women today still carry scars from the unnatural conditions the black family experienced during slavery. These scars manifest themselves clearly to the alert observer. For example, some fathers spend more time and energy chasing women than raising their children. Some mothers raise their sons to be irresponsible and dependent, but raise their daughters to be responsible and independent.

The *plantation stud* of slavery times is still alive today in the black community. He reincarnates himself as the black male who boasts about the dozen children he has fathered in the neighborhood but lets the state support them. Such family irresponsibility does not occur among African people who have not endured the ravages of slavery.[32]

One important fact needs to be pointed out, however. It is the impact of racism on black employment. Many black males would work if they could find jobs. Unable to find work, many of them give up and let the state support their children. So then, the conditions of society help to maintain this destructive scar from slavery.

Slavery kept the black man's true manhood in check. It allowed him to do physical things such as work and breed, but it didn't allow him to be a leader, planner, thinker, protector, or analyst. As a result the black man compensated by defining his manhood in terms of his sexual and physical prowess.

This slavery definition of manhood has been passed down to present-day Black America. Many black males today equate being a man with only physical things such as fathering kids and the ability to compete in sports, rather than the whole package (a combination of both physical and mental abilities). Many black males today spend much time and energy learning physical things such as how to play basketball, how to party, and how to womanize, but on the other hand, they neglect academic development which teaches them how to think, analyze, plan, and lead. Some black males, unfortunately, have been led to believe that being intelligent is for sissies or is acting white. They believe that being seen with an armload of books will threaten their masculinity. What is needed is a balance between physical and mental development. The black male identifying his manhood through sexual and physical prowess is exhibiting a handicap from slavery. African men raised in indigenous African cultures certainly didn't define their manhood this way. Theirs was a balance of physical and mental attributes.

Many black females today are continuing the destructive motherhood patterns of slavery. They are overprotective of their sons, raising them to be irresponsible and dependent, while raising their daughters to be independent. Some scholars have described this abnormality as "mothers raising their daughters and loving their sons." The pattern of black females breeding at an early age is also being repeated today in the black community. Most of these teenage mothers, some as young as thirteen and fourteen, are not prepared educationally and emotionally to successfully raise children. Some end up abusing their children. What you have is *children raising children.*

The much-talked about friction between the black man and woman has its roots in slavery. In Africa the black man and woman were bound together by mutual love, affection, and respect, but once they became slaves in America the situation changed. The slave master divided them against each other as a way of controlling them. Also their manhood and womanhood were damaged by the unnatural conditions of slavery. Scars from this traumatic experience are seen today in Black America. We see them in womanizing black males who father children but avoid supporting them, which puts a strain on black male-female relations. We see them in black males who have been raised by their mothers to be dependent, some of whom when they marry expect their wives to be second mothers in terms of providing for them. These black males sometimes even call their wives "Mama." This situation further strains black male-female relations. We see these scars in black women who have been raised by their mothers to be independent, so independent in fact that they bruise black men's egos and manly pride, which sometimes drive them away. This situation really causes problems when a very independent black woman constantly reminds her husband that she makes more money than he does and is more educated than he. By understanding history, by understanding how black male-female relations are still being affected by scars from slavery, black men and women will be able to improve their relationships. Instead of attacking and tearing each other down, they will learn to encourage each other and to turn to each other for support.

One thing that needs to be made clear is we are not implying that today's black women should not be assertive and strong. They should stand tall and be strong. We only wish to show how slavery affected the upbringing of male and female children, an imbalance that haunts blacks today.

Today the black family is under much stress from friction between black men and women, large numbers of female-headed households, large numbers of black males in prisons, teenage mothers attempting to raise children, and other serious problems. Many of these problems are rooted in slavery. The black family continues to act out destructive behavior patterns that began during the unnatural conditions of slavery. Conditions in society such as the availability of drugs and guns, high unemployment among blacks, and racism only worsen these destructive behavior patterns. By understanding how these destructive behavior patterns originated and how they are maintained, we can begin to overcome them.

▲▲▲

Blacks were both physically and mentally enslaved. The physical shackles were removed with the abolishing of slavery. However, the mental shackles have remained intact and continue to impair black people psychologically. These mental shackles—dependency, divisiveness, the feeling of inferiority, lack of respect for one another, and self-hate—are invisible to people who are not aware of them. Yet they are so powerful, so damaging, and so devastating.

Analyzing the psychological effects of slavery on black people gives us a better understanding of how to overcome the mental scars of slavery. Before we can solve any problem, we first have to understand it.

Black people survived the cruelest slavery in the annals of history. Our strength, our strong faith, our extraordinary determination, and our uncanny ability to bounce back from adversity all enabled us to triumph over slavery. Many blacks today carry scars from slavery, but many others are practically unscarred from slavery. Many blacks today stand tall, walk proud, talk courageously, and strive for excellence. In terms of our experiences since slavery, the positives outweigh the negatives. In retrospect, we have come a long way.

Chapter 12

Historical Analysis

Before approaching the final chapter, we must analyze three subjects that have had a big impact on African history: (1) invasions of Africa, (2) the mulatto, and (3) weaknesses and strengths of black people.

Invasions of Africa

Africa's great riches attracted foreigners to her from the earliest times. Africa had things that foreigners needed and desired. She had valuable minerals like copper, iron ore, diamonds, and gold. She had land in abundance, a warm climate, food, areas where soil was fertile, and lastly an abundance of humans for slave labor. Africa's great riches made her irresistible to foreigners. They came to Africa as settlers, traders, missionaries, explorers, adventurers, and as invaders and conquerors. Africa has been under relentless pressure from invaders for over three thousand years. Constant pressure from invaders made it difficult for Africans to resist conquest.

▲▲▲

Ancient Egypt, with her abundant food supply, wealth, and advanced culture, was the first African nation to come under pressure from migrants and invaders. Egypt's crossroads location in northeast Africa made her accessible to white migrants from western

Asia and Europe. This location also made her vulnerable to invasions from western Asia and Europe.

White migrants from western Asia at first trickled into ancient Egypt, settling in the Delta or elsewhere in the north. As time passed they came in increasing numbers and began to infiltrate further southward into Egypt. Foreign infiltration of Egypt grew steadier and heavier with the passing centuries. Attacking her from within and without, foreigners eventually conquered Egypt.

The nomads from western Asia who came into Egypt were masters of disguise. They presented themselves to the Africans as friendly settlers and peaceful traders. Wearing masks of friendship and brotherhood, they were able to cleverly disguise their long-range plans of eventual domination of Egypt. Some intermarried with Egyptians and rose to positions of importance and power in Egypt. Also, these nomads generally came into Egypt in a subtle and gradual way. "They...came in a manner that never caused immediate alarm: small numbers spreading out, and then gradually forming separate communities next to an African village, town or city."[1] Over the centuries these Asiatic communities grew in size and power until they became a force to reckon with. Foreigners who came into Egypt as friendly settlers and peaceful traders helped to pave the way for their brothers to come in later as invaders and conquerors. The Africans seemed to be so occupied with living in the present that only a few could see the long-range threat of the Asians, who planned to eventually take over Egypt. Also, it seemed that only a few Africans could see the Asians' clever game of disguise and subtly. The Asians moved slowly and stealthily in undermining Egypt politically, promoting internal strife and divisiveness among the Africans, thus setting them up for future conquest.

Foreigners generally came into Egypt in large numbers during periods of chaos or breakdown in central government, when they could enter without being challenged. The First and Second Intermediate Periods witnessed large migrations of settlers into the country. After the first golden age in Egypt, central government broke down. A period of civil disorder followed. During this First Intermediate Period, large numbers of foreigners came into Egypt. The First Intermediate Period (2180 to 2040 B.C.) ended when Lower and Upper Egypt were reunited by the great African king Mentuhotep II of the Eleventh Dynasty. Mentuhotep II also drove the Asians out of Lower Egypt back into western Asia. "What Mentuhotep did was to put the government to flight, along with its army and other known supporters."[2] The reunification of the country set in motion the beginning of a second golden age in Egypt. The Eleventh and Twelfth Dynasties comprised the second golden age (2040 to 1786 B.C.). The Thirteenth Dynasty brought civil disorder and chaos back to Egypt. During the Second Intermediate Period (1785 to 1544 B.C.), Asians entered Egypt once again in large numbers, taking advantage of the breakdown in central government. Mired in chaos and civil disorder, Egypt was now vulnerable to invasions from the outside.

About 1700 B.C. Egypt was invaded by a nomadic people from western Asia called the Hyksos or Shepherd Kings. These invaders burned cities, destroyed temples, and treated the inhabitants of Egypt cruelly. They settled in the Delta of Lower Egypt, making Avaris their capital. The Hyksos invasion was aided by Asians already living in Egypt. They no doubt supplied the Hyksos with information about Egypt's strengths and weaknesses. The Hyksos founded the Fifteenth and Sixteenth Dynasties in Egypt. The Seventeenth Dynasty was founded by Africans at Thebes. However, the Egyptians grew weary of Hyksos rule and during the Seventeenth Dynasty a king named Sekenenre began a war to free Egypt from foreign control. Sekenenre died fighting the Hyksos and was succeeded by Kamose, his son. Kamose continued the war against the Hyksos. After Kamose's death his brother Ahmose I came to power. Ahmose I expelled the despised Hyksos from Egypt and reunited Lower and Upper Egypt again into one nation. This brought the Second Intermediate Period to an end.

Ahmose I founded the Eighteenth Dynasty, the beginning of the New Kingdom. The New Kingdom also included the Nineteenth and Twentieth Dynasties. The New Kingdom, 1554 to 1075 B.C., was Egypt's third and greatest golden age.

During the Nineteenth Dynasty, about 1222 B.C., Egypt was invaded by a large group of migrating whites called the Sea Peoples. The Sea Peoples joined forces with the Libyans and came against Egypt in a battle at Memphis. This coalition was defeated and put to flight by the Egyptian pharaoh Merneptah.

The Sea Peoples brought trouble to Egypt again during the Twentieth Dynasty, 1192 to 1075 B.C. Comprising a huge force, they again allied themselves with the Libyans and invaded Egypt by land and sea. This very large coalition of invaders was soundly defeated by Ramses III and his Egyptian forces. Although they had been defeated, the Sea Peoples and Libyans still desired to conquer Egypt. They, therefore, formed another coalition and invaded Egypt again but were stopped a second time by Ramses III. The Sea Peoples and Libyans invaded Egypt a third time but were annihilated by an Egyptian force led by Ramses III. Ramses III also won a victory over the Libyans in 1188 B.C. at Memphis.

Ramses III of the Twentieth Dynasty was a great leader. He held Egypt together when she was being repeatedly invaded by the Sea Peoples. The kings of the Twentieth Dynasty who followed him lacked his great leadership ability. As a result, Egypt began to decline. During this period Egypt experienced problems such as robberies of royal tombs, raids by Libyans, labor strikes, and corruption among government officials and landlords. The Twentieth Dynasty ended in 1075

B.C., which brought Egypt's third golden age, the New Kingdom, to a close.

Egypt had now collapsed into her Third Intermediate Period (1075 to 715 B.C.), Twenty-first through Twenty-fourth Dynasties, a time of breakdown in central government and turmoil in the country. Egypt was once again vulnerable to invasions. The Twenty-first Dynasty had kings ruling from Tanis in Lower Egypt and high priests ruling from Thebes in Upper Egypt. The Twenty-second Dynasty was founded by Libyans; they ruled from Tanis in the North. The Twenty-third Dynasty is vague; where the kings ruled from and the time period isn't clear. The Twenty-fourth Dynasty was comprised of Tefnakhte and his son Bocchoris. Their capital was at Sais in the Delta.

In 715 B.C Piankhi, the king of Ethiopia (Nubia), invaded Egypt to stop the southern advance of foreigners. Tefnakhte, the aggressive Asian king of the Delta, and his allies had seized almost all of Egypt. Tefnakhte's aim was to bring all of Egypt under his control. To confront the Asians, Piankhi armed himself with a large fleet of ships and thousands of soldiers. As Piankhi advanced down the Nile, large numbers of black Egyptians joined him. Piankhi was victorious over Tefnakhte in a battle fought at Heracleopolis. Continuing on down the Nile, he captured town after town. After his conquest of Egypt, Piankhi returned to Nubia, his home in the South. When Piankhi's brother Shabaka came to power in 710 B.C., he had to invade Lower Egypt and subdue Bocchoris, who was causing trouble. Shabaka's victory in the Delta united Lower and Upper Egypt for the fourth time. This was the third time that a southern king had rescued Egypt from foreign domination. Ethiopians, founders of the Twenty-fifth Dynasty in Egypt, were now the rulers of two countries, Nubia and Egypt.

Meanwhile, Egypt faced a new danger: the Assyrians, an Asiatic people armed with superior iron weapons (the Africans had only bronze weapons).

Warfare between Egypt and Assyria began when Egyptian forces went to the aid of Palestine against the Assyrians about 701 B.C. The Egyptian army was led by Taharqa; the Assyrians were led by King Sennacherib. Taharqa destroyed the Assyrian army with the help of an epidemic that killed many Assyrian soldiers. In 690 B.C. Taharqa became king of Ethiopia (also Egypt). In 673 B.C. the Assyrians, led by King Esarhaddon, invaded the Delta of Egypt but were stopped by Taharqa and his forces. In 671 B.C. Esarhaddon fought Taharqa a second time and was victorious, capturing Memphis. Two years later, in 669 B.C. Taharqa recaptured the city of Memphis from the Assyrians. In 666 B.C. Taharqa was defeated by the Assyrian king Ashurbanipal, son of King Esarhaddon. After this defeat Taharqa returned to Napata, where he died in 664 B.C. Taharqa's nephew Tanutamon was his successor. Tanutamon assembled an army, moved northward, and recaptured the city of Memphis. This victory angered the Assyrians. They invaded Egypt in 661 B.C., led by Ashurbanipal, who burned and looted the historic city of Thebes, defeated the Africans, and took control of Egypt. This defeat ended the Twenty-fifth Dynasty's rule of Egypt, which was an Ethiopian (Nubian) dynasty. The Assyrians didn't control Egypt very long. The Egyptians regained their independence from the Assyrians during the reign of Psamtik I, 664 to 610 B.C., the first king of the Twenty-sixth Dynasty. The Twenty-sixth Dynasty, 664 to 525 B.C., was composed of indigenous Egyptian rulers.

In 525 B.C. the Persians, led by King Cambyses, invaded Egypt. Cambyses overwhelmed the Egyptian king, Psamtik III, in a battle at Pelusium. The Persian conquest of Egypt ended her existence as an independent nation ruled by Africans, and from hereon foreigners would dominate her. Under Persian rule, the Egyptians rebelled several times. From 404 to 341 B.C., 63 years, the Egyptians were independent of Persian rule. This period comprised the Twenty-eighth, Twenty-ninth, and Thirtieth Dynasties. Between 343 and 341 B.C. the Persians, under Artaxerxes III, reconquered Egypt. This second period of Persian rule comprised the Thirty-first Dynasty.

In 332 B.C. the Greeks invaded Egypt. They were commanded by Alexander the Great of Macedonia. Alexander the Great easily established Greek rule in Egypt. After his death in 323 B.C., one of his generals, Ptolemy, took over the reins of leadership. Ptolemy ruled Egypt as *satrap* (governor) from 323 to 305 B.C. and as king from 305 to 283 B.C. Ptolemy founded the Ptolemaic Dynasty, which ruled Egypt down to the Roman conquest. Queen Cleopatra VII was the last ruler of this dynasty.

Cleopatra tried to keep Egypt from falling into Roman hands by having love affairs with Roman leaders Julius Caesar and Mark Antony. Her tactics only delayed Roman rule. In 31 B.C. the Romans, led by Octavian, defeated the forces of Mark Antony and Cleopatra in a battle at Actium. This defeat destroyed Cleopatra's attempt to keep Egypt from falling into Roman hands.

In 30 B.C. the Romans replaced the Greeks as the new rulers of Egypt. The Romans ruled Egypt for almost seven hundred years, 30 B.C. to A.D. 642.

In 639 the Arabs invaded Egypt. By 642 they had successfully conquered Egypt. They have ruled Egypt down to the present (except during interludes with the Turks, French, and British).

Although Egypt fell in the end, she resisted foreign domination for over twenty-five hundred years. The foreigners from western Asia and Europe put constant pressure on Egypt, attacking her from within and from without. Foreigners inside Egypt undermined her leadership and pitted the Africans against one another. A weak Egypt, suffering from civil strife and decentralization, was vulnerable to foreign invasions from the outside.

▲▲▲

We turn now to the ancient North African city-state of Carthage to examine how its wars with Rome led to the African loss of North Africa.

Carthage was founded about 814 B.C. by the Phoenicians, a seafaring Negroid people who in ancient times occupied a strip of land along the eastern Mediterranean coast. Carthage, within three hundred years, had grown from a small town to a wealthy and powerful city-state. Carthage's great trade had made her powerful and rich.

The Carthaginians, like the Greeks, had an interest in founding new colonies. Their common interest eventually brought them into conflict with one another. The Carthaginians and the Greeks fought continuously over the prized island of Sicily. Yet neither side was able to deliver a knockout blow. In 280 B.C. the Greek general Pyrrhus invaded Italy and clashed with the Romans, beating them twice. However, his victories cost him a lot of men. He next invaded the island of Sicily and attempted to drive the Carthaginians from it but was unsuccessful. He had better luck, however, in forecasting the future. Leaving Sicily in 276 B.C., Pyrrhus predicted that Rome and Carthage would someday fight over the control of the island. Rome and Carthage eventually clashed over Sicily, leading to three wars between the two countries, called the Punic Wars, they lasted 118 years.

The first war between Rome and Carthage began in 264 B.C. At the beginning of the war, Carthage had the better navy and Rome had the better army. Recognizing Carthage's naval advantage, the Romans got busy and built a navy that could challenge Carthage's. The Romans won a sea battle over Carthage at Mylae in 260 B.C. and another sea battle over Carthage in 256 B.C. In 255 B.C. the Carthaginians, using elephants, whipped the Romans in a land battle in North Africa. In 249 B.C. the Carthaginians were victorious over the Romans in a sea battle at Drepanum. In 241 B.C. the Romans delivered the knockout blow—a sea victory over Carthage in the battle of the Aegates Islands, that ended the First Punic War.

The long and bitter First Punic War was costly to both Rome and Carthage. Both countries spent much money to fight the war and lost many men in battles. The peace treaty was very hard on Carthage, requiring her to hand over Sicily to Rome and also to pay Rome the large sum of thirty-two hundred talents within ten years. Scraping for money to pay Rome, Carthage was unable to pay her large number of mercenary soldiers. As a result, they rebelled and fought a war against Carthage, called the Revolt of the Mercenaries. Carthage's famous general Hamilcar Barca was able to end the revolt in 238 B.C.

Carthage's dependence upon mercenary soldiers (Numidians, Libyans, Spaniards, and Gauls) to fight her wars put her at a disadvantage against Rome. Roman soldiers were motivated by patriotism and nationalism, whereas Carthage's mercenary soldiers (hired soldiers) were fighting for money. In general mercenary soldiers, fighting for money, are not as committed as soldiers fighting for love of their country.

In 237 B.C. the Carthaginian general Hamilcar Barca, accompanied by his son Hannibal (who was to became famous), left Carthage for Spain. Hamilcar's aim was to exploit the rich territory of Spain for its wealth. He was successful in gaining control of most of southern and eastern Spain before he died in 229 B.C. His successor was his son-in-law Hasdrubal. In 226 B.C., Hasdrubal reached a territorial agreement with Rome over common interests in Spain. This treaty made the Ebro River the dividing line between Roman and Carthaginian interests. Hasdrubal was killed in 221 B.C. His successor was Hannibal. The daring Hannibal ignored Roman orders in Spain and did as he pleased. His defiance brought him into conflict with Roman interests there. In 218 B.C. the Romans, infuriated by Hannibal's actions, declared war on Carthage.

Hannibal made the first move, leading his army from Spain over the dangerous snow-covered Alps into Italy. The march to Italy cost Hannibal thousands of men. Hannibal's daring march over the dangerous Alps Mountains into Italy caught the Romans by surprise. They hadn't anticipated such a bold move from the Africans. However, when the Romans learned of the weak condition of Hannibal's army, they were certain that he could be easily defeated. The Romans were on their own terrain and could put a much larger army than Hannibal's on the field.

In his battles with the Romans in Italy, Hannibal showed his great leadership ability and tactical genius. During his fifteen years there he never lost a battle. In his first battle against the Romans at Ticinus (Ticino), Hannibal faced a much larger Roman force commanded by the Roman general Scipio. But Hannibal, using his elephants as battle tanks, his superb cavalry, and the terrain to his advantage, routed the much larger Roman force. In the next battle at Trebia in December 218 B.C., Hannibal with his forty thousand soldiers faced a Roman force of about forty-four thousand men. In this battle Hannibal baited the Romans into a carefully planned trap and slaughtered them. Only ten thousand Romans escaped from this battle which Hannibal all his life considered his most brilliant tactical success.[3] The Romans and Carthaginians fought again at Lake Trasimene in April 217 B.C. In this battle Hannibal concealed his troops and ambushed the Roman general Flaminius and his forty thousand troops as they marched along the shore of Lake Trasimene. The Romans suffered heavy losses in this attack, some fifteen thousand men, including the Roman general Flaminius. They also had fifteen thousand men taken prisoner. This defeat caused the Romans much concern. They, therefore, changed leadership of the country. They made Fabius Maximus their new leader. Fabius advocated using delaying tactics against Hannibal. The Romans avoided engaging

Hannibal in battle, hoping instead to overcome him by wearing him down and weakening him. However, the Romans soon became frustrated with Fabius Maximus' delaying tactics and selected generals Varro and Paulus to replace him.

Hannibal was now a menace to Rome. He was ravaging the country and causing all kinds of problems. As a result, the Romans decided to attack him in force and rid the country of him. They assembled an army of 90,000 men to confront him. In August 216 B.C. the Romans met Hannibal and his men at Cannae. It was called by some the most famous battle of all antiquity. In this battle, Hannibal cleverly baited the Romans into a trap and annihilated them.

Hannibal's victory at Cannae put him in control of most of Italy. The only thing that stood in the way of his complete control of Italy was the capital city of Rome. However, Hannibal chose not to attack Rome because he didn't have seige artillery and a large enough army to take the city.

Needing men and supplies to bring all Italy under his control, Hannibal sent word to Carthage to give him support. Unfortunately for Hannibal, there was infighting within the Carthaginian senate. One side supported Hannibal's war effort and the other side didn't. The anti-Hannibal side was more interested in profiting from commerce than conquering Rome. With Carthage not united behind him, Hannibal didn't receive adequate reinforcements from home. Instead he had to rely on Italy to supply what he needed.

If Carthage had been united behind Hannibal's war effort in Italy and had sent him the men and supplies that he needed, he could have followed up his victory at Cannae with an attack on the city of Rome. And Hannibal, with his military genius and a large army, would have probably captured Rome and brought Italy under his control. However, because of the lack of support from Carthage, Hannibal had to try to persuade

Italians to desert Rome and come over to his side. Some came over to his side, but they weren't enough.

Hannibal's victory at Cannae in 216 B.C. was the high point in his war with the Romans and from then on, things slowly went downhill. The Romans, having learned a very important lesson at Cannae, refused to fight Hannibal again in Italy in an all-out battle. They knew that in this type of engagement he could use his strengths, his tactical genius, and his well-trained cavalry. Instead, they chose to let time wear him down and do him in. They harassed him; they weakened him; they prevented reinforcements from reaching him. By 208 B.C. Hannibal was desperately in need of men and supplies from Carthage or Spain. Conditions grew worse for Hannibal when his brother Hasdrubal and his army, coming from Spain to join forces with him, were ambushed and annihilated by a Roman army in Italy. This tragic event was the turning point of the Second Punic War.

Meanwhile, a Roman general named Scipio was causing problems for the Carthaginians. He had already taken Spain from the Carthaginians and was now contemplating invading Africa. Scipio had a stroke of good luck. He had been able to entice Masinissa, the leader of the superb Numidian cavalry, to desert Carthage and come over to his side. Masinissa blamed Carthage for the loss of his beloved Sophonisba, the beautiful and charming woman he was going to marry. The Carthaginians had been threatened by King Syphax of Numidia, who was also in love with Sophonisba, and to prevent him from attacking them, they had allowed Syphax to marry Sophonisba. This incident angered and hurt Masinissa, and out of revenge he aligned himself with the Romans. He became a bitter enemy of Carthage. With the Africans divided against one another, Scipio believed that the time was ripe for an invasion of Africa. Scipio also believed that an invasion of Africa would force Hannibal to come home to defend Carthage. The crafty Scipio knew that

Hannibal would come home to Africa with a weak and worn-out army, after spending years fighting in Italy. Scipio knew too that Hannibal would be fighting without the famous Numidian cavalry. This time it would be on his side. With the odds in his favor, Scipio decided to invade Africa.

In 204 B.C. Scipio and his fleet arrived in North Africa. Scipio aligned himself with Masinissa, and the coalition of Romans and Numidians wreaked havoc on Carthage. In one incident Scipio and Masinissa used trickery to overcome a larger Carthaginian-Numidian force. A fire was deliberately set in both Numidian and Carthaginian camps. When the men ran out of the camps to put the fire out, they were ambushed and slaughtered by the forces of Scipio and Masinissa. Thousands of Carthaginians and Numidians were killed. Meanwhile Carthage, low in spirits, sent for Hannibal to return home from Italy and defend Carthage against the Romans. Hannibal and his small force of men arrived in 203 B.C.

In 202 B.C. the troops of Hannibal and Scipio met at Zama to engage in a battle that determined the course of history. Scipio arrived with hardened, battle-tested Roman soldiers. Hannibal's army was comprised mostly of unseasoned soldiers, with some veterans, and eighty elephants. Scipio also had the famous Numidian cavalry, led by Masinissa, on his side. Hannibal's forces gave a good account of themselves but in the end they were defeated. Masinissa's cavalry had tipped the outcome of the battle in favor of the Romans. Scipio had finally avenged his father's defeat by Hannibal, which had occurred at Ticinus back in 218 B.C. This battle at Zama ended the Second Punic War.

Although the peace treaty of 201 B.C. ended the Second Punic War, it did not end Carthage's troubles with Masinissa, the Numidian king. Masinissa felt that Carthage was to blame for his loss of Sophonisba, the love of his life. As a result, he began to punish

Carthage, and continued to punish her for a period of nearly fifty years. Masinissa raided Carthage's towns and forced them to pay tribute to him. He also grabbed Carthage's territory. A frustrated Carthage asked Rome for help. Rome, playing the role of a neutral peacemaker, sent arbitrators to Carthage to negotiate a settlement between the two sides. The arbitrators pretended not to take sides, but they generally decided against Carthage.

Unknown to Masinissa, he was being used as a tool by the Romans to carry out a subtle, hidden war against Carthage. This war was designed to weaken Carthage, keep her on the defensive, and to set her up for eventual destruction. Carthage was in the path of Rome's march toward world conquest.

In 153 B.C. a commission from Rome arrived in Africa again to arbitrate the differences between Carthage and Numidia. A year earlier Masinissa had taken some more territory from Carthage and she was again asking Rome for help. The leader of the Roman arbitrators was eighty-one year-old Senator Cato, known for his stinginess and tightness with a dollar, which made him the object of laughs back in Rome. Although he was a miser, the Romans held him in very high regard because of his dedication and service to Rome. When Senator Cato saw how Carthage was thriving, he was shocked. He hadn't expected Carthage to have made such a quick economic recovery from the Second Punic War. Senator Cato interpreted a thriving Carthage to mean that she would soon be able to challenge Rome again militarily. With Senator Cato in such an unpleasant mood, the arbitration between Carthage and Numidia broke down, accomplishing nothing.

Filled with anger, Senator Cato left Africa and returned to Rome, where he told the Roman senate about the prosperity he had seen in Carthage and the threat she posed to the Romans. To further dramatize the situation Senator Cato showed the Roman senators "some Libyan figs"[4] that he had brought back from

Carthage. The senators marveled at how large and delicious-looking the figs were. Senator Cato then told them "that the country where they grew was only three days' sail from Rome."[5] From then on, Senator Cato concluded his speeches in the Roman Senate with the cry "Carthage must be destroyed."

Senator Cato's war talk aroused fear in the Romans, bringing them closer to the final clash with Carthage. In 150 B.C. fighting erupted between Carthage and Numidia. Carthage's involvement in a war meant that she had failed to abide by the treaty of 201 B.C. In 149 B.C. the Romans decided to go to war with Carthage.

The third and final war between Rome and Carthage was shorter than the previous two, lasting only three years, 149 to 146 B.C., but it was a very bitter and hard struggle. Carthage was fighting for her survival; Rome was fighting to eliminate Carthage as a rival in her march toward world conquest. The first two years of the Third Punic War witnessed Carthage defeating the Romans a number of times. However, in the third year of the war the tide turned in favor of the Romans and Numidians, and they defeated Carthage. Afterwards, the city of Carthage was looted and burned by the Romans. Carthage's destruction brought three years of valiant resistance by her inhabitants to an end. Senator Cato's cry of "Carthage must be destroyed" had become a reality.

The three wars between Rome and Carthage lasted 118 years. During this time the two combatants were locked in a life-and-death struggle. Carthage's dependence upon mercenary soldiers to fight her wars, her disunity, and her lack of commitment to the war effort worked to her disadvantage. The Romans were more organized and more committed to the war effort than Carthage. These factors worked to their advantage.

After Rome's conquest of Carthage in 146 B.C., she later moved on the Numidians. The Numidians had played an important role in helping the Romans conquer the Carthaginians, their African brothers. But because they stood in the path of Rome's march toward world domination, they too were conquered. By 30 B.C. all of North Africa, from Egypt to Morocco, was in Rome's hands and was part of her empire. The Africans had now permanently lost North Africa. Except for an interlude by the Vandals, Rome ruled North Africa down to the Arab conquest of the region.

▲▲▲

The Arabs, inspired by religious zeal to spread Islam, invaded North Africa in A.D. 639. This Arab army was led by Amr ibn-al-As. Within three years the Muslims had completed the conquest of Egypt. The forces of Islam pushed westward, conquering Libya, and by 672 they had taken control of Tunisia. Continuing their conquest, the Arabs moved on across Algeria and Morocco to the Atlantic Ocean about 681. Oqbar ben-Nafi was the Arab general who led the conquering Muslim forces to the Atlantic Ocean. In 682 Africans, led by Kuseila of Mauritania, began a strong resistance to Arab conquest. In a battle in Algeria the Arab general Oqbar ben-Nafi was defeated and killed by Kuseila and his African forces. In 688 Kuseila was slain in battle by Muslim forces. His successor was a brave relative, Queen Kahina. Kahina led a heroic African resistance against Arab conquest. She defeated the Arabs twice in battle, but in 705 she was killed. Kahina's death ended serious African resistance to Arab conquest. By 708 the Arabs had conquered North Africa, from Egypt across to Morocco. They were now the new rulers of North Africa, replacing the Romans.

Queen Kahina, with her strong leadership and magnetic personality, was able to hold the Africans together in an alliance against the Arabs, but when she was killed in battle the alliance fell apart.

Although the Africans were just as courageous as the Arabs in battle, they lacked the Arabs' unity and organization. As a result, they couldn't sustain a long war against the well-organized Arab armies and were eventually defeated.

In the fifteenth century, a new threat appeared in Africa: white men from Europe.

Portuguese mariners, directed by Prince Henry, arrived in West Africa in the 1440s. Within ten years they had made contact with the Africans and were trading with them, exchanging European goods for African products such as gold, fruits and nuts, skins, and pepper. The Portuguese also became increasingly involved in trading for enslaved Africans. In 1482 an African king, Kwame Ansa, allowed the Portuguese to build a fort on the Gold Coast of West Africa. In 1487 the Portuguese met the king of Congo and established friendly relations with his kingdom. The Africans of Congo, however, made the mistake of allowing the Portuguese to become involved in their family disputes. Portuguese involvement in the political affairs of Congo led to internal strife and wars among the Africans, which produced an abundance of captives for sale. In the 1520s the Portuguese began to aggressively exploit the kingdom of Congo for slaves. In response, Affonso, the king of Congo, tried to stop the spread of slaving in his kingdom but he was unable to do so. About 1530 the Portuguese expanded their slave operations beyond Congo into the state of Ndongo (Angola). Portuguese slaving brought ruin and depopulation to Angola. In Angola the Portuguese were confronted by the great African leader, Queen Nzinga, who resisted their conquest for over forty years.

In addition to making contact with West Africa, the Portuguese also made contact with East Africa and the Swahili civilization there along the coast. This Swahili civilization was "predominantly African in culture...though carrying the strong imprint of Arab influence and Islamic religion."[6] The inhabitants of this Swahili civilization used a language called Kiswahili, which was African with Arabic words added.

The Portuguese were surprised when they gazed at the prosperous Swahili city-states along the East African coast in 1498. They hadn't expected to find such a flourishing African culture there. These Swahili city-states had become wealthy from their trade with Arabia, Persia, India, China, and Indonesia (Indian Ocean Trade). The Portuguese soon began to demand that these wealthy cities pay them tribute or risk being attacked. In 1503 the Portuguese attacked the city of Zanzibar and forced the sultan to pay them tribute. In 1505 the Portuguese seized the cities of Kilwa and Mombasa and looted them. The Portuguese brought ruin and decay to many of the towns and cities along the East African coast. They also took over the lucrative East African coastal trade.

The Portuguese dominated the slave trade in Africa from roughly 1450 to 1600, a period of 150 years. The 1600s witnessed other European nations challenging the Portuguese monopoly on the slave trade. The Dutch, English, and French wanted to profit from the slave trade, too. Therefore, Europeans fought bitter wars with one another over the riches of the slave trade.

As the centuries passed, Europeans became increasingly interested in Africa. Africa's wealth was the magnet that attracted them. When Europeans came to Africa they generally settled in towns and forts near the coast for protection. From their strongholds near the coast, they traded with Africans for ivory, slaves, and other commodities. European military expeditions repeatedly attempted to invade the interior of the African continent but were stopped by the fighting ability of African armies, the hot and humid climate, and tropical diseases.

Despite the obstacles penetrating the interior of Africa, Europeans in the 1780s, began to think seriously about opening the continent up for commerce. They wanted to obtain African raw materials such as minerals, wood, cotton, wool, and palm oil for use in industry. They also wanted Africa to be a new market for European goods. Exploiting Africa's huge supply of raw materials and her large market for European goods would be more profitable to Europe than just the slave trade. In 1788 the British formed an organization called the African Association, which promoted the exploration of the interior of Africa. Their best-known explorer was Mungo Park, a Scotsman. Park explored areas of West Africa and learned in 1796 that the Niger River flowed eastward. Park published a book entitled *Travels in the Interior Districts of Africa.* After Park's expeditions into inner Africa, other explorers followed him, including the German Heinrich Barth, Englishmen Sir Richard Francis Burton and John Speke, and Scotsman David Livingstone.

In the 1800s Europeans, growing in power from the Industrial Revolution, shifted their focus from trading along the Africa coast toward the conquest of Africa. In 1830 the French invaded Algeria in North Africa and by 1847 had gained control of the country. In the 1880s the drive to conquer Africa accelerated. In 1881 the French took control of Tunisia. In 1882 the British seized Egypt. At the historic Berlin Conference of 1884-1885, Europeans agreed to abide by certain rules and regulations in the scramble for African territory. The French seized the Ivory Coast and French Guinea in 1893. The British colonized the Ashanti of the Gold Coast in 1902. The French made Morocco their colony in 1912. By 1914 all Africa except Liberia and Ethiopia was under European control.

In the conquest of Africa, Europeans were aided by disunity among Africans and a technological edge in weapons. Europeans took advantage of rivalries between African groups and played one against the other. The coming of the repeating rifle in the 1860s and the Maxim machine gun in the 1880s gave Europeans a decisive weapons advantage over the Africans. Another factor that helped the Europeans was their use of African troops to conquer other Africans. Still, the Africans resisted European conquest. The Ashanti of the Gold Coast, in particular, offered stiff resistance. They won a number of victories over the stubborn British before the British finally conquered them in 1902.

Ethiopia was the lone African nation that successfully resisted European conquest. In 1889 Menelik II came to power in Ethiopia. He was a strong, able, and smart leader. He realized that a disunited Ethiopia was vulnerable to European conquest. He, therefore, united Ethiopia. Meanwhile Italy, which had made a treaty with Menelik in 1889, was becoming more and more disturbed by his independent behavior. Menelik was doing things without Italian approval. For example, he independently conducted foreign affairs with other European nations without using Italian officials. The Italians saw this as a violation of the treaty of 1889. Menelik disagreed with the Italian interpretation of the treaty. On May 11, 1893, he declared it null and void. Two years later, in 1895, Italian forces moved into northern Ethiopia and began to penetrate the country. They captured the Ethiopian "towns of Addigrat and Adowa."[7] The overconfident Italians didn't realize, however, that Menelik was cleverly drawing them into his country so he could lay a trap for them. Many stories have been told of Menelik's strategy: he prepared inaccurate maps that were allowed to fall into the hands of the Italians, and had his agents, posing as guides, volunteer erroneous information.[8] The Ethiopians engaged the Italians in battle at Adowa in 1896. In this battle the Italians were overwhelmingly defeated, losing a large number of their men.

The Italians didn't forget this humiliation, however. In the 1920s under Benito Mussolini, the Italians began planning for the invasion and conquest of Ethiopia. They eventually built up a force of over five hundred thousand troops in Africa to use against Ethiopia. In October 1935 the Italian forces of Mussolini, about 120,000 strong, invaded Ethiopia. They conquered and occupied the country until it was liberated in 1941.

Ethiopia was freed from Italian rule by a coalition of forces, including the Ethiopian Patriots, British troops, South African troops, and thousands of black troops from all over Africa.

The Mulatto

The mulatto, or colored, is a person whose parents are black and white. In some parts of the world mulattoes are classified as white. For example, in the Arab world, North Africa, and the Middle East, mulattoes are classified as white. On the other hand, in the United States mulattoes are classified as black. If a person has just a drop of black blood in the United States he is considered black. However, in some parts of the world mulattoes were put in a class of their own, serving as buffers in a caste system. Whites were at the top, the mulattoes or coloreds were in the middle, and the blacks were at the bottom. The whites of South Africa used this type of caste system to maintain power and to control the blacks and coloreds under apartheid.

A person's racial identity may be determined by political and strategic circumstances. For example, a mulatto may be white, black, or colored, depending upon where in the world he resides. A light-skinned mulatto is classified as white in Egypt, black in the United States, and colored in South Africa.

The study of the mulatto is an intriguing and very sensitive subject. The late African-American historian J.A. Rogers did extensive research on the mixing of black and white people. During his time he was no doubt one of the world's leading authorities on race mixing. His books, *Sex and Race* and *Nature Knows No Color Line,* reflect his broad knowledge. The three-volume, *Sex and Race,* deals mainly with the white race mixing into the black race in Africa, Asia, North and South America, and the Caribbean islands. *Nature Knows No Color Line* deals mainly with the black race mixing into the white race in Europe and the United

States. It is well known that many blacks have whites in their family tree, but it is not well known that many whites have blacks in their family tree. There were large numbers of Africans living in ancient Greece and Rome. The Greco-Roman world of antiquity was familiar with Africans such as Egyptians, Ethiopians, Libyans, Numidians, Carthaginians, and Moors. The African Hannibal and his troops invaded Italy in 218 B.C. The African Moors were in Europe for over 700 years. These Africans intermixed with Europeans, leaving behind an African strain in them. In the United States, during the era of segregation, large numbers of light-skinned blacks entered the white community and were able to pass for white. Still, the black strain in the white race is a very, very sensitive subject.

Race mixing has impacted the history of North Africa. The original blacks of North Africa, called by some Berbers and Moors, intermixed with Europeans and Arabs who came into the region. This intermixing modified the physical appearance of the original black people of North Africa, causing them to be lighter in color.

Today Africa is divided into two parts: (1) a white North Africa, Muslim in culture, stretching from Egypt across to Morocco and (2) a black sub-Saharan Africa. Present-day scholars often write history as if Africa has always been divided into a white Africa and a black Africa. They often portray people of North Africa such as the ancient Egyptians, the ancient Carthaginians and Numidians, and the medieval Moors as white. This is a distortion, however. These people were indigenous Africans. The intermixing of the races has clouded the picture of a North Africa that was inhabited by blacks in ancient times.

The mulatto has had a big impact on African history. In fact, an analysis of African history is incomplete without discussing the mulatto. Yet many historians have avoided this sensitive and painful subject.

Mulattoes have played many different roles in African history.

Many mulattoes have worked against blacks in history. They didn't want to be identified as African because they despised their blackness. They joined with their European and Asian fathers against their mothers' people (other Africans). Mulattoes have also been an instrument used to divide, confuse, and weaken blacks. For example, mulatto agents, disguised as loyal blacks, were used to infiltrate African states and undermine them politically. Some of the most notorious slave traders were mulattoes. Being colored, they could penetrate deep into the interior of the continent and not draw attention to themselves, whereas white and Arab slave traders' pentration into the interior would cause alarm. Perhaps, the most notorious colored slave trader was Hamid bin Muhammed, better known as Tippu Tib. Tippu Tib's mother was an African, his father was half-Arab and half-African, making him one-quarter Arab and three-quarters African. He was called a Negroid Arab by some Europeans. Tippu Tib led many raiding expeditions from Zanzibar into the interior of Africa. His men consisted of Arabs, coloreds, blacks, and whites. He wreaked havoc on the blacks of Central Africa with his murdering and raiding. Tippu Tib became rich and powerful from his slave trading and plundering. Another notorious mulatto slave trader was Cha Cha; his Portuguese name was Norbert Da Souza. Cha Cha became rich from slave trading. He "lived in a palace in Dahomey like a maharajah."[9] In Cha Cha's harem were women from races all over the globe—Circassian, American, Dutch, Asian, French, Italian, African, etc.

During the Haitian Revolution the French divided the mulattoes against the blacks. The mulatto general André Rigaud and the black general Toussaint L'Ouverture came to blows in a bitter conflict called the War Between the Castes, which was won by Toussaint. The mulattoes eventually learned, however, that they were also oppressed by the French. In the end they united with the blacks under black general Jean-Jacques Dessalines and drove the French from Haiti in 1803.

Some mulattoes have played a double role in African history. When it was advantageous to be white, they identified themselves as white and when it was advantageous to be black, they identified themselves as black. They switched back and forth between the white world and the black world, enjoying the benefits of both. According to historian Chancellor Williams, noted mulatto historian Leo Africanus of the 1500s, operated this way. He would be African when it was beneficial and then switch to being white when it was beneficial. Leo Africanus wrote a valuable book about his travels in West Africa during the first half of the sixteenth century. His book was published by Italians in 1550.

Some mulattoes today fit in comfortably in both the white and black worlds. They are respected by both sides and get along well with both sides. They also don't try to exploit the advantage of having a dual ancestry.

Large numbers of mulattoes have remained loyal to the black race in history, although they could have passed for white and benefited. In this situation blackness is determined by a *state of mind* rather than color, because the person with the blackest skin, widest nose, and woolliest hair may be the biggest betrayer of the race.

The mulattoes Adam Clayton Powell, Jr. and Walter White could have easily passed for white but they chose to remain with the blacks. Congressman Powell of New York was proud of his blackness to the point that he flaunted it. His outspokenness and arrogance ruffled a lot of feathers. Walter White was secretary of the NAACP from 1931 to 1955. He was a bold civil rights leader who sometimes went South to investigate the lynching of blacks. Walter White was so nearly white that he could go and investigate the murders of Southern blacks without whites discovering that he was a Negro. However one time they discovered his Negro identity. In 1919 White went to Phillips County, Arkansas to investigate a riot in which mobs of angry whites had killed over two hundred blacks. Blacks in Phillips County had become tired of being treated unfairly and manipulated by their landlords under the sharecropping and tenant farming system. They met at a church to discuss how to force their oppressive landlords to deal fairly with them. During the meeting a group of whites fired into the packed "church, killing a number of women and men and wounding others."[10] Some blacks fired back at the attackers and killed one of them. This killing of one of the whites had triggered the riot. While White was in Phillips County, Arkansas, investigating the riot, a black man secretly told him he had heard the whites saying that they were going to get him. White, knowing what the whites were going to do to him if they caught him, immediately hurried to the train station and bought a ticket from the conductor for Memphis, Tennessee. The conductor told White that "he was leaving when the fun was just going to start." White asked him "What's the nature of the fun?" The conductor replied, "There's a...yellow...[Negro] down here passing for white and the boys are going to get him." White asked the conductor what the boys were going to do to the yellow Negro who was passing for white. The conductor replied, "When the boys get through with him he won't pass for white no more." White made it to Memphis safely, but he said the train ride was a very long one.

Weaknesses and Strengths of Black People

It is important to know your strengths and weaknesses. Weaknesses can be overcome. Weaknesses can be avoided. Strengths can compensate for weaknesses.

Also by knowing the strengths of your foes, you can avoid playing into their hands.

Individuals have strengths and weaknesses; basketball teams have strengths and weaknesses; armies have strengths and weaknesses; peoples have strengths and weaknesses. One of the most important things a person with a weakness can do is to admit it to himself that he has a weakness rather than to keep denying it. For example, a man with a serious drinking problem would be better off admitting to himself that he is an alcoholic rather than to keep saying that he has his drinking problem under control. By admitting to himself that he is an alcoholic, he can go to the doctor, get help, and overcome his drinking problem. A weakness can be avoided. For example, if a woman trying to lose weight is weak to the temptation of food, it would be best for her to avoid dining at all-you-can-eat restaurants. If a weakness is understood, a strength or strengths can be used to compensate for it. For example, Coach Wilson of the Public High League compensated for his basketball team's lack of height by utilizing its speed, quickness, and deadly outside shooting. His short-but-quick team won the city championship. If you know your foe's strengths, you can avoid playing into them. For example, a wise general would avoid an all-out battle on an open plain with an enemy's army that has a size and weaponry advantage. Instead he would probably try to lure it into the hills and forests, where he could use the terrain to his advantage and fight it guerrilla style.

Black people, struggling to survive in a deceptively dangerous and uncertain world, must study history to learn their weaknesses and strengths. A critical analysis will answer many questions, clear up much confusion, and enable them to move forward in history. What were their weaknesses in history? What were their strengths? How were blacks able to survive the most cruel slavery known to man? What caused blacks to fall from power in history? Why are blacks such a

divided and fragmented people? Why are blacks so distrustful and suspicious of one another? By understanding their weaknesses and strengths black people
can become strong again.

We have covered over five thousand years of documented history. This probe into our past has highlighted at least five major weaknesses: (1) disunity, (2)
hospitality to strangers without caution, (3) not looking beneath the surface of things for hidden meanings,
(4) lack of long range thinking and planning, and (5)
holding onto old customs and ways of doing things
and not adjusting to change.

Many blacks are reluctant to discuss these weaknesses. Some go into a state of denial when weaknesses are mentioned; some become irritated. Others
interpret the discussion of weaknesses as talking negative. However, not wanting to deal with your weaknesses is itself a sign of weakness.

Disunity—a glaring weakness—cost blacks dearly
in history. The inability to solve internal problems and
come together as a cohesive unit made blacks vulnerable to conquest. For example, African disunity led to
the Roman conquest of North Africa. The Romans took
advantage of a rift between the Numidians and the
Carthaginians and played one side against the other
and eventually conquered both sides. The rift between
the Numidians and the Carthaginians started over a
beautiful and charming woman name Sophonisba.
Sophonisba had been promised to the brilliant Numidian cavalry leader Masinissa. When King Syphax of
Numidia, who was also in love with her, threatened to
attack Carthage, she was given to him instead.
Masinissa became very angry when he learned that
Sophonisba had been given to King Syphax. He then,
out of revenge, deserted the Carthaginians and went
over to the Roman side. In 203 B.C. Hannibal left Italy
and returned home to Carthage to defend her against
the Roman general Scipio. "Hannibal sent an offer of
alliance to Masinissa but...[he] refused it and joined

Scipio."[11] Masinissa's superb cavalry helped the Romans to defeat Hannibal at Zama in 202 B.C. Zama was one of history's most important battles because it determined the course of history. Had Masinissa forgiven the Carthaginians and aligned himself with Hannibal against the Romans, history today would probably be different. After destroying Carthage in 146 B.C., the Romans eventually conquered the Numidians, their former allies. By 30 B.C. the Romans had conquered all of North Africa. So the Romans, taking advantage of a rift between Africans and playing a clever game of divide and conquer, were able to defeat the Africans and become the rulers of North Africa.

The Arabs, and later Europeans, also used a divide-and-conquer strategy against Africans. Africans repeatedly made the mistake of allowing foreigners to become involved in their wars. The foreigners would help one African group defeat its rival, then turn on and conquer it.

The Arabs' strategy was to weaken the Africans by having them fight against one another, and when they were weakened from internal blows, they could conquer them. The Arabs also divided the Africans along religious and racial lines. The Islamic Africans would be encouraged to go to war on non-Islamic Africans to bring them into the Muslim fold. For example, the current bitter war in the Sudan is a war pitting the Islamic North against the traditional African religion and Christian South. The Arabs used their offsprings by African women to weaken and control Africans. For example, Africans with Arab blood like Tippu Tib led slave raids and wars against other Africans.

The reason the slave trade was so devastating to Africa and couldn't be stopped was that Africans couldn't settle their differences and come together against a common foe, the European slave traders. In their conquest of Africa in the late 1800s and early 1900s, Europeans again were able to take advantage of rivalries between Africans, playing one side against the other.

Although the slave traders ravished Africa, some Africans were able to resist enslavement. Chief among these were the Mossi people of West Africa. Historian Chancellor Williams calls them "the remarkable Mossi." Unlike many other African states, the Mossi states were able to unite when they were threatened from the outside. Their wise leaders were aware that in unity there is strength. This explains why "the Mossi were one of the rare peoples of the intermediate zone who successfully defended themselves against slaving."[12]

In 1914 Ethiopia stood alone as the only African nation that had resisted European conquest. Ethiopia was able to resist Italian aggression because it was united. Ethiopians, united behind their wise and able leader Menelik II, inflicted a crushing defeat on the Italians at Adowa in 1896.

Several factors made it difficult for blacks to achieve unity. One factor was the inability to put aside differences and find common ground. Instead of focusing on common problems like foreign aggression and the slave trade, African chiefs and kings often let their petty differences divide them. Some black leaders thought their personal agendas were more important than the group's agenda. For example, if a group of African kings in an area attempted to stop the slave trade, one king might continue to participate in the slave trade because he considered his personal enrichment or the enrichment of his state more important than the welfare of black people as a whole. Still another factor that worked against black unity was the lack of trust of one another. Divided against one another for centuries, blacks had become suspicious of each other's motives and intentions, which made achieving unity difficult.

For black people to move forward in history, they will have to heal internally. Centuries of being divided have left a legacy of mistrust, suspicion, and hatred among blacks. This painful legacy of mistrust, suspicion, and hatred among blacks is manifest in the form of civil wars in Africa and gang violence in the United States. The pain and hurt that many blacks carry for one another should be addressed by black leadership and dealt with, rather than ignored. Black people need to forgive one another so they can heal internally. They have forgiven other peoples for the wrongs committed against them. For example, they have forgiven whites, Arabs, and Jews for their roles in the slave trade. But they haven't been able to forgive one another for the pain and suffering they have caused one another. Blacks need to treat one another with the same humanity that they treat other peoples. They need to show the same respect, kindness, forgiveness, and love to one another that they show to other peoples. Black people are very spiritual and religious; they need to ask God Almighty to give them the strength to forgive one another so they can heal. Until black people heal internally, they will continue to be a frustrated, confused, and divided people, unable to move forward in history.

However, blacks are not the only people who have experienced internal problems. For example, Europeans have fought bitter wars with one another. World Wars I and II, which cost many lives, were mostly wars between Europeans. However, Europeans have been able to come together and heal internally from these wars. Black people need to come together and forgive one another so healing can begin. Their wounds are very deep but time can heal them. But they don't need other people mediating their healing. They alone need to mediate their healing.

Another characteristic—hospitality to strangers without caution—has made African people vulnerable in history. Hospitality to strangers shows a beautiful humanity, and it's a good characteristic for a people to have. It was a part of African culture to be warm and friendly to strangers. However, inviting strangers into one's home and allowing them to become involved in the family business without getting to know them fully can cause trouble. A sense of caution with hospitality to strangers is needed. Blind trust in strangers set Africans up for exploitation and conquest. Historian John Henrik Clarke comments on the inability of Africans to read the intentions of foreigners:

> ...Africans have never been able to access successfully the temperament and the intentions of visitors to Africa and invaders. Most of the visitors to Africa and the invaders were first accepted by the Africans as friends because, in most cases, the Africans thought their intentions were good. The invaders stayed on in Africa as conquerors and enslavers, and most of the visitors stayed on as their collaborators. The aftermath of Africans' political naivete in relationship to visitors and invaders reverberates to this day.[13]

There is nothing wrong with being hospitable to strangers. It is a good display of man's humanity to his fellow man. But one has to use caution with it. If one doesn't, he can easily be taken advantage of.

The third weakness of black people was not looking beneath the surface of things for hidden meanings. This lack of alertness has caused black people a lot of problems in history. Clever people can make things look one way when they are another way. If one doesn't look beneath the surface of things for hidden meanings, he can easily be tricked and manipulated and not be aware of it. Some things in the world are clear and obvious, and they are easy to see and understand. Other things are subtle, disguised, and gradual, harder to see and understand. Cleverly disguised traps and pitfalls are hard to see. They are made that way to catch unaware and unsuspecting victims. The slave trade was a clever trap. The tempting trade goods such as rum, fancy hats, guns, and gaudy trinkets were the bait that lured the African chiefs and kings into the slave trade. Once they got into the slave trade they became trapped in it and couldn't get out. Many times Africans weren't able to see through the smiles, handshakes, gifts, and promises of foreigners and were fooled. Many times they weren't able to see through the flowery and glittery language of tricky treaties that could be interpreted in more than one way. Many times they failed to think things over carefully before making critical decisions. Many times they failed to examine things carefully before using or adopting them. Looks can be deceiving!

Black people can learn the lessons of history by looking more beneath the surface of things for hidden meanings. By doing this they can avoid the painful traps and pitfalls of the past that blacks walked blindly into. For example, they can avoid the destructive trap of selling drugs by studying another destructive trap of the past, the transatlantic slave trade. The present drug trade and the slave trade of the past have some similarities. The African chiefs and kings were lured into the slave trade by the quick wealth obtained from it. Today black dope sellers are lured into selling drugs by the quick money obtained from it. The African chiefs and kings didn't get anything of real value for selling their people into slavery. Today black dope sellers are not getting anything of real value for selling drugs to their people. The trade goods such as watered-down rum, cheap guns, and gaudy trinkets that the chiefs and kings received for selling other Africans into slavery weren't anything that could bring progress to Africa. The materialistic goods such as sporty cars, gold chains, and flashy clothes that the black dope sellers buy with their money from selling drugs to other blacks aren't anything that can bring progress to the black community. The slave trade wreaked havoc on the African continent, turning it into a huge slave hunting ground where death, pain, and suffering were common. The drug trade is currently causing pain and suffering in the black community. By studying the slave trade and its inner operations, how it lured and forced Africans into it, blacks can learn how to avoid the current drug trade, another destructive trap.

The fourth weakness of black people was a lack of long-range thinking and planning. This lack of foresight has hurt them in history. The present is important but so is the future. Looking into the future, and analyzing the long-range effects of things can help one avoid traps and pitfalls. For example, if African chiefs and kings had looked far ahead they could have avoided becoming trapped in destructive alliances. Many times in history an African chief aligned himself with a foreigner to overcome an African rival, but the foreigner, seeing the African's weakness of not looking far ahead, played one chief against the other and conquered both of them.

Living in the present and not being concerned enough about the future has worked against blacks in history. Many times blacks were unable to see foreigners' long-range plans for the conquest of their country. The future conquest would be hidden beneath such things as trade, high positions, brotherhood, and religion. Historian Chancellor Williams describes how the focus on short-term gains blinded Africans to the Arabs' long-range plan to dominate the Sudan.

> Once again, learning nothing from even just yesterday, the Black leadership paved the way for further Arab advances into their country. For the Blacks' struggle for personal power and, above all, their own personal security and welfare...[caused them to be] neither concerned about the future of their people nor their welfare in the living present. They were quite willing and ready to welcome the Arabs and to surrender their people to them in exchange for "high" office and limited consideration.[14]

Blacks have been so concerned about day-to-day survival that they haven't found time to plan well for the future. Black people must not leave the future up to chance. They need to prepare their children for survival in an uncertain world by making sure they are properly educated.

The fifth weakness of black people was holding onto old customs and ways of doing things and not adjusting to change. For example, during a critical period in ancient history when Asians such as the Hittites and Assyrians were arming themselves with iron-weapons, Africans failed to update their arsenal and it proved costly to them. The Assyrians' iron weapons gave them a big advantage over the Africans in warfare. That is the main reason why the Assyrians were able to take control of Egypt. The ancient world was changing at this critical juncture in history. The Bronze Age was being replaced by the Iron Age, and those who didn't adjust to this technological change suffered the consequences. Bronze weapons had become obsolete. Why didn't the Africans upgrade to iron weapons? It wasn't because they didn't know how to smelt iron ore into iron. Africans had known how to make iron for a long time. It wasn't because iron ore wasn't available. Although iron ore was scarce in Egypt, it was plentiful in Ethiopia. Why the blacks didn't update their weapons is hard to answer precisely. It may have been complacency or overconfidence, two things that can lull one to sleep. Or, perhaps the Africans were blinded by the wealth they were getting from foreign trade. However, one thing is certain: the inability to upgrade to iron weapons caused Africans to lose their domination in the ancient world to Asiatics—Assyrians and Persians. Iron-working eventually got underway in Ethiopia around the city of Meroe, but it came too late to keep the Ethiopians from being pushed out of Egypt by the iron-armed Assyrians. If the Ethiopians could have produced iron weapons earlier, they probably would have kept the iron-armed Assyrians from taking over Egypt in 661 B.C.

Throughout history blacks have failed to update certain cultural traits. Their tradition of hospitality to strangers often made them vulnerable. The strangers they put blind trust in often betrayed them. Blacks need to develop a caution and alertness when dealing with strangers. They can do this and still keep their *beautiful humanity*. In addition, black people need to examine alliances with other peoples in history. They have repeatedly made alliances and have often been betrayed by them. Black people need to adjust and become more sophisticated in how they make alliances with other peoples. Historian John Henrik Clarke comments on blacks making alliances with other peoples.

> Africans are always a junior partner. If the alliance can be broken without your consent, then it is not an alliance. You are a servant of it instead of being a partner of it. If it is a genuine alliance and a genuine friendship, then collectively both of you decide how it should go and how it should not go. Why are so many of the alliances blacks make with other people dismantled to the detriment of Africans and Africans have nothing to say about them? These alliances aren't real alliances and blacks aren't partners in them in the first place.[15]

There is nothing wrong with making alliances with people. Alliances can benefit blacks. But they have to develop the political sophistication to not be used. An alliance is not worth a hill of beans if blacks become servants in the alliance rather than partners.

Holding onto old ways of thinking and doing things can sometimes be detrimental. Sometimes for their own well-being it is necessary that blacks adjust to changes.

▲▲▲

We turn now to the strengths of black people. Many present-day historians have written about the shortcomings of black people, but few have written about their strengths. Black people's strengths are a neglected subject. How were blacks able to survive the horrors of slavery? How were blacks able to overcome impossible situations and not give up? The strengths of black people answer these questions. The strengths have more than compensated for their weaknesses.

A study of black history over thousands of years highlights at least four major strengths: (1) blacks' ability to draw hope, inspiration, and strength from religion; (2) their resiliency; (3) their creativity; and (4) the ability to adapt to harsh conditions.

From the earliest times, black people have been a very spiritual and a very religious people. Their ability to draw hope, inspiration, and strength from religion has benefited them in many ways.

Religion helped black people to survive slavery. During slavery many slaves identified with the Hebrews of the Old Testament, an oppressed people like themselves. The miraculous escape of the Hebrews from bondage in ancient Egypt, with God's help, was a source of hope and inspiration for the slaves. God's deliverance of the Hebrews from bondage strengthened the slaves' belief that one day God would deliver them from bondage, too. Some slave masters wouldn't allow their slaves to hold religious services. Not being allowed to worship God openly, slaves often stole away from the plantations to the cane fields and woods, where they worshiped God secretly. In these secret meetings, the slaves would call on the Lord and tell Him all about their troubles. The slaves drew strength from their prayers, inspiration from their songs, and hope from their sermons. In addition, the religious meeting was a place where the slaves comforted one another and shared their troubles. The religious meeting served as a type of group therapy for the slaves, which helped to keep them from going insane from the pain and suffering of slavery.

During the Civil Rights Movement of the 1950s and 1960s, civil rights workers encountered many obstacles trying to combat racism in a hostile Southern environment. They faced beatings, jailings, and murders in Mississippi; snarling dogs and powerful water hoses in Birmingham; and bigoted law enforcement officers in Georgia. Facing such formidable opposition, many civil rights workers turned to their Christian faith as a source of courage, strength, and inspiration. They drew inspiration from spiritual songs like "Ain't Nobody Going to Turn Me Around" and "Joshua Fought the Battle of Jericho." They drew courage and strength from the prayers and sermons of leaders such as Dr. Martin Luther King Jr. and Rev. Fred Shuttlesworth. Armed with spiritual power and the will to struggle until victory was won, the civil rights workers were able to break down the walls of segregation in the South.

Religion inspired blacks on the battlefield many times in history. For example, when King Piankhi and his Ethiopian army invaded Egypt in the eighth century B.C., they were on a holy mission to retake Egypt from foreigners. They were inspired by the African god Amon. King Piankhi of Ethiopia was a fanatical devotee of the god Amon. He ordered his mighty army to baptize itself in the Nile River at Thebes before going into battle. He told his soldiers to have faith in Amon and Amon would give them victory over their enemies. Fired up with religious zeal, Piankhi and his soldiers defeated the Asian king Tefnakhte at Heracleopolis. Moving on down the Nile, they captured town after town and eventually conquered all of Egypt. Another example was the conquest of Spain by the African Moors in A.D. 711. The Moors were facing King Roderick of Spain and his vast army that was much larger than theirs. But Tarik, their leader, was confident and unafraid. He told the Moors to put their trust in Allah and Allah would reward them. Tarik's impassioned words energized the Moors and they defeated the much larger Spanish army in battle. After this defeat of the Spaniards in this battle near Xeres, the Moors went on to conquer Spain.

In ancient Egypt religion inspired Africans to build huge and elaborate temples, monuments, and pyramids. It was only appropriate that the temples and monuments constructed for the gods be huge in size and as close to perfection as possible. The famous city of Thebes had many splendid and huge temples. The pyramids constructed for the pharaohs in their afterlife were of massive size and excellent quality because they were supposed to stand forever. In short, religion was the dynamic force that inspired Africans to build on such a colossal scale and with such precision.

Religion has been and still is very important to black people. They have turned to religion during times of trouble or crisis, whether on a battlefield, on a slave auction block, or in jail. Religion has also inspired them to build superstructures.

Resiliency is another strength of black people. The ability to bounce back from adversity is one of their greatest strengths. Again and again, we have bounced back from hardships, setbacks, failures, and defeats. Black people's great resiliency is reflected in their history. They have shown great resiliency in the Americas and in Africa.

Blacks in Africa have withstood thousands of years of adversity. They withstood the pain and suffering of the Euro-Asian slave trade and survived. The Euro-Asian slave trade lasted over twelve hundred years. Africans fought wars of resistance against invaders for over thirty-five hundred years and survived. The invaders first came from western Asia and then Europe. The invaders destroyed African towns, cities, and states but Africans rebuilt them. Africans also withstood droughts, floods, climatic changes, and expanding deserts.

Another tragedy in African history was the migrations. They were movements of African people from one part of the continent to another. They began far back in ancient history. The expanding Sahara and Kalahari Deserts forced many Africans to migrate to other parts of Africa in search of food, water, and shelter. Having their homelands taken over by foreigners also caused many Africans to migrate to other parts of Africa in search of freedom. The migrations were often marked by pain and suffering. There were starving times during the migrations when Africans couldn't find enough food to eat or water to drink. There were dying times during the migrations when Africans weakened by hunger, thirst, and diseases perished.

Despite all the adversity African people have faced through the millennia, they have survived. Historian Chancellor Williams says, "the strength and greatness of the African people can be measured by how, in the face of what at times seemed to be all the forces of hell, they fought through to survive it all and rebuilt kingdoms and empires, some of which endured a thousand years."[16]

The blacks' survival of slavery is the greatest example of human resiliency in world history. They were able to survive the cruelest, most inhumane, and most brutal slavery known to man. Slavery was both physical and mental. Although African-Americans still carry psychological scars from slavery, our "recovery has been substantial."[17]

If the history of African-Americans was written in a manner that reflected their great resiliency, the epic would inspire oppressed people worldwide.

African-Americans have shown great resiliency in the field of sports, from baseball player Jackie Robinson to boxers Muhammad Ali and Evander Holyfield.

Jackie Robinson was tested as no baseball player had ever been tested before when he attempted to break the color barrier in major league baseball in 1947. He had to prove to doubters that blacks were qualified both mentally and physically to play baseball at the major league level. Therefore, he had to perform well on the baseball field and as well as keep his composure. He had to bounce back from hitting slumps, poor fielding plays, and bad calls by umpires. He had to ignore taunts from opposing teams; he had to ignore racial slurs from fans; he had to ignore negative comments from the press. His superiors had told him "not to fight back." If Jackie had fought back and caused negative publicity, that would have been an excuse to drop the whole experiment. Jackie knew that if he broke under pressure and failed, he would set back the desegregation of baseball for a long time. However, thanks to his strong will to succeed and his great resiliency, he was successful in his attempt to desegregate major league baseball. He was so successful in fact that he was named Rookie of the Year in 1947 and helped to lead his team, the Brooklyn Dodgers, to a pennant. Jackie Robinson was a trailblazer. He blazed the trail for other black athletes to follow.

Muhammad Ali was a great boxer during his career. He has been called by some "the greatest heavyweight champion of all time." He possessed great charisma and showmanship, superb boxing skills and ring savvy, excellent stamina and willpower, great speed and quickness. However, his greatest attribute might have been his great resiliency—his remarkable ability to bounce back from setbacks, failures, and defeats. Ali won the heavyweight championship from Sonny Liston in 1964, but in 1967 he was stripped of his title for refusing to go into the U.S. military. He wasn't allowed to fight for three and a half years. In 1970 he began a comeback by defeating boxer Jerry Quarry. In 1971 he lost a championship fight to Joe Frazier. After this defeat, many people began to doubt that Ali would ever become heavyweight champion again. They thought his ring skills had deteriorated during his long absence from boxing. In 1973 he lost again, this time to a relatively unknown boxer named Ken Norton. In 1974 Ali surprised the boxing world when he knocked out the undefeated and defending heavyweight champion George Foreman, considered by some people to be invincible. This victory made Ali the heavyweight champion of the world for the second time. In 1978 Ali lost his heavyweight championship to Leon Spinks, which was a big upset. In a rematch the same year, Ali regained his heavyweight title. This gave Ali the distinction of being the first three-time heavyweight champion in boxing history. Ali's great resiliency enabled him to bounce back again and again from defeats, failures, and setbacks. When he was tested by adversity, he didn't fall apart; instead he stood tall and strong.

Evander Holyfield is another heavyweight champion who has shown "great resiliency" during his boxing career. He has come back again and again from defeats and setbacks. At one time he was diagnosed with a heart condition, but doctors later said that his health was all right and he could resume boxing. He has come back from two defeats to Riddick Bowe and a defeat to Michael Moore to become boxing's second three-time heavyweight champion of the world. His stunning defeat of "Iron" Mike Tyson on November 9, 1996 made him a three-time heavyweight champion. Very few people gave Holyfield a chance to beat Tyson. However, the champion believed in himself.

Resiliency is deeply ingrained in black people. It is as ingrained in them as rhythm. Throughout history blacks have repeatedly bounced back from adversity. Their resiliency is amazing.

The third strength of black people is great creativity. They have the ability to use their creativity to take things to another level as black athletes have in the sport of basketball. They have added creativity to the jump shot, the lay-up, the dunk shot, and to basketball in general. A dazzling reverse dunk by "Dr. J." Julius Erving could so inspire his teammates and so excite the fans that it often changed the momentum of a basketball game. A gravity-defying, double-clutching lay-up by Elgin Baylor could leave a crowd in awe. A sky-hook by Kareem Abdul-Jabbar was a thing of beauty to watch. An in-the-air, change-of-hands lay-up by Earvin "Magic" Johnson could leave a crowd speechless. Earl "The Pearl" Monroe's 360-degree spin moves could leave his defender shaking his head and mumbling to himself in disgust. A fade-away, double-pumping jump shot by Michael Jordan that hit nothing but net, could stir a crowd into a frenzy. The creativity and energy that black athletes have brought to the game of basketball in the last forty years have revolutionized the sport, making it a much more exciting game.

The great creativity of black people is reflected in their music. With their style, emotion, imagination, and sensuality, blacks have taken music to another level. They have created spirituals, ragtime, blues, jazz, gospel, reggae, and rap, all of which have become famous the world over. Black music is a multibillion-dollar industry. Peoples throughout the world enjoy listening to it. Many ethnic groups have been inspired by black musicians and have tried to copy and imitate them.

Black music is rooted in Africa but was brought to the New World by slaves. Enslaved Africans brought their knowledge of singing, dancing, and instrument playing to the Americas. From the songs, shouts, hollers, cries, calls, and hums of the slaves came the new music of spirituals, blues, ragtime, and jazz.

Despite the obstacle of racism, blacks have been responsible for numerous inventions, another manifestation of their great creativity. Granville T. Woods, sometimes called the "Black Edison," held over thirty-five patents on electro-mechanical devices which he sold to American Bell Telephone, General Electric, and Westinghouse Air Brake.[18] Another famous African-American inventor was Lewis Latimer. He worked with Thomas Edison, the inventor of the lightbulb. In 1878 Edison asked Latimer to work with him on a filament for the electric lightbulb; on October 19, 1879, in Menlo Park, New Jersey, Latimer's inexpensive cotton thread filament passed the test, which made electric light practical for homes.[19] On September 13, 1881,

Latimer and Joseph V. Nichols received a patent for their electric lamp.[20] Latimer "also drew for Alexander Bell the plans for the first telephone."[21] Still another famous African-American inventor was Elijah McCoy. He "patented fifty different inventions relating principally to automatic lubricators for machines."[22] African-American inventor Jan Matzeliger revolutionized the shoemaking industry with his shoemaking machine. His machine made obsolete the making of shoes by hand. His machine sewed the upper part of a shoe to the sole. African-American inventor Garret A. Morgan invented a gas mask and the first automatic stoplight.

Creative genius is reflected in the great structures Africans built in the Nile Valley and elsewhere on the continent. Africans in ancient Egypt used their rich imaginations to build temples, monuments, sphinxes, and pyramids on a massive scale. The three Great Pyramids at Giza are architectural wonders. The precision with which the Great Pyramids were built still holds the modern world in awe. Of the seven wonders of the ancient world, the Great Pyramids at Giza alone remain almost intact. The Great Sphinx is another architectural wonder created by blacks. Many splendid temples were constructed at Thebes, a very important religious city in ancient Egypt. Some of these temples were of colossal size and immense beauty. In southern Africa we find still another architectural wonder, Great Zimbabwe. The ruins of this great stone city, located in the present-day country of Zimbabwe, have intrigued modern scientists for over a century.

The fourth strength of black people is the ability to adapt to harsh conditions. This strength has helped them to survive in some very difficult situations. For example, the ability to adapt to the harsh conditions of a changing environment enabled the blacks to survive the Saharan Tragedy. The Sahara seven or eight thousand years ago was not a desert; instead, it was a land of forests, grasslands, rivers, and streams. A climate change caused the Sahara to begin to dry up. Over time, the Sahara was transformed from a fertile area into an "ocean of sand."[23] "It does not appear that any Black prophets came forth to warn...African people that over three million square miles of their fertile land would be made a vast wasteland by the slowly moving sandstorms from the north...."[24] The treacherous sandstorms no doubt buried whole towns and villages, bringing death to large numbers of people. However, there were small areas known as oases that the moving oceans of sand didn't bury. These oases, containing water, became places where blacks of the Sahara could build communities. Blacks adapted to the harsh environment of the Sahara and survived. They also learned how to navigate the dangerous and trackless Sahara Desert, which is over three thousand miles wide and over one thousand miles long. Violent sandstorms and a scarcity of food and water were factors that made traveling in the Sahara very hazardous.

In another example, blacks were able to adjust to the harsh conditions of slavery in the Caribbean, whereas the Indians could not. Europeans first enslaved the Indians of the Caribbean and forced them to work in the fields and mines. The cruelty of the Europeans toward the Indians, combined with diseases like smallpox and measles to which the indigenous people had no immunity, practically wiped out the Indians in the Caribbean. With the failure of Indian slavery, Europeans then turned to Africans to do their hard labor. The enslaved Africans also died in large numbers from the cruelty of European slavery. But eventually, they were able to adjust to the harsh conditions of slavery in the Caribbean and survive.

It seems that blacks have adapted well to the new climates everywhere. Originally from a warm climate in Africa, they have adapted to the cold climate of North America, Europe, and elsewhere. On the other hand, Europeans didn't seem to fare well in the hot, humid climate of tropical Africa. "Certain parts of tropical Africa, particularly the rainy lowlands of West Africa, long had a reputation as a"[25] place where whites often perished. Here, they were vulnerable to diseases such as yellow fever, malaria, and dysentery. The parts of Africa more suitable for European settlements were the cooler highlands of southern and eastern Africa.

▲▲▲

Understanding your strengths and weaknesses is a good thing. Weaknesses can be overcome. Weaknesses can be avoided. Strengths can compensate for weaknesses. If you know your strengths you can use them to your advantage.

Chapter 13

Crisis in the Black Community: Can Black People Overcome It?

The black community today faces a serious crisis. This crisis is reflected in problems such as inadequate health care and poor housing for large numbers of blacks, crime and violence in black neighborhoods, the increasing number of households headed by black females, the increasing imprisonment of young black males, unemployment among blacks that is more then twice that of whites, the rising number of HIV/AIDs cases among blacks, and divisiveness among blacks.

However, some blacks are of the opinion that there is no crisis in the black community. They say that the talk about a crisis is just "gloom-and-doom rhetoric." They point to the economic and political gains that blacks have made the last three decades as proof that there is no crisis. They say, "Look at the growing number of black millionaires in the United States. Michael Jordan, Oprah Winfrey, and Bill Cosby are even multi-millionaires. Look at the nice homes and fancy cars that many blacks have. Look at the fine clothes and expensive jewelry that many blacks wear. Look at the expensive restaurants in which many blacks dine. Many blacks can now eat high on the hog; they don't have to eat the neckbones and chitterlings, the turnip greens and sweet potatoes, the corn bread of yesteryears. Look at the large numbers of blacks who have college degrees as compared to forty years ago. Look at the large number of black politicians we have today as compared to forty years ago. Look at the favorable conditions in the black community today as compared to seven or eight years ago. Black spending power has increased; black homicides are down; crime has decreased. Things are looking better for Black America. There is no crisis in the black community."

Blacks have certainly come a long way over the last three decades, and things are looking better than seven or eight years ago. Large numbers of blacks have been able to get good jobs and have moved into the middle class. But millions of blacks still live in poverty. These blacks haven't made it. These blacks are really suffering today. They live in both urban areas and rural areas. They have poor housing; they are unemployed or have minimum-wage jobs; they lack the income to move out of crime- and drug-infested neighborhoods; they struggle to pay their utility bills during the winter; their kids often receive a substandard education. To many blacks who haven't made it, every day is a struggle to survive. Also, the blacks who have made it are just as vulnerable to acts of racism as those blacks who haven't made it. For example, because they wear a black skin, wealthy blacks are subject to being stopped or brutalized by bigoted policemen just like poor blacks.

Although blacks have made substantial social, economic, and political gains in the last thirty years, they still can't afford to become complacent, to be lulled into a false sense of security, because danger is silently lurking. The number of HIV/AIDS cases is on the rise among blacks. Black leaders can no longer afford to remain silent about this dreaded killer. The black community urgently needs AIDS education. The increasing imprisonment of young black males is a call for alarm. For example, Watts, a black section of Los Angeles, California, has been particularly hard hit by young black males being tied up with the judicial system. An estimated 70 percent of the young black men of Watts—those between the ages of sixteen and twenty-five—are on *some kind of paper*, meaning they're in jail, on parole or on probation.[1] The increasing number of households headed by black women is also a cause for alarm.

The AIDS crisis and the black family crisis threaten the very survival of black people. If blacks continue to be silent about AIDS and allow it to continue to go unchecked, it will wreak havoc on the black community in the future just as it is currently doing to blacks in sub-Saharan Africa. If young black males continue to go to prison at the alarming rate that they are going now, it will eventually create a big imbalance between black males and females, which will further strain relations between the sexes. If the number of households headed by females in the black community continues to grow, more and more black children will be denied a father to guide and love them. Blacks need to wake up and deal with these problems now.

The crisis in the black community is real. To see the crisis in the black community, one only needs to open his eyes.

Can black people overcome this crisis? Yes. But they must first wake up and deal with it. There is no quick fix for this crisis. Solving it will take time.

Eight propositions can help black people overcome this crisis and move forward in history: (1) face problems instead of avoiding them; (2) change negative behaviors toward one another; (3) spend more time thinking; (4) educate rather than miseducate; (5) become economically empowered; (6) become more involved and more alert politically; (7) change the distorted image of self; and (8) keep hope and faith alive. The solution to this crisis will not be given to blacks on a silver platter; instead it will take thinking, planning, hardwork, and vision to solve it.

Face Problems Instead of Avoiding Them

If African-Americans are to solve these problems, they must first face up to them, rather than seek to avoid them. However, to understand why black people seek to escape their problems, one has to understand their plight in America—the pain, the suffering, and the racism over the centuries. Black people, in their hopelessness, frustration, fear, dependency, and lack of understanding, attempt to escape their problems instead of facing them.

They escape through singing, rhyming, clowning, laughing, rapping, hollering, and complaining. They escape through drinking alcohol, using drugs, acting and looking white, partying, displaying fads and fashions, and playing sports. Another escape, popular among some young African-Americans, is driving around the neighborhood in their cars with the music blasting. These behaviors help black people temporarily escape reality but don't help them solve problems of unemployment, teenage pregnancies, black homicides, poor housing, and racism.

A prerequisite to successful problem solving is to get quiet. It is very difficult to solve problems in a noisy environment. Black people are not being quiet, but black people are going to have to start getting quiet so they can think.[2] There is a correlation between quietness and thinking. Quietness helps thinking; noise is a distraction to thinking. A person can concentrate better in a quiet environment than in a noisy environment.

Another benefit of getting quiet is that it helps one relax. If black people get quiet and relax, they can free themselves of unwanted tension. Tension is a dangerous menace to society. It can bring on strokes, heart attacks, and nervous breakdowns. Many people use drugs, alcohol, tranquilizers, and cigarettes to relieve themselves of tension. Black people can free themselves of tension by relaxing the mind and body, bringing themselves into harmony with one another.

When the mind and body are relaxed and are in a harmonious relationship, the true self is revealed. In this state, the mind is calm and poised, free of stress. When people are in tune with their true selves, they can better use their creativity and imagination to help them solve problems.

Good things will happen to black people if they get quiet. They will be able to think better, plan better, and analyze better. Getting quiet will also enable them to better see and understand the hidden and the unseen. There are things in the world that are hidden, masked, and disguised such as clever tricks, traps, and pitfalls. Unless blacks get quiet and look beneath the surface of things for hidden meanings, they will never see them.

Many things distract black people and keep them from getting quiet, things which in turn prevent them from doing serious thinking. They are distracted by loud music, sporting events, television, partying, and fads and fashions. Black people spend too much of their time involved in sports and entertainment and not enough of their time thinking about their future in an increasingly complex, sophisticated, and computerized world.

After black people get quiet and face up to their problems, they can begin to try to solve them. Solving their problems won't be quick or easy, however, because there are so many obstacles in the way. Prejudice and racism are examples of external obstacles. Disunity, lack of respect for one another, naïveté, indifference, and mistrust are examples of internal obstacles.

To overcome their problems, black people need to come together to set goals and make plans that will improve their lives, rather than come together to talk, complain, and make speeches. Present actions such as fiery speeches that denounce past wrongs, marches, boycotts, conventions, and mass meetings are not enough to help them overcome their problems, but they are a step in the right direction.

Setting goals and making plans require much thinking, analyzing, and planning, which is a lot of work. Black people can't afford to rely on other peoples to do their thinking, analyzing, research, and planning for them. Instead, they need to do these things for themselves. Many blacks, because of the slave experience, have become comfortable in their state of dependency. They rely on other people to do things for them that they should be doing for themselves. Black people need to become more self-reliant and do things for themselves. Being more self-reliant will boost their self-confidence.

If black kids see their parents and other blacks in the community working hard, setting goals, and making plans for the future, it will no doubt really inspire them.

After black people set goals and make plans, they need to work as hard as they can to accomplish them. Accomplishing goals and plans will require cooperation and mutual respect among black people.

Change Negative Behaviors Toward One Another

Black people's negative behaviors toward one another are major obstacles that prevent them from overcoming their problems and moving forward in history. These negative behaviors include being disrespectful to one another, being selfish to one another, being slick toward one another, being envious of one another's success, and not being able to forgive one another.

Disrespect is a behavior rooted in slavery. Slaves were conditioned to respect and honor their slave masters and at the same time to feel unimportant and helpless. As a result of this programming, slaves over time came to believe that whites were superior and they were inferior. The slaves passed their feeling of inferiority on to their children. This feeling of inferiority causes blacks to disrespect one another. To blacks, people from their own race are less important than people from other races. For example, a black foreman will sometimes walk all over the factory to solve his white employee's problem but won't show the same sensitivity to his black employee's problem. In another example, black cashiers in grocery stores will sometimes show more courtesy to white customers than to black customers. Backstabbing and calling one another names are also examples of being disrespectful. Furthermore, many blacks show a lack of respect for black leadership, expertise, and knowledge.

Disrespect toward one another is very destructive to the black community and needs to be dealt with. It breeds hurt feelings and anger, which leads to disunity and divisiveness among black people. This disunity and divisiveness among blacks is one reason why their businesses fail and their organizations split up.

Proper training and reeducation can foster respect among black people. Black children, at a very young age, should be trained to respect themselves and to respect others. Their training in self-respect should include exercises in teaching love and kindness to one another. Adult blacks can also be reeducated to respect one another. Unless black people develop a deep respect for one another, overcoming their problems will be very difficult.

A second negative behavior that many blacks manifest today is being selfish to one another. For example, in a classroom, a frustrated black teacher was overheard telling one of his students, "I have my education and you have to get yours." He should have told his student, "I have my education and I am going to help you get yours."

Selfishness in the black community is a rather recent phenomenon. It is an indicator of how times have changed since the 1960s when black people were more generous toward one another. Americans in general have also become more selfish toward one another in the last thirty-five years. In America today people are not as caring and as helpful as they were thirty-five years ago. Perhaps because society has become more dangerous in the last three decades people are more reluctant to help others, afraid that it might be to their detriment. Also people are not as appreciative of others helping them as they once were.

From the 1960s and on back into slavery, black people in the South practiced a concept called *sharing and caring*. Black people looked out for one another and helped one another to survive. They shared food and clothing, cars and trucks, televisions and radios, tools, and other things. For example, if a woman was preparing to bake a cake and needed some eggs, she could borrow them from her neighbor. And when she received her paycheck and bought groceries, she would repay the neighbor with the eggs she had borrowed. This concept of sharing and caring that black people practiced in Tennessee where the author grew up was a beautiful thing. Black people depended upon one another for mutual survival.

Some blacks today seem to have forgotten how hard their parents and forefathers struggled for them so they could be successful. They say, "I made it on my own." However, that statement is untrue. They didn't make it on their own. They benefited from those who sacrificed to get them where they are today.

Successful blacks who have made it—athletes, entertainers, and professionals—need to reach out and help the brothers and sisters who haven't made it. These successful blacks didn't make it by themselves, either. People such as Jackie Robinson, Dr. Martin Luther King, Jr., Rosa Parks, and many others struggled and sacrificed to get them where they are today.

The Civil Rights Movement paved the way for many present-day blacks to be successful. It was a group effort, an unselfish effort. Many civil rights workers showed their unselfishness when they sacrificed their jobs, their careers, and even their lives for others. Had they been selfish, the Civil Rights Movement would have never gotten off the ground.

African-Americans of 2002 need to reflect on their history and not forget the rocky roads they have traveled and the trouble they have seen as a people. The concept of sharing and caring in the black community needs to be restored because it was such a beautiful thing. It helped blacks survive the difficult times of slavery, the difficult period after Reconstruction, the rough times of the Great Depression. It can help them survive in the future.

A third negative behavior that black people manifest today is being slick toward one another. Slickness is using people's kindness, trust, or naïveté to get over on them. It includes blacks working con games on one another, stealing from one another, and manipulating one another. Slickness breeds mistrust, suspicion, selfishness, and fear among black people.

Slickness is rampant in the black community today, but it hasn't always been this way. There was a time when the black community held values and morals in high regard. For example, in the Southern community where the author grew up in the 1960s, slickness was frowned upon. Then, black people looked out for each other's welfare and shared with one another. A black person back then who stole from other blacks and manipulated them was often isolated from the black community. The word soon got around the neighborhood that the person couldn't be trusted. The concept of sharing and caring back in those days was based upon trust. If you couldn't trust a person, how could you depend upon him for survival in the hostile and intimidating Southern environment, where disrespecting a white person could get you killed?

Slickness in the black community needs to be talked about and dealt with. Although it isn't often mentioned, this behavior is the reason why some blacks—especially if they have been burned—are apprehensive about helping other blacks, contributing to black causes, joining black organizations, and patronizing black businesses. If black people are to build trust with one another, an ingredient that is vital to successful group functioning, they must avoid the self-destructive behavior of being slick with one another.

A fourth behavior that is destructive to the black community is black people being envious of one another's success. Too many brothers and sisters become envious of other brothers and sisters' success and try to bring them down. This destructive behavior causes rivalries and divisiveness in the black community.

A fifth behavior that is destructive to black people is the inability to forgive one another. This negative behavior has haunted them since ancient times. Many times in history, forgiveness would have made the difference between enslavement and freedom, victory and defeat, and subjection or independence. For example, during the Second Punic War if the Africans—Numidians and Carthaginians—could have reconciled their differences, the Romans would not have been able to exploit their differences and defeat Hannibal at Zama. The Numidian, Masinissa, could not forgive Carthage, whom he blamed for the loss of the woman he loved. Hannibal sent word to Masinissa, asking him to reconsider the situation and join forces with him against the Romans, but Masinissa was so filled with anger that he couldn't forgive the Carthaginians. Masinissa's alliance with the Romans tipped the balance in the Romans' favor and they defeated Hannibal at Zama in 202 B.C. Hannibal's defeat at Zama set in motion the eventual Roman conquest of North Africa. If Masinissa could have forgiven Carthage and joined forces with Hannibal against the Romans, history would no doubt be different today.

Although black people have a difficult time forgiving one another, they can very easily forgive other races and ethnic groups. Historian Chancellor Williams comments on this baffling phenomenon.

> For they are, as a race, too ready to forgive and forget past evils committed by foreigners; whereas, on the other hand, a fellow African tribe can easily become a "traditional enemy" and continue as such for so many generations that no one remembers what the original quarrel was all about![3]

We as a people not only need to forgive other ethnic groups but also need to learn to forgive one another. It seems that it is hard for blacks to ask for forgiveness when they have wronged one another. Telling a brother or sister "I am sorry if I hurt your feelings" could be the difference between continuing a warm friendship or making a bitter enemy. Asking one another for forgiveness for a wrong committed could be the difference between a church splitting up or becoming more united. Many times egos and pride keep blacks from asking one another for forgiveness. Some blacks also think that apologizing to other blacks is a sign of weakness.

The inability to forgive and reconcile differences can lead to bitter rivalries. One of the bitterest rivalries in sports over the last thirty years has been the rivalry between Muhammad Ali and Joe Frazier. It began with their first boxing match back in 1971 and has continued down to the present. It would be a beautiful thing if these two famous brothers could forgive one another and let time heal their deep wounds. A reconciliation between Muhammad Ali and Joe Frazier would no doubt inspire other blacks that have differences to come together and forgive one another.

The whole world needs more forgiveness and reconciliation. It would be a much better world to live in if different races and ethnic groups could forgive one another and reconcile their differences.

Dr. Frances Cress Welsing, an African-American psychiatrist, has studied black people's negative behaviors toward one another. She is keenly aware of how destructive these behaviors are to the black community. In her book, *The Isis Papers: The Keys to the Colors*, she comments on black people's negative behaviors toward one another.

> All of these patterns of self- and group-negating behavior, in addition to many others, become the invisible chains and shackles around the necks and ankles of the Black oppressed, holding all of us in a continuously destructive enslavement...These behaviors prevent group unity and efficient group effort. When parents, teachers and other adults practice these behaviors toward one another, they teach children how to practice them also. Black children learn that Black people do not respect each other, which also means Black people do not and should not respect themselves. The children, in turn, will teach those of following generations how to disrespect themselves and each other—thus, how to remain oppressed.[4]

Black people's negative behaviors toward one another are self-imposed chains that keep them from overcoming their problems and moving forward in history. It is important that black people address these negative behaviors and deal with them.

Spend More Time Thinking

If black people are going to overcome their problems, they need to spend more time thinking and less time involved in sports and entertainment. Dr. Welsing emphasizes this point: "Black people are not thinking, but Black people are going to have to begin thinking. Black people are not being quiet, but Black people are going to have to start getting quiet so they can think."[5] These statements may sound too critical and perhaps a little hard, but they are true. If black people were thinking critically, they wouldn't be in the adverse condition they are in today. Dr. Welsing's statements, unfortunately, also speak for the past. If our ancestors had taken the time to think things over carefully and critically, they could have avoided many traps and pitfalls that devastated them. They could also have avoided making hasty decisions that came back to haunt them.

If black people are going to survive in this confusing and deceptively dangerous world, they need to do more critical thinking. Critical thinking will help them make wiser decisions and enable them to see through things that are disguised and hidden.

The critical thinker examines things carefully. He is alert. He is focused. The critical thinker also uses foresight, hindsight, and insight to enhance his thinking ability. Foresight is the ability to look into the future and predict the results of things. A businessman uses foresight when he moves his store out of a neighborhood that shows signs of deterioration and relocates it in a neighborhood that shows signs of future prosperity. The businessman, looking long range, foresees financial losses in a neighborhood that is beginning to deteriorate. He may lose money in the short term, but over the long term he will make it all back and much more. Hindsight is the ability to analyze the past and see the mistake that was made. An example of hindsight is when a mother encourages her daughter to finish high school and avoid dropping out like she did. The daughter learns from her mother's mistake. Insight is being able to see and understand things that are hidden beneath the surface. For example, the wise old man of the village used his insight into human behavior to see through the smiling face and smooth talk of the trader.

Critical thinking is essential for many roles. For example, the wise general must be a critical thinker. The wise general must think critically because so much is at stake. His thinking affects the outcome of wars and battles which in turn impact the fate of nations and even the course of history. The wise general uses good judgement and makes sound decisions. He often overcomes his foe with tactical and strategic thinking. The wise general uses tactical thinking when he lures his foe into dense, woody terrain where his troops are hiding and ambushes them. He uses strategic thinking when he fights a guerrilla war against a larger and better-equipped foe and confuses and frustrates them, and eventually wins the war. The wise general uses tactics such as deception and manipulation to overcome his foe. He pretends to be weak when he is strong, thereby inviting his foe to attack him. He makes his foe overconfident and complacent by pretending to be weak. He often moves with quietness and stealth so he won't alarm his foe. He attacks his foe's weaknesses instead of strengths. The wise general can also make necessary adjustments to overcome his foe. By thinking critically, the wise general can overcome his foe with his mind.

In certain games like checkers and chess, much thinking is needed to be successful. In these games, a player tries to beat his opponent with moves and countermoves. The master checker player or chess player has to be a great tactician and strategist.

My experience with the game of checkers goes back to elementary school, but the summer of 1972 is when I came into my own as a checkers player. That summer I worked as a warehouseman in a depot, and the thing to do during breaks was to play checkers. We played checkers in the breakroom. There was always a lot of trash talking, a lot of good-natured teasing, and a lot of laughing going on while we played. Everyone was having lots of fun! My opponent was usually an older man named James, a good checker player. Old James would beat me in checkers and talk *plenty smack* while he did it. He would say things to me like "I'm putting a good whipping on this young scrub... Move fish, don't take all day to move now" and "Study long, study wrong." The brothers in the break room would laugh at his trash talk and say, "Old James is putting a good whipping on that young blood." However, after about four weeks of playing against Old James, I had him all figured out. Old James' strategy was to unnerve his opponent with his trash talking and then pressure him into moving his checkers fast without thinking. An opponent moving his men fast without thinking is easy to beat. I countered Old James' strategy by slowing the game down and then thinking carefully on every move. As a result, I began to consistently beat Old James, and the brothers then began teasing him about losing to me. They would say, "That young blood is tearing Old James up." Their laughing and teasing hurt Old James' pride and after a while he wouldn't play me anymore.

In addition to Old James, another brother with a reputation played in the break room. His name was Wade. He was a master checker player, the best that I have ever seen. He beat his opponents with his great tactical and strategic thinking ability. I never saw him lose a game; no one could beat him. He took advantage of his opponent's mistakes. He would bait his opponent into clever traps. He would give his opponent the impression that he was winning, but all the time he was setting him up for defeat. Wade always thought at least three or four moves ahead. Eventually, Wade would get his opponent in a trap from which he couldn't escape. He would then tell his opponent that the game was over, although half of the pieces might still be left on the checkerboard. Wade's opponent had a choice: continue to play the game or submit. Sometimes his opponent couldn't think far enough ahead to see that the game was over and would continue to play Wade until it was clear that the game was over. But when Wade said the game was over, it was over. Watching Wade play checkers was a thing of beauty.

Checkers and chess are excellent games for practicing exercises in tactical and strategic thinking. Once tactical and strategic thinking is learned, it can be applied to business, careers, sports, and life in general.

We turn now to the increasing imprisonment of black males, a serious crisis. If this trend continues, it threatens the long-range survival of black people in the United States. Today there are more black males in prison than in college. One-third of young black males between the ages of eighteen and twenty-eight are either in prison, on probation, or in some way tied up with the judicial system.

Unfortunately, young black males are becoming increasingly involved in crime and violence, which leads them to prison. Why are black males becoming increasingly involved in crime and violence? There are a number of reasons: racism, which denies them equal employment opportunities; female-headed households, where the father is absent and discipline is lacking; and high levels of hopelessness and frustration, which cause them to give up and vent their negative emotions inward. Another reason for the increasing involvement of black males in crime and violence is their lack of critical thinking. They are not taking the time to think things over carefully before they act. In essence, they are acting without thinking. As a result, they are making bad choices and are using poor judgement, which is leading them down the road to self-destruction. However, before we analyze the black male's lack of critical thinking, we must examine still another reason for the increasing involvement of black males in crime and violence—the breakdown of morals and values in the black community.

The massive imprisonment of black males is rather recent. Thirty-five to forty years ago, black males were not incarcerated in large numbers like they are now. There is a correlation between the increasing imprisonment of black males and the breakdown in morals and values in the black community. This breakdown has made illegal hustling activities more acceptable. And, of course, these illegal hustling activities such as selling drugs, selling hot items, and burglary send many black males to prison.

At one time the black community held morals and values in high regard. Although illegal hustling activities went on, they were frowned upon by most people in the black community, more so than now.

Growing up in the South in the 1960s and on back, black children were trained by their parents to respect themselves, to avoid trouble, and to do what was right. Parents warned their kids to stay away from *bad houses*—places where illegal activities such as gambling, prostitution, and the selling of bootleg whiskey occurred. Fathers warned their sons to avoid trouble and to do what was right. Mothers warned their daughters to be careful with their boyfriends and not to do everything they wanted them to do. They were trying to prevent teenage pregnancies. If Sister Jones saw a boy acting mannish or a girl acting fast, she warned them to straighten up or else she would tell their parents on them. When black kids went to church, the preacher warned them about the pitfalls if they disobeyed their parents. The preacher also warned them that hellfire awaited sinners and backsliders in the next life. At school, teachers warned kids that if they didn't study hard, try to make something of themselves, and walk a straight path, their future would be bleak.

While growing up in the South, I remember my grandmother warning my sisters and me to avoid trouble and to do what was right. In fact, every time we went to visit her, she always gave us a firm warning before we left her house. She would say, "Children, we are living in some very dangerous times. You have to be careful and watch out for trouble. And, most importantly, do what is right."

The late 1960s and early 1970s were times of turmoil and change in the United States. This period witnessed riots, protests, and demonstrations; the shocking assassination of Dr. Martin Luther King, Jr.; a new cultural awareness among blacks; and new job opportunities for blacks, including roles as actors and actresses in black movies.

Exploitive movies of the early 1970s gave blacks starring roles in movies that glorified characters such as pimps, drug pushers, and hustlers. Those movies had a big impact on the black community in terms of desensitizing it to crime and violence. These movies made illegal activities more acceptable to the black community, further breaking down its high morals and values.

The most watched, the most talked about, and the most damaging of these movies was Superfly, which hit the movie theaters in 1972. Superfly was no doubt one of the most powerful movies ever made. It glorified the criminal activity of the drug pusher, the pimp, and the prostitute, making them sensational and colorful. Superfly impacted the black community immediately. Large numbers of black males identified strongly with the character Priest, a super-pimp and drug pusher. Priest drove a fancy Cadillac and wore flashy clothes. He was cool, hip, and slick. Overnight, black males began to snort cocaine like him, dress flashy like him, walk cool like him, talk hip like him, wear their hair long and processed like him, and act cold like him. It became more acceptable in the black community to make large amounts of money selling drugs, pimping women, and hustling. Some blacks said, "It was all about survival, and the brothers had to do what they could do in order to survive."

Another movie that had a big impact on the black community was *Colors* (1989) which glorified gangs, drugs, and violence. Overnight, gangs sprang up in black communities across the nation.

Black males are not taking the time to think critically, but to survive they must begin to spend more time thinking critically. While thinking critically, they must use hindsight, insight, and foresight.

Thinking with hindsight will enable young black males to learn and benefit from past experiences. For example, young black males aspiring to become pro athletes can learn from the bad experiences of black athletes who neglected the books in college, instead spending hours developing their game, and still failing to make the pros. They ended up with shattered dreams. The negative experience of these athletes can serve as a warning to young black males, telling them if they are fortunate enough to get an athletic scholarship, they must also hit the books and get a college education. This way, if they don't make the pros, they will have a degree on which to fall back. In other words, thinking with hindsight can help young black males use sports instead of letting sports use them.

Thinking with insight will enable young black males to look beneath the surface of things for hidden meanings. For example, if a young black male is attracted to the quick money and glamour of the underworld and desires to become a hustler, he can look at the hustler's life with insight, see the drawbacks, and avoid becoming one. There is an old saying, "Everything that looks like gold isn't gold." The hustler's life from the surface looks very attractive—fancy cars, rolls of hundred dollar bills, gold jewelry, expensive clothes. But stripping away the glitter and glow from the surface of the hustler's life reveals it to be risky and dangerous. A hustler can be killed or sent to prison at any time.

Thinking with foresight will enable young black males to foresee trouble and avoid it. For example, by long-range looking into the future, black males can foresee the risks and dangers of selling drugs. They can foresee destructive consequences such as prison time, being killed by a rival dope dealer, or a future as a criminal because many employers are shy about hiring people with criminal records.

Critical thinking—the use of hindsight, insight, and foresight—will benefit many young black males. They will be able to make smarter decisions, wiser choices, and use better judgment. They will choose to become teachers or lawyers instead of hustlers, even though it will take years of hard studying. They will decide to sell themselves to an employer rather than to sell drugs, even though they might make less money. They will decide to settle a quarrel peacefully rather than with a gun, although their judgment may not seem macho.

The legendary Malcolm X used critical thinking to turn his life around. He was sent to the Massachusetts State Prison in 1946 for burglary. While in prison Malcolm was able to get quiet so he could think. He also began to read. His reading helped to expand his mind beyond the ghetto and beyond the black man's slave history. Malcolm soon realized that there were many interesting things in the world to do besides hustling. He also learned that the black man had a glorious history, one that went back far beyond slavery. Armed with knowledge from extensive reading and his new religion (Islam), Malcolm began to think critically. Thinking with hindsight enabled him to see the mistakes he had made in his life when he went the route of hustler, thief, and pimp. Thinking with insight enabled him to see through the quick money and glitter of the hustler's life and to see it for what it really was, risky and dangerous. Thinking with foresight enabled him to foresee his own self-destruction if he continued down the dangerous road of hustling. As a result of his critical thinking, Malcolm chose to turn his life around. When he was released from prison, he became active in the Nation of Islam and rose to a position of leadership. His transformation from a hustler to an internationally known black leader was amazing. Malcolm's ability to turn his life around inspired other blacks to pull themselves out of the muck and mire of self-hate and self-destruction and turn their lives around also.

Racism causes poverty, high unemployment rates, and despair in the black community, but in the final analysis it is black males' poor judgement, bad choices, and unwise decisions that lead them down the road to self-destruction. They choose to sell hot items, steal cars, join gangs, rob stores, or kill, all of which can get them in trouble with the law. By thinking critically, they will be able to avoid trouble and stay out of prisons.

Emotions can dull people's thinking and cause them to do things they wouldn't ordinarily do. Love and anger are emotions that can make highly intelligent people do stupid things. An intelligent professional woman, without hesitation, withdrew five thousand dollars from the bank and gave it to her boyfriend, with whom she was deeply in love. After getting the money her boyfriend dumped her. An intelligent college professor was so madly in love with a young, attractive woman that he would challenge any man who flirted with her to a fight. He also paid her car note every month. She eventually quit him. A teenaged boy became involved in a heated argument with his mother over the use of her car. When she refused to let him drive it, he became so enraged that he shot and killed her. He later regretted that he did it, but it was too late.

Black people sometimes get very emotional, which impairs their thinking and they don't think clearly. As a result, blacks say and do things that are regretted later.

If black people are going to overcome their problems and move forward in history, they must spend more time thinking. They need to think tactically and strategically like the master checker or chess player. They need to think critically like the wise general.

Educate Rather than Mis-educate

More than 60 years ago, African-American historian Carter G. Woodson observed that blacks were being mis-educated rather than educated. In his book, *The Mis-education of the Negro*, he points out that blacks were being trained to serve and follow others instead of being trained to think and do for themselves. He also points out that "so-called educated blacks" were not trained to apply their knowledge to develop and uplift their race. Woodson's book, although published in the 1930s, is still relevant, because blacks today face many of the same problems.

Slavery took away black people's historical memory and self-confidence. A people without their historical memory won't know what they have done in the past and, as a result, won't know what they are capable of doing in the present. A people without self-confidence will imitate others and seek their approval of things because they don't believe that they are capable of doing things for themselves.

Inferiority is one of the most destructive psychological scars that black people have inherited from slavery. It makes them believe that they can't do well in school because of their black skin. As a result, many black kids don't put forth their best efforts in school, falsely believing that they can't learn. This negative thinking even affects teachers. Some say, "Black kids can't learn. The situation is hopeless." This negative attitude toward black kids causes some teachers not to put forth their best efforts trying to teach them.

Historian Woodson recognized this same feeling of inferiority in black students over sixty years ago. He observes: "to handicap a student by teaching him that his black face is a curse and that his struggle to change his condition is hopeless is the worst sort of lynching. It kills one's aspirations and dooms him to vagabondage and crime."[6]

Today, unfortunately, many school systems are still guilty of portraying blacks in a negative light. For example, American history books generally emphasize blacks' contribution to America as slaves, while generally ignoring their contributions to America as inventors, scientists, and leaders.

Black children today need a school curriculum that will help them overcome this feeling of inferiority. The school curriculum must include teachings and activities that build pride and self-esteem in black children. It must also teach them that if they work hard they can learn as well as anyone else.

Being educated means more than being trained to work at a company. It also means being trained to apply what was learned to help oneself. If blacks can't apply what they have learned to help develop themselves, then they have not been educated properly. An education that teaches a person that he is inferior and robs him of his common sense is doing him more harm than good.

Woodson maintains that in terms of helping their people, blacks with little or no education have had a bigger impact than those who have been highly educated. He observes:

> Practically all of the successful Negroes in this country are of the uneducated type or of that of Negroes who have had no formal education at all. The large majority of the Negroes who have put on the finishing touches of our best colleges are all but worthless in the development of their people.[7]

The late A.G. Gaston was the type of successful black man that Woodson had in mind. A.G. Gaston was a wealthy businessman in Birmingham, Alabama, who owned a bank and motel and other businesses. Dr. Martin Luther King Jr. and other civil rights workers often stayed at his motel when they were in Birmingham. Mr. Gaston used a common sense approach to business. He didn't have a degree in business administration or economics. He would create a business where there was a need for one. He treated common black people with respect and they in turn supported his businesses and made him wealthy.

A number of blacks have masters and doctorate degrees but their education hasn't trained them to apply their knowledge to help uplift their people. I heard a story while in college about a black professor who had a Ph.D. in economics but he didn't know how to apply it to help his people. This economics professor was one *heavy man*. He amazed his students with his ability to quote theory after theory, authority after authority, and book title after book title. But one day in class, a student asked the professor how to apply his economic theories to solve economic problems in the black community. Instead of answering the student's question, the professor got upset, went berserk, and turned the class out. He said to the class, "You all just get out of here. Just get out of here and leave me alone!"

This story is an illustration of the mis-education of the Negro. This economics professor's education had taught him how to memorize, but not how to think, analyze, and apply what he had learned. Therefore, he didn't understand how to answer the student's question. He didn't understand how to apply his education to solve economic problems in the black community.

Blacks with degrees in economics and business need to know how to apply their education to empower the black community economically. If Chinese immigrants can come into the heart of the ghetto and establish thriving businesses selling rice, surely blacks can establish thriving businesses in the ghetto. Some black writers publish books and write articles that describe how bad and hopeless conditions are in the black community, but they offer no hope, no advice, no solutions.

Woodson was an advocate of education for self-reliance. He believed that a man's education should teach him how to think and do for himself. Another advocate of education for self-reliance was Booker T. Washington of Tuskegee fame. Black leaders Marcus Garvey of the UNIA and Elijah Muhammad of the Nation of Islam also stressed education for self-reliance.

Booker T. Washington wanted blacks to acquire land and skills and build institutions. He was laying an economic foundation on which blacks could be self-reliant. He knew that unless blacks could do things for themselves, they would never be respected in the eyes of the world. Washington knew that many whites were against the idea of blacks building schools to educate themselves, acquiring land to grow food and build homes, and learning skills. To quiet white opposition, he took a humble and submissive approach. Sometimes you have to swallow your pride and humble yourself to get what you want. Washington's strategy didn't fare well with some blacks. They interpreted his strategy of *shuffling to the white man* to help his people as a sign of weakness. They wanted him, if he was going to lead the race, to take stands on issues and demand equality and justice. Men such as W.E.B. DuBois and William Monroe Trotter had big problems with Washington's strategy of humbleness to quiet white opposition.

DuBois was an advocate of the *Talented Tenth* philosophy, a belief that elite blacks such as politicians, preachers, professionals, and educators should lead the masses to a better life. The concept of the Talented Tenth failed because the black elite did not assume the responsibility expected of them.[8] Humbling oneself to get what one wants is an old strategy. It buys time and it quiets the opposition. Why go to the lion's den and wake up the sleeping lion? This strategy has been used by other ethnic groups to get themselves together and to get what they want. Sometimes if you don't come humble to people who can help you, they won't help you. However, many blacks have problems with this humble strategy. They interpret it as being weak and cowardly.

If more black people had continued Washington's program of education for self-reliance, blacks would be in better shape economically as a people today. There would be more black banks, grocery stores, and insurance companies. Black unemployment would be down because blacks would know how to create their own jobs. For example, large numbers of blacks would now be employed in ghetto areas renovating dilapidated homes and buildings, thus working for themselves in revitalizing the black community.

"Time brings about changes" is an old expression. That certainly is true when it comes to the nation's schools. Things such as students bringing guns to schools, students killing other students in schools, metal detectors in schools, and policemen stationed in schools were practically unheard of thirty-five to forty years ago.

Today we hear complaints that black kids can't learn. We hear excuses that *explain* why they can't learn. However, if black kids could learn thirty-five to forty years ago in segregated schools, using inadequate facilities and second-hand books, then why can't they learn now? The difference is, thirty-five to forty years ago there was more discipline in the schools, there were more dedicated parents and teachers, there were more kids who had the desire to learn, and there was more support of schools by parents.

Presently, there is an atmosphere of pessimism surrounding the education of black children. Problems in school systems such as high dropout rates among black students, low scores on achievement tests among black students, school violence, and lack of school discipline serve to feed this pessimism. Yet there is hope.

To combat this growing pessimism and hopelessness, there needs to be a change in attitude in the black community toward education.

The first place to begin this change is in the homes. Parents should begin reading to their children when they are one year old or younger. This will create in them a love for books and a desire to learn. Parents should let their kids see them reading newspapers, books, and magazines. This will show the kids that reading is important. Parents should teach their kids that an education is something of value. Parents should spend time talking to their kids about the future and life in general, instead of spending most of their time watching television and listening to loud music. A family's home reflects its priorities. If a family has more televisions, boom boxes, CDs, and cassette tapes than books at home, then education has a low priority in that home. The second place to begin this change in attitude toward education is in the schools. There needs to be teamwork between parents and teachers and parents and school administrators. The parents should let the teachers know that they care about their children's education. Parents should let teachers know they want to be made aware when their children aren't doing well in school. The parents should let the teachers and school administrators know that they are concerned about their children's behavior, and if their children misbehave, they want to be made aware of it. The parents and teachers need to become more dedicated to the education of black kids. For example, teachers need to make sure that kids have homework to do and parents need to make sure that they do it. Parents and teachers should encourage kids and let them know that they believe they can succeed in school. Parents and teachers should let kids know that, in terms of schoolwork, they expect commitment, hard work, and striving for excellence. Children should be awarded for academic achievements. This will teach them that education is something to be valued and held in high regard. As a result, in time, a scholar will be as respected and adored in the black community as an athlete or entertainer.

The third place to begin this change in attitude toward education is in the black community as a whole. Everyone in the black community needs to become involved in the education of black kids, from the preacher to the radio disc jockey to the school dropout. The preacher can encourage black kids to strive for excellence during his sermons. The radio disc jockey can emphasize to the kids that "a mind is a terrible thing to waste" while he is playing music. The school dropout can be an inspiration to kids by returning to school and graduating. A change of attitude in the black community toward education will no doubt benefit black kids. It will lead to better academic performance, which will in turn boost blacks' self-confidence and self-respect.

Education means more than book learning. It also means being trained how to survive. If blacks can't survive, knowledge and training are worthless. In the 1960s and earlier, down South, black children were taught survival skills, called by some *Survival 101*. Survival 101 was an informal course that taught black kids how to survive in the hostile and intimidating Southern environment. In those days blacks could be beaten, imprisoned, or killed for disrespecting a white person or acting uppity. The Ku Klux Klan would often punish blacks who got out of their place. Parents taught their kids how to behave properly around white people and to humble themselves when it was necessary to do so in order to survive. For example, if a sheriff and his deputy stopped a black man for speeding on an isolated country road late at night, the black man's life could depend upon how he behaved and his ability to think tactically. If the black man humbled himself and had a good reason for speeding or quickly made up a good reason for speeding that satisfied the sheriff, he might get by with a firm warning. On the other hand, if the black man denied he was speeding or spoke to the sheriff defiantly, he would probably be in trouble and at the mercy of the sheriff. Not being trained in Survival 101 could have cost a black male his life down South years ago. For example, in 1955, a fourteen-year-old Chicago teenager named Emmett Till, who was in Money, Mississippi, visiting his grandparents, was brutally murdered by some white men for allegedly whispering at a white woman. Evidently, while growing up in Chicago rather than in the South, Emmett Till wasn't taught Survival 101 skills like how to properly behave around a white women back then, and it cost him his life.

Survival 101 taught blacks other survival skills besides proper behavior and tactical thinking. It also taught black kids how to respect others, how to get and hold a job, how to read people and size them up, how to make and keep friends, how to avoid trouble, and other important skills. Growing up down South in those days, you heard old sayings like "Trouble is easy to get into but hard to get out of," "A chip doesn't fall far away from its block," "Birds of a feather flock together," and "If you mess with trash, it will get into your eyes." These old sayings could help you if you followed the advice they gave. If a person was trained properly in Survival 101, he could go anywhere and survive.

Today, parents rarely teach their children these survival skills. They have been forgotten by lots of black people, yet they are an important part of black history. One of the reasons why so many young black men are in trouble with the law and are going astray is that they haven't been properly trained how to survive. Without Survival 101, they are vulnerable in today's deceptively dangerous world.

Become Economically Empowered

If black people are going to overcome their problems, it is imperative that they become economically empowered. They can accomplish this by using their money more wisely and by supporting and developing black businesses. In 1992 African-Americans collectively had an income of about three hundred billion dollars, equal to the gross national product of Canada. By the end of 1996 their income as a whole had increased to about four hundred billion dollars. Also African-Americans spend more than four hundred billion dollars a year as consumers. The point here is, African-Americans aren't poor as a whole. They have much money to spend. In fact, they have more spending power than people in many countries of the world. The problem is, however, they are spenders rather than sellers and producers. As a result, they don't keep money long enough for it to work for them in terms of creating wealth, capital, and jobs. Blacks comprise about 13 percent of the U.S. population, yet they own only 2 percent of the nation's businesses. If they had more businesses they could employ themselves and reduce their high unemployment rate. Sales by black businesses account for about 0.5 percent of total U.S. business sales. One-half of 1 percent is a very small number. If black business sales could generate more capital, it could be used to empower the black community economically and blacks wouldn't have to beg other peoples for money. Until blacks use their money more wisely and support and develop black businesses, they will be unable to acquire wealth and build economic muscle. As a result, they will remain disproportionately impoverished in the United States.

African-Americans are not using their money wisely. Many blacks, instead of using their money to empower themselves economically, are misusing it to their own detriment. For example, they spend millions of dollars every year on items that will harm their health such as cigarettes, liquor, and drugs. These items may provide a temporary escape, but won't help solve their problems. The money they spend on cigarettes, liquor, and drugs could be better spent on education and business training. Blacks throw away millions of dollars every year gambling at racetracks and casinos and on other get-rich-quick schemes. They also spend millions of dollars every year buying things that are associated with power—luxury cars, fine clothes, expensive jewelry—instead of investing their money in banks and businesses, which will give them real economic power.

There is a long list of black athletes and entertainers who, unfortunately, have let fortunes slip through their hands, from boxer Joe Louis to singer M.C. Hammer. They lost their fortunes in various ways, including overspending, bad investments, mis-management, and through naïveté.

Many African-Americans spend more money than they make, which keeps them in debt. To avoid economic hardships they need to change their spending habits and the way they think about money. They would be better off to save some of their money for a rainy day. Their money could better serve them invested in saving bonds, saving certificates, IRAs, thrift saving plans, and in other places. Many African-Americans need education in how to manage and invest their money more wisely.

Although African-Americans spend over four hundred billion a year, their spending power isn't always respected by the people with whom they spend their money. They are sometimes treated differently than others when they patronize restaurants, stores, banks, and other businesses. In some instances blacks have responded to this mistreatment with boycotts, economic sanctions, and class-action discrimination suits. For example, the well-publicized Denny's restaurant incident in which black secret service agents were refused service was followed by "the successful class-action discrimination suit against the Denny's restaurant chain...."[9] Despite this victory against discrimination and others like it, black spending power is still not fully respected by those who benefit from it. Blacks need to be more selective. They need to spend their money where they will get a benefit in return. Why spend your money with a business that mistreats you, won't hire you, and won't support you? In many instances the money from black consumers is the difference between profit and loss for businesses and consumer products.

Blacks are under-represented in the United States in terms of business ownership, comprising about 2 percent of the country's businesses but 13 percent of the country's population. This low number gives the impression that blacks aren't interested in owning businesses. However, this is not the case. Blacks do want to own businesses. The problem is, many blacks lack self-confidence when it comes to starting businesses. They view starting businesses as difficult and risky as climbing a steep mountain.

While many blacks are reluctant to start businesses, others are not. The ones who take a chance sometimes succeed and they sometimes fail. This leads us to the following question, why do black businesses fail? Answering this question is not as simple as it seems. Scholars who have studied black businesses identified the following reasons for their failure: (1) lack of capital to operate a business; (2) inability of owners to borrow adequate loans from banks; (3) a small market that sells mostly to blacks; (4) inability of owners to get products from suppliers at a reasonable price, which causes black businesses to charge higher prices for products in order to turn a respectable profit; (5) lack of accounting, planning, and managing skills; (6) hiring employees such as friends and relatives who are not committed to working the job; (7) lack of networking; (8) racism, which makes it difficult for blacks to buy goods cheaply in bulk. Lastly, there is another reason why black businesses fail but it is seldom mentioned, and it is blacks' disrespectful attitude toward other blacks. This disrespectful attitude is a ghost from slavery.

Only a small percentage of blacks' annual collective income of four hundred billion dollars is spent with black businesses. They spend about 95 percent of their income with white businesses. There are black businesses in most black communities but many of them are not supported whole-heartedly by blacks. Why blacks don't support black businesses more is an intriguing question. There are a number of reasons. Black businesses don't always provide the products and services needed by blacks. Black businesses are often located in places that are perceived to be unsafe. Black businesses often are not competitive; the prices for their goods and services are too high. Blacks often lack confidence in black businesses or mistrust them. For example, some blacks are fearful of putting their money in a black bank, believing that it might fold at any moment. Blacks often complain that black businesses provide inadequate service and products of poor quality. Finally, the employees of black businesses are often disrespectful to their black customers.

If the black community is to build economic muscle, blacks must patronize black businesses more. At the same time, black businesses must make themselves more attractive to the black community. Blacks can make their businesses more attractive by improving three critical areas: competitiveness, service and quality, and treatment of customers. The complaint that black businesses are not competitive is often heard. For example, some black women say that they buy their hair products from Asian stores because black stores charge too much for their products. Another complaint often heard is that black businesses provide inferior services and goods. This is true to a certain extent. Some black businesses do provide inferior services and goods. On the other hand, many blacks are so brainwashed that they automatically think anything all-black is inferior. There is an old saying "Some black people think that the white man's ice is colder." To correct this misconception, black business owners need to strive to operate the best businesses they possibly can. Because of their recent enslavement, some blacks have developed an attitude of "indifference to high standards of excellence in all-Black situations, the idea that efficiency and expertise are unnecessary in all-Black situations...."[10] Black people can overcome this negative attitude by striving for excellence in whatever they do. Still another complaint often heard is black businesses are often disrespectful to their black customers. Black business owners can correct this complaint by making sure their employees (1) greet all customers with a hello and a smile, (2) thank all customers for patronizing their businesses, and (3) kindly ask all customers to please come back again. By treating their customers with respect, black businesses can develop warm and lasting relationships. If customers feel appreciated, they will sometimes support a business even though the prices are a little too high.

Studies have shown that black people will support black businesses if they are competitive and are managed efficiently. There are black businesses such as restaurants, lounges and clubs, barbershops and beauty salons, auto repair shops, and funeral homes that do well in the black community. In fact, black businesses that provide good services and products, have competitive prices, and establish warm relationships with their customers generally thrive in the black community. But on the other hand, black businesses that provide inadequate services and poor-quality products, and are disrespectful to their customers generally fail in the black community. The blacks who own these sub-par businesses don't seem to understand that a satisfied and pleased customer is the best advertisement that they can have. If a customer is pleased with a business, he will spread good things about it, and if he is displeased with it, he will spread bad things about it. In the final analysis, black people won't support black businesses just because they are black, but they will support them if they are competitive and are managed efficiently.

Black dollars need to circulate more than once in the black community. Generally once blacks cash their checks, they spend most of it with non-black businesses. If this money could turn over six or seven times with black businesses, it would really help to build economic muscle within the black community.

Black America needs to become more conscious economically and aspire for economic empowerment. Blacks must use their money more wisely. They must establish and support black businesses. Blacks also need to set economic goals. For example, one of their long-range goals should be to increase black owner-ship of businesses from the current 2 percent to at least 13 percent of U.S. businesses, which will reflect the percentage of African-Americans in the U. S. popu-lation. Empowered economically, African-Americans will witness a brand-new day. They will be able to cre-ate jobs for themselves. They will have money to edu-cate and train themselves. By not having to beg other peoples for money and jobs, blacks will boost their self-esteem and pride.

Become More Involved and More Alert Politically

The Voting Rights Act of 1965 guaranteed African-Americans the right to vote without restrictions. Since the passage of this law, blacks have made remarkable strides politically. They have been elected mayors of large cities such as New York, Chicago, Los Angeles, Philadelphia, Detroit, and Washington, D.C. In 1989 L. Douglas Wilder was elected governor of Virginia. He was the first African-American to be elected governor of a state in U.S. history. In 1992 a black woman, Carol Moseley-Braun of Illinois, was elected to the U.S. Senate. This history-making event made her the sec-ond black U.S. Senator since Reconstruction and the first black woman senator in U.S. history.

Despite their political gains during the last thirty-five years, African-Americans still need to become more involved politically. Blacks struggled long and hard for the rights to vote and hold office. However, large numbers of blacks in the United States are not registered to vote. There need to be voting drives to get as many of them registered as possible. Many blacks who are registered don't vote, even during critical elec-tions. Some blacks think that their votes won't make a difference. They are mistaken. In many instances the black vote has decided close political races at the national, state, and local levels. African-Americans need to be encouraged to vote because their votes can make a big difference. For example, their votes can be the difference between electing a staunch conservative or an ultraliberal. If elected, the staunch conservative will generally fight tooth and nail against affirmative action, job programs, welfare benefits, and other programs that benefit minorities and the poor. On the other hand, if elected, the ultraliberal will generally support programs that benefit minorities and the poor. Some blacks complain about how bad things are, but they won't go to the polls and vote to try to change things. Also, more blacks need to run for public offices in order to increase the number of black public officials.

African-Americans need to become more alert politically. They must know what type of people they are electing to offices. It is counterproductive to elect African-Americans to offices if they become more conservative than the most conservative white politicians. These types of black officeholders frustrate African-Americans and kill their spirit. It is also disappointing to elect people who turn out to be more concerned about helping themselves than their constituents. Some of these slick politicians rarely come around their constituents until it is time to be reelected, then they make themselves quite visible. These politicians cause voter apathy in the black community. Many blacks say, "What's the use in voting when the people you elect do very little to help you once they get in office?" Increased political education will enable blacks to better evaluate and choose office seekers. With increased political education they will no longer vote for Joe Williams just because he is black. Voting for Joe Williams just because he is black can backfire. Once Joe Williams gets into office, he may become so conservative that he will vote against all legislation that will benefit minorities and the poor. Increased political education will enable blacks to vote wisely. They will judge political candidates more by their political history and track record than by what they say and how they smile. They will be able to see through political gimmicks.

African-Americans need to use their political strength to their advantage. They should support politicians and the political party that will help them and not take their votes for granted. Increased political education can teach blacks how to vote and run political campaigns more tactically and strategically. By voting more tactically and strategically they can put politicians and political parties on the defensive, forcing them to pass legislation that will benefit minorities and the poor. Blacks can put pressure on politicians and political parties by withholding their votes if their interests are ignored. Knowing how to put pressure on politicians or political parties can make the difference between having black interests supported or taken for granted. By running political campaigns more tactically and strategically, blacks can win more elections, even when they are less than 50 percent of the voters. Knowing how to plan ahead, how to get the voters out to the polls, how to campaign, and how to take advantage of the opponent's weaknesses can make the difference between winning or losing an election.

By becoming more involved and more alert politically, blacks can increase their political strength and use it to help solve their problems.

Change the Distorted Image of Self

"How you see yourself influences what you will do for yourself." The following story bears witness to the truth of this old saying. A teacher once became very angry with a student for disrupting his class. The teacher told the student that he was stupid and ignorant and would never amount to anything. Unfortunately, the student believed his teacher and began to see himself as stupid and ignorant, and therefore began to act that way. He began to dress sloppily and use profanity. He began to hang out with students who had discipline problems. He stopped doing his homework and began to cut his classes. Soon afterward he dropped out of school and became a hustler. His hustling life was filled with crime and it eventually led him to prison. The teacher's negative comments about the student became a self-fulfilling prophecy. How the student saw himself influenced what he did for himself.

Images are powerful. They can teach one how to think. They subliminally plant thoughts in the mind and influence thinking. They can influence thinking positively or negatively.

Images of black people in books, newspapers, and other literature have been mostly negative during the past five hundred years. This negative portrayal of black people is rooted in the slave trade and slavery. To justify the exploitation of African people, the concept of black innate inferiority was created. Supported by volumes and volumes of literature, it has been accepted as the truth by many people. Although it is propaganda, it is deeply rooted in the modern world.

Slavery stripped Africans of their self-respect. Made to feel powerless and helpless, enslaved Africans over time developed a feeling of inferiority. This feeling of inferiority was used by the slave masters to control the slaves. It has been passed down from generation to generation, and many blacks today still manifest it.

Clowning is another destructive inheritance from slavery that is still affecting blacks. This behavior was used by some slaves to get on the good side of their masters. Slaves who could make their slave masters laugh were generally favored by them. They were often granted privileges that weren't given to other slaves. Clowning was used as a survival tactic by slaves. If they could manipulate a cruel and evil slave master by making him laugh it was to their advantage.

Today some blacks are still clowning, but instead of doing it on the old plantation, they are clowning on television and at the movies. Some of the black comedies currently on television are so degrading that they need to be taken off the air. Others are not as offensive. Laughing is good for the soul, but when it degrades one, it is harmful. There is a thin line between making people laugh and making a fool of oneself. Some of the black comedies on television today are so embarrassing that people are laughing at us instead of laughing with us.

The image of black people has been distorted over the past five hundred years. History books show blacks as slaves and servants but seldom as great leaders and thinkers. Movies portray blacks as clowns, hustlers, pimps, and criminals but rarely as heroes. Even when blacks are portrayed as heroes they generally manifest comic or physical ability but rarely show leadership ability, mental sharpness, and power.

This distorted image of black people has been very damaging. It has caused blacks to be looked upon negatively in the eyes of the world. Even worse, it has caused them to see themselves in a negative way.

Movies that portray blacks as clowns, buffoons, criminals, and villains are not as harmless as they appear. Many people of the world are heavily influenced by these movies. They see black people joking, laughing, clowning, or doing someone in and they think blacks are like that in real life. These negative images reinforce the belief in peoples' minds that black people are inferior.

The Tarzan movies, about the exploits of a white man in the African jungle, distorted the image of black people tremendously. These movies portrayed the continent of Africa as a huge jungle and its inhabitants as backward, ignorant, and easily frightened. This image influenced many peoples' thinking, causing them to look at Africa and black people in a negative way.

Blacks are not the only people whose image has been distorted. Asians, Native Americans, and Jews have often been ridiculed and misrepresented.

Forty-five to fifty years ago, goods produced in Japan were considered so inferior that they were laughed at. The Japanese, however, didn't like seeing their goods being laughed at in the eyes of the world. They had a lot of pride and, as a result, they decided to do something about it. Within twenty to twenty-five years, Japan became an economic giant, producing goods of high quality. Today people don't laugh at Japanese goods, they admire them. Today Japanese goods such as automobiles, televisions, textiles, and computers are sold worldwide.

Now that Japan is an economic giant, she is looked at more favorably than she was fifty years ago. In fact, she gets respect and admiration from many of the same people who once laughed at her. Japan's successful image influences people, causing them to want to trade and do business with her.

How people see you is important. For example, it can determine whether a person gets hired. If a woman interviews for a job and is seen as intelligent, poised, and orderly, the interviewer will probably think she will be an asset to the company and will probably hire her. On the other hand, if the woman is seen as slow witted, shy, and untidy by the interviewer, he will probably think that she will be a liability to the company and will probably not hire her. Being seen as wealthy can benefit you, whereas being seen as poor and destitute can be to your disadvantage. A wealthy businessman once said that because people saw him as wealthy, they were always giving him things and offering him business opportunities. On the other hand, if a person is seen as poor and destitute, people will often avoid him because they think he will ask them for something. If a people are seen as wealthy, powerful, and intelligent, they will benefit in terms of respect, prestige, and admiration. Also peoples will want to associate, do business with, and emulate them. On the other hand, if a people are seen as poor, backward, and naïve, it will be to their detriment. Such a negative image can cause other peoples to exploit and look down upon them, and also not want to do business or associate with them. The point here is, how people are seen is very important, but many people don't realize it.

Even more important is how people see themselves. How people see themselves influences what they will do for themselves. If a child is taught to see himself in a negative way, his negative image of himself can serve to check his aspirations. Although he has above-average intelligence, his low self-esteem and lack of confidence can cause him to give in to adversity and underachieve, becoming a drug addict instead of a successful dentist. If a child is taught to see himself in a positive way, his positive image of himself can serve to boost his aspirations. Although he has average intelligence, his high self-esteem and high level of confidence can cause him to overachieve, becoming a successful businessman instead of a bus driver. The point here is, how one sees himself influences what he will do for himself.

Black people need to change their distorted image because it demeans them in the eyes of the world. The television programs in which blacks are involved are overwhelmingly comedies. Even in commercials that involve blacks, there is often some humor. In the real world, however, no one laughs all the time. Life has a serious side. People often judge a person by how they see him. If they see him laughing and clowning all the time, they will get the perception that he is a perpetual clown. "People...[will] not take you seriously if you don't take yourself seriously."[11] Black people need to change their image to reflect a serious side. In the eyes of the world, blacks are good at entertaining (playing sports, singing, dancing, and making people laugh) but are out of their league when it comes to serious endeavors like solving the world's problems, leading others in times of crisis, producing and selling products, and seeking to understand the universe. Blacks need to change the image of their heroes to reflect qualities such as intelligence, leadership ability, courage, and creativity. Generally black heroes only possess two qualities—physical ability and comic ability. Black people also need to put pressure on school boards to change the distorted history books that their children use. The history books used in most school curriculums generally discuss black people's period of enslavement and colonialism but ignore their thousands of years of achievements and contributions to the world. A people's history is the sum total of their ups and downs, their positives and negatives. It is neither all good nor all bad.

Another thing that needs to change is the message of rap music. Presently, rap music sends a mostly negative message to its listeners—a message of violence, disrespect, and foul language. It needs to send a positive message, one that will inspire and give hope. Rap music is not bad; its negative message is what many people find repulsive. Some rap artists are very talented and creative. They could be valuable to the black community if they cleaned up their music. They could serve as teachers with their music, teaching kids dignity and self-respect, understanding about life, knowledge about black history and black heroes, and other pertinent information.

By changing their distorted image to a more positive one, blacks will be defining their own image, instead of letting other peoples do it for them. This new image change will result in blacks being seen in a more positive light in the eyes of the world and, what is even more important, seeing themselves in a more positive light. Blacks will benefit in many ways from this new image of themselves.

Keep Hope and Faith Alive

Hope and faith are inspirational words. Hope is a feeling that what you expect to happen will happen. Faith is a complete belief in something, and as applied to religion it is a complete belief in God. Some people say "faith is in the heart and hope is in the mind."

If black people are going to overcome their problems, it is important that they keep hope and faith alive. The Rev. Jesse Jackson of civil rights fame often used this expression some years ago. His words were inspirational and also meaningful because it is difficult to make it through rough times without hope and faith. And we as a people have seen our share of rough times during the past five hundred years.

Hope and faith were the two ingredients that helped black people survive the cruelest slavery known to man. As a kid, I heard slave stories that had been passed down from generation to generation. I once heard a man say that when he was a kid, he asked his grandmother why her hands were all scarred up. She told him that her slave master used to whip her and she would put her hands up to shield the blows from his whip. The blows she caught on her hands, when healed, left ugly scars. During slavery our forefathers were praying and hoping for a brighter day. They believed it was coming, even though they might not live to see it. They felt that freedom was coming, and it finally came. Hope and faith kept them strong during the most terrible days of slavery, enabling them to survive until freedom finally came.

Faith anchors a man like roots anchor a tree. When a strong wind blows, a tree's roots anchor it to the ground and keep it from being blown away. When the storms of life rage, a man's faith in God anchors him and keeps him from being swept away. Without faith to anchor him, a man is as vulnerable as a tree without its roots.

Faith is one of the most powerful things in the universe. It can help one deal with all kinds of adversity. There have been many intelligent, talented, and gifted people who, because they lacked faith, gave up when adversity struck them. As a result, they failed to achieve their aspirations. Many times people did well under favorable circumstances, but when adversity came their way, they gave up because of a lack of faith. Faith can help a person in a time of trouble. It can give him the strength, confidence, and inspiration to overcome adversity.

Faith can help people face adversity and enable them to win in the end. There are many success stories about people who overcame setbacks and failures to win in the end. One such success story is about a boy named Johnny.

Johnny was such a slow reader that he was diagnosed as mentally retarded by his teachers at school. Because he read so slowly, he rarely could pass his tests. The time limit would be up on the tests before he could finish. But somehow Johnny never lost faith and continued to believe that one day his reading speed would improve. He therefore began to visit the library and borrowed books to read. He read book after book and eventually his reading speed improved. This inspired Johnny and he went on to finish high school.

After working as a laborer for four years, Johnny decided he wanted to open a small restaurant and work for himself. Filled with excitement Johnny told his relatives, friends, and associates about his new idea. Some of them scoffed at his plans, however. They told him that he was lucky to have a job as a laborer and he would never succeed as a businessman. Johnny was hurt by their negative comments, but he didn't let them discourage him. He subsequently went to the bank and applied for a loan but was denied it. Refusing to give up, Johnny applied for a loan with several other banks but was turned down each time. Fortunately for Johnny, there was a wealthy man in the neighborhood who admired his determination. This wealthy man loaned Johnny the money to open the restaurant. To everyone's surprise Johnny's restaurant was a success.

Although Johnny was slow mentally, he compensated for it in other ways. For example, he had a good sense of humor, he liked people, and he also knew how to treat people with respect. Because Johnny was likable and operated a good business, people supported him. Over time he became a wealthy businessman. Despite numerous setbacks and failures, Johnny never lost faith. In the end he won.

Today millions of African-Americans are mired in poverty. Others are doing well. These successful blacks have good jobs, nice homes, fine cars, and money in the bank. Black people have come a long way since the early 1960s. Back then, the black middle class was much smaller than it is now. Of course there were teachers, preachers, and other professionals, but there were also many blacks struggling as field workers, domestic servants, laborers, and factory workers.

In the early 1960s, when I was a little boy, I remember attending services at a Baptist Church in the country outside Memphis, Tennessee. Its members were predominately common people—laborers, field workers, and domestic workers—people who were struggling to make it financially. The religious services at this church were generally lively and emotional. During services people would get up and testify about how good God had been to them. They would thank God for providing them basic things such as food to eat, clothes to wear, and a house to live in. Some people would get up and testify about the power of faith. They would say that they had made it on faith. It seems like faith was a big thing in the black community back then. Ministers would preach about the faith of Job. People would say that if you had faith, you could make it.

The black community has changed a lot in the last thirty-five to forty years. Black people now are not as humble and as thankful as they were when I was a little boy. Today many successful blacks take for granted what their parents and grandparents only dreamed about. Many of these successful blacks don't want to hear about the rough times of the past. They say,

"Those old rough times are gone. We are living in a new day now." But we as a people should never forget about the rough times that we have experienced, because "if a people are not mindful of history, they shall repeat it."

We turn again to adversity, which affects people in different ways. Faced with adversity, some people give up or fall apart. Others face adversity with faith and confidence and overcome it.

Adversity can get in the way and prevent or delay plans. This happens to many people. It happened to me back in 1974.

While in college, I looked forward to the year 1974 for four years. That was going to be the year I graduated from college and I got the good job. After getting the good job, I was planning on celebrating by buying some of the things that I had always wanted, including a brand new Buick Riviera. However, things didn't work out as I had planned, and 1974 turned into a year of frustration.

After graduating from college in June 1974, I left Nashville, Tennessee, and went home to Memphis. About mid-June my cousin Willie Nunley and I decided to begin job hunting. We both were very enthusiastic and thought we had a lot to offer a potential employer. My cousin Willie had just retired from the army and was a Vietnam veteran, and I was a young man with a college degree. We began to job hunt, but after about three weeks we hadn't come close to finding a job. We then realized that getting a job wasn't going to be as easy as we had thought. The problem was, Memphis had been hit hard by the recession of 1974 and very few companies were hiring. However, we continued to job hunt, driving all over town, dropping applications wherever we could.

One day while job hunting, we went to a factory in North Memphis and asked the man at the desk if he was accepting applications. To our surprise he never looked up at us. He just mumbled something and kept fumbling around in a drawer at his desk. My cousin Willie told me, "Come on, man, let's get out of here." This is an incident I will never forget.

By mid-August my cousin Willie and I were so tired and frustrated from job hunting almost every day that we quit to rest for a while. After resting for a week or so, we began to job hunt again, but could find nothing. Then my cousin Willie said to me, "Man, I've about done all the job hunting I'm going to do for a while. I'm going to sit back and let some of the places where we dropped applications call me." Someone did call him; he got a job working at the airport. Meanwhile, I continued to job hunt, going wherever I heard they were hiring to drop applications, but still could find no job. Despite the frustration that I was feeling, I continued to job hunt. One day while job hunting another incident occurred that I will never forget. I went to this company and filled out a job application. After the personnel man reviewed my application, he burst out laughing, and said "You have a degree in history, huh?" He then told me that they weren't hiring people with degrees in history. Being laughed at hurt my spirit and I began to have doubts about finding a job. My spirit got even lower when I learned that certain people were beginning to talk negatively about me. They were saying that I had spent four years studying in college and had a college degree but still couldn't find a job.

However, when I told my Uncle Boo (Silas Scott) about my bad experience with job hunting, he encouraged me. He said, "Junior, don't give up. Something will break after a while." Uncle Boo's words were a big psychological boost to me. They lifted my spirits. His words also proved to be prophetic because in January 1975 I finally began working on a job. And by December 1975 I was working two jobs.

My point here is, faith helped me to stay strong when I was faced with adversity. I didn't give up when

I couldn't find a job, I continued to look for one, and in the end I found that job.

I hope my frustrating job-hunting experience of 1974, which was eventually successful, will be an inspiration to young black men who are struggling with adversity. Do not give up and turn to crime out of frustration if you cannot find a job. Instead, keep on looking and keep on believing that you will find a job, and you will.

It can be very difficult for young black men to get started in life. Sometimes people don't expect much from young black men who come from broken homes and impoverished backgrounds. People will sometimes discourage them. Others won't help at all. This happened to me. Yet you can't give up. You have to hang tough. Keep the faith.

If black people keep hope and faith alive, they will win in the end. An old African proverb states, "No matter how long the night, the day is sure to come." This old African proverb speaks to the condition of black people. If they don't give up during the night, they will see the bright sunshine of tomorrow.

▲▲▲

We have examined eight propositions that can help black people overcome the crisis that is currently impacting the black community: (1) face problems instead of avoiding them; (2) change negative behaviors toward one another; (3) spend more time thinking; (4) educate rather than mis-educate; (5) become economically empowered; (6) become more involved and more alert politically; (7) change the distorted image of self; and (8) keep hope and faith alive. If black people implement these eight propositions, they can overcome this serious crisis in the black community, although it will take time. Of these eight propositions, changing negative behaviors toward one another and becoming economically empowered are probably the most important.

Now is the time for black people to wake up, stand up, and meet the challenge of solving the crisis in the black community. We have the power within to accomplish what we wish, if only we believe.

Conclusion

We have opened the pages of history and traveled down the corridors of time to investigate and analyze the history of African-Americans. We began our investigation and analysis on the African continent, the ancestral home of African-Americans. The history of Africa is also the history of African-Americans because that is where our enslaved forefathers came from. In our probe into the prehistory of Africa we learned that Africa is the birthplace of mankind and that civilization began in Ethiopia. We also learned that Ethiopia was the mother of Egypt, the greatest civilization of antiquity. We discussed the rise and fall of ancient Egypt, her African beginning, her rule by black pharaohs, her golden ages, and her eventual conquest by foreigners. We discussed the rise and fall of the ancient North African city-state of Carthage, her Phoenician founding, her years of glory and power, and her eventual conquest and destruction by the Romans. We discussed North Africa under Roman and Vandal rule to the coming of the Arabs, and their subsequent replacement of the Romans as the new rulers of North Africa. We discussed the African Moors—their conquest of Spain, their period of glory in Spain, and their fall from power in Spain. We discussed empires and states of West Africa, including the famous medieval empires of Ghana, Mali, and Songhay. We discussed the Arab slave trade in Africa. We also discussed the European slave trade in Africa, which brought millions of enslaved Africans to the Americas. We discussed blacks' period of bondage in the Americas to their eventual emancipation, and down to the present. We analyzed the psychological impact of slavery on blacks today. We analyzed three subjects that have had a big impact on black history—invasions of Africa, the mulatto, and the weaknesses and strengths of black people. In the final chapter, we discussed the crisis in the black community and things we can do to overcome it.

In our journey down the corridors of time to investigate and analyze the history of African-Americans, we have covered a time period of many, many years. We began our probe in prehistory, examining man's origin in Africa and his early history, and then sweeping across thousands of years of documented history to the present.

Black People at the Crossroads

A traveler on a long journey will eventually come to a crossroads. The road he chooses to travel is very important because it will determine whether he continues on his journey or gets lost.

Today we find ourselves standing at the crossroads of history, wondering which way to go. We want to choose the road that will lead us to a brighter tomorrow, but we are not sure which road is the right road.

Standing at the crossroads of history, large numbers of blacks are confused about their identity. They identify themselves as mixed, black, African-American, Black Muslim, American, and Creole. Some blacks even identify with fads like a particular brand of sneakers, a particular sports jacket, or a type of jewelry. Their confusion is rooted in slavery, which took away their historical memory. Blacks can regain their historical memory by studying their true history. Knowledge of their true history will reveal their true identity. It will also tell them who they were before slavery and what they still can be.

Standing at the crossroads of history, large numbers of blacks are divided against one another. Blacks are divided by class. Many poor blacks believe that the black middle class has abandoned them in the inner city and won't help them like they could. Blacks are divided ideologically. Some militant and liberal blacks have become frustrated with black conservatives, calling them *Uncle Toms* and *handkerchief head Negroes*, and *sell-outs*. Black conservatives have fired back, charging that their opponents are exploiting race and poverty and are out of touch. There is divisiveness among black men and women. Some black women complain about black men's womanizing, irresponsibility, and disrespectfulness. Some black men complain that black women are bossy, too independent, and don't understand their problems. However, instead of complaining about each other and putting each other down, black men and women urgently need to come together and analyze their problems so they can better understand the causes of their friction and alienation.

Black people can overcome their divisiveness by working with one another to find common ground, by being more tolerant of one another's differences, and by showing more respect for one another's differences.

Standing at the crossroads of history, large numbers of blacks are frustrated. They are frustrated with racism that won't go away. They are frustrated with the crises in Black America that won't go away. Young blacks are probably the most frustrated group in Black America. Young blacks between the ages of twenty and twenty-four have a higher unemployment rate than blacks overall. Young blacks have a higher imprisonment rate than blacks overall. Because their lack of experience in life makes them vulnerable, young blacks probably suffer more than any other group in Black America.

Older blacks must share some of the blame for the frustration of young blacks. They haven't provided black youth with the appropriate leadership, nurturing, and teaching that they should have during the last twenty-five years, and it shows. For example, many young blacks haven't been properly taught about black people's history of struggle in America and how this struggle enabled blacks to make significant economic, political, and social gains that many enjoy today and take for granted.

Many young blacks are frustrated with older blacks who complain about their self-destructive behavior but won't reach out to help them. On the other hand, many older blacks are fearful of young blacks with their *gangsta rap* culture. Many feel that they don't know how to relate to today's black youth. Many older blacks see young blacks as irresponsible, disrespectful, and rebellious.

Trapped in poverty in the inner cities, many young blacks feel hopeless and abandoned. They are a part of Black America that hasn't made it. Their hopelessness and frustration are reflected in their rebellious behavior and in the gangsta rap music they listen to.

Gangsta rap is a product of the ghetto. It grew out of high unemployment, crime and violence, a breakdown of morals and values, and the hopelessness and frustration of blacks who didn't benefit from the movement and were left behind. Gangsta rap glorifies violence and is generally laced with profanity. Two of its biggest stars—Tupac Shakur and Notorious Big—were killed in drive-by shootings, 1996 and 1997, respectively.

In the meantime, many young blacks are still frustrated with their problems of unemployment, trouble with the law, hopelessness, and alienation. What can we do about their problems? Well, there is no quick fix. Older blacks, instead of denouncing young blacks as rebellious and irresponsible, need to reach out to them and try to understand their feelings and problems. They also need to try to inspire young blacks and give them hope for the future. Young blacks also need to try to help themselves. It's a two-way street. Young blacks need to try to take advantage of the educational and job-training opportunities that are currently available.

Standing at the crossroads of history, large numbers of blacks are apprehensive about the future. They are aware that they need leaders who will work hard to prepare them for the future. Looking around, they see a crisis in leadership in the black community. Of course, they see some black leaders who are preparing their people to survive in a complex, computerized future, but they also see many who are not. Blacks want real leaders, people who will work hard to improve the conditions of black people. Blacks are sick and tired of leaders who look good, talk good, dress good, and know how to *stir emotions to empty pocketbooks* but do very little to improve the lives of the masses of black people. Therefore, wanted in the black community are leaders who are dedicated, have vision and foresight, and are respected by the people.

Meanwhile, black people are still standing at the crossroads of history, confused, divided, frustrated, and apprehensive, wondering which way to go. "How long, [we will stand at the crossroads], only [the] future...will tell."[1] However, one road can lead us to a brighter tomorrow. The road I am talking about consists of the eight propositions we examined in chapter 13: (1) face problems instead of avoiding them; (2) change negative behaviors toward one another; (3) spend more time thinking; (4) educate rather than miseducate; (5) become economically empowered; (6) become more involved and more alert politically; (7) change distorted image of self; and (8) keep hope and faith alive. This road of eight propositions is not an easy road. It will require that black people work hard thinking, planning, and analyzing. It will require that black people cooperate with one another. It will require that black people show one another mutual respect.

If You Believe It, You Can See It

Some years ago, I listened to an old lady in church deliver one of the most touching testimonies that I have ever heard. She got up and told the congregation how sick she had been, and how it looked as if she would never get well. But the old lady had believed that she would get well, and God had helped her to overcome her sickness. She also told the congregation that she was so happy to be back in church one more time. She ended her beautiful and touching testimony with the expression "If you believe it, you can see it."

African-Americans have a rich historical legacy of believing it and seeing it. During the past five hundred years we have been able to overcome overwhelming odds and do things that seemed impossible because we strongly believed that we could. Many times when faced with adversity, we didn't give up. Instead we hung tough, continued to believe, and overcame that adversity.

Our strong faith and belief is reflected in our songs. Back in the 1960s when I was a kid, blues singer Little Milton Campbell sang "We Are Going to Make It," a song that reflected a strong belief in making it against the odds. It was a very popular song and lots of black people could be heard singing it all over town. Little Milton sang, "If we don't have a cent to pay the rent, we are going to make it, and if a job is hard to find and we have to go on the welfare line, we are going to make it." The Mighty Clouds of Joy, a famous gospel group, used to sing "Bright Side," a beautiful song that reflected a strong belief in making it against the odds if you didn't give up. The Mighty Clouds of Joy sang, "There is a bright side for you somewhere if you don't give up or turn around." (Note: I may not have the words of these songs exactly right, but this is how I remember them.)

Harriet Tubman, the famous conductor on the Underground Railroad, was a woman of much courage and strong faith. Harriet believed that she could escape to freedom despite the great risks of being caught, and in 1849 she did. She also believed that she could lead other slaves North to freedom. She subsequently made nineteen daring trips to the South and was successful on each trip in leading slaves to freedom. Because she strongly believed that she would be successful, Harriet took great risks and faced much danger while working on the Underground Railroad, but she was never captured. Harriet, with her bravery and strong faith, made the expression "If you believe it, you can see it" a reality.

My point here is, Harriet Tubman made what she believed a reality. She didn't sit around waiting on a miracle to happen. Instead she went out and worked and made freedom for herself and others a living reality.

Dr. Martin Luther King, Jr., the celebrated civil rights leader, was a man of great courage and strong faith. He believed that he could succeed when the odds were stacked against him. The forces of history thrust Dr. King into leadership of the Montgomery, Alabama, bus boycott of 1955-56. It ended in a big victory for the blacks of Montgomery, enabling them to ride the city buses on a first-come, first-served basis for the first time. After the victory in Montgomery, Dr. King's successes continued. In 1957 he spearheaded the founding of the Southern Christian Leadership Conference. Also in 1957 he received the prestigious Springarn Award from the NAACP, given for contributions toward improving race relations. By the end of 1957, Dr. King had emerged as Black America's main leader. In February 1960 he was charged with income tax evasion in the state of Alabama. Surprisingly, an all-white jury found him not guilty. In October 1960 Dr. King was arrested in Atlanta, Georgia, for participating in a sit-in at a department store. He refused to pay the bond and, therefore, remained in jail. After about a week, Dr. King was put in handcuffs and chains and taken to Reidsville State Penitentiary. However, thanks to Senator John F. Kennedy's intervention in the matter, Dr. King was released from prison. Less than two weeks later, November 8, 1960, blacks returned the favor to John F. Kennedy by helping him defeat Richard Nixon in a very close presidential election.

In 1961-62, Dr. King and other civil rights workers attempted to desegregate Albany, Georgia, but were unsuccessful. The failure to desegregate Albany was a big setback for Dr. King and the Civil Rights Movement. One reason for the failure was that Dr. King was suddenly invited into the Albany battle, a battle he didn't start and therefore wasn't adequately prepared to fight. Another reason for the failure was divisiveness among the various civil rights workers in Albany. This divisiveness was exploited by Albany's sheriff, Laurie Prichett, and other city officials.

Dr. King's defeat in Albany was a low point in his civil rights career. Before Albany everything had seemed to go his way, but now, all of a sudden, he found himself a failure. People were casting doubts on nonviolence as an effective weapon to combat injustice, inequality, and segregation in the South. The doubts, the criticism, the defeat all combined to discourage Dr. King and shake his confidence. However, he refused to give up. He chose to keep on believing in the struggle against injustice, inequality, and segregation.

In April 1963, Dr. King and other civil rights workers launched an attack on Birmingham, Alabama, "the most thoroughly segregated city in America." Their aim was to desegregate Birmingham. However, they faced a formidable foe in Commissioner of Public Safety Eugene "Bull" Conner, a racist and segregationist. Conner and his firemen and policemen were determined to stop the civil rights movement in Birmingham. The struggle to desegregate Birmingham was a bitter one, but in the end Dr. King and his civil rights workers prevailed. The desegregation of Birmingham was a great victory for Dr. King and the Civil Rights

Movement. It was the turning point of the Civil Rights Movement because it broke the back of segregation in the South.

After Birmingham, Dr. King moved his civil rights activities on to St. Augustine, Florida, in 1964; Selma, Alabama, in 1965; Chicago, Illinois, in 1965-66; Mississippi, in 1966; Cleveland, Ohio, in 1967; and finally to Memphis, Tennessee, in 1968.

In March 1968, Rev. James Lawson asked Dr. King to come to Memphis, on behalf of black sanitation workers who were striking because of poor working conditions. Dr. King, of course, agreed to visit Memphis to support the striking sanitation workers. When he came to Memphis on March 18, 1968, he spoke at Mason Temple before a large crowd. On March 28, 1968, he led a march in downtown Memphis that turned into a riot. However, he hadn't been told all the details about the situation in Memphis, including information about a militant black group called the *Invaders* who were believed to have started the riot. Meanwhile, Dr. King returned home to Atlanta. But on April 3, 1968, he returned to Memphis to lead another march. Delivering a very emotional speech that night at Mason Temple, Dr. King seemed to sense that the forces of evil were closing in on him and he was nearing the end of his journey. Dr. King states as follows:

Well, I don't know what will happen now. We've got some difficult days ahead. But it really doesn't matter with me now, because I've been to the mountaintop. And I don't mind. Like anybody, I would like to live a long life. Longevity has its place. But I'm not concerned about that now. I just want to do God's will. And He's allowed me to go up to the mountain, and I've looked over, and I've seen the Promised Land. I may not get there with you. But I want you to know tonight that we, as a people, will get to the Promised Land. And so I'm happy tonight. I'm not worried about anything. I'm not fearing any man. Mine eyes have seen the glory of the coming of the Lord.

The following day, April 4, 1968, Dr. King was assassinated in Memphis. Although the bullet silenced him, his spirit lives on. Dr. King died believing that black people would see the Promised Land, "a brighter tomorrow."

Dr. King was a remarkable man. He had compassion for the poor and oppressed everywhere. He was dedicated to the struggle against injustice, inequality, and segregation. He inspired people to overcome their fear and stand up for their rights. He worked to make America and the world a better place in which to live. He faced constant death threats and criticism, yet he never gave up. He kept on believing in his cause to the end.

The success of the Civil Rights Movement against overwhelming odds proves that it is not impossible to change your condition. The civil rights workers faced opposition that seemed too formidable to overcome, but they overcame it. The civil rights workers were surrounded by walls of segregation that seemed impregnable, but they tore the walls of segregation down. Armed with courage, willpower, and a strong belief in their cause, they accomplished what seemed impossible.

If black people work hard, don't give up, and continue to believe, we will see "a brighter tomorrow." "If you believe it, you can see it."

Notes

PREFACE

1. John Henrik Clarke, *Notes for an African World Revolution: Africans at the Crossroads*, Africa World Press, Inc., Trenton, New Jersey, 1991, p. 402.

CHAPTER 1
THE SIGNIFICANCE OF BLACK HISTORY

1. Frank Snowden, Jr., *Blacks in Antiquity*, The Belknap Press of Harvard University Press, Cambridge, Massachusetts, sixth printing, 1982, p. vii.
2. J.A. Rogers, *Nature Knows No Color-Line*, Helga M. Rogers, New York, New York, 1952, third edition, p. 55.
3. Rev. Sterling M. Means, *Ethiopia and the Missing Link in African History*, originally published by The Atlantis Publishing Company, Harrisburg, Pennsylvania, 1945, (1980), p. 133.
4. Chancellor Williams, *The Destruction of Black Civilization*, Third World Press, Chicago, 1976, revised edition, third printing, p. 94.
5. Ibid., pp. 94-95.
6. Ibid., p. 359.
7. Ibid., p. 207.
8. John Henrik Clarke, "Ancient Civilizations of Africa: The Missing Pages in World History," *Egypt Revisited, Journal of African Civilizations*, editor Ivan Van Sertima, November 1982, (Vol. 4, No. 2), p. 121.

CHAPTER 2
AFRICA: BIRTHPLACE OF MANKIND

1. Richard E. Leakey, *The Making of Mankind*, E. P. Dutton, New York, 1981, pp. 145-146.
2. John G. Jackson, *Introduction to African Civilizations*, Introduction by John Henrik Clarke, The Citadel Press, Secaucus, New Jersey, 1970, p. 45.
3. Ibid., p. 41.
4. Ibid., p. 41.
5. Ibid., p. 42.
6. Ibid., p. 45.

7. Ibid., p. 45.
8. Ibid., p. 46.
9. John Tierney, "The Search for Adam and Eve," *Newsweek*, Vol. CXI (January 11, 1988), p. 46.
10. Ibid., p. 46.
11. Allen Wilson, "The Mother of Us All," *World Press Review*, Vol. 35 (November 1988), p. 54.
12. Ibid., p. 54.
13. John Tierney, "The Search for Adam and Eve," *Newsweek*, Vol. CXI (January 11, 1988), p. 46.
14. Allen Wilson, op. cit., p. 54.
15. Ibid., pp. 54-55.
16. John G. Jackson, op. cit., p. 55.

CHAPTER 3
ETHIOPIA: MOTHER OF CIVILIZATION

1. Frank Snowden, Jr., *Blacks in Antiquity*, The Belknap Press of Harvard University Press, Cambridge, Massachusetts, sixth printing, 1982, pp. vii-viii.
2. John G. Jackson, *Introduction to African Civilizations*, Introduction by John Henrik Clarke, The Citadel Press, Secaucus, New Jersey, 1970, p. 66.
3. Bertram Thomas, *The Arabs*, Doubleday, Doran & Co., Garden City, New York, 1937, p. 339, cited by John G. Jackson, in *Introduction to African Civilizations*, p. 71.
4. Runoko Rashidi, "Dr. Diop on Asia: Highlights and Insights," Great African Thinkers, Vol. 1, *Journal of African Civilizations*, editor Ivan Van Sertima, Transaction Books, New Brunswick, New Jersey, June 1986 (Vol. 8, No. 1), p. 138.
5. Ibid., p. 138.
6. V. T. Rajshekar, "The Black Untouchables of India: Reclaiming Our Cultural Heritage," African Presence in Early Asia, *Journal of African Civilizations*, edited by Runoko Rashidi and Ivan Van Sertima, Transaction Publishers, New Brunswick, New Jersey, August 1995 (Vol. x, No. x), p. 236.
7. Lady Flora Shaw Lugard, *A Tropical Dependency*, Barnes and Noble, New York, 1964, p. 221, cited by John G. Jackson, in *Introduction to African Civilizations*, pp. 65-66.
8. John G. Jackson, op. cit., p. 65.
9. Chancellor Williams, *The Destruction of Black Civilization*, Third World Press, Chicago, 1976, revised edition, third printing, p. 47.
10. *Histoire universelle*, translated by Abbe Terrasson, Paris, 1758, Bk. 3, p. 341, cited by Cheik Anta Diop, in *The African Origin of Civilization: Myth or Reality*, pp. 1-2.
11. Alexandre Braghine, *The Shadow of Atlantis*, E. P. Dutton & Co., New York, 1940, pp. 213-214, cited by John G. Jackson, in *Introduction to African Civilizations*, pp. 80-81.
12. John G. Jackson, op. cit., p. 73.

13. Ibid., p. 71.
14. Harry H. Johnston, *The Negro in the New World*, Methuen & Co., London, 1910, p. 27, cited by John G. Jackson, in *Introduction to African Civilizations*, p. 72.
15. G. Elliot Smith, *Human History*, Norton & Co., New York, 1929, pp. 365-368., cited by Runoko Rashidi, in *Journal of African Civilizations*, African Presence in Early Asia, p. 25.
16. Will Durant, Our Oriental Heritage, New York, 1935, p. 396, cited by John G. Jackson, in *Introduction to African Civilizations*, p. 75.
17. John G. Jackson, op. cit., p. 75.
18. Charles S. Finch, "Further Conversations with the Pharaoh," Great African Thinkers, Vol. 1, *Journal of African Civilizations*, editor Ivan Van Sertima, Transaction Books, New Brunswick, New Jersey, June 1986 (Vol. 8, No. 1), p. 234.
19. Ibid., p. 234.
20. Ibid., p. 234.
21. John G. Jackson, op. cit., p. 95.
22. Charles S. Finch, op. cit., p. 235.
23. Godfrey Higgins, *Anacalypis*, Book 1, Chapter 4, Section 10, p. 59, cited by Gershom Williams, in *Journal of African Civilizations*, African Presence in Early Asia, "Ancient Kushite Roots in India: A Survey of the Works of Godfrey Higgins," pp. 118-119.
24. Godfrey Higgins, *Anacalypis*, New York, 1927, Volume 1, p. 286, cited by J. A. Rogers, in *Sex and Race*, Volume 1, New York, 1967, p. 266.
25. Godfrey Higgins, *Anacalypis*, New York, 1965, Volume 1, p. 51, cited by John G. Jackson, in *Introduction to African Civilizations*, The Citadel Press, Secaucus, New Jersey, 1970, p. 69.

CHAPTER 4
EGYPT: GREAT CIVILIZATION OF THE NILE VALLEY

1. Herodotus, *The History of Herodotus*, Book II, pp. 114-115, translated by George Rawlinson, cited by John G. Jackson, in *Introduction to African Civilizations*, p. 92.
2. Lucian, Navigations, paras 2-3, cited by Cheikh Anta Diop, in *Journal of African Civilizations, Egypt Revisited*, 1982, "Origin of the Ancient Egyptians," p. 17.
3. Aristotle, Physiognomy, 6, cited by Cheikh Anta Diop, in *Journal of African Civilizations, Egypt Revisited*, 1982, "Origin of the Ancient Egyptians," p. 17.
4. Ivan Van Sertima, "African Origin of Ancient Egyptian Civilization," *Egypt: Child of Africa, Journal of African Civilizations*, edited by Ivan Van Sertima, Transaction Publishers, New Brunswick, New Jersey, Spring 1994, (Vol. 12), second printing, 1995, p. 4.
5. Ibid., p. 5.
6. Ibid., p. 5.

7. Ibid., p. 5.
8. Ibid., p. 5.
9. Ivan Van Sertima, "Egypt Is in Africa but Was Ancient Egypt African?" *Egypt: Child of Africa, Journal of African Civilizations*, edited by Ivan Van Sertima, Transaction Publishers, New Brunswick, New Jersey, Spring 1994, (Vol. 12), second printing, 1995, p. 77.
10. Keith W. Crawford, "The Racial Identity of Ancient Egyptian Populations Based on the Analysis of Physical Remains," *Egypt: Child of Africa, Journal of African Civilizations*, edited by Ivan Van Sertima, Transaction Publishers, New Brunswick, New Jersey, Spring 1994, (Vol. 12), second printing, 1995, p. 69.
11. Ivan Van Sertima, *They Came Before Columbus*, Random House, New York, 1976, p. 109.
12. C. F. Volney, Voyages en Syrie et en Egypte, Paris, 1787, I, 74-77, cited by Cheikh Anta Diop, in *The African Origin of Civilization*, p. 27.
13. Ibid., p. 27.
14. Ivan Van Sertima, *They Came Before Columbus*, p. 109.
15. J. A. Rogers, *Africa's Gift to America*, Helga M. Rogers, New York, 1961, (revised edition), p. 11.
16. C. F. Volney, *Voyages en Syrie et en Egypte, Paris*, 1787, I, 74-77, cited by Cheikh Anta Diop, in *The African Origin of Civilization*, p. 28.
17. Arnold Heeren, *Historical Researches: African Nations*, cited by William H. Ferris, in *The African Abroad*, Vol. 1, pp. 492-493.
18. Gerald Massey, *A Book of the Beginnings*, Williams and Norgate, London, 1881, Vol. 1, p. 4, cited by John G. Jackson, in *Introduction to African Civilizations*, The Citadel Press, Secaucus, New Jersey, p. 153.
19. Ibid., p. 18, cited by John G. Jackson, in *Introduction to African Civilizations*, pp. 153-154.
20. Baron Viviant Denon, *Travels in Upper and Lower Egypt*, vol. 1, 1803, p. 140, cited by J. A. Rogers, in *Africa's Gift to America*, p. 11.
21. John Henrik Clarke, "Ancient Civilizations of Africa: The Missing Pages in World History," Egypt Revisited, editor, Ivan Van Sertima, *Journal of African Civilizations*, November 1982, (Vol. 4 and No. 2), p. 114.
22. Rev. Sterling M. Means, *Ethiopia and the Missing Link in African History*, originally published by The Atlantis Publishing Company, Harrisburg, Pennsylvania, 1945, (1980), p. 29.
23. Arnold Heeren, cited by Rev. Sterling M. Means, in *Ethiopia and the Missing Link in African History*, p. 29.
24. Chancellor Williams, The Destruction of Black Civilization, Third World Press, Chicago, 1976, revised edition, third printing, p. 73.
25. Ibid. p. 73.

26. Cheik Anta Diop, *The African Origin of Civilization: Myth or Reality*, trans. by Mercer Cook, Lawrence Hill and Company, Westport, Connecticut, 1974, p. XIV.

27. R. A. Nicolaus, p. 11, cited by Chiek Anta Diop, in *Journal of African Civilizations*, Egypt Revisited, November 1982, (Vol. 4 and No. 2), p. 15.

28. Cheik Anta Diop, "Origin of the Ancient Egyptians," *Egypt Revisited, Journal of African Civilizations*, editor, Ivan Van Sertima, November 1982, (Vol. 4 and No. 2), p. 15.

29. Wayne B. Chandler, "Of Gods and Men: Egypt's Old Kingdom," Egypt Revisited, *Journal of African Civilizations*, editor, Ivan Van Sertima, Summer 1989, (Vol. 10), revised edition, third printing, 1993, p. 122.

30. Bruce Williams, "The Lost Pharaohs of Nubia," Egypt Revisited, *Journal of African Civilizations*, editor, Ivan Van Sertima, November 1982, (Vol. 4 and No. 2), p. 40, (Reprinted from *Archaeology Magazine*, 1980, Vol. 33, No. 5).

31. Ibid., p. 38.

32. Ivan Van Sertima, *Egypt Revisited*, audiotape, Legacies Inc., 1988.

33. Ibid.

34. Ibid.

35. Ibid.

36. Ibid.

37. Asa G. Hilliard III, "Waset, the Eye of Ra and the Abode of Maat: The Pinnacle of Black Leadership in the Ancient World," *Egypt Revisited*, editor Ivan Van Sertima, Transaction Publishers, New Brunswick, New Jersey, Summer 1989, (Vol. 10), revised edition, third printing, 1993, p. 211.

38. John G. Jackson, *Introduction to African Civilizations*, Introduction by John Henrik Clarke, The Citadel Press, Secaucus, New Jersey, 1970, p. 96.

39. Chancellor Williams, *The Destruction of Black Civilization*, Third World Press, Chicago, 1976, revised edition, third printing, p. 67.

40. Ibid., p. 73.

41. Wayne B. Chandler, op. cit., p. 138.

42. John G. Jackson, op. cit., p. 13.

43. Ibid., p. 106.

44. Ibid., p. 13.

45. Ibid., p. 106.

46. Chancellor Williams, op. cit., p. 86.

47. Ibid., pp. 86-87.

48. Ibid., p. 84.

49. Ibid., p. 87.

50. Ibid., p. 87.

51. Ibid., p. 85.

52. Ibid., p. 88.

53. Ibid., p. 112.

54. James E. Harris and Kent R. Weeks, *X-raying the Pharaohs*, Charles Scribner's Sons, New York, 1973, p. 134, cited by Legrand H. Clegg II, in *Journal of African Civilizations, Egypt Revisited*, November 1982, (Vol. 4 and No. 2), p. 91.
55. Chancellor Williams, op. cit., p. 113.
56. J. A. Rogers, *World's Great Men of Color*, Vol. I, Introduction by John Henrik Clarke, Macmillan Publishing Co., Inc., New York, 1972, revised edition, p. 53.
57. Ibid., p. 53.
58. Ibid., p. 53.
59. James Henry Breasted, cited by J. A. Rogers, in *World's Great Men of Color*, Vol. I, p. 54.
60. J. A. Rogers, *World's Great Men of Color*, Vol. I, p. 54.
61. John G. Jackson, op. cit., pp. 109-110.
62. J. A. Rogers, *World's Great Men of Color*, Vol. I, p. 57.
63. Ibid., p. 61.
64. Ibid., p. 61.
65. Margaret A. Murray, *The Splendor that Was Egypt*, Hawthorn Books, Inc., New York, New York, 1963, revised edition, p. 56.
66. John G. Jackson, op. cit., p. 112.
67. Ibid., p. 115.
68. J. A. Rogers, *World's Great Men of Color*, Vol. I, p. 89.
69. Cheik Anta Diop, *The African Origin of Civilization*, p. 219.
70. Ivan Van Sertima, *They Came Before Columbus*, p. 131.
71. Chancellor Williams, op. cit., p. 121.
72. Rev. Sterling M. Means, op. cit., pp. 50-51.
73. Ivan Van Sertima, *They Came Before Columbus*, p. 129.
74. A. J. Arkell, *History of the Sudan to A.D. 1821*, London, The Athlone Press, 1935, p. 128, cited by Ivan Van Sertima, in *They Came Before Columbus*, p. 129.
75. Chancellor Williams, op. cit., p. 123.
76. Ibid., p. 123.
77. Ibid., p. 91.
78. Cheik Anta Diop, *The African Origin of Civilization*, p. 221.
79. Chancellor Williams, op. cit., p. 124.
80. John G. Jackson, op. cit., p. 13.
81. Ivan Van Sertima, *They Came Before Columbus*, p. 124.
82. Ibid., p. 123.
83. Ibid., p. 124.
84. Ibid., p. 124.
85. Chancellor Williams, op. cit., pp. 138-140.
86. Cheik Anta Diop, *The African Origin of Civilization*, p. 10.
87. Margaret Murray, op. cit., p. XVII.
88. Ibid., p. XVIII.
89. Ibid., p. XVIII.
90. Ibid., p. 255.
91. Wayne B. Chandler, op. cit., p. 153.
92. Asa A. Hilliard III, op. cit., p. 212.
93. Chancellor Williams, op. cit., p. 91.
94. Ibid., p. 94.

95. Margaret Murray, op. cit., p. XVIII.
96. Ibid., p. XVIII.
97. Ibid., p. 276.

CHAPTER 5
CARTHAGE: CELEBRATED CITY-STATE OF NORTH AFRICA

1. Saul Israel, *Introduction to Geography*, Holt, Rinehart and Winston, Inc., New York, 1964, p. 131.
2. John G. Jackson, *Introduction to African Civilizations*, Introduction by John Henrick Clarke, The Citadel Press, Secaucus, New Jersey, 1970, p. 157.
3. J.C. degraft-Johnson, *African Glory: The Story of Vanished Negro Civilizations*, Walker and Company, New York, 1954, p. 7.
4. Harry H. Johnston, *A History of the Colonization of Africa*, Cambridge University Press, London, 1899, p. 2, cited by J. C. degraft-Johnson, in African Glory, p. 4.
5. James Wellard, *Lost Worlds of Africa*, E. P. Dutton & Co., Inc., New York, 1967, p. 13.
6. Ibid., p. 19.
7. Ibid., p. 23.
8. Ibid., p. 23.
9. David Soren and others, *Carthage: Uncovering the Mysteries and Splendors of Ancient Tunisia*, Simon and Schuster, New York, New York, 1990, p. 31.
10. John G. Jackson, op. cit., p. 147.
11. Cheikh Anta Diop, *The African Origin of Civilization*, translated by Mercer Cook, Lawrence Hill and Company, Westport, Connecticut, 1974, p. 107.
12. John G. Jackson, op. cit., p. 147.
13. Donald Armstrong, *The Reluctant Warriors: The Decline and Fall of the Carthaginian Empire*, Thomas Y. Crowell Co., New York, 1966, p. 7.
14. J. C. degraft-Johnson, op. cit., p. 15.
15. Donald Armstrong, op. cit., p. 2.
16. Ibid., p. 2.
17. J. A. Rogers, *Sex and Race*, Vol. 1, Helga M. Rogers, New York, ninth edition, 1967, p. 88.
18. L. Bertholon and E. Chantre, Recherches Anthrop. dans la Berberie., cited by J. A. Rogers, in *Sex and Race*, Vol. 1, p. 88.
19. Cf. Eugene Pittard, *Les Races et l' histoire* (Race and History), Renaissance du Livre, Paris, 1924, p. 410, cited by C. A. Diop, in *African Origin of Civilization*, p. 122.
20. Cheik Anta Diop, op. cit., p. 122.
21. Gilbert C. Picard and Colette Picard, *The Life and Death of Carthage*, translated from the French by Dominique Collon, Taplinger Publishing Co., Inc., New York, 1969, p. 59.
22. Donald Armstrong, op. cit., p. 19.
23. David Soren and others, op. cit., p. 65.
24. Gilbert C. Picard and Colette Picard, op. cit., p. 96.

25. Donald Armstrong, op. cit., pp. 18-19.
26. Ibid., p. 21.
27. Donald Harden, *The Phoenicians*, Frederick A. Praeger, Inc., Publishers, New York, New York, second edition, 1963, p. 70.
28. Donald Armstrong, op. cit., p. 16.
29. J. C. degraft-Johnson, op. cit., p. 18.
30. Ibid., p. 19.
31. Donald Harden, op. cit., p. 70.
32. Donald Armstrong, op.cit., p. 24.
33. Picard and Picard, op. cit., p. 191.
34. Ibid., p. 191.
35. Donald Armstrong, op. cit., p. 27.
36. Ibid., p. 27.
37. Donald Harden, op. cit., p. 71.
38. Donald Armstrong, op. cit., p. 37.
39. J. C. degraft-Johnson, op. cit., p. 20.
40. David Soren and others, op. cit., p. 102.
41. R. Garrucci, *La Monete dell' Italia Antica*, Parte Secunda. t. LXXV, 11, 12, 13, 14, 15, Roma, 1885, cited by J. A. Rogers, in *Sex and Race*, Vol. 1, p. 88.
42. Donald Armstrong, op. cit., p. 38.
43. J. A. Rogers, *World's Great Men of Color*, Vol. 1, Introduction by John Henrik Clarke, Macmillan Publishing Co., Inc., New York, 1972, revised edition, p. 99.
44. Donald Armstrong, op. cit., p. 38.
45. Ibid., p. 39.
46. Ibid., p. 39.
47. Ibid., p. 39.
48. Ibid., p. 40.
49. Ibid., p. 40.
50. David Soren and others, op. cit., p. 107.
51. Ibid., p. 105.
52. J.A. Rogers, *World's Great Men of Color*, Vol. 1, p. 103.
53. Ibid., p. 104.
54. Ibid., p. 104.
55. Ibid., p. 105.
56. Donald Armstrong, op. cit., p. 41.
57. Theodore A. Dodge, *Great Captains*, Kennikat Press, Inc., Port Washington, New York, 1889, reissued 1968, pp. 57-58.
58. Donald Armstrong, op. cit., p. 42.
59. Ibid., p. 42.
60. Ibid., p. 43.
61. Josef ben-Jochannan, *Africa: Mother of Western Civilization*, Alkebu-Lan Books Associates, New York, New York, 1971, p. 536.
62. David Soren and others, op. cit., p. 111.
63. J. A. Rogers, *World's Great Men of Color*, Vol. 1, p. 106.
64. David Soren and others, op. cit., p. 112.
65. Donald Armstrong, op. cit., p. 45.

66. Picard and Picard, op. cit., p. 264.
67. J. A. Rogers, *World's Great Men of Color*, Vol. 1, p. 106.
68. David Armstrong, op. cit., p. 52.
69. J. A. Rogers, *World's Great Men of Color*, Vol. 1, p. 111.
70. Ibid., p. 111.
71. Donald Armstrong, op. cit., p. 57.
72. J. A. Rogers, *World's Great Men of Color*, Vol. 1, p. 114.
73. Donald Armstrong, op. cit., p. 57.
74. Ibid., p. 57.
75. Ibid., pp. 57-58.
76. Theodore Dodge, op. cit., p. 65.
77. Donald Armstrong, op. cit., p. 53.
78. Ibid., p. 53.
79. David Soren and others, op. cit., p. 105.
80. Ibid., p. 117.
81. Donald Armstrong, op. cit., p. 65.
82. David Soren and others, op. cit., p, 119.
83. Charles H. Hapgood, *Maps of the Ancient Sea Kings: Evidence of Advanced Civilization in the Ice Age*, Chilton Book Co., New York and Philadelphia, 1966, p. 196, cited by John G. Jackson, in *Introduction to African Civilizations*, p. 149.
84. Yosef ben-Jochannan, op. cit., p. 544.

CHAPTER 6
NORTH AFRICA UNDER ROMAN AND VANDAL RULE

1. J. C. degraft-Johnson, *African Glory: The Story of Vanished Negro Civilizations*, Walker and Company, New York, 1954, p. 29.
2. Ibid., p. 29.
3. Ibid., p. 31.
4. Ibid., pp. 34-35.
5. Ibid., p. 35.
6. Ibid., p. 35.
7. Jane Soames Nickerson, *A Short History of North Africa*, The Devin-Adair Company, New York, 1961, p. 27.
8. Ibid., p. 32.
9. Mark Hyman, *Blacks Who Died for Jesus*, Corrective Black History Books, Philadelphia, 1983, p. 18.
10. Ibid., p. 25.
11. Ibid., p. 26.
12. Ibid., p. 28.
13. J. C. degraft-Johnson, op. cit., p. 45.
14. Mark Hyman, op. cit., p. 33.
15. Ibid., p. 3.
16. Ibid., p. 20.
17. J. N. D. Kelly, *The Oxford Dictionary of Popes*, Oxford University Press, Oxford and New York, 1986, p. 12.
18. Frank J. Coppa, editor, *Encyclopedia of the Vatican and Papacy*, Greenwood Press, Westport, Connecticut, 1999, p. 439.

19. Mark Hyman, op. cit., p. 21.
20. Ibid., p. 21.
21. Frank J. Coppa, op. cit., p. 439.
22. J. N. D. Kelly, op. cit., p. 12.
23. Ibid., p. 27.
24. Ibid., p. 27.
25. Mark Hyman, op. cit., p. 21.
26. Ibid., p. 21.
27. Ibid., p. 21.
28. Ibid., p. 23.
29. Ibid,, p. 23.
30. Ibid., p. 23.
31. Ibid., p. 23.
32. J. N. D. Kelley, op. cit., p. 49.
33. Mark Hyman, op. cit., p. 23.
34. Ibid., p. 25.
35. Frank J. Coppa, op. cit., p. 172.
36. J. C. degraft-Johnson, op. cit., p. 53.
37. Ibid., p. 54.
38. Ibid., p. 55.
39. Mark Hyman, op. cit., pp. 35-36.
40. E. Jefferson Murphy, *History of African Civilization*, Thomas Y. Crowell Company, New York, 1972, pp. 71-72.

CHAPTER 7
THE MOORS OF NORTH AFRICA
AND THEIR OCCUPATION OF SPAIN

1. John G. Jackson, *Introduction to African Civilizations*, Introduction by John Henrik Clarke, The Citadel Press, Secaucus, New Jersey, 1970, p. 167.
2. J. A. Rogers, *World's Great Men of Color*, Vol. 1, Introduction by John Henrik Clarke, Macmillan Publishing Co., Inc., New York, 1972, revised edition, p. 144.
3. Ibid., p. 145.
4. John G. Jackson, op. cit., pp. 16-17.
5. J. C. degraft-Johnson, *African Glory: The Story of Vanished Negro Civilizations*, Walker and Company, New York, 1954, p. 65.
6. Jamil M. Abun-Nasr, *A History of the Maghrib*, Cambridge University Press, New York, New York, 1971, p. 68.
7. Ibid., p. 68.
8. J. C. degraft-Johnson, op. cit., p. 66.
9. Ibid., p. 66.
10. Ibid., p. 66.
11. Ibid., pp. 66-67.
12. Ibid., p. 67.
13. Ibid., p. 68.
14. John G. Jackson, op. cit., p. 174.
15. Ibid., p. 174.
16. James E. Brunson and Runoko Rashidi, "The Moors in Antiquity," *Golden Age of the Moor, Journal of African*

Civilizations, edited by Ivan Van Sertima, Transaction Publishers, New Brunswick, New Jersey, Fall 1991, Vol. 11, second printing, 1993, p. 28.

17. Ibid., p. 28.
18. J. A. Rogers, *Nature Knows No Color-Line*, Helga M. Rogers, New York, 1952, third edition, p. 78.
19. Preston E. James, *All Possible Worlds: A History of Geographical Ideas*, The Odyssey Press, Indianapolis, Indiana, eighth printing, 1977, p. 37.
20. Dana Reynolds, "The African Heritage & Ethnohistory of the Moors: Background to the Emergence of Early Berber and Arab Peoples, from Prehistory to the Islamic Dynasties," *Golden Age of the Moor, Journal of African Civilizations*, edited by Ivan Van Sertima, Transaction Publishers, New Brunswick, New Jersey, Fall 1991, Vol. 11, second printing, 1993, p. 93.
21. Brunson and Rashidi, op. cit., p. 43.
22. *The Song of Roland*, trans. F. Goldin (New York: W.W. Norton, 1978), 99., cited by Brunson and Rashidi, in *Journal of African Civilizations, Golden Age of the Moor*, p. 43.
23. *The Song of Roland* (New York: Heritage Press, 1938), 58, cited by Brunson and Rashidi, in Journal of African Civilizations, *Golden Age of the Moor*, p. 43.
24. *The Song of Roland*, trans. F. Goldin (New York: W.W. Norton, 1978), 107., cited by Brunson and Rashidi, in *Journal of African Civilizations, Golden Age of the Moor*, p. 43.
25. John G. Jackson, op. cit., pp. 175-176.
26. Philip K. Hitti, *History of the Arabs*, St. Martin's Press, New York, 1964, p. 534.
27. Ibid., p. 534.
28. Ibid., p. 535.
29. J. A. Rogers, *World's Great Men of Color*, Vol. 1, p. 223.
30. Ibid., p. 219.
31. Stanley Lane-Poole, *The Story of the Moors in Spain*, first published in 1886, new introduction by John G. Jackson, Black Classic Press, Baltimore, Maryland, 1990, p. 179.
32. J. A. Rogers, *World's Great Men of Color*, Vol. 1, p. 220.
33. Ibid., p. 220.
34. Ibid., p. 220.
35. Ibid., p. 220.
36. Ibid., p. 220.
37. Ibid., p. 221.
38. Ibid., p. 221.
39. Stanley Lane-Poole, op. cit., p. 213.
40. Galbraith Welch, *North African Prelude*, William Morrow and Company, Publishers, New York, 1949, p. 315.
41. Rom Landau, *Islam and the Arabs*, The Macmillan Company, New York, 1959, p. 123.

CHAPTER 8
EMPIRES AND STATES OF WEST AFRICA

1. Lady Flora Shaw Lugard, *A Tropical Dependency*, Barnes & Noble, New York, 1964, p. 157, cited by John G. Jackson, in *Introduction to African Civilizations*, p. 196.
2. Ibid., p. 157, cited by John G. Jackson, in *Introduction to African Civilizations*, p. 196.
3. Ibid., p. 161, cited by John G. Jackson, in *Introduction to African Civilizations*, p. 197.
4. John G. Jackson, *Introduction to African Civilizations*, Introduction by John Henrik Clarke, The Citadel Press, Secaucus, New Jersey, 1970, pp. 199-200.
5. Ibid., p. 200.
6. Ibid., p. 202.
7. Ibid., p. 202.
8. Chancellor Williams, *The Destruction of Black Civilization*, Third World Press, Chicago, 1976, revised edition, third printing, p. 210.
9. Stanlake J. Samkange, *African Saga: A Brief Introduction to African History*, Abingdon Press, Nashville, Tennessee, 1971, p. 113.
10. John G. Jackson, op. cit., p. 206.
11. Ibid., p. 206.
12. Ibid., p. 206.
13. G. T. Stride and Caroline Ifeka, *Peoples and Empires of West Africa*, Africana Publishing Corporation, New York, New, York, 1971, p. 33.
14. Ibid., pp. 33-34.
15. Stanlake J. Samkange, op. cit., p. 115.
16. Ibid., p. 115.
17. G. T. Stride and Caroline Ifeka, op. cit., p. 34.
18. J. C. degraft-Johnson, *African Glory: The Story of Vanished Negro Civilizations*, Walker and Company, New York, 1954, p. 82.
19. G. T. Stride and Caroline Ifeka, op.cit., p. 38.
20. J. C. degraft-Johnson, op. cit., p. 86.
21. Ibid., p. 86.
22. Ibid., p. 86.
23. Ibid., p. 86.
24. Stanlake J. Samkange, op. cit., p. 123
25. J. C. degraft-Johnson, op. cit., p. 97.
26. John G. Jackson, op. cit., p. 210.
27. Ibid., p. 210.
28. J. C. degraft-Johnson, op. cit., p. 98.
29. Ibid., p. 98.
30. John G. Jackson, op. cit., p. 210.
31. Ibid., p. 209.
32. J. C. degraft-Johnson, op. cit., p. 100.
33. Ibid., p. 100.
34. Stanlake Samkange, op. cit., p. 125.

35. Nancy Cunard, *Negro: An Anthology*, Introduction by Hugh Ford, Frederick Ungar Publishing Co., New York, third printing, 1984, p. 362.
36. G. T. Stride and Caroline Ifeka, op. cit., p. 55.
37. Ibid., p. 55.
38. J. C. deGraft-Johnson, op. cit., p. 102.
39. John G. Jackson, op. cit., p. 215.
40. G. T. Stride and Caroline Ifeka, op. cit., p. 70.
41. Stanlake Samkange, op. cit., p. 136.
42. John G. Jackson, op. cit., p. 217.
43. Stanlake Samkange, op. cit., p. 141.
44. Basil Davidson, *The African Past: Chronicles from Antiquity to Modern Times*, Little, Brown and Company, Boston and Toronto, 1964, p. 24.
45. Ibid., p. 91.
46. Ibid., p. 91.
47. Ibid., p. 92.
48. J. C. deGraft-Johnson, op. cit., p. 108.
49. Ibid., p. 111.
50. Ibid., p. 111.
51. G. T. Stride and Caroline Ifeka, op. cit., p. 77.
52. J. C. deGraft-Johnson, op. cit., p. 115.
53. Ibid., p. 115.
54. Ibid., p. 117.
55. Ibid., p. 118.
56. Ibid., p. 118.
57. E. Jefferson Murphy, *History of African Civilization*, Foreword by Hollis R. Lynch, Thomas Y. Crowell Company, New York, 1972, pp. 145-146.
58. John G. Jackson, op. cit., p. 371.
59. Basil Davidson, op. cit., pp. 18-19.
60. Ivan Van Sertima, "The Lost Sciences of Africa: An Overview," *Blacks in Science: Ancient and Modern, Journal of African Civilizations*, edited by Ivan Van Sertima, Transaction Books, New Brunswick, New Jersey, April & November 1983, (vol. 5, nos. 1&2), p. 11.
61. Ibid., p. 11.
62. Ibid., p. 11.
63. Hunter Havelin Adams III, "African Observers of the Universe: The Sirius Question," *Blacks in Science: Ancient and Modern, Journal of African Civilizations*, edited by Ivan Van Sertima, Transaction Books, New Brunswick, New Jersey, April & November 1983, (vol. 5, nos. 1&2), p. 29.
64. Van Sertima, op., cit. pp. 11-12.
65. Ibid., p. 12.
66. Ibid., p. 12.
67. Ibid., p. 12.

CHAPTER 9
THE ENSLAVEMENT OF THE AFRICAN

1. Chancellor Williams, *The Destruction of Black Civilization*, Third World Press, Chicago, 1976, revised edition, third printing, p. 168.
2. J. A. Rogers, *Sex and Race*, Vol. 1, Helga M. Rogers, New York, ninth edition, 1967, p. 97.
3. Ibid., p. 97.
4. Daniel P. Mannix, in collaboration with Malcolm Cowley, *Black Cargoes: A History of the Atlantic Slave Trade, 1518-1865*, The Viking Press, New York, seventh printing, 1968, p. 241.
5. Ibid., p. 242.
6. Sidney Painter, Mediaeval Society, Cornell University Press, Ithaca, New York, fifteenth printing, 1967, p. 16.
7. Stanlake Samkange, *African Saga: A Brief Introduction to African History*, Abingdon Press, Nashville, Tennessee, 1971, p. 180.
8. Basil Davidson, *Black Mother: The Years of the African Slave Trade*, Little, Brown and Company, Boston and Toronto, 1961, p. 22.
9. E. Jefferson Murphy, *History of African Civilization: The Peoples, Nations, Kingdoms and Empires of Africa from Prehistory to the Present*, Thomas Y. Crowell Company, 1972, p. 254.
10. Preston E. James, *All Possible Worlds: A History of Geographical Ideas*, The Odyssey Press, Indianapolis, Indiana, eighth printing, 1977, p. 84.
11. Ibid., p. 84.
12. Chancellor Williams, op. cit., p. 267.
13. Preston E. James, op. cit., p. 85.
14. Ibid., p. 85.
15. Ibid., p. 85.
16. Ibid., pp. 88-89.
17. Ibid., p. 89.
18. Ibid., p. 89.
19. Basil Davidson, *Africa in History*, Collier Books, Macmillan Publishing Co., New York, New York, revised and expanded edition, 1991, p. 203.
20. Ibid., p. 203.
21. Ibid., p. 203.
22. Ivan Van Sertima, *They Came Before Columbus*, Random House, New York, 1976, p. xiii.
23. J. A. Rogers, *Africa's Gift to America*, Helga M. Rogers, New York, 1961, p. 17.
24. Rev. Sterling M. Means, Ethiopia and the Missing Link in African History, originally published by the Atlantis Publishing Company, Harrisburg, Pennsylvania, 1945, (1980), p. 95.

25. John G. Jackson, *Introduction to African Civilizations*, Introduction by John Henrik Clarke, The Citadel Press, Secaucus, New Jersey, 1970, p. 305.
26. Daniel P. Mannix, op. cit., p. 3.
27. Ibid., p. 3.
28. Ibid., p. 3.
29. J. A. Rogers, Africa's Gift to America, p. 125.
30. Daniel P. Mannix, op. cit., p. 22.
31. Basil Davidson, *Black Mother: The Years of the African Slave Trade*, p. 82.
32. Chancellor Williams, op. cit., p. 271.
33. Basil Davidson, *Black Mother: The Years of the African Slave Trade*, p. 241.
34. Daniel P. Mannix, op. cit., p. 100.
35. John Hope Franklin, *From Slavery to Freedom*, Alfred A. Knopf, Inc., third edition, 1967, p. 55.
36. Daniel P. Mannix, op. cit., p. 76.
37. Ibid., p. 76.
38. Ibid., p. 47.
39. Ibid., p. 48.
40. Ibid., p. 104.
41. John Hope Franklin, op. cit., p. 56.
42. Daniel P. Mannix, op. cit., p. 111.
43. Stanlake Samkange, op. cit., p. 190.
44. Daniel P. Mannix, op. cit., p. 119.
45. Ibid., p. 120.
46. Ibid., p. 117.
47. Chancellor Williams, op. cit., p. 268.
48. Ibid., p. 256.
49. Helen Miller Bailey and Abraham P. Nasatir, *Latin America: The Development of its Civilization*, Prentice-Hall, Inc., Englewood Cliffs, New Jersey, third edition, 1973, p. 159.
50. Chancellor Williams, op. cit., p. 274.
51. Basil Davidson, *Black Mother: The Years of the African Slave Trade*, p. 119.
52. Chancellor Williams, op. cit., p. 264.
53. Ibid., p. 268.
54. Basil Davidson, *Black Mother: The Years of the African Slave Trade*, p. 238.
55. Ibid., p. 150.
56. Ibid., p. 151.
57. Basil Davidson, *Africa in History*, p. 158.
58. Chancellor Williams, op. cit., p. 280.
59. Ibid., pp. 280-281.
60. J. A. Rogers, *World's Great Men of Color*, Vol. 1, Introduction by John Henrik Clarke, Macmillan Publishing Co., Inc., New York, 1972, revised edition, p. 247.
61. Chancellor Williams, op. cit., p. 281.
62. Ibid., p. 283.
63. Ibid., p. 283.
64. Ibid., p. 283.

65. Ibid., p. 284.
66. Ibid., p. 285.
67. Ibid., p. 285.
68. Ibid., p. 288.
69. Ibid., p. 288.
70. Basil Davidson, *Black Mother: The Years of the African Slave Trade*, p. 151.
71. Chancellor Williams, op. cit., p. 237.
72. Basil Davidson, *Black Mother: The Years of the African Slave Trade*, p. 8.

CHAPTER 10
BLACKS IN THE UNITED STATES AND LATIN AMERICA: BONDAGE TO FREEDOM

1. Daniel P. Mannix, in collaboration with Malcolm Cowley, *Black Cargoes: A History of the Atlantic Slave Trade, 1518-1865*, The Viking Press, New York, seventh printing, 1968, p. 128.
2. Ibid., p. 129.
3. Ibid., p. 14.
4. Ibid., p. 15.
5. Ibid., p. 15.
6. Ibid., p. 17.
7. Ibid., p. 17.
8. Ibid., p. 17.
9. Ibid., p. 17.
10. Governor Codrington to the Council of Trade and Plantations, December 30, 1701, Calendar of State Papers, Colonial Series, America and the West Indies, Cecil Headlam (ed.) XIX (London. 1910), No. 1132, pp. 720-721, cited by Monica Schuler, in "Akan Slave Rebellions in the British Caribbean," *Caribbean Slave Society and Economy*, Hilary Beckles and Verene Shepherd, editors, The New Press, New York, New York, 1993, pp. 374-375.
11. Daniel P. Mannix, op. cit., p. 21.
12. Basil Davidson, *Black Mother: The Years of the African Slave Trade*, Little, Brown and Company, Boston and Toronto, 1961, p. 79.
13. Helen Miller Bailey and Abraham P. Nasatir, *Latin America: The Development of its Civilization*, Prentice-Hall, Inc., Englewood Cliffs, New Jersey, third edition, 1973, p. 162.
14. E. Jefferson Murphy, foreword by Hollis R. Lynch, *History of African Civilization: The Peoples, Nations, Kingdoms and Empires of Africa from Prehistory to the Present*, Thomas Y. Crowell Company, 1972, p. 275.
15. John Hope Franklin, *From Slavery to Freedom*, Alfred A. Knopf, Inc., New York, 3rd edition, 1967, p. 61.
16. Ibid., p. 65.
17. Ibid., p. 65.
18. Ibid., p. 67.
19. Ibid., p. 65.

20. Basil Davidson, *Africa in History*, Collier Books, Macmillan Publishing Co., New York, New York, revised and expanded edition, 1991, p. 211.
21. John Hope Franklin, op. cit., p. 66.
22. James Pope-Hennessy, *Sins of the Fathers: A Study of the Atlantic Slave Traders 1441-1807*, Alfred A. Knopf, Inc., New York, 1968, p. 143.
23. Bailey and Nasatir, op. cit., p. 169.
24. Richard A. Haggerty, editor, Dominican Republic and Haiti, country studies, Federal Research Division, Library of Congress, Washington, D.C., 1991, p. 207.
25. T. Lothrop Stoddard, *The French Revolution in San Domingo*, Houghton Mifflin Company, The Riverside Press Cambridge, Boston and New York, 1914, p. 65.
26. John Hope Franklin, op. cit., p. 68.
27. T. Lothrop Stoddard, op. cit., p. 66.
28. John Hope Franklin, op. cit., p. 68.
29. T. Lothrop Stoddard, op. cit., p. 82.
30. Richard A. Haggerty, op. cit., p. 209.
31. David Geggus, "The Haitian Revolution," *Caribbean Slave Society and Economy*, Hilary Beckles and Verene Shepherd, editors, The New Press, New York, New York, 1993, p. 408.
32. T. Lothrop Stoddard, op. cit., p. 219.
33. David Geggus, op. cit., p. 410.
34. Richard A. Haggerty, op. cit., pp. 210-211.
35. David Geggus, op. cit., p. 413.
36. Lerone Bennett, Jr., *Before the Mayflower: A History of Black America*, Penguin Books USA Inc., New York, New York, sixth revised edition, 1993, p. 123.
37. Ibid., p. 123.
38. Bailey and Nasatir, op. cit., p. 283
39. John Hope Franklin, op. cit., p. 150.
40. Ibid., p. 46.
41. Bailey and Nasatir, op. cit., pp. 155-156.
42. J. A. Rogers, *Sex and Race*, Vol. 2, Helga M. Rogers, New York, seventh printing, 1980, p. 79.
43. Michael L. Conniff and Thomas J. Davis, *Africans in the Americas*, St. Martin's Press, Inc., New York, New York, 1994, pp. 272-273.
44. Ibid., p. 113.
45. John Hope Franklin, op. cit., p. 120.
46. Bailey and Nasatir, op. cit., p. 425.
47. Ibid., p. 169.
48. Ibid., p. 169.
49. Ibid., p. 610.
50. Conniff and Davis, op. cit., p. 285.
51. J. A. Rogers, *Sex and Race*, Vol. 2, p. 60.
52. Ibid., p. 60.
53. Ibid., p. 69.
54. P. Aguado, *Historia of Venezuela*, Vol. 2, pp. 99-131, 1915, cited by J. A. Rogers, in *Sex and Race*, Vol. 2, p. 69.

55. John Hope Franklin, op. cit., p. 124.
56. Conniff and Davis, op. cit., p. 98.
57. Abdias do Nascimento, *Brazil: Mixture or Massacre?*, The Majority Press, Dover Massachusetts, 1989, p. 29.
58. John Hope Franklin, op. cit., p. 123.
59. Ibid., p. 124.
60. Ibid., p. 124.
61. Ibid., p. 125.
62. E. Bradford Burns, *A History of Brazil*, Columbia University Press, New York, New York, second edition, 1980, pp. 50-51.
63. J. A. Rogers, *Sex and Race*, Vol. 2, p. 153.
64. William Loren Katz, *The Black West*, Open Hand Publishing Inc., Seattle, Washington, third edition, 1987, p. 7.
65. Bailey and Nasatir, op. cit., p. 105.
66. Ibid., p. 105.
67. Ibid., p. 105.
68. Ibid., p. 155.
69. John Hope Franklin, op. cit., p. 46.
70. Ibid., p. 47.
71. Ibid., p. 71.
72. Ibid., p. 85.
73. Ibid., p. 102.
74. Ibid., p. 103.
75. J. A. Rogers, *Africa's Gift to America*, Helga M. Rogers, New York, revised and enlarged edition, 1961, p. 42.
76. Ibid., p. 106.
77. John Hope Franklin, op. cit., p. 135.
78. J. A. Rogers, *Africa's Gift to America*, p. 110.
79. John Hope Franklin, op. cit., p. 178.
80. Ibid., p. 178.
81. J. A. Rogers, *Africa's Gift to America*, p. 216.
82. John Hope Franklin, op. cit., p. 85.
83. Ibid., p. 188.
84. Ibid., p. 189.
85. Ibid., pp. 208-209.
86. Ibid., p. 268.
87. Lerone Bennett, *Before the Mayflower*, sixth revised edition, 1993, p. 206.
88. Ibid., p. 206.
89. J. A. Rogers, *Africa's Gift to America*, p. 188.
90. John Hope Franklin, op. cit., p. 292.
91. Lerone Bennett, *Before the Mayflower*, sixth revised edition, 1993, p. 201.
92. Ibid., p. 224.
93. John Hope Franklin, op. cit., p. 305.
94. Lerone Bennett, *Before the Mayflower*, sixth revised edition, 1993, p. 251.
95. Ibid., p. 333.
96. Ibid., p. 344.
97. Ibid., p. 347.

98. Ibid., p. 347.
99. John Hope Franklin, op. cit., p. 502.
100. Ibid., p. 502.
101. Ibid., p. 503.
102. Lerone Bennett, op. cit., p. 354.
103. John Hope Franklin, op. cit., pp. 503-504.
104. Ibid., p. 504.
105. Ibid., pp. 504-505.
106. Lerone Bennett, op. cit., pp. 389-390.

CHAPTER 11
PSYCHOLOGICAL EFFECTS OF SLAVERY ON BLACK PEOPLE

1. Na'im Akbar, *Chains and Images of Psychological Slavery*, New Mind Productions, Jersey City, New Jersey, seventh printing, 1987, p. 7.
2. Amos N. Wilson, *The Developmental Psychology of the Black Child*, Africana Research Publications, New York, New York, sixth printing, 1987, p. 9.
3. Carter G. Woodson, *The Mis-education of The Negro*, Hakim's Publications, Philadelphia, Pennsylvania, first published in 1933, p. 122.
4. Chancellor Williams, *The Destruction of Black Civilization*, Third World Press, Chicago, 1976, revised edition, third printing, p. 359.
5. Ibid., p. 359.
6. Ibid., p. 359.
7. John Henrik Clarke, *Notes for an African World Revolution: Africans at the Crossroads*, Africa World Press, Inc. Trenton, New Jersey, 1991, p. 398.
8. Ibid., p. 402.
9. Ibid., p. 398.
10. Yosef ben-Jochannan, *Africa: Mother of Western Civilization*, Alkebu-Lan Books Associates, New York, New York, 1971, p. 97.
11. Basil Davidson, *Black Mother: The Years of the African Slave Trade*, Little, Brown and Co., Boston and Toronto, 1961, p. 159.
12. Daniel P. Mannix, in collaboration with Malcolm Cowley, *Black Cargoes: A History of the Atlantic Slave Trade, 1518-1865*, The Viking Press, New York, seventh printing, 1968, p. 44.
13. John Henrik Clarke, op. cit., p. 62.
14. Ivan Van Sertima, "The Lost Sciences of Africa: An Overview," Blacks in Science: Ancient and Modern, *Journal of African Civilizations*, edited by Ivan Van Sertima, Transaction Books, New Brunswick, New Jersey, April & November 1983, (vol. 5, nos. 1& 2), 1983, p. 15.
15. Na'im Akbar, op. cit., p. 27.
16. Chancellor Williams, op. cit., p. 364.
17. Carter G. Woodson, op. cit., p. xiii.
18. Na'im Akbar, op. cit., p. 20.

19. Ibid., p. 20.
20. Ibid., p. 20.
21. Daniel J. Leab, *From Sambo to Superspade: The Black Experience in Motion Pictures*, Houghton Mifflin Company, Boston, Massachusetts, 1975, p. 88.
22. Ibid., p. 90.
23. Na'im Akbar, op. cit., p. 10.
24. Ibid., p. 10.
25. Kenneth M. Stampp, *The Peculiar Institution: Slavery in the Ante-Bellum South*, Vintage Books, New York, 1956, p. 104.
26. Ibid., p. 104.
27. Na'im Akbar, op. cit., p. 11.
28. Ibid., p. 13.
29. Ibid., p. 32.
30. John Hope Franklin, *From Slavery to Freedom*, Alfred A. Knopf, Inc., 3rd edition, New York, New York, 1967, p. 178.
31. Na'im Akbar, op. cit., p. 34.
32. Ibid., p. 33.

CHAPTER 12
HISTORICAL ANALYSIS

1. Chancellor Williams, *The Destruction of Black Civilization*, Third World Press, Chicago, revised edition, third printing, 1976, pp. 84-85.
2. Ibid., p. 87.
3. Donald Armstrong, *The Reluctant Warriors: The Decline and Fall of the Carthaginian Empire*, Thomas Y. Crowell Co., New York, 1966, p. 40.
4. Ibid., p. 67.
5. Ibid., p. 68.
6. Basil Davidson, *Black Mother: The Years of the African Slave Trade*, Little, Brown, and Co., Boston and Toronto, 1961, p. 171.
7. E. Jefferson Murphy, *History of African Civilization: The Peoples, Nations, Kingdoms, and Empires of Africa from Prehistory to the Present*, Thomas Y. Crowell Co., New York, 1972, p. 343.
8. Ibid., p. 343.
9. J. A. Rogers, *Africa's Gift to America*, Helga M. Rogers, New York, revised and enlarged edition, 1961, p. 62.
10. Walter White, *A Man Called White: The Autobiography of Walter White*, The Viking Press, New York, 1948, p. 48.
11. J. A. Rogers, *World's Great Men of Color*, Vol. 1, Introduction by John Henrik Clarke, Macmillan Publishing Co., Inc., New York, revised edition, 1972, p. 115.
12. Basil Davidson, op. cit., p. 276.
13. John Henrik Clarke, *Notes for an African World Revolution: Africans at the Crossroads*, Africa World Press, Inc., Trenton, New Jersey, 1991, p. 325.
14. Chancellor Williams, op. cit., p. 161.

15. John Henrik Clarke, *Notes for an African World Revolution: Africans at the Crossroads*, pp. 413-414.
16. Chancellor Williams, op. cit., p. 36.
17. Na'im Akbar, *Chains and Images of Psychological Slavery*, New Mind Productions, Jersey City, New Jersey, seventh printing, 1987, p. 39.
18. Robert C. Hayden, "Black Americans in the Field of Science and Invention," *Blacks in Science, Ancient and Modern*, edited by Ivan Van Sertima, Transaction Books, New Brunswick, New Jersey, April & November 1983 (vol. 5, nos. 1&2), 1983, p. 220.
19. Ibid., p. 222.
20. John Henrik Clarke, "Lewis Latimer—Bringer of the Light," *Blacks in Science, Ancient and Modern*, edited by Ivan Van Sertima, Transaction Books, New Brunswick, New Jersey, April & November 1983 (vol. 5, nos. 1&2), 1983, p. 232.
21. J. A. Rogers, *Africa's Gift to America*, p. 228.
22. John Hope Franklin, *From Slavery to Freedom*, Alfred A. Knopf, Inc., 3rd edition, 1967, p. 400.
23. Chancellor Williams, op. cit., p. 198.
24. Ibid., p. 196.
25. Jesse H. Wheeler, Jr., and others, *Regional Geography of the World*, third edition, Holt, Rinehart and Winston, Inc., New York and other cities, 1969, p. 562.

CHAPTER 13
CRISIS IN THE BLACK COMMUNITY:
CAN BLACK PEOPLE OVERCOME IT?

1. Ellis Cose, "The Good News About Black America," *Newsweek*, Vol. CXXXIII, No. 23, (June 7, 1999), p. 39.
2. Frances Cress Welsing, *The Isis Papers: The Keys to the Colors*, Third World Press, Chicago, 1991, p. 183.
3. Chancellor Williams, *The Destruction of Black Civilization*, Third World Press, Chicago, revised edition, third printing, 1976, p. 71.
4. Francis Cress Welsing, op. cit., p. 243.
5. Ibid., p. 183.
6. Carter G. Woodson, *The Mis-education of The Negro*, Hakims Publications, Philadelphia, Pennsylvania, first published in 1933, p. 3.
7. Ibid., p. 2.
8. John Henrik Clarke, *Notes for an African World Revolution: Africans at the Crossroads*, Africa World Press, Inc., Trenton, New Jersey, 1991, p. 53.
9. Marjorie Whigham-Desir, "The Real Black Power," *Black Enterprise*, Vol. 26, No. 12, (July 1996), p. 61.
10. Chancellor Williams, op. cit., p. 359.
11. Na'im Akbar, *Chains and Images of Psychological Slavery*, New Mind Productions, Jersey City, New Jersey, seventh printing, 1987, p. 22.

CONCLUSION

1. Chancellor Williams, *The Destruction of Black Civilization*, Third World Press, Chicago, 1976, revised edition, third printing, p. 348.

Selected Bibliography

Abun-Nasr, Jamil M. *A History of the Maghrib*. New York, New York: Cambridge University Press, 1971.

Akbar, Na'im. *Chains and Images of Psychological Slavery*. Jersey City, New Jersey: New Mind Productions, 1987.

Andrews, George Reid. *The Afro-Argentines of Buenos Aires, 1800-1900*. Madison, Wisconsin: The University of Wisconsin Press, 1980.

Armstrong, Donald. *The Reluctant Warriors: The Decline and Fall of the Carthaginian Empire*. New York: Thomas Y. Crowell Co., 1966.

Bailey, Helen Miller and Abraham P. Nasatir. *Latin America: The Development of its Civilization*. Englewood Cliffs, New Jersey: Prentice-Hall, Inc., 1973.

Beckles, Hilary and Verene Shepherd. *Caribbean Slave Society and Economy*. New York: The New Press, 1991.

ben-Jochannan, Josef. *Africa: Mother of Western Civilization*. New York, New York: Alkebu-Lan Books Associates, 1971.

Bennett, Lerone, Jr. *Before the Mayflower: A History of Black America*. Chicago: Johnson Publishing Co., 1962.

Bennett, Lerone, Jr. *Before the Mayflower: A History of Black America*. New York, New York: Penguin Books, 1993.

Bennett, Lerone, Jr. *What Manner of Man: A Memorial Biography of Martin Luther King, Jr*. New York: Pocket Books, 1968.

Blakely, Allison. *Russia and the Negro*. Washington, D. C.: Howard University Press, 1986.

Brown, Claude. *Manchild in the Promised Land*. New York, New York: A Signet Book, New American Library,1965.

Brunson, James E. and Runoko Rashidi. "The Moors in Antiquity." *Golden Age of the Moor*. Edited by Ivan Van

Sertima. New Brunswick, New Jersey: *Journal of African Civilizations*, 1993.

Burns, E. Bradford. *A History of Brazil*. New York, New York: Columbia University Press, 1980.

Chandler, Wayne B. "Of Gods and Men: Egypt's Old Kingdom." *Egypt Revisited*. Editor, Ivan Van Sertima. New Brunswick, New Jersey: *Journal of Africa Civilizations*, 1993.

Caven, Brian. *The Punic Wars*. New York: St. Martin's Press, 1980.

Clarke, John Henrik. "Ancient Civilizations of Africa: The Missing Pages in World History." *Egypt Revisited*. Editor, Ivan Van Sertima. New Brunswick, New Jersey: *Journal of African Civilizations*, 1982.

Clarke, John Henrik. "Lewis Latimer—Bringer of the Light." *Blacks in Science, Ancient and Modern*. Edited by Ivan Van Sertima. New Brunswick, New Jersey: *Journal of African Civilizations*, 1983.

Clarke, John Henrik, editor. *Malcolm X: The Man and His Times*. Trenton, New Jersey: Africa World Press, Inc., 1991.

Clarke, John Henrik. *Notes for an African World Revolution: Africans at the Crossroads*. Trenton, New Jersey: Africa World Press, Inc., 1991.

Conniff, Michael L. and Thomas J. Davis. *Africans in the Americas*. New York, New York: St. Martin's Press, Inc., 1994.

Cose, Ellis. "The Good News About Black America." *Newsweek*. Vol. CXXXIII, No. 23, June 7, 1999.

Crawford, Keith W. "The Racial Identity of Ancient Egyptian Populations Based on the Analysis of Physical Remains." *Egypt: Child of Africa*. Edited by Ivan Van Sertima. New Brunswick, New Jersey: *Journal of African Civilizations*, 1995.

Cunard, Nancy. *Negro: An Anthology*. Introduction by Hugh Ford. New York: Frederick Ungar Publishing Co., 1984.

David, Rosalie. *Discovering Ancient Egypt*. New York, New York: Facts On File, Inc, 1994.

Davidson, Basil. *Africa in History*. New York, New York: Collier Books, Macmillan Publishing Co., 1991.

Davidson, Basil. *Black Mother: The Years of the African Slave Trade*. Boston and Toronto: Little, Brown and Company, 1961.

Davidson, Basil. *The African Past: Chronicles from Antiquity to Modern Times.* Boston and Toronto: Little, Brown and Company, 1964.

degraft-Johnson, J. C. *African Glory: The Story of Vanished Negro Civilizations.* New York, New York: Walker and Company, 1954.

Diop, Cheikh Anta. *The African Origin of Civilization: Myth or Reality.* Westport, Connecticut: Lawrence Hill & Company, 1974.

Diop, Cheikh Anta. "Origin of the Ancient Egyptians." *Egypt Revisited.* Editor, Ivan Van Sertima. New Brunswick, New Jersey: *Journal of African Civilizations,* 1982.

Dodge, Theodore A. *Great Captains.* Port Washington, New York: Kennikat Press, Inc., 1968.

Dorey, T. A. and D. R. Dudley. *Rome Against Carthage.* New York: Doubleday & Company, Inc., 1972.

Du Bois, W. E. B. *The Negro.* With a New Introduction by Herbert Aptheker. Millwood, New York: Kraus-Thomson Organization Limited, 1975.

El-Amin, Jamilah. *Empowering the Black Woman: Through the Development of Healthy Relationships.* St. Louis, Missouri: New Generation Publishing Co., 1995.

Franklin, John Hope. *From Slavery to Freedom: A History of Negro Americans.* New York: Alfred A. Knopf, Inc., 1967.

Franklin, V. P. *Martin Luther King, Jr.* New York, New York: Park Lane Press, 1998.

Harden, Donald. *The Phoenicians.* New York, New York: Frederick A. Praeger, Inc., Publishers, 1963.

Hayden, Robert C. "Black Americans in the Field of Science and Invention." *Blacks in Science, Ancient and Modern.* Edited by Ivan Van Sertima. New Brunswick, New Jersey: *Journal of Africa Civilizations,* 1983.

Hilliard, Asa G. III. "Waset, the Eye of Ra and the Abode of Maat: The Pinnacle of Black Leadership in the Ancient World." *Egypt Revisited.* Editor, Ivan Van Sertima. New Brunswick, New Jersey: *Journal of African Civilizations,* 1993.

Hitti, Philip K. *History of the Arabs.* New York: St. Martin's Press, 1964.

Hutchinson, Earl Ofari. *The Crisis in Black and Black.* Los Angeles, California: Middle Passage Press, 1998.

Hyman, Mark. *Blacks Who Died for Jesus.* Philadelphia, Pennsylvania: Corrective Black History Books, 1983.

Israel, Saul. *Introduction to Geography.* New York, New York: Holt, Rinehart and Winston, Inc., 1964.

Jackson, John G. *Introduction to African Civilizations.* Introduction by John Henrik Clarke. Secaucus, New Jersey: The Citadel Press, 1970.

James, Preston E. *All Possible Worlds: A History of Geographical Ideas.* Indianapolis, Indiana: The Odyssey Press, A Division of Bobbs-Merrill Educational Publishing, 1977.

Johanson, Donald and Lenora. *Ancestors: In Search of Human Origins.* New York: Villard Books. 1994.

Karenga, Maulana. "Towards a Sociology of Maatian Ethics: Literature and Context." *Egypt Revisited.* Editor, Ivan Van Sertima. New Brunswick, New Jersey: *Journal of African Civilizations,* 1993.

Katz, William Loren. *The Black West.* Seattle, Washington: Open Hand Publishing Inc., 1987.

King, Coretta Scott. *My Life with Martin Luther King, Jr.* New York: Henry Holt and Company, 1993.

King, Martin Luther, Jr. *Why We Can't Wait.* New York and Ontario: A Mentor Book, New American Library, 1964.

Kunjufu, Jawanza. *Developing Positive Self-Images and Discipline in Black Children.* Chicago, Illinois: African-American Images, 1984.

Lane-Poole, Stanley. *The Story of the Moors in Spain.* Introduction by John G. Jackson. Baltimore, Maryland: Black Classic Press, 1990.

Leab, Daniel J. *From Sambo to Superspade: The Black Experience in Motion Pictures.* Boston, Massachusetts: Houghton Mifflin Company, 1975.

Leakey, Richard E. *The Making of Mankind.* New York, New York: E.P. Dutton, 1981.

Leakey, Richard E. *The Origin of Humankind.* New York, New York: BasicBooks, 1994.

Let's Make a Slave. Speech of Willie Lynch, 1712. The Black Arcade of Liberation Library.

Lewis, Bernard. *The Arabs in History.* New York: Oxford University Press, 1993.

Mahmud, S.F. *A Short History of Islam.* New York: Oxford University Press, 1988.

Malcolm X, with the assistance of Alex Haley. *The Autobiography of Malcolm X.* New York: Ballantine Books, 1992.

Mannix, Daniel P. *Black Cargoes: A History of the Atlantic Slave Trade, 1518-1865.* In collaboration with Malcolm Cowley. New York, New York: The Viking Press, 1968.

Means, Rev. Sterling M. *Ethiopia and the Missing Link in African History.* Harrisburg, Pennsylvania: The Atlantis Publishing Company, 1945.

Murphy, E. Jefferson. *History of African Civilization:* The Peoples, Nations, Kingdoms and Empires of Africa from Prehistory to the Present. New York: Thomas Y. Crowell Company, 1972.

Murray, Margaret A. *The Splendor that Was Egypt.* New York, New York: Hawthorn Books, Inc., 1963.

Nascimento, Abdias do. *Brazil: Mixture or Massacre?* Dover, Massachusetts: The Majority Press, 1989.

Neill, Thomas P. and Raymond H. Schmandt. *History of the Catholic Church.* Milwaukee: The Bruce Publishing Company, 1957.

Nickerson, Jane Soames. *A Short History of North Africa.* New York: The Devin-Adair Company, 1961.

Painter, Sidney. Mediaeval Society. Ithaca, New York: Cornell University Press, 1967.

Picard, Gilbert C. and Colette Picard. *The Life and Death of Carthage.* New York: Taplinger Publishing Co. Inc., 1969.

Pope-Hennessy, James. *Sins of the Fathers: A Study of the Atlantic Slave Traders 1441-1807.* New York: Alfred A. Knopf, Inc., 1968.

Prevas, John. *Hannibal Crosses the Alps: The Enigma Re-examined.* Rockville Centre, New York: Sarpedon,1998.

Rajshekar, V. T. *Dalit: The Black Untouchables of India.* Atlanta and Ottawa: Clarity Press, 1987.

Rajshekar, V. T. "The Black Untouchables of India: Reclaiming Our Cultural Heritage." African Presence in Early Asia. Edited by Runoko Rashidi and Ivan Van Sertima. New Brunswick, New Jersey: *Journal of Africa Civilizations,* 1995.

Randall, J. G. and David Donald. *The Civil War and Reconstruction.* Lexington, Massachusetts: D. C. Heath and Company, 1969.

Rashidi, Runoko. "Dr. Diop on Asia: Highlights and Insights." Great African Thinkers, Vol. 1. Editor, Ivan Van Sertima. New Brunswick, New Jersey: *Journal of African Civilizations,* 1987.

Reynolds, Dana. "The African Heritage & Ethnohistory of the Moors: Background to the Emergence of Early Berber and Arab Peoples, from Prehistory to the Islamic Dynasties." *Golden Age of the Moor.* Edited by

Ivan Van Sertima. New Brunswick, New Jersey: *Journal of African Civilizations*, 1993.

Rogers, J. A. *Africa's Gift to America*. New York: Helga M. Rogers, 1961.

Rogers, J. A. *Nature Knows No Color-Line*. New York: Helga M. Rogers, 1952.

Rogers, J. A. *Sex and Race*, Vol. 1. New York: Helga M. Rogers, 1967.

Rogers, J. A. *Sex and Race*, Vol. 2. New York: Helga M. Rogers, 1980.

Rogers, J. A. *Sex and Race*, Vol. 3. New York: Helga M. Rogers, 1972.

Rogers, J. A. *World's Great Men of Color*, Vols. 1 & 2. Introduction by John Henrik Clarke. New York: Macmillan Publishing Co. Inc., 1972.

Samkange, Stanlake J. *African Saga: A Brief Introduction to African History*. Nashville, Tennessee: Abingdon Press, 1971.

Sertima, Ivan Van. "The Lost Sciences of Africa: An Overview." *Blacks in Science: Ancient and Modern*. Edited by Ivan Van Sertima. New Brunswick, New Jersey: *Journal of African Civilizations*, 1983.

Sertima, Ivan Van. *They Came Before Columbus*. New York: Random House, 1976.

Shillington, Kevin. *History of Africa*. New York: St. Martin's Press, 1989.

Snider, Denton J. *The Father of History*. St. Louis, Missouri: Sigma Publishing Co., 1907.

Snowden, Frank Jr. *Blacks in Antiquity*. Cambridge, Massachusetts: The Belknap Press of Harvard University Press, 1982.

Soren, David and others. *Carthage: Uncovering the Mysteries and Splendors of Ancient Tunisia*. New York, New York: Simon and Schuster, 1990.

Stampp, Kenneth M. *The Peculiar Institution: Slavery in the Ante-Bellum South*. New York: Vintage Books, 1956.

Sterling, Dorothy, editor. *The Trouble They Seen: Black People Tell the Story of Reconstruction*. Garden City, New York: Doubleday & Company, Inc., 1976.

Stoddard, T. Lothrop. *The French Revolution in San Domingo*. Boston and New York: Houghton Mifflin Company, The Riverside Press Cambridge, 1914.

Stride, G. T. and Caroline Ifeka. *Peoples and Empires of West Africa*. New York, New York: Africana Publishing Corporation, 1971.

Tierney, John. "The Search for Adam and Eve." *Newsweek* Vol. CXI, January 11, 1988.

Volney, C. F. *The Ruins or, Meditation of the Revolutions of Empires: And the Law of Nature.* Chesapeake, Virginia: ECA Associates, 1990. (Originally published, 1793).

Ward, W. E. F. *A History of Africa.* Nashville, Tennessee: Aurora Publishers, Incorporated, 1970.

Watterson, Barbara. *The Gods of Ancient Egypt.* New York and Oxford: Facts On File Publications, 1984.

Welch, Galbraith. *North African Prelude.* New York: William Morrow and Company, Publishers, 1949.

Wellard, James. *Lost Worlds of Africa.* New York: E. P. Dutton & Co., Inc., 1967.

Welsing, Frances Cress. *The Isis Papers: The Keys to the Colors.* Chicago: Third World Press, 1991.

Wheeler, Jesse H., Jr. and others. *Regional Geography of the World.* New York and other cities: Holt, Rinehart and Winston, Inc., 1969.

Whigham-Desir, Marjorie. "The Real Black Power." *Black Enterprise.* Vol. 26, No. 12, July 1996.

White, Walter. *A Man Called White: The Autobiography of Walter White.* Foreword by Andrew Young. Athens, Georgia: Brown Thrasher Books, The University of Georgia Press, 1995.

Williams, Chancellor. *The Destruction of Black Civilization.* Chicago: Third World Press, 1976.

Williams, Chancellor. *The Rebirth of African Civilization.* Chicago: Third World Press, 1993.

Willis, Delta. *The Leakey Family: Leaders in the Search for Human Origins.* New York, New York: Facts On File, Inc., 1992.

Wilson, Allen. "The Mother of Us All." *World Press Review.* Vol. 35, November 1988.

Wilson, Amos N. *The Developmental Psychology of the Black Child.* New York, New York: Africana Research Publications, 1987.

Woodson, Carter G. *The Mis-education of the Negro.* Philadelphia, Pennsylvania: Hakim's Publication, 1933.

Index

About the Author

Robert L. Bradley is a historian, short story writer, and a cartographer (mapmaker). He was born in Memphis, Tennessee. He holds a B.A. degree in history from Tennessee State University of Nashville, Tennessee, and an M.S. degree in geography from the University of Memphis (formerly Memphis State University). Bradley lives in St. Louis, Missouri and works as a cartographer. He has been studying the history of black people since the fourth grade. He also loves to write short stories and poetry.

Other works by Robert Bradley include *Stories about the Black Experience: The Lord Will Make a Way, Volume 1* (2001) and *Stories about the Black Experience: They All Came Together to Uplift the Community, Volume 2* (2001).

WAKE UP!

An Analysis of African-American History
From a Glorious Past to the Present Crisis

To order a copy of this book, write to:

Robert L. Bradley

P. O. Box 25768

St. Louis, MO 63136